Magdalena Wasiura

Les Berbères et Moi

A Story of Poverty and Suffering,

Elation and Hope.

Edited by Neil Baylis

Magdalena Wasiura

Les Berbères et Moi

Print ISBN 978-1-908419-96-5   Ebook ISBN 978-1-910110-604-1

Book copyright © 2014 Cv Publications

Text copyright © Magdalena Wasiura All rights reserved

Printed and bound by Blissett: Design.Print.Media www.blissettdigital.co.uk

Cv Publications www.tracksdirectory.ision.co.uk

Magdalena Wasiura
Les Berbères et Moi

Acknowledgements

All my gratitude goes towards friends whose financial support made my journey less stressful; but first I shall bow in front of Dorothy Mitchard. Her immense generosity that exceeded all my expectations made me cry on a few occasions. THANK YOU DOROTHY. Further thanks goes to:Alex Russell Flint, Allysa Cigarroa, Anna Rosa Paladino, Bembenek's family, Frank Rekrut, Huguette, Rene, Gilles Couteleau, John Fairley, Joshua Press, Julian Lees, Laura Thompson, Michael Richman, Pascal Métayer, Pierre de Chevilly, Sheldon Hutchinson, Ted Seth Jacobs, Tomasz Rajfura, Trevor Bedeman and Yanan Par.

A big thank you to Hannah and Hmad Naatit for their generous support and the opportunity to work with the Hannan charity, to my Moroccan family who hosted me and cared for me, and to all the good people that I've met in Morocco. A special thank you to Mohamed Ijmar for his immense help and care.

A massive thanks also to Neil Baylis for his incredible help with editing this book and making me understand all those troublesome quirks of the English language - every rule has an exception! The same gratitude goes to my editor Nicholas James for his everlasting support, patience, and encouragement; and to my mum for looking after me.

Certain words, events or quotes are explained in the notes section which follows each part of the text.

Magdalena Wasiura

Introduction

After my holiday in Morocco in 2012, I felt a terrible need to go back there and for over a year I had been looking for a way to fulfil such desire. It was simply out of my sympathy, admiration and love for those people who have suffered immense poverty and yet who managed to be so generous and hospitable. During my research I stumbled upon a charity called "Hannan" that has been helping the Berber people in the Middle Atlas Mountains. It was established by a couple called Hannah (British) and Hmad (Moroccan); they built a school from scratch in a village called El Borj, where Hmad was born and raised, that now accommodates about 30 children aged 2-5 years old, and currently they are going through tough regulations and money raising (circa £150.000) for the new school for children aged 5-12 years old. They desperately need volunteers to co-ordinate the existing school by helping teachers, managing the paper work, running extra French classes, basically anything that could help children and the organization to progress.

Magdalena Wasiura

It's more out of the ordinary than the ordinary. Life as it has been experienced, simply lived. This journal presents a fresh look at life in Morocco, gives you an insight as to how the Berbers live, what problems they face, their attitudes, what they know about us Europeans and what they think about us. This book is written by a young woman, who as a voluntary worker travelled to the Middle Atlas Mountains to help the Association Hannan, a charity that has been helping mainly children, but has also been generous to others in need. "The instant discovery of such a different world, led me to want to prove to myself and perhaps others, who doubted that my mission would be successful, that Muslims can be open-minded, amiable, feel the need of love, and that they want more from us than money or a visa." My focus was on helping others. However, living with a Muslim family and having Muslim friends turned the whole experience into a simple but also complicated series of events which I had never anticipated to live through. Casualties of this five month 'experiment' have vividly been portrayed in the book. "Am I one of them?" This journal aims to be funny, quirky, knowledgeable and authentic. "Reach out for it and it is yours."

The Author: Magdalena Wasiura gained a MA degree in journalism and media studies and then worked as a television presenter and reporter in Poland. Multi-lingual she has worked as a dancer, model and actress in France, Italy and England. Her previous contribution to Cv Publications includes an interview about Andy Warhol's Brigitte Bardot portraits at Gagosian Gallery 2011, and a profile of the artist Daniel Graves published in 2012.

"LES BERBÈRES ET MOI" CONTENTS

Part One

Part One of "Les Berbères et moi" describes the author's first step into the life of her Moroccan family hosts, takes you to the souk and hammam, explains the importance of Fridays for Muslim society, sulks itself in whisky and the problems caused by it. In this Part we are introduced to countless opportunists and amiable characters, and we visit a rather lavish circumcision party.

Part Two

The second part of Magdalena's journal recording her life with the Berber community in Khénifra, in the Middle Atlas of Morocco, their homes, social gatherings and her work with their children in the Association Hannan. Get a good wash in hammam, eat boucheyar, drink shiba, meet her friends Mohamed and Ali and go with them to Arougou, wakha?

Part Three

Part Three of Magdalena's journal describes broadly 'the forbidden' subjects: intimacy and drinking in the context of Islam that is supported by numerous tales from the Quran, and how young people will turn the prohibited into pleasure. She depicts the growing tension between her and her Muslim family and the cultural clash, something that one will not get in package holidays. "Lasciate ogne speranca, voi ch'intrate," it's Dante's invitation to Hell, here however, it invites one to hammam.

Part Four

What about the fatalism? Should women wear tight jeans? What about swimming? Our God or My God, whose then? Some of those issues are discussed in Part Four of Magdalena Wasiura's account of her stay in Morocco. She also describes a rather stressful Christmas time spent there, the overprotective nature of her Muslim family and her trip to Meknès where she will get arrested.

Part Five

Love and marriage...does it really go together like a horse and carriage? In Part Five of Magdalena Wasiura's journal one can read about marriage and love, and in the context of a strange encounter in Beni Mellal about hashish and L'eau de Vie. The author travels to the Plateau de Tadla and discovers an amazing Bin El Ouidan barrage, and dances to Berber music at a newborn baby's party.

Part Six

The tales in Part Six of "Les Berbères et moi" consist of the author's attempts to build her life in Morocco by accepting a certain proposal, but meeting obstacles on both the personal and professional level; living thorough a major crisis at home relating to the lack of money, lack of work, and deteriorating health of both grandparents and seemingly everyone else including the author; spending weekends in the mountains and enjoying family outings in the forest of Ajdir.

Part Seven

New projects, new ideas along with matchmaking in Timdghass are just a small part of Part Seven of "Les Berbères et moi." What is all the fuss about kissing? The author explains zina and how Sharia punishes you for that. You feel the blisters on the author's hands when she beats the dirt out of sheep skin as well as the discomfort and cold during her night voyage to Casablanca.

Part Eight

It's far from easy to say goodbye but before the author bids them farewell, she goes on a long physically and emotionally draining journey. The countless hours in the buses to Chefchaouen, then Raba, then Marrakesh are a significant component of Part Eight, the last part of "Les Berbères et moi." The author meets obstacles at Raba airport that make her return to Khénifra, to the police station. And someone dies in this Part.

******

Part One

At Fés airport, around 9.30 pm, I was greeted by two, tall, skinny guys with moustaches who were holding my name written down on a big piece of paper, in capital letters, MAGDALENA WASIURA, and down below, in small writing, Mohamed Naatit. I smiled at them while dragging through the hallway my meticulously packed fifteen kilograms backpack and another nineteen kilograms of hand luggage that had cost me an additional £60. The smile was genuine but contained a tinge of anxiety, a pinch of fear accompanied by a single thought: "What the hell am I doing here?" "Bonsoir. Ça va? Magdalena? Magdalena?" They kept repeating my name while taking my suitcases. When we got out of the airport, the breeze greeted me warmly. Straight away I melted under the five layers of clothing that I had not been able to fit into my suitcase. The heat here, as opposed to the heavy rain and strong wind that bid me farewell in Nantes, had cheered me up at once. We packed everything into a car that was parked just outside the airport and drove through the small part of Fés towards Khénifra - our destination, one hundred and sixty kilometres away. We tried to chat in French but there was obviously some fluency missing in all of that. I knew from that very moment that communication could be our biggest problem. "Tu parle Arabe?" "I wish I could." I was looking at the world from the back seat while responding to their first questions. "Quel âge, toi? Française? Ah Polonaise, Pologne... Pologne... Ou est ça?" Mohamed, to my surprise, was only twenty-eight years old. Despite his beautiful smile which showed a full set of white teeth, he appeared to be much older. His very skinny face and moustache aged him a great deal. Regardless of the linguistic struggle we managed to understand each other. His friend was constantly on the phone while driving usually in the middle of the road or on the wrong side of it. When he wasn't on the phone and still driving like a maniac, he was trying to show me photos of his Italian wife and, I guessed, his children. "Regarde! Regarde! Elle est belle, no?" Had she been a bit slimmer she would indeed have been a good looking girl, but even if she wasn't, I couldn't have said "no." This is one of the questions which makes me feel uncomfortable and forces me to lie occasionally.

The condition of the road was surprisingly good and the whole journey was going smoothly. We were driving through numerous small villages which carried a strong feeling of abandonment or desolation, with no sign of human inhabitants, only cats and dogs and the policemen. We were stopped twice and checked over quite thoroughly. The policeman stuck his head through the window, nodded, and kept asking questions about me. The checks continued with opening the boot and examining my suitcases. "Shall I get out?" "No, no, reste ici, ça va, c'est normal." Finally, we were able to get back on the road and stopped at another road blockade. The same questions, the same control, and back on the road again. Occasionally, we had some radio-signal and music which very much reminded me of my last trip to the Sahara Desert. "Première fois au Maroc? Toi, mariée? Tu veux marier Mohamed?" "Well," I thought, "that was a good start."

Around forty kilometres from Khénifra we stopped to get something to eat. It was one of those places by the road, very strongly lit that displayed massive chunks of meat hanging off the roof with: black and white headed dead goats with tails and bowels still attached to their naked bodies. I asked if this was also going to be on our plate but they did not get my sense of humour. Actually, I considered my question perfectly normal, Italians, for example, pay 1.95 Euro for one hundred grams of *pisellino cinghiale* - testicles of wild boar. When my question did not evoke any reaction, I shifted my attention onto the butcher who was busy cutting bits and pieces of meat and roasting them on the open-fire. I could only see his bushy dark moustache through those hanging chunks of meat while we were sitting at the table waiting patiently for our feast. As I was observing the numerous cats and dogs running around, as well as plunging my thoughts into the unknown, I had forgotten to wash my hands realising it afterwards. I remembered, it was one of the pieces of advice that a woman who I met at Nantes airport had given me: "Wash your hands before each meal, eat only with your right hand and never with your left - this one is reserved for cleaning yourself only, eat what is in front of you, never reach out for something that is not on your side of the plate." I kept asking questions and she kept responding. "If you ever wanted to come to Rabat and stay with me and my husband, we would be very happy to have you." She talked about her husband Steve, a sweet loving man from Manchester, a lot. After his first unsuccessful marriage followed by divorce, he came to Morocco and found her, his soul mate, in Rabat, in a shop where she was working at that time: "He looked at me, I looked at him and we felt in love. Soon after we got married." "Sounds extremely romantic; how long have you been married for?" "For two years," she responded. They had a farm full of peacocks, with a swimming pool and a constant flow of visitors, mainly foreigners. For some reason, perhaps all those over-exaggerated adjectives of sweet, loving, charming, handsome, brilliant, wonderful, fantastic Steve from Manchester, I suspected the opposite; you don't really praise your husband to a total stranger unless there is something completely wrong with him. I had the pleasure to meet the Steve from Manchester at Fés airport: "Hello," his accent took me straight back to Huddersfield where I spent over three years. "Come and see us. I'll call you." We said goodbye and never saw each other again.

Going back to that meal. We were served one big portion of nicely grilled lamb which was scrumptious, well-flavoured, and *succulent*. We shared the meat served with bread, a glass of water from the outside tap, and mint tea. The butcher with the big moustache was extremely nice to me. He got out of his little place, sat in front of it, and kept glancing and smiling at me saying something in Arabic, which I translated in to my own language: "I hope you like the meal." "It is delicious," I said and put my thumb up. Incidentally, just couple of weeks ago, there was the religious celebration of the sheep slaughter called *Eid al-Adha*, a very important holiday in the

Muslim world. Muslim families sacrifice their own sheep in remembrance of Abraham who was to forgo his first newborn son to obey God.

It was after 1.00am when we left the place and we still had one hour's drive ahead of us. Around 2.15am we finally reached our destination driving through narrow streets and pulling up just outside the front door of the house. A young man came to help us and showed me in saying: "Salut, bienvenu." Everybody in the house was fully awake. "I'm sorry for being so late, it was a long drive." They all greeted me warmly and invited me to a small room where most of them were gathered. Immediately, my whole attention was drawn to an old man who was sitting on his single mattress bed in a far corner of that room, wearing a turban wrapped loosely around his head. This was a face of a man who I could only have seen on TV in some exotic tribal programmes or adventures of Bruce Parry. He was a very tall and dry-looking man with conspicuously wrinkled face and hands, massively long eye-catching ears, and rather dissimilar eyes: one looked whiter than the other and the right one seemed to be popping out more than the left one. When I was shaking hand with him, he glanced at me pronouncing my name few times, whereupon he kissed me on the forehead and welcomed me in his house. "He is almost hundred years old," said the young man. On the opposite side of that room, there was an old woman lying down on the mattress, tiny and fragile looking, with the voice that did not carry well. She grabbed my head, pulled it close to hers and kissed me repeatedly on the forehead.

I was physically and mentally exhausted and felt overwhelmed by the drastic change that occurred. In that moment, I was dreaming of a hot shower and a good night's sleep knowing that the hot shower would not happen soon. Abdellah, the young man, took me to the first floor where my room was. Tiny but sufficient, the only one with a door and a proper king size bed that was covering eighty per cent of that space. The big chest of drawers with a mirror and two small chiffoniers placed on top of each other were facing the bed leaving a small space for my suitcases. There was a big open hole in the wall through which I saw another open space overlooking the rooftop. The very moment that I saw my room I was grateful for this little privacy that no one else seemed to have it.

I was called to come downstairs to eat with everybody else. "But I have just eaten. I'm not hungry, thank you." They weren't interested in my story. I had to eat. Later on I found out it was a sign of hospitality and welcome. It's simple: If you get the food you are welcome, if not, you better look for an alternative shelter. Over a huge plate of tagine, we exchanged some laughter and basic information. "Mangez! Mangez!" they kept repeating. I was warned before that I would be forced to eat.

It was around 3.00am when I had to excuse everyone saying how exhausted I was. Then I took my sleeping bag out and got additional three massive woollen blankets. I even had a bed sheet and a pillow wrapped around in a big piece of a bed cover. Just looking at the bed was making me feel happy.

******

I woke up at around 10.00am thinking how late it was and that they might all be waiting for me with breakfast. I was still feeling a little bit drowsy though. On the one hand, the massive breeze coming through that wide gap in the wall was discouraging me from getting up. On the other hand, a bird peeping though that gap, tweeted some encouraging tunes, 'it's a brand new day, get up, get up!' So I did. The family was waiting downstairs with a home-made cake and hot milk. There was a young man looking very much in pain whom, I guessed, was not living here permanently. He was holding a tiny sachet of Nescafe. "Would you like some?" Except for a strong cup of coffee in the morning, I don't think there is anything else that I'm addicted to hence I gladly accepted his offer. "What do I do with this?" I was asking myself looking at the quantity. I didn't want to appear fussy demanding some boiled water, hence I rushed the tiny bit of coffee into the hot milk as everyone else did and drunk it as if it was the same daily intake of a strong Italian coffee from my stainless steel Sardinian coffee-maker. Nevertheless, I was functioning quite well throughout the whole day without fatigue or headache. For a split second, I thought I may be willing to give up coffee, but the first shop that we passed by that day, supplied me with four small jars of Nescafe. It was inevitable; my addiction to coffee was much too strong and pleasurable to give up so easily.

I was looking around my new home. It was very basic here. I shared the three-storey house, including the rooftop, with at least nine people as I counted. The fairly spacious corridor on the ground floor led to three rooms: a kitchen and two living/dining/sleeping rooms and the squat toilet. When it came down to sleeping, one room accommodated at least four people who occupied single mattresses that were laid around each room. Except for my space on the first floor, there was a big area that served as a bedroom or the living room, then a small storage with a gas oven, and a quite spacious bathroom-lavatory. As a breeze would come through every window, every door, all cracks, and the *open-air aperture*, the house felt very cold. "It's better to stay outside," I was told.

After breakfast, I asked for some hot water to wash myself and was nicely surprised with a massive kettle of boiling water. The bathroom-toilet room contained of a normal modern flushing toilet and that nasty squat one. There was a tap with cold water as well as a washing machine which made me feel spoiled already. I mixed up the hot and cold water in a bucket and began my "douche" as they call it here. In case of some peeping Tom, the small window that was overlooking the main street had to be literally stuffed with some fabrics; but no matter how awkward and cold it felt to be standing naked in that icy room at first, it truly was a blessing afterwards. I was clean, content and ready to plunge myself into the unknown. Because I was told we were going out, and I had to take my passport with me, I was rushing to get dressed. "Tiens! It's a present for you," said Meryam. "What is that beautiful thing?" "Pyjama," she said. "Shall I wear it now?" "*Bsha!*" It was a black, long, sleeveless, simple design with an orange pattern blazoned around the neck and the chest area. I put it on, covered my head with a scarf and went out.

A young woman called Leila who lived on the same street had joined us. She looked slightly too big for her height which revealed itself through her gait: wobbly, unstable, almost painful as if she was catching up with our steps but it was all too fast for her. She was a very pleasant, chatty and smiling girl. "Comment trouves-tu Maroc? Qu'est-ce que tu va faire ici?" She asked in French and then added in English. "I love English, I like singing in English." "I could help you with that if you want?" She sounded positive about my offer and happy to share on the spot some English words with me. We carried on walking through some narrow, pretty, colourful streets where all the people, whether they were young or old, women or men, poor or rich, miserable or elated were staring at me. "They might not have many foreigners here," I said to myself.

It was a jolly hot day and by the time we had reached our destination my cheeks were burning red. "Tu es rouge, le soleil, le soleil," Leila kept repeating it and laughing. When we finally made to the Registry Office in the fourth district of Amelou, first we had to answer a few questions, then we were asked to make a copy of my passport, and finally, we were asked to wait outside. We sat on the staircase and were observing people passing by. "What is the difference between pyjama and djellaba?" I asked Meryam. Silence. "Is it a hood that makes it djellaba?" She nodded. "Is this a djellaba or pyjama?" I continued pointing out at a woman in front of us. "Djellaba," she answered. "It doesn't have a hood though," I expressed my confusion. The explanation did not come. For some reason, and djellaba had nothing to do with it, I sensed that friendship with Meryam, if we would manage to get that close, may be a little bit arduous. It wasn't on the cultural level that I was thinking of but more on a personal one, a character-wise that it seemed judgmental and self-righteous making her harsh and uneasy to get on with. Anyhow, after thirty minutes of waiting, we got back in. I was registered and official here in Khénifra.

When we came back home, there were a couple of new people in the living room downstairs. The two women, beautifully dressed up, greeted me with an overt joy, warmth and kindness. The older one had a very handsome face, strong conspicuous features with full lips and big smile. Likewise, the young one was equally affable and cordial to me. I was invited for tea and sat around the table with them. "You have a very beautiful face. It would make a great portrait," my past was haunting me. "You are all beautiful, I mean," I corrected myself swiftly adding some smile to the perplexed faces of six other women round that table. I tried to apologise for not speaking their language as the gawking part was making me feel awkward. "Mangez! Mangez!" I heard it instead. Grandma beckoned me from her corner to come over, then pulled me hard to her laying down position, kissed me repeatedly in the forehead, and kept pointing at the cake, then at me, and yet again at herself and her moving lips, and said: *"Koul! Koul! Koul!"*

After a little "chat" I was told we were off to the medina. "Go and get changed." "Can't I go like this?" I was looking at my pyjama. *"La! La! La!"* My confusion with this pyjama continued. We headed off to the centre of Khénifra, a very vibrant and colourful place crammed full of cafés, souks with food, clothes, shoes, carpets, blankets, and people: poor people, beggars, homeless with children on the streets. When we stopped by an olive stand, a beggar had approached me. I only found one dirham in my pocket, which I gave to him, and came across a rather peculiar reaction: he raised it, looked at it with disbelief and frustration, and then was mumbling something, as if he were expecting more. What a cheek!

After the medina I had a short moment for myself, but soon after I was called to come downstairs to have some soup. Food again. I sat down around the table and tortured Meryam with my phrases in *Darija* while she was watching Arabic soap opera on television. I was also observing *Äami* Lahcen and his enormous ears while he was falling asleep panting, when all of a sudden he woke up. "I want to go to bed," he said it, and I guessed it by watching him moving. I rushed to get on my feet in order to help him stand up, but to my surprise, I got "no-no" for the answer. Instead, he turned himself on both knees and crawled along across the room through the corridor to the other room where his bed was. It was heart-breaking to watch this tall, large, almost hundred-year-old man on his knees like a baby. Don't we make the full circle? We are born inept and we die inept.

Mohamed, the dad, looked in pain, so dry, so skinny, and so tired. Apparently both, him and the cousin that I met over breakfast, suffered the same stomach problem which was caused by smoking too many cigarettes and hashish. They showed me his medicine: a bottle of liquid with a high-dose of magnesium and written in French "for constipation!" I fetched some painkillers that he claimed later on to have helped him ease the pain. He was asking many questions about Poland, the distance between Poland, France and my home and the hours on the plane. He mentioned how difficult life was here in Morocco, but he did not make a single complaint. Perhaps he was too busy listening to my Darija and laughing his head off, "better therapy than painkillers," I thought.

******

From the recording: "My second day in Morocco. The poverty is alarming. I don't know if I'll mange to stay here the whole period of five months. I feel emotional. They suffer. I cry. The soil is dry. It seems as if it has not been raining for a long time. *People, donkeys, sheep, goats, "all human life is here.""*

I was woken up by the noise of a hammer banging on continuously from 7.30am until now - 9.00am. They were fixing the roof. As soon as I came downstairs, grandma Halima waved at me and was showing me, in her sign language, tiredness and lack of sleep. She kept making a gesture as if she was crying all night long. I got emotional looking at this tiny, fragile and immobile lady in her, at least, late eighties. Not only did she stay in bed all day long, but also hardly participated in any conversation with the family. She sat, observed, and looked as if she was bothered by something. I was watching her wiping her tears off with a blanket when my own eyes started producing those giant drops. I really didn't know what was happening. I might have been moved by the image that came suddenly to my head of my own grandma who is already ninety-four years old, or simply, I was touched by senility as such. Otherwise, I might have been projecting on myself my own fear of getting old. Apart from the present moment, there would be nothing else left for me as there is nothing else left for them, same room, same routine, same faces, same objects that repeat themselves over and over again, day by day, night by night. *"Nihil novi sub sole,"* or as it was called by Brandon Mull: *"A curse of mortality."* He writes:

"You spend the first portion of your life learning, growing stronger, more capable. And then, through no fault of your own, your body begins to fail. You regress. Strong limbs become feeble, keen senses grow dull, hardy constitutions deteriorate. Beauty withers. Organs quit. You remember yourself in your prime, and wonder where that person went. As your wisdom and experience are peaking, your traitorous body becomes a prison."

Whatever was the reason for my rather odd behaviour, I knew I had to leave the room to regain my composure. The other room cheered me up as the table was laden with delicious *boucheyar*, exquisite and simple, some jam, coffee and teas. And I must say that *boucheyar* deserves, at least, one separate page.

After a quick wash in cold water, Abdellah agreed to take me to El Borj - the village where I was going to work for the next five months for the Association Hannan. "There are plenty of buses," he assured me. Perhaps there were but today they seemed to be rather ghostly, so in that case, we had to take a taxi. There were two types of taxi: le grand taxi, the one that went outside the city, and le petit yellow licensed only for the city. The grand taxi pulled out in front of us and seated us both at the front leaving four other passengers on the back seat. The distance was short; within ten minutes we were there. "Le centre d'El Borj" said the sign and led me to a minuscule, destitute-looking village, where some shepherds were running after a herd of hungry sheep; men were hanging around the local shop or outside their shelters; women with their babies wrapped around their backs were sitting outside and watching their grown-up children playing. There was so much peace in this place and the surroundings added a great deal to the feeling of tranquillity. The sheer vast Atlas stretches the dirty-orange colour everywhere, continuously and without stopping for about three hundred kilometres. Amazing. The crashing state of ruins of those houses looked as if they'd been bombarded a few weeks ago and was still in a process of rebuilding. Shocking and disconcerting that one could live one's whole life in such conditions. How do they survive winter? It was one of the first questions that came into my head.

It was a week off holiday here, but Mohamed, the caretaker, showed me inside the school. There were two classrooms on the ground floor with a kitchen and the dining room, four rooms on the first floor including Mohamed's sleeping room, the staff room, the playroom with a computer, printer, books and all sorts of toys, and the open rooftop floor with its spectacular view over the mountains and with enough space for children to play. The place was freezing cold and the ground floor wasn't getting much natural light coming in. However, one cannot underestimate the great achievement that this school is. How can I express my first impression of this place? Perhaps admiration would be a good word. I wholeheartedly admire Hannah and Hmad, the founders of this place, for what they have accomplished throughout the twelve years. It's not easy to bring education or hope to a region like this one, but the mission is on and it's working. They have lent a helping hand to many families and many more children will benefit from schooling as they have been raising the funds to build a school on the 1.000sq meters of land that they had bought. "We are making small steps to make a difference and maybe in the future as this grows, we might be able to have a school in the village that takes children right through to Baccalaureate stage, and maybe some hostel accommodation for those that live further away so they can get a decent education," wrote Hannah.

When I walked out of the school, the village people were greeting me with joy, smiles, and curiosity. I was lost for words faced with such hospitality. It moved me and disturbed me at the same time making me feel useless. I felt as if I was capable of nothing. What went wrong that they have so little and we have so much? If there was hope, would it be enough for everybody? How much suffering one could cure if one would find a remedy for it all? What is the solution? Money? More money? Education? Work? How to start? How to give them better lives? I believed that the impotence that I felt, before even commencing my mission, had something to do with a conversation that I had had with Abdellah. "Would you like to learn English?" I asked. "No," he replied without hesitation. "There would be time in the future to do that." The same answer went for the French language. What future is he talking about if he doesn't want to take care of the present moment and grab the opportunity of what is now and here? For me, the fairly well-educated European, statements like this one make me doubt if some people want to change. They do dream and talk about a different world, better, easier, where the struggle is not served on a plate each day. However, the words are empty ones if they lack any follow up action.

Coming back from El Borj, I got plunged straight into the deep waters of *hammam*, the steaming walls and sweating, "sautéed" all body types, colours, ages, characters that were spread all over floors in each room. It was after lunch. Meryam, kindly insisted on paying the entry fee for me – 10DR each. "I pay the next time." She nodded. We walked into a "reception room" where everyone stripped off to their underwear and deposited their clothes, including towels, to a lady in charge, and then taking only the essentials: a bucket, a mat, a plastic stool, soap, shampoo, and some scrubbing devices. The heat, when getting inside the *hammam*, struck one immediately even when walking through the first and the second rooms that were supposed to be the most comfortable temperature wise. The third room had the only access to water: the hot water that came directly from the wall to a separate basin was controlled by the lady in charge, I believed. On the contrary, the cold water was coming from the tap and it was used as often as it was needed. The women were observing me, whereas I was observing the whole ritual starting off with: finding a comfortable place, sanitising it by pouring some water over the chosen spot, placing the mat, filling the bucket with water, and putting it in front of us. I could get settled now. The upper body got washed first. "Savon?" Meryam took some brown soft grease and placed on to my sponge. It took me no longer than five minutes when she took over my scrub and started scouring hard my back. That was painful! My back felt red-hot! "Would you like me to do it for you?" I asked and got "no" for answer. At first, I thought that was weird, then I forced myself thinking that perhaps there is some sort of religious issue to it: Muslim, Christian, nudity, and then the cultural one, perhaps Europeans cannot rub Moroccans backs? Hmmm…, it doesn't add up, does it? I did not insist and I still don't know why she refused it. I was ready to wash my hair. "No, no, no!" She strongly disagreed with my next move. "What do I do now?" I was thinking. She took another sort of scrubbing sponge, and starting from arms and finishing on the back, she was rubbing until the skin came off. I was the appalling copycat. "How do you do that? It does not work on my body." It really didn't. I tried hard but not a single layer of my skin was willing to shed itself off. "Look!" She took her scrubber and voilà, it was more than the natural peeling, the skin was rolling itself and coming off like crazy! I tried it again and guess what? I failed again. Now it was definitely the time to wash my hair, but as soon as I reached out for some water, it was taken away from me. "Not in this water," she said. My water was perfectly fine but I tried to respect the full ritual of the bath and did not oppose any suggestions or any change. Within five minutes my hair was shampooed and conditioned and I was ready to get back home. However, Meryam's still dry, untouched head baffled me slightly. "Don't you wash your hair?" I asked politely. She did. One hour later, after a very deep and long cleanse of her body. I have to admit: I felt overheated, dehydrated, and bored. I wasn't entangled in any social aspect of it and I might have suffered the European "in a hurry" attitude. I wasn't even brave enough to look at those naked bodies that were parading in front of me coming perhaps too close without any shyness whatsoever. It struck me how comfortable they were in that room, how free and relaxed in comparison to the outside world that requests the thorough, from the head to the toe, cover. Once, the underwear got washed, we were done and ready for some fresh air.

At home I was entertaining Papa Mohamed by repeating some newly-learned words: *brit n'koul, tcharafna, ajbani, mezyan, zwina, khayb, tsbah-ala-khir.* Papa Mohamed looked in pain, but as soon as I recited them, he cheered up and laughed out loud. He called Hakima, my Moroccan mum, to scratch his back, then he called her again as he was thirsty, and yet again with some other petty things. Here is the rule: men are the breadwinners and hardly do anything in the house, women totally in charge of it: cleaning, cooking, washing, shopping, looking after children and elderly. Hakima was the best example: the mother, wife, and the cook. This beautiful human being of a peaceful nature took care of everybody in this family, and she hardly complained. "Hakima, Hakima…." her name was bouncing off every wall in this house during the day and the night time.

Before each meal, one member of the family went around the room with a kettle of hot water so everybody could wash their hands. Although I was feeling hungry, I couldn't eat a lot. I had this weird, unjustified feeling that if I ate as much as I wanted, I might have deprived someone of his

15

or her portion. For now, I decided to stick to my Japanese rule: eat until you satisfy your first hunger. Anyhow, the dinner was exquisite: a tasty tender chicken with vegetables sautéed in a pressure cooker, with some finely chopped and well-seasoned tomatoes and bread on the side. Over dinner, I had the pleasure to meet another young man whose name I didn't catch. He appeared unclean and acted as if he was on drugs. He said something about European women, beautiful but wrong for this country as they don't have a heart for it. Owing to the fact that he could only express few words in French, I might have misunderstood his utterance. Then he mentioned Armstrong highlighting strongly his intelligence, and in the same breath - Putin - not a very good man. "What language do you speak?" I asked him. "Berber," he replied. "Arabic?" He strongly opposed. "I'm not Arab. I'm Berber. I hate Arabs." His face looked irate. He really meant it. *"Tsbah-ala-khir,"* I said goodnight and left the table around the usual 1.00am.

******

From the recording: "There's a saying in Islam that our external form impacts our internal state, just as our internal state has an impact on our external form."

The very early, five o'clock call to prayer, named *al-Fajr*, woke me up every single morning. The *Muadhdhin's* powerful voice carried strong for about two minutes and it was repeated four more times during the day. My Christian response to such an early call was: "Would God like me to get up so early? Wouldn't He rather let me stay in bed and enjoy the deep REM state?" "It's not hard to get up to pray," I hear Muslims saying. "Allah gives you the energy, you feel very connected with Him, especially in the morning." In our house, the young Abdellah prayed out loud five times a day and went to the mosque at least three times a week. Although I had not heard him praying early mornings, I was becoming familiar with his daily routine: he got up, heated up some water, *washed himself*, and prayed out loud while singing and reciting the Quran during his morning *Sobh's* implore.

It was Wednesday, the market day in our district, La Scierie. This massively crowded and boisterous place offered everything: vegetables, fruits, fish, meat, sweets, clothes, shoes, mobiles, toys, and odds and ends for the house. Most of the things were placed on the ground, some had a big plastic platform protecting them from the heat. The Moroccan crowd seemed hectic, and the Moroccan men - desperate. They kept gazing at me, and if lucky enough to catch my eye, they first tried to sell themselves, then their phone numbers, and then whatever was left. One very weird man was following me. I saw him looking. I changed the alley and foresaw his next move. He was a few meters behind me pretending to be interested in potatoes, suddenly. I carried on walking when abruptly, from behind, I felt someone's hand on my leg. The same man passed me, and straight away, like chameleon, mingled with a busy crowd. What a cheek! I couldn't believe he did that!

In the midst of that crowd, I was spotted by another disturbing individual, young with the face of a psychopath, rather creepy looking. He circled around the stands and clearly was spying on me.

He saw me buying some grapes, talking to salesmen and other men who were offering their phone numbers, but had no courage to approach me. I then decided to go for a walk, to the garden just outside our district. No surprise that the local psychopath decided to do the same; he had followed me until he stumbled upon his friend on a bicycle. When I stopped by the bridge to take some photographs, they both approached me. The boy on a bike was interested in some private French lessons, and the psychopath, called Mustapha, wanted to "faire connaissance avec moi." Although I doubted their intentions, I agreed to help the man on a bike by scheduling the first lesson for the following Monday. He bid me farewell, but his friend insisted on staying. There was something disturbing about him, the way he walked, moved, and talked; it was like seeing the spitting image of the character in the Taxi Driver played by Al Pacino, and no, he was not as handsome as Al Pacino. "Either he is mad or on the way to turn into a serial killer," I was disturbed by my own thoughts. He wanted to accompany me to the garden and respond to the standard set of questions, i.e., name, age, profession, country etc. "I thought you were twenty-two years old," he paid me rather a startling complement and carry on saying, "L'âge, c'est ne pas grave." "Pardon?" "I'm twenty-four years old and it doesn't matter if you are older, vraiment." Has he just proposed something to me, or was I missing the whole point of this conversation? He talked about his diplomas, schools, lack of work, and money. O Goodness me! He was so mind-numbing! I had to find an excuse for to be left alone and lunch was a good one.

For lunch we had chicken tagine and home-made bread. This time I allowed myself to eat a little bit more as my Japanese rule was making my stomach rumble and my energy level - low. After lunch, I spent some time in my room reading. All of a sudden, I heard people screaming, moving about, running up and down the stairs, a real commotion. Meryam and Hakima came upstairs to report what the whole tumult was about. I ran downstairs with them and saw a group of people gathering around Achraf who had cut his foot-open. It was looking dramatic; the gushing blood was creating a little pool around his foot while women holding some sort of infectious-wet-looking fabric were trying to clog the dribbling blood. "No!" I screamed inside, and in terror, ran upstairs to get a proper bandage. They wrapped it around his foot and carried him to the local doctor. The medic stitched the troublesome cut and as soon as he did it, Achraf was back on his feet. "I don't think it's a good idea. You better let the wound rest." He didn't listen to me, nor to anybody else who gathered around the dinner table that evening. There were: Mustapha, the twenty-nine-year-old lunatic who seemed to be rather keen on my company, Lahcen another cousin in the family, Mohamed from El Borj, and some friends of Papa Mohamed. I had the feeling that Mustapha may even appreciate my company and his comment regarding heartless women from Europe might be a simple misunderstanding. He kept spending more and more time with me asking all sorts of questions, including my email address, and was keen on learning French. Perhaps, he was not as crazy as I thought. Perhaps his bad temper and low self-esteem had something to do with heavy drinking and cigarettes. Lahcen, on the other hand, the thirty-something mechanic, a specialist in repairing only lorries, divorced with no children, his mother--in-law hated him apparently, appeared to be stable. He was an entertainer, some even called him a comedian. Talking about a comedy, when we were done with tagine, there was a plate with fresh pomegranates waiting to be consumed. Each of us got a significant portion and enjoyed eating those little healthy bubbles; so *Äami* Lahcen did. However, the bits and pieces of this fruit stuck in his mouth unwillingly, but willingly and with some force, were spat out and landed purely by chance on me. "What the hell? What was that?" At the very moment that I reflected on possibilities, I got attacked by another spit but this time I could clearly see the culprit. "*Baba* spits really well," I commented and made everyone break into laughter.

******

My family. They cared for me. They didn't make me feel like a stranger. In spite of all the cultural and linguistic obstacles, we had so far managed to create a decent atmosphere. We laughed but sometimes we didn't even know why we laughed; we hugged each other; we played some sort of silly games, we ate together, and we shared everything. In the mornings, I was always greeted with a cup of Nescafe and a cup of tea at the same time. I believe this needs some explanation. Those two mugs in which coffee and tea were served came from France as one of the presents. The tea I got each morning also came from France as one of the presents. I thought it would make an excellent gift: all sorts of flavoured, fine see-through pyramid tea bags. What an idiot! What was I thinking! I felt exactly like a bunch of people from the "Apprentice" who, in one of those episodes, brought cheese and sausages to France to promote England. Bringing teas to the tea country, what would you call that? A great tea-pas or simply a tea faux-pas?

Unfortunately, the poor little boy was very sick during the night and continued to be sick during breakfast. Not only did he cover the carpet and the mattress with his vomit, meaning a glass of aspirin, vitamin C and ibuprofen that were given to him few minutes before, but he also had a temperature. He was feverish and his wound looked swollen, sore, bloody, and infected. "Why is the blood still coming out? It is not supposed to with the stitches?" "He will be ok. Ça va," they reassured me. The visit to a pharmacy was apparently unnecessary. "Are you sure?" I kept insisting while walking to the medina with Meryam and two young men from the same street. She was, and there was no point on insisting. Instead, we got to the centre: idle, unoccupied, quiet. "It is a good time to do some shopping unlike in the evening where one has to squeeze through the busy, narrow streets full of shoppers," I was told. Meryam wanted a pair of pyjama trousers. "How much are they?" "Too expensive," she said. "You don't negotiate?" I took over remembering the golden rule: always negotiate. The trousers cost 35DH. "I give you 25DH," I said. "*La! La!*" The stubborn salesman kept refusing. "What about if we take two pairs of trousers for 55DH?" Another refusal. When we were walking away he shouted, "60 DH for two!" "Forget it, we'll get somewhere else." Shopping generally is not my cup of tea, here was even worse as prices were not set and the salesmen were not open to negotiation. We forgot about the trousers and bought a wristwatch for someone in the family and a gun-toy for Achraf. I thought it would cheer him up a little. And it really did. As soon as he saw it, he jumped on his left leg and absconded the house hobbling supporting himself with the wounded one.

I was craving for some rest and solitude. My room was my solitude. I disappeared for a while. I read, wrote, and talked to my recorder. Half an hour later I had Meryam in my room with a piece of cake and a cup of tea. "Mangez!" she said. I wasn't keen on eating by myself, hence I rushed downstairs. I walked into the room and as soon as I sat down I had to run upstairs to get my camera. I saw something moving. The whole family spread all over the floor, was resting while watching Arabic soap opera. *Baba*, after his meticulous shave and good body scrub done by Meryam who was leaning against him, was fast asleep. Hakima's mum, Rkia, was also having a little snooze and Hakima was finally dosing on the other side with petit Achraf in the corner of that room. Likewise, grandma Halima was in her bed on the opposite side. This was a moment that I felt a strong unity of the family, love, peace and extraordinary calmness that I don't see much in the Western world as we are far too busy with formulating new goals, creating a new flow of activity so that we forget to get involved with easy details of our lives. In other words, are we as a family linked in any way, or are we *"like string puppets whose wires rest in separate hands?"*

******

Allhu Akbar

Ashhadu Ana La ilaha illa-Llah

Ashhadu Ana Muammadan Rasulu-Llah

Hayya Ala Salat

Hayya Ala Falah

Allahu Akbar

La ilaha illa-Llah

It's Friday, the special day for Muslims. It is a day of compulsory gathering praying and it's proceeded by the sermon. "O you who believe! When the call is made for prayer on Friday; then hasten to the remembrance of Allah and leave off trading that is better for you if you know. But when the prayer is ended, then disperse abroad in the land and seek of Allah's grace, and remember Allah much, that you may be successful." It is also a day when Allah's special mercies are granted. Muhammad ibn Isa at-Tirmidhi, a widely recited Islamic scholar said: "The best day the sun rises over is Friday; on it Allaah created Aadam. On it he was made to enter paradise, on it he was expelled from it, and the Last Hour will take place on, no other day then Friday." The prophet al-Bukhaari said the sins are forgiven on Friday: "Any man who performs *Ghusl* on Friday, perfumes himself if he has perfume, wears the best of his clothes, then goes to the mosque and offers as many prayers as he wishes while not harming anybody, then listens quietly while the

Immam speaks until he offers the prayer, will have all his sins between that Friday and the next forgiven." Whoever dies on Friday, said the Prophet al-Tirmithi and Ahmad, will be protected from the trial: "Any Muslim who dies during the day or night of Friday will be protected by Allaah from the trial of the grave." The Muslims say that it is a good occasion for them to meet together and listen to sermons and feel equality when praying all together in rows without any distinction between the rich and the poor or any other kinds of differences.

The prayer time depends on the sun rise and it changes accordingly. However, the Friday midday prayer, which is called *Zuhr*, gathered them together between 12.00 and 13.00am and was preceded by the usual call to prayer. The mosque was usually overcrowded and the holy gathering extended on to the outside space where they sat, listened, bowed, contemplated, and simply prayed.

When men were back from the mosques, they ate couscous for lunch, the traditional Friday meal. This Friday we were visited by other members of the family. As usual, the number of people outnumbered seats around our little table, but then again nine of us had managed to eat from the same plate. When I say plate, I mean a massive ceramic tagine dish which was as big as a table and as hot as a burning stove, but still the women managed to eat the couscous with their hands; first they grabbed a handful; and then tossing and rolling it quickly they were making perfect little balls ready to eat. Fortunately, this exertion was not obligatory: men, children and foreigners were allowed the spoon. The couscous that was poured over with some tomato sauce or hot milk was usually served with vegetables mainly carrots, pumpkin, chickpeas, potatoes, and meat. The most delicious of all were those tiny "barrels" of sheep meat - tender and mouth-watering. There was a rule which also applied to eating tagine: the meat was consumed last, and usually women in charge were taking it out and sharing it between everybody - in this case each one had a tiny piece. *"Koul! Koul!"* Apparently, I ate too slow and took too little. "You have to eat properly, like us, *chouf!*" Papa Mohamed took a spoonful of couscous and shovelled it down his mouth, and then demonstrated my way of eating. "I suppose I have a little stomach," I responded. As the couscous did not come with bread, some Moroccans did not like it for that reason. "You satisfy your stomach but soon after you feel hungry again," said Papa Mohamed.

It was the first time since my arrival that I went out in the evening, with Abdellah, and got connected to the internet in a local café, which was only occupied by men. The pleasure of getting out and seeing people was immense! On the way back home I saw a young crowd coming out of the school dressed up in white pinafores. Perhaps there is some life here? Perhaps I'll make some friends?

******

From the recording: "I have so far enjoyed this journey. I'm overwhelmed by my family's generosity and warmth towards me."

After the usual morning coffee, tea, and some bread with olive oil, I was ready to go out. It was the big souk on the suburbs of Khénifra in the fourth district of Amelou today. The day was hot, and Meryam, Leila, and I strode, beaten by the sun, for thirty minutes. First a cloud of dust that was seen from the distance struck me when walking past the Registry Office, and then a vast field of widely spread out tents, people, donkeys, mules, horses and cars that were struggling to get passed it all were emerging slowly exposing more and more of what the dust had covered so scrupulously. Papa Mohamed was supposed to be there. Therefore, we marched towards his lorry not far-off from the souk. Papa, Mustapha and another young man, with a prominent cut on his face, were the guards of sheaves of straw. The lorry which was packed full of straw seemed to have bent under its weight. "How much does one cost?" "25 DR each," Mustapha explained to me later. He and his friend were happy to pose for the photo when a man on a mule stopped to make a deal. "C'est un vrai, vrai, vrai Berbèr. Je veux un photo," he insisted. They might have sold or might have not, but they packed everything back on to the *camion* and drove off leaving us waiting there for quite a long stretch of time, and what we were waiting for I did not know, I guessed it was money. "I can give you some money or pay for the shopping," I proposed but she refused. Another hour got passed. We went to the souk. Leila was holding my hand like my girlfriend and wasn't willing to let go of it until we went back to our "straw station." After three hours of useless waiting we headed back home with no money, no shopping, and no straw. As soon as we got back Meryam received a phone call from Mohamed the caretaker who was keen on meeting me, but where, how, when and for what reason I had no idea and the answer wasn't clear. Meryam walked me to the main road, sat on its kerb, and waited with me. He arrived twenty minutes later in a taxi with another man. From the correspondence to Hannah:

Dear Hannah,

I met Mustapha, the chairman of our Association today. Fortunately, we had an interpreter. Now I have a clearer view of the whole situation.

Well, I don't think it will be that easy to do things for the school or the children.(…) Mustapha sounds rather sceptical explaining that the children have little time for any other activities (extra French or English) than school; he highlights how tired they are after the school and how difficult it would be to find some extra time. I proposed to do it during weekends, but yet again he told me how worn-out they may be.

In order to do anything, I have to go to Mr. Important and explain everything. If this official agrees on what I want to do, it would be a big step forward. If not, I have to go to someone else (this is where the madness starts).

The other thing is that the teachers in El Borj hardly speak French, and they do not teach children French. They said they have to learn Arabic first because majority of them speak Berber. So for me to sit in a classroom, observe, and then try to explain things in French sound like a "mission impossible" task, and the same would probably go for the teachers.

The chairman sounded very complacent to me, what is the world I'm looking for, hmm"the doesn't really matter" attitude. He sounded like this: this is our reality and you are not Moroccan, he actually said that, so you know hardly anything, which is maybe the truth. However, with such attitude any change would be impossible. From the onset, he puts everyone into the same basket: they are poor, illiterate, they have a little bit of crops that they grow or some chickens. This is what I should write down about the family background of each child. This really frustrates me.

I had this idea of getting to know the families (maybe it will be impossible), spending some time with them, observing how they live, maybe trying to communicate, but straight away I got the response: you have to go the local authorities to get the permission to do that.

Perhaps I should not have mentioned the idea of writing a book, but as I said, it may bring some sponsors for the school, and as you said, it's better to be honest. In the end, they understood that I'm not going to be a crazy, creepy reporter who runs around with a microphone and takes photos of everything but just a friend who wants to observe the reality and write about it. I will try my best to become their friend and not an intruder.

You see, here in the village I have already met young people who would like to continue learning French and English. Leila, my young neighbour, told me how much she would like to be taught French and English by me. Today we went to the big souk and we practised both languages. Yesterday I met another young man who'd like to do the same. Therefore, I was thinking perhaps Hmad could write a letter for me in Arabic that I could present to that important official. Perhaps that man could help me to find a venue if Hmad could mention it in his letter (…)

Mustapha also kept saying that the children need to follow their curriculum. I said I don't want to change any of it; this could be additional to what they had learned already.

They will choose two children from the school who are not sponsored yet. Mustapha thinks it's a better idea as it would encourage the rest of the children to attend the school instead of looking for new ones in the village. What do you think? I will take photos and find out a few things about them. Hopefully it will be done the same day with a bit of luck.

My best wishes, M

After that disappointing meeting, which gave me nothing but obstacles to overcome, I happily sat down at the dinner table with my family: a very delicious plate of tagine followed by two litres of Coca-Cola and the same quantity of something tropical - equivalent of Fanta.

The dinner was interrupted by drunken Mustapha, who could hardly stand on his legs but managed to sit at the table mumbling something that irritated *Baba* Lahcen. He was the wise one, and from the tone of his voice, I guessed, he wasn't very impressed by muttering, intoxicated Mustapha. He raised his voice and made him listen, but this young man couldn't keep his mouth shut. "What an idiot!" I thought. "He must have earned some money today by selling the straw and spent it all on alcohol." He then got up, left the room, and one minute later came back to *Baba's* bed, grabbed his head, and kissed it repeatedly. While *Baba* was getting more and more furious with him, Mustapha decided on calming him down by crawling up in front of him pretending to be funny and apologetic. Whatever he had expected from *Baba*, he got rather the opposite. *Äami* Lahcen grabbed his stick and spanked his back, once, twice, three times until he warded him off. In hindsight, it looked quite comical and entertaining but it wasn't funny at all when it was happening. It brought nothing but a great deal of upset. The prayer initiated by *Baba* and joined by Rkia, Halima, and Papa Mohamed came straight after Mustapha's angry disappearance and was followed by a rather intimate barbecue party in our upstairs living room with me, Papa, and Hakima. The small ceramic pot filled with incandescent red-hot charcoal fried tenderly pieces of chicken, and although they seemed to have been rather too tender for consumption, it really did not matter. What did matter in that moment was the company, laughter and the warmth coming from both: my parents and the pot.

******

Around midnight, Mustapha came back banging on the door. Someone let him in. He kept talking out loud in a very angry manner and left a few minutes later. The door was locked. Half an hour later he was at the doorstep jolting it as roughly as he could. I heard another man's voice. I believed it was Abdellah. They were both arguing and Hakima was called to come downstairs. It sounded violent. Papa Mohamed did not get up. I imagined he was too sick and too fragile to confront the boozer. The loud voices and Mustapha's fiery words were disappearing in the distance. The metal door was locked again, the lights went out. It became silent once more. Around 1.30am the drunk lunatic appeared in front of the door yelling and roaring trying to get inside. Bang! Bang! No one moves. Bang! Bang! "Hakima! Hakima!" Bang! Bang! No reaction. He moved on to the window. Bang! Bang! Luckily, there was a metal bar that prevented him from breaking in. He had no intention of leaving and Abdellah could no longer stand this spectacle, so both, him and Hakima, went to confront him. There was that silent moment followed by another flood of fury which sounded like total blasphemy. Then the shouting yet again became distant, the door was locked and the lights went out for the third time. Finally, there was some peace and quiet. The extremely uncomfortable feeling went through my body living me almost paralysed. I knew it very well as my father was an alcoholic. I wanted to react but I had no idea what to anticipate? Would it be appropriate to get involved? If I did, what language would I use to get my message across? All sorts of questions ran through my head, but in the end I said to myself: "If Papa stays in bed so should I."

The next morning my family was very troubled by the whole incident. They were crying and praying looking rather anxious. "He had not come back nor had he been seen today at all," I was told. Papa took me to the district of Amelou in the afternoon and asked around. No one knew where he was. While looking for Mustapha, Papa and I were running some errands, that is, trading some metal wire for money and getting a big fat 500DH. "Good job! Hakima will be very pleased!" I said. "The medina? Coffee?" asked Papa. "Avec plaisir!" Strolling with Papa Mohamed always made me feel safe. In spite of his rather nasty habit of sniffing *nafha* and more appalling way of spitting everywhere, there was something rather compelling about him. Perhaps it was a combination of both: poverty and pride, cordiality and harshness which were adding up to the authenticity. He might have been simple but authentic and good-hearted, and one could never underestimate such attributes. Anyhow, the medina offered us few things including a very, very second hand pair of boots that looked used and abused, worn out from walking, running or even crossing the whole Atlas; then a bag of nuts and sweets worth 75DH, a really giant fish for 30DH and 1kg of apples for another 15DH. Instead of having coffee, we sat down in a scruffy but charming place for *iben*, home-made yoghurt, and a piece of cake. *Hrira* came next; we chose another tatty but likable place where women's curiosity called 'who is she and what is she doing here?' had to be satisfied. "Do you speak Arabic?" The investigation continued and the truth had to be stretched a bit. "*Chwya*," I responded proudly. Our rendez-vous was sadly over and we had to head back home. I felt speechless and moved by Papa's gesture of inviting me out. He knew I had not a single dirham on me that evening and yet again he, the man without a proper job who struggled each day to provide for his wholeheartedly loved family, was more than happy to stand me a meal.

The fish was delivered to Rue 11, No 8, La Scierie, in very skilful hands of Hakima and landed on our dinner table along with tagine, apples, some pomegranate and one kilogram of nuts. I noticed one thing: no matter how much food was on the table, there were hardly ever any leftovers and one was always pushed to eat more. Was it a simple philosophy that said: eat when it's on the table as you don't know if, or when, the next meal will be?

******

Men introduced themselves every single day, sometimes they strolled with me, sometimes they sat in the park or in a café telling tales. Today, two young men on bikes accompanied me to the garden. They were charming and positively beaming with pleasure but at the same time, there was so much sorrow in their eyes. I often thought about my life and how lucky I was and still am; I never suffered hunger or poverty, I always had a choice, study or work, stay at home or travel. There was never lack of drinkable water, Coca-Cola or Fanta if I wished to drink it. And what choice did most of them have?

When they had gone, another man who didn't look at all Moroccan, neither his pale skin nor the way he was dressed up, invited me for a quick lunch with mint tea and some *boucheyar*. "The life in

Morocco is much more enjoyable, much more tranquil, people here actually smile, whereas in Europe everyone is stressed out and panics rushing around and not having time for a normal human interaction, a smile, a bonjour, a spontaneous laughter," he recalled. The European paranoia of having and not being seemed to have had upset him a great deal. Paris is conceited, and like all Parisians, it raises his nose at him. "I stay in Paris only for work and always anticipate holidays here, with people, and not robots out there." He drove me back home, to the "gates" of La Scierie, left me there with his mobile numbers and follow up question: "Would you like to go to Aglmam to see the big lakes and monkeys?" The temptation to say 'yes' was greater than common sense, and although I trusted his intentions, I was not able to respond without my family consent. I believed, the desire to act as I was free was greatly succumbed by the respect I had for my family and cultural rules imposed on me. They neither approved nor disapproved. They looked perplex. "We will have our family outing to Aglmam next Sunday," Meryam convinced me and got me excited. But we never did, and I never saw my "one afternoon friend" again. Instead, Lahcen was becoming friendlier and friendlier and that evening he turned up in my room. Although it was nothing new for me, here, however, it was treated as cultural faux-pas. Never had a man come to a woman's bedroom unless he was married to her. The rule-breaker was very much aware of his cheeky and senseless rather visit in my room and was as confused by his own appearance there as everybody else in the house. "Ça va? Ça va bien, tu marchez aujourd'hui?" He was standing in the door not knowing whether he should come or go, but eventually he went away pressed by his own confusion. "Au-revoir," he said and disappeared.

******

Going out after 6.00pm required a strategy, a sort of convincing and worry-free plan that was safe for both, my family and me - the truth-stretcher.

I had to allow myself a bit of flexibility. I had to response to my own desire, to my own unfulfilled curiosity about the nightlife in this city. It's not safe for you; the phrase repeated itself. What is safe for me here? Would it be better to stay in Europe and let all my desires of travels and adventures drown in the deep and rough waters of my imagination? That would be safe, cowardly safe. I prefer risk, happenings, action, the real journey that eventually calms my mind. "I'm sensible and strong," I responded. "I will not be stupid. In any case, I will protect myself by making fair judgement. Don't worry." The understanding of my liberty was non-existent yet, and the given and well-developed sense of freedom and independence had nothing to do with their strict rules. Women here cannot go out after dusk, and if they do, they must be always accompanied by someone, preferably a man, it's for their own safety. I have never underestimated safety as my own heavy baggage of fear and panic attacks keep haunting me, and depending on the environment, might even paralyse me. Nevertheless, locking myself at home would not resolve the problem. On the contrary, it would add more anxiety and distrust towards humans. In spite of my own misfortune that one human being brought upon me, I have the tendency to look positively on the whole spectrum of human existence. In any case, I managed to sneak out after

5.00pm, and I must thank the sun that was still exuding life for giving me an easy explanation. I took a book with me and went off to the garden to read for a while, whereupon the lights of the medina were beckoning me inside. I accepted the invitation and returned it as soon as I entered the gate of busy souks. I was squeezing myself through the crowd and suffocating under heavy looks and shallow talks of curiosity. Bonsoir, Holla… Française… Anglaise… Italiano… que yeux… salut… donnez moi ton numero, hihihi… bella…. I was about to go back home when I heard someone speaking English. "Hi, your eyes are really beautiful. Can I talk to you for a moment, please?" A young man's voice squeezed itself thought that busy crowd first and then his body popped out unexpectedly in front of me. "You must be the only person in Khénifra who speaks English. How do you feel?" "Fine," he responded as if my joke wasn't even taken into consideration. "You are so beautiful. Where do you come from?" This very charming young man was flooding me with compliments and insisted on walking me back home. We were swapping languages like a very used pair of gloves, so that when *Simo's* English was failing him then the French was coming handy. The contact with this young, curious and intelligent human being was almost rejuvenating making me realise how much I missed my real friends. Unfortunately, when he was about to write down his number, we were interrupted by the presence of Mohamed, my neighbour. "Are you ok?" "Fine, don't worry. He was walking me back home." Mohamed took over and delivered me home in one piece just after 7.00pm. Straight away Meryam's eyes were punishing me for coming in late, and demanding explanation. "Where have you been?" "I was just sitting in the garden and reading."

******

In order to get from place A to place B outside the city of Khénifra one had to take a grand taxi or patiently wait for buses that never came. Each visit to the Association Hannan started off with a "grand tour" around the centre of Khénifra so that the "grand l'espace" could be filled up with six passengers, at least. One could not swing a *cat* in there, I can assure you of that. I had my preferences: I was going for the front seat. Although I was always crushed by someone, whether it was at the front or at the back seat, I preferred to sit on the gear stick than on my fellow passengers who suffered some sort of chronic staleness which was difficult to breathe in. When I got to El Borj, I started updating files by gathering necessary information regarding the background to the children's families, identifying the poorest for new sponsors and following up on their progress at school. "I could kiss you and hug you for that," Hannah was very pleased. Mohamed Ousbigh, one of the trustees and as he called himself - the vice-president of the Association - seemed rough and bullish, but he also gave me the impression of having the welfare of the children on his mind. I was raising my eye-brows when he was reciting, entirely off-the-cuff, information on each single child, whether he has carried his education in the primary school in El Borj, or had left to find his calling through the high school in Khénifra, then their ages, fathers, mothers, siblings, animals… at a certain point I was doubting the truth behind all of it thinking he could have told me anything and I had no choice but to trust him. However, my stay here would not make sense if from the onset I would distrust or doubt the honesty of a man who practically ran our school. Not only had he provided me with the information needed, but also had not been opposed to running extra French lessons here. "You can start after 1.00pm. We only need the primary school director's approval. "And we did. I presented myself to the director: a fat, arrogant, unpleasant, full of himself man who without Mohamed's intervention would not have given me his blessing. "O dear child! You don't understand our reality, do you?" It was written down on his face but pronounced rather unequivocally. "You have to go to Mr. Important to get his permission." Apparently, the previous director was even worse. He took a computer to his home given to the school as a present from our Association to be used by children saying it was for security reasons, and before he left the school, he had replaced the brand-new computer, which the school never saw, with some crappy old one. Nevertheless, the full of himself director had agreed on extra French lessons offering me children's schedule and planning the best time for it. As my rumbling stomach reminded me of lunch, I rushed back home to discover a special family's gathering to which I was also invited. "Put your black pyjama on," I was told off by Hakima for looking too European. The gathering must be special as Hakima, Fadma - our neighbour and a relative, and another Fadma - Hakima's best friend, they all were dressed up and had their make-up done in a local beauty salon.

The house where we were going, from outside, looked like nothing but an old scruffy building; the inside told a very different and rich story, a story of splendour, pomp, and extravagance; a story of people who, with no doubt, did better than the rest. A custom tells you to take something with you; it could be chocolate, tea, sugar, yogurts, fruits, something that says how much one appreciates the invitation. Although I appreciated the invitation, I regretted the supply of sugar and milky chocolate to this household; as soon as it was delivered it melted in the splendour of this extravagant event, the party-people, and the silver service that was provided. "The sitters" - women only, were occupying sofas in two large leaving rooms and were spreading on the already existing luxury more luminosity coming from their djellabas, headscarves, and the jewellery. *"Salam ali-koum. La bas? Bikhir? Henya?"* A handshake. Kiss. Hand on the mouth. And again. Round the room. The other one. Sit. Wait. More women. More handshakes. More kisses. More hand on the mouth.

"You can all go upstairs now," the announcement made us all moved in a pronounced multi-coloured vivid wave. The rooftop, where the whole event was taking place, was as large or even larger than the first floor of our house; layered with red carpets that with contact with heavy plastic rooftop covers, supported by wooden beams, and strong sunbeams were illuminating orange and blue colour all over the space. Comfortably, there were eight tables and more than eighty women, some with children, some with their parents, some singles. I had this misfortune to be seated by a woman with a baby who kept staring at me, and as soon as I responded to that gaze, the baby was going hysterical making me feel like some kind of monster. Not only was it getting hotter, with more women coming and more breeze escaping, but also the baby was getting on my nerves. "You don't need to look at me baby, yes everyone sees that I'm different here, I really don't need more attention; if you want to carry on looking my question is: what the hell are you crying for?" But the baby did not understand my inner voice. Instead, it was giving me a headache. A kind woman from the family, who I had just met, sat in between me and the baby. "Don't look at her." "I don't. It's her that is looking at me. Tell her that." The baby did not comprehend the whole point of our discussion nor did that woman. After over one hour of waiting and grilling in that space, we heard some particular noise: music, chanting, cheering, and singing. The chanting was distinct; it was produced by a singular sound broken by a vibrating tongue making one hell of a resonance, and whoever felt like joining the orchestra - joined. Soon after, a young woman called Zahra, who I had already met, appeared in our room with her singing entourage, like some kind of diva who everybody awaited in anticipation. She was glowing with joy and the melting make-up while walking around a room shaking hands with everybody. I had no idea what the party was about and I knew nothing about her. When she came up to me I kept asking: "Did you just get engage or married?" "No, no, baby, baby," she responded. "Ah! You are pregnant!" I congratulated her not even knowing if my guess was right. The party was about to start. It was announced by plates of roasted chicken tagine that laid the tables, followed by another bursting with quantity platters of tiny sweet pasta. What a delight! Wait a minute. It's almost gone. Are we in a hurry? Is this some kind of "who finish first contest?" If it was, the woman next to me would have a surprisingly good timing; she wasn't eating, she was devouring piece by piece nervously, and at the same time, was grabbing and throwing the chicken's parts on to the side of my plate saying: *"Koul! Koul!"* All the leftovers were quickly taken away by the eaters, placed on the bread, wrapped up in the serviettes and hidden away. It is a very normal behaviour here; food is precious and it would be considered a crime throwing it away. I did the same thinking of *Baba* and Halima back at home.

Our table looked like a chicken battlefield as everything that was not consumed landed on the tablecloth, which after the meal was quickly removed, easy and simple, not much washing up for them. The feast needed to be digested; another plate full of fruits was served. That was more than enough; I could hardly move when I was rushed to wash my hands and get my shoes ready to walk back home. *"Blatti! Blatti!"* Zahra's mum was trying to sit us down for a cake and some tea. *"Je me suis remplie le bidon,"* I said and they all agreed with me. The cake was packed and the whole trophy, including the chicken and fruits, were given to my grandparents.

Before the food was served, I came downstairs for a little look around. In the kitchen the "You Tube" was on and a few young women, including Meryam, were dancing. "What are you doing here?" Meryam looked bewildered. "Nothing, just looking." The young man came with a very different attitude and dragged me to the kitchen floor: "Dance! Dance!" he said. They were all lined up performing a traditional, well-synchronised Berber dance; the shoulders moved up and down with the legs and hands followed. I had fun but soon was reprimanded by Meryam. "It's not like this, it's like that," she was laughing at my puny effort. "Give me a chance, I have to practise it." Fortunately, the music stopped and my hapless shoulders, not used to such movement, were ready for a little rest.

When I went back upstairs, some women were interested in finding out who I was. As soon as I introduced myself as a voluntary worker, they were giving me their phone numbers to teach their children and kept saying: "Do you really work for free?"

******

That night I had very eerie dreams. I was getting to know someone in a supermarket, someone who claimed to be in love with me but I kept saying, "Listen, we are not compatible." Later I was surrounded by animals, dogs precisely that were having a real human chat with me.

The dreams were in tune with the morning call for prayer: rare, loud, shrill and terribly discordant. The voice wasn't singing but drilling like a pneumatic hammer pressing me to use my ear plugs. The previous week's *Muadhdhin's* voice was waking me up gently, touching my ears and cradling me back softly into my sleep; his voice was light and graceful; it had carried peace and warmth and through his voice one could have felt the spirit of God. This melody, however, was too rough, too loud and too violent for such early hour. Not only did I badly desire a good-night sleep to feel fully rested the next morning, but also regained the energy consumed by the latest events. I craved for a sleep without any disturbance or any background noise which so far proved to have been impossible.

The next day I was continuing with the files update; lucky day for two children who got a sponsor. The poverty was beyond anyone's recognition and only by living such experience I could comprehend the scale of it. My goal was to find good-hearted souls for eighteen more children who desperately needed financial support. "What about if we make contact with the Moroccan Embassies in Paris, London, etc? These embassies may know friendly businesses through import/export trade?" I was asking Hannah in one of my emails. "Perhaps contacting Moroccan Airlines and asking them if their suppliers would sponsor our children would be a good idea, or directly approaching charities like UNICEF inquiring for a grant or some help with finding sponsors?" The ideas were great but they had already been tested without much of a success, not even extra luggage or free flights were considered by British Airways or Royal Air Morocco - those giant corporations that are making billions each year. "How on earth did it happen that we have so much and they have so little? What went wrong?" I repeated the questions in one of my emails sent to my wonderfully "ancient" and supportive friend Michael Richman. "Who is responsible for such mess? Is it still possible to fix it, and if so, how?"

The whole afternoon I spent in the company of my mum Hakima, Fadma and a family that we paid a visit to that day: Halima, and her mum, whom I met at the party, the one who sat in between me and that screaming baby. By the way, the whole mystery behind that celebration was explained to me by Hannah in one of her emails to me. It turned out it was not pregnancy but a *circumcision* party for her little boy. The house was icy cold and after one hour of not moving and not having a hot drink, I was properly frozen. It was noticed and I was given a blanket. Soon after my poor blood circulation was improved by mint tea and *boucheyar* that were served when Halima came back from the market. I looked at her thinking how attractive she was with her pure healthy skin complexion touched by the sun, finniest wrinkles and her upper teeth that were coming out a little bit too far out adding even more charm to her rather shy character. She was forty-two years old and not married yet. There was someone in her life, someone that she loved, but it turned out to be a dodge, disappointment, and a drunken-scam.

The winter finally paid us a visit dropping loads of rain and taking away the sunshine. Our house felt even colder. The temperature dropped down by a few degrees and although the open-air aperture was covered by a blanket, it did not prevent the chill from coming in. Hakima gave me another warm pyjama and a dressing-gown, it was necessary to put more layers on in order to survive winter here. The sudden change of climate made me feel nostalgic, the yearning to be with my own family or friends, sitting in front of a fire, sipping hot chocolate, or having a glass of mulled wine over a film or some chit-chat.

******

Notes:

1 (p. 8) 'Succulent' - one of my favourite words in English language as reminds me of my best-loved playwright Harold Pinter and his "Birthday Party" (1958).

2 (p. 9) Eid Al Adha - Abraham had a dream in which God told him to sacrifice his first newborn son. When the day came he told his dream to his son who agreed to obey God; when Abraham was about to kill his son, God sent him a sheep to slaughter instead of his son. This is where the commemoration comes from.

3 (p. 10) The open-air aperture in typical Moroccan houses or riads is no accident. It serves two purposes. Firstly, the obvious focal point but more importantly, the natural air-conditioning that has been prevalent in Morocco for millennia and is remarkably successful.

4 (p. 11) Bsha/bessaha, in Darija, the Moroccan dialect, "in good health." It's a very common word and one hears it often.

5 (p. 12) Koul! In Darija, Eat!

6 (p. 12) La, in Amazigh/Tamazigh, the Berber language means no.

7 (p. 12) Darija - Moroccan Arabic dialect. It's not an official language but it has a strong presence in Morocco. This year it has stirred some linguistic debates whether it should be taught at schools. The proposal has been rejected by Moroccan Prime Minister Abdelilah Benkirane as "a threat to the very foundations of the Moroccan state."(Al Jazeera, 27 April 2014).

8 (p. 12) Äami, in Darija, my paternal uncle. In this case, when preceded a name, it expresses a great deal of respect for that elderly person.

9 (p. 13) "All human life is here" - an advertising slogan for the News of the World in late 1950s. The quotation comes from the book "The Madonna of the future" (1879): "Cats and monkeys – monkeys and cats – all human life is here."

10 (p. 13) "Nihil novi sub sole" - "There is nothing new under the sun," "Ecclesiastes" (1:9).

11 (p. 13) Brandon Mull, "Fablehaven. Teacher's Guide," prepared by LuAnn B. Staheli, M.Ed, p.7-8.

12 (p. 13) Boucheyar/ Mssemen - Moroccan pancakes.

13 (p. 15) Hammam - it derives from Arabic word 'al hamim' - 'the force of the summer heat,' in Western World it is known as the Turkish bath.

14 (p. 15) In Darija: Brit n'koul - I want to eat; tcharafna - nice to meet you; ajbani - I like it; mezyan - good; zwina - pretty, beautiful; khayb - bad; tsbah-ala-khir - good night.

15 (p. 16) Al-Fajr - lit. "when the sky begins to whiten/ the first light of dawn," is the first of the five salat prayers.

16 (p. 16) Muadhdhin/Muazzin/Muezzin/Moaadin - a person who is appointed at a mosque to lead and recite the call to prayer (adhan).

17 (p. 17) Before each prayer, Muslims perform a ritual ablution called 'wudu.' The process involves washing the hands, face, arms and feet in a very particular way. 'Wudu' symbolises a state of physical and spiritual purity required to stand before God.

18 (p. 17) Sobh - the morning prayer.

19 (p. 18) Baba, in Amazigh, grandfather.

20 (p. 20) "Letters on life," Rainer Maria Rilke, The Modern Library, 2006, p. 37.

21 (p. 20) Allah, the Almighty; I declare, there is no God but Allah; I declare that Muhammad is the Messenger of Allah; Come to pray, Come to success (salvation); Allah, the Almighty; There is no God but Allah.

22 (p. 20) Quran, chapter 62/verses: 9-10.

23 (p. 20) Aisha Stacy, from the article, "The religion Islam. The significance of Friday in the life of a believer," 2010.

24 (p. 20) "Ghusl" - is an Arabic term referring to the full body ritual ablution required, if the adult loses the state of body cleanness; mandatory for any Muslim after having sexual intercourse, orgasmic discharge, completion of menstrual cycle, giving birth, and death by natural causes.

25 (p. 20) Immam - a person who learns the Quran by heart and conducts Islamic worship service, and provides religious guidance. It is also a title that is given to every person that leads in Muslim society, e.g. the King of Morocco is called the Immam.

26 (p. 20) Aisha Stacy, Op. cit.

27 (p. 20) Zuhr or Dhuhr - the midday prayer, the second of the five salat prayers.

28 (p. 21) Chouf! In Darija, Look!

29 (p. 25) Nafha - black tabacco.

30 (p. 25) Iben - white cheese.

31 (p. 25) Hrira - the traditional Moroccan soup.

32 (p. 25) Chwya/ chwiya, in Darija, a little.

33 (p. 27) The name Simo equals Mohamed.

34 (p. 27) "Daunbailo" (1986), a fantastic film with Robert Benigni who goes to prison, takes out of his pocket his notes and reads out loud, "Excuse me, excuse me, not enough room to swing a cat."

35 (p. 28) Salam ali-koum, La bas? Bikhir? Henya? The greetings, hello, how is going? How are you? Is it going well? The verbal greeting is usually accompanied by a hand-shake (between men and women and strangers); then the hand is either placed on the mouth (if one greets elderly persons) or on the chest. The close family and friends (only between men) kiss each other three times – one kiss on one side and two kisses on the other side.

36 (p. 30) Blatti! In Darija, Wait!

37 (p. 30) "Se remplir le bidon" - "to be full up," this French idiom does make French people laugh.

38 (p. 31) Circumcision is practised nearly universally by Muslims in Morocco. It is a tradition established by the Prophet Muhammad and so its practice is considered very important in Islam. There is also a matter of cleanliness and purification. According to a systematic and critical review of the scientific literature, the health benefits of circumcision include lower risks of acquiring HIV, genital herpes, human papilloma virus and syphilis. Circumcision also lowers the risk of penile cancer over a lifetime; reduces the risk of cervical cancer in sexual partners, and lowers the risk of urinary tract infections in the first year of life. (New Evidence Points to Greater Benefits of Infant Circumcision, But Final Say is Still Up to Parents, Says AAP, American Academy of Paediatrics, 2012). Risks associated with male circumcision depend on the type of study (e.g., chart review vs. prospective study), setting (medical vs. nonmedical facility), person operating (traditional vs. medical practitioner), patient age (infant vs. adult), and surgical technique or instrument used. The most commonly reported complications were pain, bleeding, infection, and unsatisfactory appearance. There were no reported deaths or long-term sequelae documented. Well-designed studies of sexual sensation and function in relation to male circumcision are few, and the results present a mixed picture. Taken as a whole, the studies suggest that some decrease in sensitivity of the glans to fine touch can occur following circumcision. However, several studies conducted among men after adult circumcision suggest that few men report their sexual functioning is worse after circumcision; most report either improvement or no change. (Risks associated with male circumcision, Centre for Disease Control and Prevention).

End of Part One

Itto Azziz with Meryam in front of their house.

Part Two

"Two things are infinite: the universe and human stupidity; and I'm not sure about the universe."

I left Europe exactly two weeks ago. Although I missed some of the commodities that I was used to, I had not made a single complaint. Amongst the most missed were my shower and bath, and BBC Radio 4 with the stories on Desert Island Discs, and the countryside drama on The Archers. Some form of entertainment, including the cinema and decent meaningful conversations were top of my list. Despite the occasional craving for a glass of Bordeaux or Côte de Lyon, my body felt lighter and my thinking clearer. The popularity that I had been gaining here through all those countless opportunists with such transparent intentions made me ponder writing my own phonebook.

Today I was perturbed by the appearance of two young men who seemed older but acted like teenagers. The one who spoke a little bit of English and French was a twenty-eight-year-old school bodyguard. The second one, called Said, had no particular skills. Wait a minute! I'm missing two: drinking and smoking. If he wasn't sipping whisky, hidden in the inside pocket of his jacket, he was smoking either hashish or cigarettes. He was a handsome man but not the brightest crayon in the box. In fact, both of them weren't playing with the full deck and were full of clear intentions. "What about a walk along the river?" They were asking questions and at the same time praising my curves. "Going where, exactly?" "Mountains," they said. "They are quite far away," I was alert. "We could stop at Said's house if it gets too much," suggested the bodyguard. I got more alert but there was no reason to panic - it was a bright sunny afternoon in a public garden. Although I knew I was safe, I was troubled by the energy they were sending: clearly abusive, uncanny, and spine-chilling. When I was on the way to the medina, I had this weird feeling that I may see them again. Perhaps it was all a coincidence that a man called Abdellah paid attention to me and offered to walk me home that day, when out of blue, Said and his friend happened to be behind us pretending not to know me at all. "Merde! Now he knows where I live!" I cursed this fortunate encounter. "Please, call me. I'd like to take you out," said Abdellah, "If you don't, I'll come and get you. I know where you live." That meaningless but creepy remark taught me a lesson today.

Fadma, the very best friend of Hakima, dragged me out of the house over to hers. *"Aji! Aji!"* she shouted adding, *"hrira... koul!"* The level of my hunger was down below zero but the pleasure of this invitation was greater than the appetite. Despite of all the conservative attributes towards life that Fadma was gradually revealing, there was also another side to her which was illuminated by the beaming warmness towards her family and close friends. It was easy to see how much she was loved by her own children. In fact, the warmth generated by that family was the only form of heating in the entire house, there was no wood-burning stove or gas heater. It seemed like TV was the biggest modern commodity here as well as each household that I had so far visited displayed one TV screen, at least. Perhaps it was the only way of keeping in touch with reality or entertainment, and certainly football - the national obsession spread out on at least ninety-five per cent of Moroccan men.

I have to own up. *Hrira*, the refined by chickpeas minestrone soup, did not work for me at all. No matter where or by whom it was prepared, there was something tasteless about the whole combination of chickpeas, tiniest pasta, and tomatoes sauce. Nevertheless, I ate it every time out of politeness, respect, and gratitude for the food that was on the table each day. "Fadma…baby," Hakima was pointing at Fadma's belly. "Is she pregnant? Congratulations!" Hold on, there was no trace of the father, where was he? Apparently he was constantly away working and only occasionally was coming back home. Having had two boys she desperately wanted a girl. "She will call the baby after you," I was told by Hakima.

It could have been the *hrira* that gave me a splitting headache which turned into a bad migraine, or it could have been something else. No matter what caused my temporary illness, it certainly required a little snooze. "What's going on?" Incredibly loud yells suddenly woke me from my nap. I rushed downstairs and saw Lahcen's father against Papa Mohamed boozing with disagreement over something. I sat down thinking that perhaps the company of a stranger could prevent further arguments, but as soon as I sat down I had to stand up again as everyone else did. Papa Mohamed was erect in fury and was on the verge of punching Lahcen's father in his face, but here was grandma Halima who raised herself swiftly standing between them two and preventing any violence from erupting. They kept shouting for a while, and the quieter Papa Mohamed was becoming, the louder Lahcen's father behaved. Whatever was said that evening caused a red-hot debate after the furious man was gone. Soon after, his son Lahcen arrived joining in a debate, this time in rather a peaceful manner.

******

From the correspondence to Hannah:

"Today, Mustapha, Mohamed and Mohamed the caretaker did a great job bringing almost all the children to the school. I think that only sixteen did not turn up. One of our sponsored children, Mohamed Oulabi, came with his mum asking for help. It must have been some time ago since the boy broke his arm, but they had never had money to get it fixed. His arm looks awful and the photos I attached do not even show it. Apparently, they need 10.000DH for the operation and asked if I could help. Perhaps, you could make some sort of appeal? If this would be of any help, I could donate the £100 that John Fairley sent to me through your website."

I had an immediate response from Hannah saying: "This is a bit tricky. Basically we have had to stop helping with medical needs because there are so many; when you do for one you end up with everyone asking for money. We literally had a queue outside Hmad's dad's house, and *Baba* said he was going to put Halima at the door to sell tickets!"

They had paid for an operation to help a boy with club feet, a cataracts removal for a man with Downs Syndrome, and an operation for a three-year-old boy who had a massive lump on his face that looked like a tumour. It took them three years to find a doctor who would perform the operation. It was hugely successful and the boy who is now eight years old, still financially supported by Hannah and Hmad, in a good form. The Association has also been facing a real problem. How to trust all the people who have been approaching them and asking for very large sums of money without any formal medical verification? The people need to produce a document that could prove the cost of an operation and diagnose the problem which is easy to obtain. Unfortunately they never do.

******

The day started off with a drive around Khénifra in a taxi with Halima's mum and a few other curious passengers who talked about me while smiling and praising me by tapping my shoulders.

Then on the way back home from El Borj, I got a lift from a man who drove a brand new-looking 4x4 car. He was dressed up in djellaba and introduced himself as a retired military officer and the mayor of El Bojr, the position that he wanted to resign from this year, 2014. "The bureaucracy is far too annoying," he said. This man, without a doubt, was rich and comfortable and sounded as corrupt as the people he was referring to. He then started bombarding me with questions of diplomas that I did not have, and was crushing my enthusiasm for teaching children French. "Everything has to be authorised," he barked. "What a buffoon!" I thought while explaining, unnecessarily, to him that diplomas have nothing to do with skills. This man was showing off his wealth in front of everybody driving his 4x4 car that, if sold for cash, could feed the whole of El Borj for a minimum of two years. "Has he actually done anything for those people?" I wondered. He dropped me off wishing me good luck.

While I was getting ready to go to the café, a man from the family: smiling, chatty, happy, passed over an invitation to his place for this forthcoming Saturday for me, Hakima, and Fadma. What a charming and friendly man he was!

In spite of the rain, I walked to my favourite "Omega" café where the two waiters were showing off, Simo - with his phone number; Zouhir - with a promise of taking me to the Sahara Desert to introduce me to his family. I obviously nodded and smiled.

"Salut Magdalena, je suis ton voisin," a young man with glasses on, dressed up in a long, dark and quite a fashionable coat performed in front of me. "I'm very pleased," I said, and he disappeared. A few minutes later, he was back again asking to sit with me. As the conversation wasn't flowing, pure fault of a language, he vanished again coming back with another friend who was supposed to be better in French. "Are you both students?" That didn't go well either. He left again and ten minutes later he was standing in front of me with another friend, Mohamed. This time the conversation was on. The full set of standard questions was asked but this time the dialog felt different from any other I had: very European, mature, smooth, easy-going, normal. I was surprised how normal it was. They did not ask me if I was married or whether I would like to get married, nor did they query my age. "What a pleasure to have met someone normal," I said to myself. Ali, my neighbour, was unemployed searching for work for over a year; Mohamed was studying accountancy. While walking me back home, Ali suggested going for tea at his place and meeting his mum. I was more than happy. His mum, Mina, was at home preparing tea and *boucheyar* for us. She struck me as a warm, friendly and easy-going woman, and on top of that, an excellent cook, her *boucheyar* were exquisite! Laughing, chatting, looking at photographs, it was simply an enjoyable time. Mina gave me a present, a pair of earrings with a necklace. She insisted. We scheduled coffee for tomorrow. It was time to go home and share today's excitement with my family. "I have met Ali, his mum, and Mohamed!" I was over the moon behaving like I had never seen a human being before, but they certainly had and weren't as delighted as I was. In fact, they did not show the slightest enthusiasm, and that pressed me to calm down while waiting for dinner.

******

There was no specific time for people to go to bed or get up. The talk went on until they got tired of talking. The background noise that seemed to have been hidden in every single nook of the house was as awake as its inhabitants.

Hakima was up and about from 7.00am each morning. The children, Achraf and Moad, needed to be fed and sent off to school. Bread needed to be baked and tea needed to be made. Then everybody else needed to be fed. The two friends, both Fadmas, were visiting her in the mornings while she was making *boucheyar* or already preparing lunch. I might have said that before but it would be worth repeating: she was an extraordinary human being and I loved her wholeheartedly. Never had she complained and worked as hard as a dog. Her life as a married woman, she had tied the knot with Mohamed when she was eighteen years old, looked to me as a mad circle that was spinning around cooking, baking, cleaning, shopping, and looking after everybody. For the past twenty-eight years there was not much entertainment in her life, and I bet that her adolescent life had looked similar. Here was the morning procedure: Hakima made teas, coffee, heated up milk, then served us *boucheyar* or a cake, and if not, some bread with olive oil. No matter how delicious the bread was my stomach couldn't digest more than a few tiny pieces a day, so I was always looking forward to *boucheyar* or *rfissa* both, delicious, buttery, and satisfying. "Demain, Hakima, *Inchallah*…," it sounded like a coded message but it was clear to everybody. It was Papa

Mohamed who each night, before the bed time, was saying it out loud to me in front of Hakima. Obviously, it was treated as a joke but the expectations were serious and unambiguous.

This morning I met some children in El Borj who would definitely come to the extra French lessons. I had this cliché in my head that girls were always better-behaved than boys. Wrong. Here they appeared as difficult as boys, cheeky and not terribly clever, curious but not enough to drop the mischievous and resistant attitude. Then, while waiting for a taxi in El Borj, I talked to a man who had this European dream in his head. Europe, for him, was one fat paradise occupied by only rich people. "How much can you earn?" he enquired. "How much does it cost to rent a house in London?" The sudden drop of his mouth showed a real disbelief. "Perhaps it's not such a paradise as you think?" He mentioned Edith Piaff and was familiar with Jack Brell's "Ne me quitte pas" song.

Waiting for a taxi or any form of public transport was time-consuming and the same went for appointments or outings. The daytime did not have a real value for people here and I had to be prepared to wait, for example, the 3.00pm medina outing with Meryam and Fadma happened to be at 5.00pm. Before then, I had stumbled upon Ali who gave me a letter.

Chère Madeleine,

C'était un plaisir pour mon ami et pour moi de faire ta connaissance. Le fait de t'inviter boire un verre de thé chez moi était un geste spontané et ne portrait aucune mauvaise intention. Les gens d'ici ne perçoivent pas les choses de la même façon.

Nous sommes à ta disposition pour toute aide. Laisse-toi à nous. Si tu voudrais qu'on prenne un café ensemble ou bien faire un tour à la médina appelle moi sur mon portable ou bien viens pour me chercher chez moi.

Cordialement,

Ali

As I anticipated nothing except for an occasional coffee or chat, I was rather moved by such a cordial message. This letter also made me deliberate a much divided Moroccan society suggested by Ali: "Le gens d'ici ne perçoivent pas les choses de la même façon."

The feeling of vulnerability and powerlessness struck again. While I was standing in front of a shop in the medina awaiting Meryam and Fadma, a clochard walked past me, turned around, and stopped. He picked up a piece of vegetable that was soaked up in a puddle of dirty water on the street, and mumbling something threw that piece at me saying: "*Koul! Koul!*" I did not move. I just watched him coming closer. The temptation was to say, "I'm not hungry, thank you," but for a couple of reasons I restrained myself. Firstly, I did not want to get into any trouble with that poor man, and secondly, I felt as if I had no right to engage in any verbal or physical attack against someone more vulnerable than me. However, the clearly diminishing distance between me and him was suggesting some form of intentional aggression. It was lucky that the whole scene was observed by a couple of young men from across the street. They reacted, and their verbal interruptions warded him off. The whole scene appeared funny to them though, they were entertained and had neither any sympathy for this poor homeless man nor for me, his potential victim.

The change of the weather brought a change in our house, a smoky one at first, suffocating, making us all cry, unwillingly. The smoke produced by the malfunctioning *forno* was slowly taking over the whole house looking for escape everywhere but through the chimney. The chimney was made of five long metal pipes that were running through the open-air aperture up to the rooftop. For a couple of hours it was a real palaver, but eventually smoke found its way out through that metal pipe and we all could sit around it enjoying each other's company. Photo-click. Hakima attacks Papa Mohamed pretending to stab him in his head. Photo-click. *Baba* gets angry, the noise and Mustapha's laughter, precisely, gets on his nerves. "Ha, ha, ha, ha, ha, ha," he imitated Mustapha's cheerfulness. If only I could understand his monolog! Another photo. A good-working stove. Click. Enough. Mustapha was keen on seeing a movie on my computer. "*Wakha.*" When I was going through hundreds of films on my hard-drive, I stumbled upon the documentary on Lucian Freud. "Have a look; this man was a very famous painter." My intentions were to educate him and never to embarrass, or make him feel uncomfortable, and his reaction wasn't something that I had anticipated. He looked at the painting, "Benefits Supervisor Sleeping," and with hinted anger turned his head away. The nudity shown on the painting was for him equal to some other nude acts, which were not to be exposed publicly. *Awrah*, the intimate parts of the body must, according to Islam, be covered from the sight of others with clothing, and exposing any of it is regarded as a sin. "Modesty is part of faith." Although I did not understand his reaction then, I apologised for making him feel awkward. I do now, with hindsight.

******

The midday service seemed louder and longer than usual. The lack of sleep from 5.30am onwards made everything longer and louder, even the Abdellah's prayer seemed that way.

After Friday's couscous I was ready to go and meet up with Ali and Mohamed. The same place and same variety of drinks: coffee, tea or hot chocolate. Mohamed, reminded me of one of my best friends Tomasz, intelligent, funny, with great sense of humour. However, my intuition was telling me that he had not yet fully identified his own being, not yet fully recognised himself. His eyes were searching, but what they were searching for I didn't yet dare to ask. His smile, honest and authentic, kept disappearing under a heavy weight of thoughts and although he beamed with joy, he also kept, consciously, subduing his cheerful attitude. He was fully aware of the whole different world around him, as his intelligence and curiosity were stretching itself out beyond this town or this country. The discussions were stimulating, giving me the whole new spectrum of life here.

Ali, who constantly talked about Islam, seemed to be religious and devoted to his beliefs making me feel like a complete atheist. He looked lost though and however much he tried to hide it, it flew back on to the surface in a big wave. They both appeared kind and helpful offering their assistance with everything from petty things like finding me a mobile phone, to the more adventurous like taking me places or even organizing the New Year's Eve celebration.

This time, it was Mohamed's turn to invite us both to his place: freezing cold and dark. While we were sitting in his room awaiting tea and *boucheyar* that were being prepared by his mum, kind and friendly-looking, I was inspecting his room when my gaze, all of a sudden, stumbled upon some books. I was nicely surprised. It was the first household that exposed some literacy. His mum joined us for tea. She was clearly expressing her compassion for my situation, which at first I did not understand. I forgot the sentiments and took a very literate meaning of the word "poor" that she articulated. "How does she know that I'm not well-off?" I was thinking. Her comment baffled me but was quickly explained. Ahh, yes! I'm far away from home, the whole family and friends, I don't have a father, and I don't have a paid job. Perhaps consolidation was well-deserved, but it has never crossed my mind to see myself that way. Although I was going through some hardship in life, I have never had much compassion for myself. The things I chose were the things that shaped me, and I have been grateful for them. This subject led us to a deeper conversation about freedom, choice, letting go of material things, accumulating less and fully embracing the present moment, the acceptance of what we are and what we want from life. "Are you happy?" asked Mohamed. "I have learned how to be happy. It's almost like everything else in life, like a song or a poem, if it pleases me I learn it by heart, sometime I forget some lines but quickly enough recall them to sustain the joyful moments. The earlier hardship gave me no choice and the constant travelling has opened my mind making me realise what really matters in life. It's not what you carry in your luggage, it's what your heart experiences, what your eyes see, what your mind consumes. You have to feed your happiness as life is hard, and you two know it very well."

Along with the *boucheyar*, tea, and apples we had some *dactyls*. "Do you know that you can only eat dactyls in odd number?" I had no idea but did exactly what I was told, I eat three. My complaint of a very disturbing morning call for prayer did not come across as blasphemy but it did not evoke any sympathy either. It was considered a blessing for them. "Another day has come, another day given by Allah," confirmed Ali. They were trying to make me understand the significance of their beliefs and what religion and Allah meant to them picturing it through a marriage. It was a secret act and a strong connection between husband and wife could only be developed with Allah and in the name of Allah. It seemed to me that the whole religious connection had nothing to do with the custom. If a man decides on marrying a girl he must come first to her house and ask her parents for permission. He must bring *a bag of sugar* with him. If he is accepted then the two families get together to negotiate further arrangements. Within a few weeks the marriage is organised. If the marriage for some reason does not work, one looks for the answers in the Quran. The Quran is supposed to bring answers to every single problem in one's life. Divorce is the last thing that one considers. "Religion is supposed to unite families and make them stronger," added Ali.

******

The typical breakfast:

30g of bread

1 teaspoon of jam

2 spoonful of olive oil

one cup of instant Nescafe

one cup of normal tea

They strongly believed in Allah and were fully aware of the devil. The temptation of stealing was explained to me in a very simple manner by Lahcen. "It is not you who steal." "How do you explain that to the police when caught red-handed?" "It's the hand of the devil that pushes you to do so." "Who would go to prison, you or the devil?" Lahcen and Mustapha strongly opposed. "Tu regardez diable?" Actually, if I were to follow their way of thinking I would say, yes, many times. They also believed that any form of features like tattoos were done by the hand of the devil. "Why is that?" "Because it cannot be washed off." I doubted that grandma Halima was aware of the fact that her forehead, chin and hands had been kissed by the devil. She had a tattoo across her face, chin and hands – a strong, symbolic affiliation with Berber culture. I couldn't clearly read the symbol that ran through her forehead, but I believed it was either the symbol of the *"olive tree"* or *"wheat."* Her hands were also revealing another Berber representation which was a simple but meaningful *"tree."*

"Can you have a boyfriend and you don't have to marry him? Can you live with him? Can you also have sex with him?" Lahcen and Mustapha sounded bewildered and anxious placing the devil's horns on my head. "I want to see a film," said Lahcen. "I'm sorry, I don't have any films in Arabic." "It doesn't matter, we can watch some action film." I don't have any action films." The disappointment struck again. I searched though the collection of my films for something amusing and light that would not require linguistic understanding and would not reveal any nudity, kissing or sex scenes. I let them down. I had neither Charlie Chaplin nor Mr. Bean; there was nothing with Bruce Lee nor with Arnold Schwarzenegger.

******

"The rainy season continues making the rough waters of the river look mad, and the ground - orange brown - like never before."

The first day of teaching. Nightmare. Pure and simple nightmare. Between twenty-five to thirty savage, uncontrollable, sweet little monsters aged from ten to thirteen years old turned up that day. There was no choice but to try to accommodate them in the largest classroom which was still not big enough. They had to be seated in five round tables that usually accommodated two children. The possibility of controlling them was slim and I realised that as soon as they had entered the room. The idea of teaching French through funky dancing and singing video lessons was destroyed by talking, shouting, pardoning, hand-pointing, screaming, laughing, fidgeting, kicking, pushing, pulling, simply devouring the small room and leaving me for dessert. I was looking but my eyes were shouting: "Shut up!" Mohamed, the caretaker, calmed them down and I took advantage of the two minute silence explaining the rules on the table. "Respect. Do you know what it means?" I was looking at them and their completely blind faces thinking how pointless the whole explanation was.

I was keen on introducing them to Paris through very basic video conversations, and although they paid some attention at first, the logistics then failed me badly. The screen of my laptop was far too small and the loudspeakers far too week. As soon as the children opened their mouths, the sound from the videos was impossible to hear. My third attempt that day was to familiarise them with some singing cartoon-characters of a very simple melody and text: "Bonjour, bonjour, comment ça va? Bonjour, bonjour, très bien, merci." Although this part went well, the following change of rhythm and lyrics added more confusion and chaos to the existing one. Whatever they had learned at school it did not manifest itself in practice. At first it sounded comical. "Ça va?" "Oui" "Comment tu t'appelles?" "Oui." "No, I've asked your name." Confusion. "Pourquoi es-tu ici?" "Oui." It was becoming less comical, rather tiring and pointless. Another attempt, this time I wrote the questions down on the blackboard. "Quel âge as-tu?" "No, no," I pointed out at a boy. "Don't repeat the question, just give me the answer." "Alors, quel âge as-tu?" The voices carried the same response: "Quel âge as-tu?" To a certain extent they were amusing and making me laugh by provoking a very human contact giving me no choice but to hug them, dishevel their hair, or shake hands with them. I was far too weak and my formula that "life is hard on them, so why should I be" failed me terribly. That was my weakness and they could sense it, they could sniff it from a distance like well-trained dogs. The challenge wasn't the teaching in itself but bringing the order back to the classroom.

I lasted one hour that day. On the way back home I was pondering two things: a glass of wine and all the devoted teachers. "How admired I them! This is an exhausting job!" I was thinking out loud. "How do they do that? How do they control those little, hungry for mischief vultures ready to peck you any moment?" That day I discovered in my mail box a message from Somaya, one of our trustees, which perked me up:

41

"We've not had the chance to meet yet but I just wanted to drop you a line and say, as one of the trustees of Hannan, without volunteers like you we wouldn't be making the progress we are. Thank you so much for all your hard work so far. I hear you're doing a fabulous job and that you've fitted in perfectly with the locals. Do keep us all updated with your progress and if you need anything at all, please just let us know."

Back at home, there was a pleasant family gathering around the wood-burning stove that night with the usual tagine, and popcorn, a massive amount of different flavours: salty, spicy and sweet shared between fifteen people. Mustapha wasn't himself that night. "What is bothering you?" I asked. "You look sad." "Regardez maman et papa," he said. "Is there something wrong with them?" The explanation wasn't easy to understand as every single sentence started off with: "Il y a" and was followed by "regarder" or "pour arriver." When he didn't drink, he appeared intelligent, thoughtful and very sensible, and although he loved *Baba* to bits, he was getting upset with his constant reprimands, "Don't drink, don't smoke, don't laugh, go to the mosque, pray." "Margarena, papa Mohamed and Mustapha called me Margarena, *Baba* est Hitler," he joked meaningfully. Mustapha wholeheartedly hated Arabs and wholeheartedly expressed it while sulking drunk and being impossible to control as either he laughed hysterically or shouted some nonsense. His body did not stay still for a long time and his energy was scattered around places. Eating for him meant: grabbing, chewing, spitting and speaking with a mouthful. The food was never served spicy but a chilli pepper, the ingredient that could only be touched by bread as it was so hot, was always on the side. Mustapha consumed the whole chilli pepper at once. He was a character: difficult and big-hearted at the same time.

******

With an occasional wash in cold water, and once per week in hot, my body yearned for a good hebdomadal scrub in the *hammam*. I set off straight after breakfast packing everything but the towel. "Merde!" I spat it out when being stripped off to the underwear. "I'm sorry, I forgot something." I apologised to a couple of women who were sitting next to me. I was trying to recall the word "towel" in Darija while performing charades when, all of a sudden, they both shouted triumphantly *"Fota! Fota!"* One of the women offered me her own towel. My imagination went wild. *"Chokrane,"* I showed number two, walk, and house.

There were no rules in the *hammam*, or maybe there was one: whoever went first to the tap, if there was not much hot water left in the basin, occupied it for as long as all buckets were filled up, sometimes four or less, this time, there were eight lined up. I was standing there waiting my turn and being irritated by their manners, or lack of them. It was definitely their territory marked by "allowing me to use it" gesture when they were done.

They all had the tendency to stare. I understood the street, the outside world where I was and looked like a stranger, here however, there was nothing that made me stand out, I was more equal here than anywhere else and yet again, they gawped; they gawped when I washed, scrubbed, moved, sat or stood up. This time was even worse. While I was washing my hair, a middle-aged woman sat down next to me, in spite of all the space in that room, she chose to sit close to me. With the corner of my eyes I had followed hers, firstly, I saw her gaze right at my face, and then at my breast. She was actually starring at my boobs! I looked straight into her eyes and smiled expecting an embarrassing smile back. Instead, her dead-straight looking face turned away almost angrily, and she was carrying on with scrubbing. A minute later her eyes were on me again. I gave her another look, this time a dead-serious one which was saying "I've got enough of this game!"

Here one could see all body types from corpulent to slim, ugly to beautiful, neglected to healthy-looking. However, today, there was one image that disturbed me and rushed me back home. Here was an elderly woman sitting on the bare floor brushing her long, thin, damaged, henna-dyed hair. Her minuscule body looked particularly undernourished. Her ribcage was sticking out so much that her stomach was disappearing under the mass of that ribcage. She was tiny, vulnerable and illness-stricken. The image did upset me. It accompanied me home and took a taxi with me to El Borj. But as soon as I left the taxi, that mental picture was chased away by the screaming children who were already waiting for me in the front yard of the school. Yet again, the number of children exceeded the number of places: instead of sixteen we had to accommodate twenty-five. Although they were younger and better behaved, in comparison to the previous group, I was unable to control them without the presence of Mohamed, the vice-president. Apparently, this was how they behaved with foreign teachers: they treated them badly by disrespecting them. "They respond with only the severest discipline as that is all they know," I heard this statement on few occasions. I could actually sense the fear in them when a Moroccan person was walking into a classroom. Today, one sweetly annoying-disturbing individual was sent back home. "Silence! Who's next?" shouted Mohamed. They had to be threatened to become silent. Was this right? The lack of respect was disturbing. "Shouldn't they be taught respect at school?" I was asking myself. And why do they have such attitude towards us? We give them our time and money and in return we get this? "They have to fear you in order to respect you," I was told. Madness. It goes both for the girls and the boys. They were equally vicious and sweet at the same time. "Madam, Madam!" they kept shouting and booing as soon as Mohamed's feet were beyond the classroom's doorsteps. Voilà! Here, I would repeat after Mustapha who kept saying, "Il y a le system de Maroc, le system d'Europe, le system de Pologne, le system de Mustapha et … le system des enfants!"

Ah,…. il y a le system de *forno*. As soon as I walked away from one challenge, I jumped into another, the smoky, uncontrollable and rebellious wood-burning stove in our house. I was not sure when the pleasure of having the wood-burning stove would turn into a nightmare? Perhaps it was already happening? Something was definitely not working and it was bothering me, my lungs, eyes, and all my clothes. No one else seemed to have been bothered though. On the contrary, Papa Mohamed kept everyone in the dark saying that smoke was good for one's eyes.

******

A few days ago in the medina, I was noticed by a young man of a sleepy eye and pale skin, tall and handsome. While walking me back home he kept asking questions. "Are you happy? What is important for you in life?" Oh boy! I knew where it was all going. How did it happen? He called it love at first sight. I should have been flattered at least, instead, I was bursting with laughter while he was declaring his perpetual love for me. I suddenly had become the most important person in his life. What a sweet and charming man he was! Cutting the love story short, I promised to see him again. We were supposed to meet in the centre at 11.30am in the same place where he had spotted me the first day. The day was dry and warm. When I arrived Hassan wasn't there, but there were handfuls of opportunists circling around and sending me some sorts of signals by winking, tapping, and tracing down my steps. Bizarre! My friend was running late and I had no intention of waiting for him. I felt more than relieved. The heavy burden of getting to know another "chancer" was buried. Done and dusted. But as soon as I left the medina, I was chased by someone else who shouted, "Bonjour, bonjour, minute, minute." It was a face of that winking man who very much wanted to know where I lived, and kept insisting on coffee with me. As he was as stubborn as donkey and unresponsive to "no," I had to do my usual: I took his number and promised to call him.

Within a minute or two there was another man on the opposite side of the pavement who was trying to make eye contact with me. When this failed, he changed his tactic by overtaking me, crossing the street and waiting for me on the other side of the street. He was beckoning me mumbling "faire connaissance, faire connaissance." "*Wakha.*" Beautiful eyes he had; but the very short conversation left him disappointed, he walked off empty-handed with no contact number, no Facebook name or email.

In the meantime, Hassan called me apologising for the delay. He was now in Khénifra and badly wanted to see me. I unburied the burden and met him for coffee later that day. He sounded as desperate to me as was his brother who paid 10.000 Euros for the arranged marriage with a Spanish girl. "It's has been five years since he left Morocco," he recalled. "Is there any love between them?" I asked. "Not at all, they only live together." "What kind of a solution is this?" He said it was better to live unhappy in Europe than happy here. How did he manage to save up so much money? This is the equivalent of 100.000DH. "Our family has some animals and we had managed to save up from selling meat," he added.

He knew how desperate he was but he didn't know how badly his eyes and his body were betraying him: he was tense and nervous. "I can go to Poland with you," he made me laugh again. "When my family and yours meet, I'm sure they would get on very well." When he realised how weak this argument was, he knew he had to play the stronger cards: he hit the triumph one. "My heart belongs to you, I cannot do anything about it, I love you. Do you love me?" "No, sorry, I've known you for two hours, and besides you are far too young for me." His very sweet and handsome face brightened up as the age did not matter to him. He gave me an example of a young Moroccan man who married a very old Swiss woman. "I agree with you but I still don't love you." When he was walking me back home, he identified his last chance. "I'm sick of games that Moroccan women play with me. I will not settle down with a Moroccan woman, I'm tired of looking for one. They are not fun, you are fun and you are in my heart!" "What about friendship?" I suggested. "We don't have to get married straight away but have a romantic relationship, if you agree." I didn't. I turned down his senseless offer which he straight away tried to justify. "I don't want to create a problem for you, I don't like police. I'm just honest and straightforward." He compared Moroccan women to zigzags making me go hysterical with laughter again. "They are like zigzags," he said. "They are not straightforward and you are straightforward." He recognised it straight away, and I had no choice but to take the same straightforward road back home.

The recent tension between me and my family made me go first over to Ali's: "Frappe and monte, any time you want," so I knocked and climbed up the stairs. Mina invited me in for some scrambled chilly eggs served with tea while waiting for Ali who showed his face ten minutes later. There was a difficulty in communicating as the words were turning into a guess and the guess into laughter. There was no substitution for it, and no matter how much I wanted to get to know Mina through the alphabet I had to discover her through her simple acts of kindness, gestures, look or touch. If I looked at Mina through colours and the *Chinese* representation of them, I would use red, yellow and white to describe this superb woman; all her spontaneous acts that were fully grounded and level-headed but still flexible, were making her a very desirable woman, wife, mother, and a friend, a very generous friend. She yet again offered me two pairs of trousers, which I refused saying it would be better to give it to some poor people. She agreed, and instead took out a box full of glittery objects like earrings, bracelets, necklaces and was trying them out on me. The necklace, a pair of earrings and a bracelet were a gift. I liked it and she gave me no choice but to accept them. In exchange I copied some French lessons for Ali and a couple of films, "A Dangerous method" and "Love in the time of Cholera," having had in mind one of his favoured singers, Shakira.

The anxiety of going home was growing fast, forcing me to leave. How did it happen, I was thinking, that the time spent in a company of other people was turning itself into a sheer thought that I may be betraying my own family? Why was I feeling such fretfulness? Perhaps because I anticipated the reaction to my overtly impulsive, exultant way of sharing with my family the new, the exciting, the stimulating, the uplifting that was happening, and observing the previous retorts, I now sensed nothing but resentment and more suspicious questions which only stirred a great deal of misunderstanding. The funny and entertaining Hassan's story, in my opinion, was the very opposite in the eyes of my family. "He has to come here first so we could see his intentions clearly." I laughed not understanding the whole cultural issue behind it. They all, including drunken Mustapha, were convinced that I wanted to marry Hassan. "I have no intention to marry

45

anyone," I shouted. "But he wants to marry you," Lahcen was adding more fire to the already burning. "Who is Hassan?" Mustapha joined the surreal discussion. "Toi, mariez Hassan? Hassan, qui est Hassan?" He slummed the door and walked off. I got confused and baffled by the whole blown-up scene which was supposed to be nothing more than a humorous episode in my life. Once again, there was that very worrying and sad fact that was slowly emerging making it all clear that perhaps sharing every detail of my life with my family was not a good idea as instead of releasing some tension, it was only adding more to the existing one.

******

This morning I was invited over to Ali's for breakfast. "Are you going to eat there?" asked Meryam. The truth made her raise her eyebrows, so I quickly changed my attitude by eating as much as possible adding. "It's just a quick cup of tea." At Mina's we had heavenly delicious *boucheyar* with a tiny bit of scrambled eggs. It was 10.00am. As Mohamed overslept, Ali and I decided to walk around the town, take photos, talk and listen to the music while walking and sharing the headphones, moving to the rhythm of the music and singing out loud. It felt normal. I forgot about all the people who were staring, we were simply happy in that particular moment. The change of a café was refreshing and the purchase of "*Liberation*," stimulating; it provoked discussions that soon became our weekly routine and then a daily addiction. The deliberations about the Quran and the Bible were to be continued tomorrow over a glass of wine and followed by a film, we all decided.

Ali's dad, Mohamed, was a tailor. He couldn't hear a thing and talking to him was like having a chat with a person with headphones and loud music on. "Ça va? Toujours ça va?" He was shouting each time he saw me. His small tailor parlour was at the corner of our street where he used to spend most of his time sewing, reading the Quran, and drinking tea. The pyjamas, which he used to make were traditional, simple and old-fashioned and yet charming, and I wanted to buy one. "It's old-fashioned," said Ali. "It doesn't matter. I like it." When I shared my excitement of purchasing the pyjama with Meryam and other women who were sitting outside the house that afternoon, I got the "ça m'est égal" look followed by the "really?" guise. We disappeared into the garage and I examined the far too big, the far too old-fashioned and the far too-covered with dust pyjama deciding on purchasing that particular one.

"I don't understand why you are so angry with me?" I raised the Mina-Ali topic over lunch. "What is the problem?" I asked Meryam. I explained to her the simplicity of our relationship, the friendship and joy that comes with it. "Where I come from, I have male friends, close male friends and this is normal to me." Apparently, there was no problem; she was fine with it as long as I was safe. We hardly spoke over supper, which consisted of bread, eggs, milk and tea, and some meat that another member of the family had brought in. The room was yet again covered with smoke coming this time from the barbecue which was prepared inside the house. My eyes were watering, the breath was short, but the meat was tasty. I started giving some French lessons to Achraf as Papa Mohamed wanted him to learn and eventually handle a simple conversation. This was his fourth year at school and despite all his efforts, hardy could he differentiate letter "A" from letter "O". I wondered how on earth he had passed his exams.

I received a distressing email from my mum regarding my grandma's illness that when the ambulance came, she refused to go to hospital insisting on dying at home. I prayed. I wanted to see her again. Badly.

******

"My name is Krystyna Magdalena Margarena Hannah *Zahra* Wasiura."

At this point, I was desperate to get my message across. Before I put my faith into Hannah, I had used the Google translator creating a little message to which Meryam paid particularly long attention.

I was hoping she would understand my contemplation regarding friendship, freedom, and trust. "Please do trust me, and don't worry about me. I feel safe, you cannot protect me from everything and if I made a mistake you would not be blamed for it." I thought that my discourse would make the next one much smoother. It didn't. Damn Google! "What time will you be coming home tonight?" "Around 10.00 or 11.00pm." Her face was not accepting it, but she nodded.

When the Google translation did not help, the whole cultural misunderstanding was also discussed over a telephone with Hmad who had tried to explain it in their own language. They confirmed that the family was very controlling for a reason. They didn't want me to get exploited as basically no one in Morocco really trusted anyone else. It was hard for the family to understand the freedom that Western women had. "You are doing a great job and you will have these issues come to the surface living and working so closely in such a different culture, but I don't think you will have more problems with the family," Hannah assured me adding, "This is what you do not pick up, when you are on a package holiday!"

Whoever in the house was not involved in my problems was very much occupied by their own little agendas, for example, grandma Halima and her small plastic bottle of water. Let's play the charades. Here is grandma Halima sitting up in her bed and showing me her half-empty bottle pressed hard on to her stomach and making a gesture, with her hands, as if she was putting a spell either on me, her stomach or the bottle. Is she in pain? Is the bottle of any consolation? Why is the bottle half-empty?

Then her little plastic box with the unscrewed top that was by her bed all the time. My simple thinking was leading me to something equally banal: urine. Maybe she does pee in that little box. And when emptying it, I convinced myself to my prior discourse. It was then, when grandma gave me a full pictorial explanation: she unscrewed it and spat into that box. I felt relieved. Sometimes, however, the saliva ended up on her blanket as the top was not properly screwed, making my own stomach turn upside down. Nonetheless, her little habits of spitting, climbing up the stairs and not being able to descend, or arguing with *Baba* Lahcen, all those little elements were adding more charm and charisma to her character. Whatever tiniest favour I did for her, she paid back handsomely through her gratefulness that was bigger, wider and larger than grandma herself. She kissed my hands repeatedly three times and then always went four times for the forehead. Every time I was passing though that room, she called me "Hannah, Hannah" and performed her own ritual with my forehead and hands. Just to clear out the confusion: My name is Krystyna Magdalena Margarena Hannah Zahra Wasiura.

Nevertheless, all the efforts of going out tonight to watch a film over a glass of wine went down the drain. The evening was poisoned by a rather unreasonable amount of L'eau de Vie. All of a sudden Ali called sick. He was well and in good form the night before and in bed looking and feeling jolly miserable the following morning. The story didn't add up, but yet again, my naivety forced me to ask if he was in need of some aspirin or syrup. The explanation soon arrived with Mohamed who was familiar with the consequences of heavy drinking of "the water of life." What is this?" "It's wine." "Wine? He got poisoned by wine?" I couldn't believe it. He was rushed to the hospital this morning feeling as if he was dying. L'eau de Vie it was not wine, here everything which was alcoholic was called wine for some reason. L'eau de Vie it's a spirit as strong as Italian grappa or Polish home-made vodka called "bimber." It is usually served as a digestive. On the black market, this home-made alcohol goes into hands of young, usually unemployed men seduced by the lower price and the higher content of the spirit, what could it be better? And yet, *dangerous*; if the alcohol is not properly distilled and if the consumption is of a big quantity, it can kill.

The story went that Ali was poisoned by food, some fish, perhaps rotten, difficult to say as he did not pay any attention to what he had eaten that night. We left him in his recovery bed in good hands of Mina and on the telephone with Fatima Zahra, his sister who was to become a doctor.

Mohamed invited me over to his place for tea. With his mum, his sister and him as the interpreter, we touched on the subject of violence and aggression especially towards women. Once again, I was warned not to go out in the evenings as the possibility of getting robbed or even killed was very high. If so, there must always be a man with me. The scale of poverty and unemployment here were greater than anywhere else and the opportunities - minuscule. The theory was that those people would take revenge for their misfortune on anyone who would cross their path.

The sex discrimination that was limiting women's liberty was also evident. Rarely did I see women strolling down the street in the evening; they would not take their chances but would rather call a taxi that would deliver them home safely. The number of "dragueurs" in this part of Morocco was incredible, and if it was converted into kilometres, for sure, it would go beyond the long stretch of the Middle Atlas. There were not only "the singles" who were harassing women, the great number, if not greater, were the married men. Does the polygamy allow men to treat them badly? Does the polygamy allow men to disrespect them? I doubt. The respect, the etiquette, the manners, the whole set of values that allow human beings to grow, to experience, to be fearless, to expand, to let go of prejudices and stereotypes had little in common with the culture and the living traditions. There was a young educated generation of women that were rebelling against such hurtful and unjustified models of living by taking the initiative in their hands because they were fully aware of the transformation that this country must face. Unfortunately, the majority of women were being manipulated and cleverly controlled. The usual form of running was fear, fright, and distress. That group was chained by their own reactions, responses, and their verbal do's: don't go out, don't sit in a café, don't walk, don't wear anything that could make you attractive, otherwise you may become a victim. They all were bombarded by such messages and becoming victims of their own fear that they, and no one else, were passing on to the others in a form of care, percussion, obviously, and yet, they had not realised that their own fear that was passed on to the others in the form of care, could only transformed itself into more fear and panic.

The very stereotypes reigned in Morocco have been pointed out by *Tahar Ben Jelloun*. The very controversial intellectual who became the president of the jury of the cinema festival in Zagora in 2013 has spoken the truth that was not easy to embrace. Not many Moroccans want to face the problem with racism or the lasting stereotypes in Moroccan families: the clearly divided responsibilities for men and women or the very controversial subject of the *offspring*.

As the conversation continued, I was nervously looking at the clock. Having had no intention to turn up at home late, I had bid everyone farewell and was walked home by Mohamed. Always accompanied by a man.

****

A woman and two children turned up at my place during breakfast, one was already sponsored by our Association, the second - a girl - wanted to be, or rather her grandma who was trying to convince me that Wishal was chosen for a sponsor. "Where do you get the information from?" "Hmad, Hannah, on the phone," she was making the calling gesture. "Really? I don't know anything about it but will certainly find out." She was kissing and hugging me as if some kind of deal was made. Neither had I trusted her nor her words. I doubted her story and sniffed some kind of trick called, "pushing her own lack." She was indeed lying. In comparison to all the sponsored children they seemed to have been doing well. Although they didn't have mother, they still had one parent who worked and provided for the family, and a big house in Khénifra which they were renting out and getting additional income from it. The greediest always tried their luck; it was the poorest that would never come to me for help.

Another invitation for a Friday couscous. This time from a young retired policeman, who after his five years of service, gave it up all for running his little boutique with organic produce: coffees, teas, nuts, biscuits. "Are you religious?" I asked when hearing the call for prayer. "I am but I don't practise." "Why not?" "I smoke hashish, so when I smoke my mind is not clear, one can only pray with his pure and clear mind, otherwise it doesn't make sense," he explained. "Why do you smoke then?" "It's a habit, a social thing."

******

I don't snack.

The half a litre of coffee consumed every morning has been substituted by a small cup. The same goes for tea. Although the intake of tea is enormous and regular, the cups are tiny.

Having tea with no sugar for over twenty years, I have now been drinking very sweet tea each day. The tea with no sugar is unbearably tasteless here.

I don't drink milk. Milk is always heated up and sweetened by sugar.

I sleep at least eight hours every day.

I don't have to rush to get to work.

I don't have to be anxious when I'm late for work or any other appointment. I don't think the phrase: "I'm sorry for being late" is often used in this country.

I don't feel hungry any more. I'm used to eating bread.

I don't feel cold that much. Although the temperature in my room does not exceed a few degrees, I have learned to put as many layers on as possible to keep me warm.

When Meryam prepares pizza, a Moroccan pizza, I crave for a glass of wine.

I still don't know how to respond to the question: "Do you like to get married here?"

I still don't understand why people think that I may want to stay here.

It didn't even cross my mind to complain about anything that I was used to, like the ambient light in my room, BBC Radio 4, a shower or bath before bed, "calm nuit" tea in bed with a snack over book or film.

I don't complain if I don't wash for three days in a row.

I'm used to the cold water now if I need a wash.

It frustrates me how narrow-minded some people are.

It frustrates me the way they talk to each other and children and how the children talk to adults. It's a vicious circle.

It frustrates me that there is so little freedom for women.

It frustrates me how they are fearful.

It annoys me that despite the immense poverty, they spend so much money on cigarettes.

It frustrates me immensely the lack of ambition in young people. The few things they do are: smoking, drinking, chatting-up, and watching football.

It frustrates me the lack of respect towards foreigners.

It frustrates me how they turn this beautiful country into a rubbish bin.

It frustrates me how lazy some are.

It frustrates me that the ninety-eight per cent of Moroccans see me as a visa.

It frustrates me that most women have little ambition.

It frustrates me how resistant they are to any change.

******

Alla, one of Papa Mohamed's brothers warned me today saying: "Lock up your room every time you leave it, and hang the key around your neck with your passport. It's not the family but strangers who you should be aware of." This is the second time that a small amount of money disappeared from my purse. Not a big deal but it made me ponder Alla's warning.

Last night I couldn't sleep. Perhaps it was Alla talking, or it was all happening. I turned the lights off around 00.30am and kept hearing noises coming from the rooftop floor. The open-air aperture that was covered by some thick plastic mat was giving me a massive fright. I was convinced that there was someone on the roof trying to break into the house. I could hear voices whispering and lights moving. I turned the lights on, held my breath, and observed the roof. The noise disappeared. I was getting paranoid thinking that I may be watched. All sorts of bad scenarios went through my head starting off with a simple break-in and ending up with men throwing in some sleeping gas. I turned the lights off. The noise started again. This time it was more pronounced as if they were getting under the mat and stepping on to the metal bars. Without turning the lights on, I got up and gently opened the door thinking of catching them red-handed. I went downstairs. Everyone was fast asleep. "Meryam, Meryam," I whispered. No response. "Meryam, Meryam," I repeated and jerked her. She mumbled something. "There is someone on the roof," I said. She didn't understand. "Come with me, I show you." While I was beckoning her to follow me, she got up and turned the light on. "What a mistake!" I thought. They would have disappeared by the time we had got there. Meryam woke Hakima up. We all went upstairs searching for a torch. Hakima was ready to investigate the rooftop while Meryam was trying to prevent her by repeating *"la, la."* All of a sudden, we heard a knock at the door. It was Abdellah. "What is going on?" he asked. "There is someone up there," I said. He took the torch, unlocked the door and looked around by jumping on both sides of the roof. No one was there. I knew we wouldn't find anyone. If there was someone, they would have gone by now. They said that it was probably a cat but I didn't believe in the cat story, it was far too noisy for a cat. I went off to bed relieved but at the same time disappointed that I had not managed to catch the culprit.

******

"Are you coming today?" Mohamed, the vice-president, was on the phone. "In the afternoon, around 2.00pm," I said. His response was incomprehensible but his phone call was apparently urgent, which I found out two hours later when turning up in El Bojr. "Why did it take you so long?" I found Mohamed and Samira the teacher standing inside a classroom contemplating. "What happened? What is so urgent?" "Fatima resigned," he responded "And what can I do?" I really did not know what to do. Fatima was our second teacher. She handed in her resignation the day after she had received her monthly salary, which was today. What was the reason for her resignation? No one knew. We only speculated different scenarios over a cup of coffee that we all had together. She was twenty-eight years old and allegedly was looking for a husband, and working here wasn't giving her the right opportunities. Besides, having a job while married was, for Berber women, something contradictory, something against their beliefs as it could create a conflict between her and her husband who was the only provider and not the woman. There was a possibility that she might have left the village or might have gone abroad. Taking into account an element of superstition, no one would share such news with anybody in case of the evil eye that may curse those plans and they would not come to pass. One of the first teachers in our school didn't turn up one day, just like Fatima. She left for France on her aunt's documents with her uncle, not saying a word to anyone. The speculation went on and on, but the truth was she left us with no teacher, which the children desperately needed.

******

"We are not surprised Fatima has put in her resignation; is she going to Canada? We heard a relative, who is now in Canada, was trying to get her there? Who is the new teacher? No one has said anything to us. Have you met her? If you feel able to would you have a short interview with her in French and find out experience and what you think?" wrote Hannah.

The Factor's family. The new teacher was very quickly appointed. Today was her first day. She was a nice girl but unfortunately her father wasn't. In fact, she was one of the first girls who was interviewed by the Association few years back and scored badly; she was painfully shy and did not have much idea on teaching children; so when she was turned down the position her father bullied the organization insisting on employing his daughter. When Samira, the existing teacher, was chosen, he got the parents to boycott the school. His oppression went on for a week and then when it all settled down, he carried on with his daily nastiness, for example as a mail collector for the village, he had stopped distributing the packages. "For this reason we are a bit confused as to how all of a sudden she gets the job so quickly and wonder if some corruption or bullying has gone on?" concluded Hannah.

My task was to monitor her and give my best opinion on whether she should stay or go. In the meantime, I had carried on with the challenging task of trying to teach the children French or rather, trying to control them. After today's lesson I drew a simple conclusion: I was a useless teacher, hopeless and weak. I wanted to terrorise those little monsters, I wanted to spank them, I wanted to be ruthless and give them orders, I wanted to be like any other teacher in this country, but I couldn't. I was weak. Instead, I hugged them, made them laugh, and pulled faces when explaining words, joked or sung songs. And they loved it, but carried on misbehaving and responding to everything with chaos and destruction. What a terrible example of a teacher I was! They disobeyed the kindness because they knew they would not be punished for it. My role here so far was to control the outburst of undesirable chat in the classroom rather than teaching them.

This afternoon, as soon as I got out of the taxi, I was surrounded by children who were giving me flowers. Malak, a beautiful young girl, clever but mischievous brought me a rose. "This was a rather cunning element of public relations," I thought, but they didn't know that yet. They all shook hands with me while humming the song that we had played last time: "Bonjour, bonjour, comment ça va….." Perhaps there was some light in that dark tunnel of their disobedience? We started all over again with the alphabet but the letters were slowly being eaten by those little creatures until it all was devoured by the ruling mouth of dismay. I called for help and the terror arrived. Mohamed's presence did calm them down but as soon as he started interrupting and conducting the lesson, the children were turning into little soldiers. "A" "A…" "W" "W…" "W…" "You, letter B," "B…" "G…" "No! Again, what is this litter? "G…" "No! Concentrate." They were shrinking under the tables from protecting their heads.

The stress of this "traditional" method of teaching brought upon me a massive craving for steak, some blood, some flesh. My nervous system could not cope with the dread, the hysteria that was wrapped up tightly in the luxurious Pandora's Box along with the catch 22 situation: without Mohamed I was unable to control them, and with him I was unable to teach. My cravings for steak were replaced by a plate of tagine, *forno* and drunk Mustapha. Yet again, he could hardly stand on his feet, his T-shirt was burst, his words - insignificant. The spectacle started when he sat down next to a woman who was breastfeeding, pretending to be the "breast-feeder" or rather the "breast-taker. He was crying like a baby demanding some milk. "Mustapha, whisky does not come from the breast," I said. He laughed. "Regardez photo de Dieu? Margarena, il y a deux photos de Dieu." "I don't know what you mean. I have not seen them, sorry." His nonsense was getting on my nerves and it was time to seek for some asylum in my room. "Margarena, Margarena," I heard a knock at my door. "I'm in bed, good night." "No, no, no," he forced his way in. "Il y a beaucoup de famille de Margarena ici. Naatit et toi kif-kif." *"Wakha."* "Mangez,

mangez," he said. "J'ai déjà mangé." "*Wakha*, bonne nuit." Five minutes later he was knocking at my door again. This time he was taking about a "sœur." "*Wakha*, à demain." "Margarena, gentille. Bonne nuit." He came back one more time, sat on my bed and kept grumbling. The rescue finally came from Meryam who managed to fetch him out.

******

Ali, Mohamed and I made a solid arrangement. Every Wednesday we would go somewhere to explore more and through that we would get to know each other better. *Arougou* was the first place we visited. That day, Mohamed was remarkably quiet and rather curt towards me. His affection that I had observed growing every day was gone. Is he trying to protect himself? The quick-thinking led me to believe that he was repressing some sort of sentiments that were increasing with every day's cup of coffee and unsoiled, innocent laughter. "You seem a little bit different." "I'm just having a quiet day, that's all." I was not trusting his answer but happy to be going somewhere. The taxi was a simple van, which was also used for transporting animals. The capacity was quite impressive; it could fit in at least ten people in a standing position. Today we shared the space with two other men who instead of getting inside were clinging on to the van from the outside. Despite the fact that they were young-looking, they seemed old, their faces were fumed up profoundly and their blurred-looking eyes were hardly opened. They were also overwhelmingly generous sharing hashish with my friends. Within fifteen minutes we were dropped off by a café in Arougou, a charming place by the road that was made of nothing but a few small plastic chairs, tables and chickens that were running between the tables demanding food by furiously bouncing off the ground and stealing whatever was on it. I forgot to mention the owner, a young, single man of smiling eyes and agreeable nature. During the summer time his place offers more than coffee; one can set a tent there, right in the middle of the café, and have a menu with tagines or couscous. The price would vary but would not exceed 100DH for the camping and 30 to 40DH for the menu. It's a brilliant idea taking into account its location, in the middle of the forest with drinkable water streaming down the grazing land, and possibilities of making a fire. The menu of the day consisted of some bread, eggs, yogurts, tea and a joint - a giant joint stuffed with chemicals. I inhaled it once and had no intention to do it again.

This vast stretch of land, wild and intact, inhabited mostly by olive trees and cactuses invited us for a little exploration. The olive picking season started, picturesque to watch but we carried on walking until we reached a place that offered a billiard table, a quick couple of rounds and we were off again. We strolled across the fields until we reached a posh place with a swimming pool. Although we stopped for tea there, I felt very much out of place. Places like this one were not attractive to me at all. The charm was disappearing under the intentions that were burdened with heavy consumerism and greed: 'get more tourists, rip them off!' For me, the whole experience, no matter where I ended going, was not about the comfort but the authenticity. The feeling of being seen as a tourist had made me choke and gave me no alternative but to camouflage it by settling there for a while. Here, it was a little bit tricky. Although I saw a few people with eyes of a different to brown colour, mine - were cursing me and neither pyjama nor djellaba could conceal it. It was creating a constant problem, for example the prices were always increased, or my friends had suffered a social injustice. Anyhow, when we left that place we got a lift from another fumed up character who offered his mobile number. "If you wanted to go anywhere else, call me."

******

There was an ambiguous fellow in our house a few days ago. As soon as he came and sat down in our living room, Meryam and Hakima went over to the other side. He asked questions about me and my work and was recalling his online dating experience with a foreigner. He also studied psychology and was interested in psychoanalysis, mainly in Freud and Young. Either there was something wrong with him or with Meryam who was sitting all that time in the kitchen with Hakima and was whispering and signalling to me that I should not be talking to him. When the man was gone, the opinions about him were uncovered and summed up by the word "dodgy." "Be aware," they warned me. He was also working as a teacher for a charity which was located right in the centre of Khénifra. Although, the very next day, I had intentions to go and see how they functioned, I was kept in bed by Sunday's heavy rain. A few days later our Association in England received an email from the same man. He was called Said.

 "C'est avec un grand plaisir que j'ai découvert votre site sachant que nous avons déjà une petite idée sur vos action sur le village El Borj situé à 10 Km de Khénifra. Ce message est une invitation à la coopération et échange d'expertise dans le domaine de développement local. En attendant de vous lire veuillez agréer nos salutations et respects."

Apparently, Said had rung up the Association in England a couple of times before sending off emails and using different email addresses, but he had no intention to respond to any of our inquiries. Bizarre. I was told not to be bothered with finding who this chap or that association was. "It seems a strange one," said Hannah.

Mohamed had continued behaving weirdly convincing me that it was all fault of the lack of dopamine in his body. It may be the case. He had been depriving himself of it through smoking and drinking for quite number of years. "Be careful with those cigarettes, they not only rob you of happiness but eventually they will kill you. What's the point of smoking?" *Smoking* has been a massive problem in this country. Disregarding the health aspect, one talked mainly about the social one, which seemed to have been domineering. Men appeared to have not had control over it. Smoking became an integral part of their socio-economic status, a very popular aspect of virtually all social gatherings in Morocco. It was like fashion - it was trendy to smoke. Tons of cigarettes were available all over the place, in cafés, on streets, in boutiques, and on a large scale were distributed by individuals who devoted their time to walking across the town and selling them. They tempted everyone with a choice; either you buy the whole pack: Moroccan brand for 20DH, Marlboro for 30DH, or by item: one cigarette cost 1.50DH, Marlboro - 2DH.

Another phone call from Hassan; for the past three days he made fifty-two attempts of which none was answered. Instead he wrote:

"Tu me manques trop, je me demande maintenant si je peux supporter ton absence (…) Je brule de curiosité de connaitre ta réponse et tes sentiment envers moi, c'est nécessaire (..) mon cœur a choisi."

Despite all the warmth and romanticism behind that message, I would never find out his real intentions. Perhaps it was only me who doubted love from first sight, perhaps it did exist.

In the meantime papa Mohamed was getting more and more ill. His stomach could not bear food and quickly after each meal was disposing it all. He also created his own language in order to communicate with me: "Lo camion la da li? Ce qla ce tu El Borj? No, moi je ne travaille pas mais lo.....lo... " followed by sign language. Grandma Halima was still spitting into her small plastic box and kept her small plastic bottle of water on her stomach. The palaver with the new teacher Siham was to be continued.

******

Fatima, the previous teacher wasn't brilliant. There were complaints of her always being on the phone and treating the children badly. I did see it myself. She smacked them when they misbehaved and raised her voice on a number of occasions. It did not make her stand out though. She was the same as the other teachers. Her approach was rather conventional and predictable. She was not the first one who had left the school without any notice. In the same circumstances the previous teachers had vanished without a single warning, without a hint of complaint. Such practice made the Association think of changing the employment contract. The first salary was now to be paid after the second month of work, this way it would prevent them from leaving without notice.

The main concern of the trustees in England was Siham's father who may be using her position in the school as a form of controlling the organization. I had never met him in person, only heard stories. I knew that the bullying and nastiness in the past made everyone in the Association aware of him. Never to be trusted again "he smiles in your face and stabs you in the back."

Mohamed, the vice-president, called an urgent meeting this afternoon. It was him, Mustapha and Mohamed the caretaker who were waiting for me in a café in Khénifra looking tense and angry when I walked in. "What's wrong?" He was reading the newspaper and not wanting to talk. "Wait a minute, we'll order drinks and we'll talk," Mohamed carried on reading ignoring my presence completely. I was irritated by his odd behaviour so I grabbed the paper and took it away. "Now, we can talk," I said. The problem was the communication between the trustees back in England and the president Mustapha who felt disappointed, deceived, and wanted to resign from his presidential chair. So did Mohamed. "Wait a minute. Firstly we have to clarify few things." There was a huge discrepancy between who made a decision to appoint Siham for the teaching position and how it actually happened. They both, personally, felt accused by the trustees of some corruption that conceivably might have taken place. "Given the history, there was something fishy about how she got this job so suddenly," Hannah raised her suspicions. "The simple people in the village would not comprehend if we fired Siham right now," they were arguing. I was listening and taking into account both, the trustees and theirs point of view. I did not want to see them go. Despite all the problems that were mainly down to misunderstanding on the telephone line between here and the UK, they were so far pulling their weight. I suggested a solution to this problem and sent over to Hannah with essentially everything discussed. Firstly, a probation period which sounded like a fair option, if she passes, she stays, if not she will have to go, secondly, monitoring her performance for that period of time, and finally, making honest reports back to our trustees in the UK. It all had been accepted with one exception, she would have to sign in confidentiality an agreement which stated that if her father would do anything to harm or jeopardise the charity, she would be dismissed instantly.

I was pleased that we left the café still as a team.

Back at home, I was told that tomorrow Hakima, Fadma, Achraf and I would be going somewhere. It would be a family visit within a walking distance from El Borj that was all I understood. Rkia, Hakima's mum, was also ready to go somewhere. When she was wrapping around her back a small fabric stuffed with some other fabrics, it always signified a change – her moving somewhere else. She was a trooper. I believed she must have been in her late eighties or early nineties, and from what I had seen, she moved around places all the time, from one daughter to another, every few weeks. She was still very strong but often complained about the pain in her shoulders. Although she knew that I could not comprehend a word of what she was saying, she had often talked to me, and I sometime had had a guess making her laugh, and I never knew whether I was guessing it right or wrong.

******

Notes:

1 (p. 35) Albert Einstein.

2 (p. 35) Aji! In Darija, come!

3 (p. 39) Rfissa - a very finely torn boucheyar mixed with olive oil and sugar.

4 (p. 39) Inchallah - "if God wills/permits."

5 (p. 39) Dear Magdalena, It was a pleasure for me and my friend to have met you. The fact of inviting you over to my place for a cup of tea was a spontaneous act that has not portrayed any bad intentions. People here don't perceive things

in the same way. We are at your service with every help you need. Leave yourself to us. If you want to have coffee or go to the medina, call me on my mobile or come to my place.

6 (p. 40) Forno, in Darija, wood-burning stove.

7 (p. 40) Wakha, in Darija, also in Amazigh, yes, ok.

8 (p. 42) Eating dactyls in odd numbers is connected with Islam and the Prophet Muhammad. It was him who consumed dactyls that way.

9 (p. 42) In traditional Berber society, a man is expected to present the finest white sugar to the father of the girl whose hand he wishes to secure in marriage. The very refined high quality sugar acknowledges the innocence, purity and virginity of the focus of his intentions whilst at the same time evoking pride and power in the father as having a prized daughter who is valued enough to be coveted. To purchase the bag of sugar with its impurities in lumps, uneven grain and colour then present this, however exquisitely wrapped, to a father of a prospective bride would be equivalent to calling his daughter a prostitute. This would be not looked upon at all favourable. ("An overview of sugar culture in Morocco, particularly within a Berber community in Rastabouda," Gorgia-Rose Travis, December 2007).

10 (p. 43) The "olive tree" symbolises strength because of its Berber name "azemmur," diverted from the term "tazmat" which means - strength. "Wheat" is associated with Life (because of it sheath) and Death (because of the seeds being in the ground).

11 (p. 43) "Tree" is related to an easy life, happiness and fertility. It symbolises the centre of the world surrounded by Beings, objects and spirits. It also means Life (because of the roots) and knowledge (because of the leaves).

12 (p. 45) Fota, in Darija, towel.

13 (p. 45) Chokrane, in Darija, thank you.

14 (p. 48) In Chinese philosophy: red represents-fire, yellow-earth, white-metal.

15 (p. 49) Liberation - the daily French newspaper.

16 (p. 50) Zahra: I was given this name, which means flower in Amazigh, during my first trip to the Sahara Desert and it has been used amongst some Moroccans since.

17 (p. 51) In September 2012 two young men, a Czech and a Slovak, killed almost 30 people in Czech Republic leaving more in a critical condition in hospitals. Those two men, having no interest in chemistry but money, had decided to dilute methanol with ethanol and sell on the black market. A deadly mistake!

18 (p. 52) Tahar Ben Jelloun is a contemporary Moroccan writer whose entire collection of book is written in French, although his first language is Arabic.

19 (p. 52) "L'enfant de sable" ("The Sand Child") is a story told by a man who failed to bring a son into the world, hence is determined to raise his eighth, youngest daughter as a boy.

20 (p. 57) Arougou, a place 13 km from Khénifra on a way to Oum Rabia a popular source of drinkable water.

21 (p. 58) Having had a little idea about your work in village of El Borj, situated 10 km from Khénifra, with a great pleasure we have discovered your website. This message is an invitation to a co-operation and exchange of the expertise in the domain of local development. Yours Sincerely.

22 (p. 59) Imperial Tobacco Maroc remains the only significant player operating in smoking tobacco in Morocco and accounted for 98% of total retail volume sales in the category during 2012. The company continues to invest in offering customers a variety of different types of smoking tobacco in various different flavours, which has so far been the key to the company's success in the category. Following the liberalisation of the Moroccan tobacco industry, no player has entered the smoking tobacco, which remains dominated by the Nakhla brand, imported by Imperial Tobacco.

23 (p. 59) I miss you too much, and now I wonder if I can support your absence. I'm burning with curiosity to know your response and you sentiments towards me, it is necessary (...) my heart has chosen.

End of Part Two

The children from the Association Hannan

Part Three

"Hmad has just told me you are up in the mountains and having a sheep

slaughtered in your honor."

I was prepared for nothing but a short walk and dinner with my extended family. Prior to our outing, there was a slight change of plan: Hakima was staying at home and Meryam was to come with us instead. Also, my suspicion that Rkia was on the move was confirmed by her joining our little group. The bag of food including a dozen Danone yogurts, mandarins, bananas, various second hand clothes and some other bits and pieces were divided between me, Meryam, and Fadma for us to carry. The taxi that drove past El Borj took us to the furthest possible point on our journey leaving the rest of it for us to complete on foot. "Where is the house?" Fadma pointed to the mountains in front of us making a walking gesture accompanied by a very specific "eyeyeyeyey" noise which meant, unequivocally, a long walk ahead of us.

For about ten pointless minutes we waited for a donkey which was supposed to take grandma Rkia close to the mountains saving her energy for the more challenging parts of the journey. But the transport did not come and we all had to start walking. It was past midday. The day was sunny and hot and a light breeze that was stroking us gently wasn't spoiling us either. At first Rkia, supporting herself with a stick, was keeping a steady pace occasionally stopping to get a breather. Then the steeper it went, the more exhausted she became taking breaks more often and extending the stopovers by lying down on the open soil. She was incredibly strong though. I was watching her trekking along the rough path and could not believe my eyes – her intensity, force and stamina were not only inspiring, but also contagious, and I still don't know how she did it and where the strength was coming from. We kept climbing higher and higher but the peak started deceiving us and what at first looked like a five minutes' walk turned into a thirty minutes hike. It was time to stop and get a proper rest with some snacks and water. I was feeling dehydrated as foolishly, for the first time, I had not taken any water with me. Instead Fadma offered me a sip. "Aren't you thirsty?" I asked. "No, I'm fine," she responded. They all seemed to be like camels capable of strolling long distances and yet feeling fine. Even grandma was taking tiny sips rinsing her mouth rather than drinking it.

It took us over one hour to get to the top which then surprised me by revealing nothing but a flat land, a wild and infinite-looking plateau with random tufts of greenery and scarce stones scattered around those landscape. And yet the uninhabited land was bringing to light some form of life indicated by several ploughed fields and odd houses seen from a distance. "Is this the house?" I pointed at one on the horizon. "*La! La! La!* Eyeyeye..." I knew that sound and its unambiguity very well. The quietness and calmness of nature were only interrupted by grandma's panting and

Fadma's outrageous acts of vandalism shown towards nature. Without any thought or hesitation she threw away a plastic bottle filled with some water. Not only did she make me feel more dehydrated, but also infuriated by the lack of appreciation and respect towards the environment. This beautiful country has been turning into a rubbish bin because acts like this one have been copied by millions of other people who are disposing of rubbish anywhere. Besides, what example was she giving to young Achraf? My own lack of reaction disturbed me as much as this whole incident, but there was no time for personal disputes as we had to get moving.

While walking through that upland, I was pondering the way back home. How were we going to be able to return before dusk? It was around 2.00pm and there was not a sign of the house that we were to visit. The vast stretch of land revealed another house seen through the lens of my camera with some people and two dogs standing outside it and observing us walking past. The most surprising element of it all was the satellite dish; it was not the first time that I saw a satellite dish attached to a house or its ruins. However here, in the middle of nowhere, it looked even more conspicuous proving a very sad fact to me that whatever standards of living they had to conform to, the satellite dish was the most desirable commodity of all.

We crossed one field and then another and then one more; a little break. This time it was me who tried to keep up with grandma's pace. But then she stopped again, and one minute she was sitting on bare ground, and the next minute she collapsed holding on to the stick. Her whole body was on the ground, her face in the soil; nature seemed to have embraced her by trying to take away her exhaustion, soothing the pain, the discomfort, the anguish that she must have been familiar with as she certainly knew where she was going, how long would it take and when would it end. *"Amen, amen,"* the breeze carried the weak request. *"Amen, amen,"* I fetched some water for her. All of a sudden, she regained an upright position but her whole body was still fighting the fatigue giving her a real fever; she was trembling and her hands could hardly hold the bottle; her eyes were watering and I couldn't say if they were tears or exhaustion. I felt powerless; I couldn't help her. She then rose up and carried on walking hunched, weak, but fearless. What courage! I thought.

Someone on a mule was slowly emerging and Meryam's pointing fingers convinced me that help was finally coming. First, a beaming smile was seen from a distance, and then a girl's beautiful face showed up closer. What a relief! Having said that, Rkia refused to get on the mule, but another twenty minutes walking made her change her mind. As much as I worried about grandma, I also had a great deal of sympathy for the mule when the sudden change of weight occurred: from almost nothing at all in the form of grandma to ninety kilograms, at least, in the form of Fadma and the shopping. On top of that, the ground was getting more and more hilly and the poor animal looked more and more exhausted.

The more the milieu was changing the more spectacular it was becoming; the plateau was disappearing substituting the monotonous flatness for a set of entangled hills patched with more sporadic green bushes and trees of *idrens* - the edible acorns; the soil looked dry but its structure was prominently marked by the dashing waters of the previous week's torrential rain.

Finally, there was a house looming and it was our destination, the Azlal as they called it. "You don't have many visitors here, do you?" I asked but the joke was not understood.

The turkeys, donkeys and dogs were singing a loud "we don't know who you are" serenade. Three children were running around the house and two very skinny women with strong sharp facial features acknowledged our presence by hugging us and asking to sit inside a room, with a table that was soon laid with bread, olives, and water. The floor was fully covered with coloured carpets, walls showed pictures of the ruling King Mohamed VI and couple of other religious images. Although my body was boiling hot, the low temperature in the room made me shiver. Also Rkia, who was too tired to eat and drink, collapsed on the floor and was quickly covered with a few blankets to try to calm down her own body. "Is she going back with us tonight?" I asked. "No, she is staying here," they made that gesture. "We should hurry up if we want to get back before the sunset." "No, we will be sleeping here. Ça va?" Although I liked the taste of the adventure, I wished they had informed me before, so I could have taken a jumper or a toothbrush.

Everybody was friendly and forcing me to eat and drink. However, amongst them, there was a woman whom I found out to be one of Rkia's daughters and Hakima's sisters. Usually, the first impression offers an instant intuitional opinion, but her persona stirred in me rather strange feelings; her face was confusing me; she seemed kind and mean, honest and deceitful, trustworthy and unreliable at the same time. The other two women had every appearance of being exceptionally unavailable, rushing around, constantly preparing food, watching the children and animals. Bahssa, the shepherd, with his herd of sheep, goats and few cows, the only man at home, had come to greet me and went back to his work. I recognised his face; he was that happy individual who had visited us the other day.

I guessed there was no toilet, so instead of asking a direct question I posed the secondary, "where can I pee here?" and got the less deviated response, "everywhere, wherever you want" accompanied by laughter and the "land is your toilet" gesture. It reminded me of a joke that Mohamed told me when we were strolling in Arougou. A woman from Europe comes to Morocco, to a village. She goes off to a local bar and orders tea. A few minutes later she calls the waiter and asks: "Excuse me, where is the toilet?" The young man, comes up to the window, opens it widely and says: "Here is your toilet, madam."

In the meantime I went out. I had to keep moving as I was feeling cold. I watched the little boy playing with stones and wooden sticks. I climbed up the roof to be even closer to that spectacular sunset that was rapidly changing the whole landscape painting it with dark-orange but reflecting pink on its celestial backdrop. In this moment the whole planet seemed to have been motionless exhaling nothing but stillness and calm.

"Aji! Aji!" Fadma was pressing me to follow her, Suad the young girl, and Meryam, and I tagged along without asking any questions. To my surprise, they all were going out in search of toilet which I realised far too late when stumbling upon a naked bottom sticking out of bushes. Then I

turned around and saw another one. "Ahh!" What a surreal picture. I was searching for a way out trying to reverse like a car that first got lost, then trapped, and then embarrassed by what it had seen. Keeping in my mind the lack of toilet paper or any paper at all, I was awoken from my internal monolog, "You better keep an eye on what you eat and how much." Awoken as such, I was called to the table and panicked. "Oh my goodness! *Hrira*!"

"These two women are they sisters?" I asked Meryam. "No, they are the wives of Bahssa." "Really?" Itto, Hakima's sister, was the older one; his second wife was younger, and one year ago gave Bahssa another baby; all together they had nine children and sadly had lost one. There was not a tinge of jealousy or any negative feelings displayed between them two, they looked to me like sisters as they behaved like sisters. As much as I was curious about the intimate part of sharing the marital bed, I did not dare to ask. When we finished with the soup and the man came back home, we moved to the other room that had a simple fireplace and a tiny TV screen. The fire place, blankets, and a very energetic boy, Khalid, kept us warm. We fried the *idrens* in the fireplace and were being entertained by Bahssa, the fifty-two-year-old man who was probably looking for a third wife. "How old are you? How old is your mum? Could I come to Europe?" He asked questions "What would you do with your wives here?" "Only for regarder," he answered. "*Inchallah*. Perhaps you need a passport?"

I went out again to take photographs of the remarkable view over the mountains and made a friend with a dog that was not supposed to be friendly at all. He had never come to people as his job was to bark at them and make them scared. The dog looked extremely unfriendly when he was coming towards me and that did get me worried. "You don't want to bite me, do you?" I asked. He wagged his tail instead and sniffed my hands allowing me to tap his head, and when that happened, he jumped on me stretching his forelegs like he was ready to perform a dance. What a spectacle he gave in front of everybody who was watching his little show!

The children, Sefia, Suad, Khalid were still running about; they were beautiful and although they did not get many fellows to play with, they seemed like they had bravely embraced the solitude. The fifteen-year-old Suad never went to school and never made friends. She could speak Amazigh and Darija, but not write or read; the distance between the school and their home was far too great to be walked every day. Her parents were illiterate and so were her siblings. The little ones, calm and almost too mature for their age, were helping at home with some chores and taking the animals out and in the open, becoming their little shepherds. "If one could bring a boarding school for them would it function?" I asked myself. "Would their parents be happy? Would they let them go? Would they be pleased to give their children an opportunity for the better meeting future challenges? Would they understand the need for education, if they themselves weren't involved in any social system and the one that they were engaged in now seemed to function remarkably well?" While pondering, I got surprised by another meal; this time a sheep had been slaughtered in my honour, I was informed the following day, and lamb tagine was served. It was delicious, but the toilet question was popping occasionally into my mind controlling scrupulously the amount of digested food. The lack of electricity, dimming light, and complete darkness outside were slowly encouraging us over to the first room where beds had already been made. There were enough blankets laid on the floor for six people. As soon as I went to my bed fully dressed and covered by a few thick woollen blankets, I was slowly taking off some layers - it was getting hot. Although the temperature was right, I was tossing and turning and having real difficulties to fall asleep on that hard floor. When I finally lulled myself to sleep, I was rudely awakened in a form of chit-chat from Rkia and her daughter in the middle of the night. I cursed the ongoing chatter silently by carrying on with tossing, turning, and panting but nothing seemed to have worked as they continued talking. There was a longer pause that suggested the chat was over, but yet again was broken by Rkia's persistent, far too loud whispering. I didn't know at what time I managed to fall asleep, but the wake-up call appeared too early making the whole night too brief. As soon as I opened my eyes I felt exhausted; firstly, I craved for a shower; secondly, I was desperate to brush my teeth, and finally, to change my clothes.

The sun was waking itself up glancing through the haze and the morning dew that was seen on all the cobwebs. After breakfast we went searching for *idrens*; it was easy, almost every tree was bowing to its fertility quickly filling up our plastic bags. The next chore was to bring some water home. Suad took the empty cans of water, hung them around the donkey's back and marched down the valley to the nearest well. Each cylinder could contain thirty litres of water, I guessed, and was quite rapidly filled up. The system was manual, simple and proven: an empty bucket was lowered down the well and a full one brought out overflowing and ready to be taken back home. The donkey knew his job well and shot off by himself stopping occasionally to catch his breath, while Meryam and Suad were picking up leaves from the olive tree to use as henna on their hair.

It was past midday and it was time to head back home. Grandma was staying here for a few days, but Suad was insisting on taking the donkey and walking with us until the end of the plateau. Achraf was the first one to claim it. The sun was unbearable and we had no water as the empty bottle was still waiting to be filled. The donkey was strong but not strong enough to carry Fadma, Achraf, and an additional twenty kilograms in bags. The poor little beast crossed all the hills and suddenly collapsed on the flat ground under the weight and the heat. As soon as he got up, Achraf was on his back again. *"La! La! La!"* I shouted. "Leave this donkey alone; don't you see he is exhausted? You have one pair of legs, why don't you use them?" They all looked at me surprised and said nothing when Achraf was on his back few minutes later.

We finally reached the place where we could get some drinkable water. I was thirsty and had a headache, but they seemed to have been getting on with the heat like with their best friend, they were bothered neither by the heat nor the thirst. We stopped again just before the mountain, and I was thirsty again. "Where is the bottle?" Meryam walked away with it and came back with the empty one. I could not believe she wasted all the water for toilet! When we got to the bottom of that mountain, my head was exploding with pain and there was no taxi to catch. When a car stopped, they refused to get in saying: "You can't do that." "Why not? There is nothing wrong with someone giving you a lift." They did not accept the ride so we had to wait one hour for the bus to come.

The moment we got off the bus I saw another horror. This time Achraf who was holding an empty bottle, threw it on the pavement. "What are you doing?" I shouted. "Does the road look like a bin to you?" He grabbed it and a few seconds later threw it into the river adding, "it may be better there." I had no words. Nothing of what I said was getting into the head of that boy; he seemed to have no sympathy for nature or animals, and very little empathy for his parents.

******

After the urgent meeting last week, I went to school a little bit earlier than usual. The taxi arrived. There was only one seat left, or actually, there was no seat left but some space that two men and one woman made for me by sandwiching my body between a man and the door.

Both men had not been to *hammam* for quite some time nor had their clothes seen water for a very long time. Everything was dark brown. The man next to me gazed and smiled. I smiled back. I looked at him asking myself: "Could the layer of the dirt possibly be working as extreme sun cream protection?" He was wearing a baseball hat along with a very heavy, four sizes too big for him, filthy-looking jacket and a mucky pair of trousers. He eyed at me again and said bonjour. With his bonjour came a beautiful smile which uncovered his intact perfect white teeth. Owing to the poor dental hygiene, cigarettes, and massive sugar intake, to catch sight of a man with intact teeth here was almost like spotting a tiger in Africa. If only someone gave him a good scrub and some decent clothes to wear, visually, he would make a great candidate for a husband. Nevertheless, his set of perfect teeth revealed the cavities in a language, and despite the fact that his French was very poor, he kept asking all sorts of questions regarding my stay here, and not forgetting the most essential: the phone number request. This terribly smelly and rather sweet man got off the taxi with me, welcomed me in Morocco, wished me good luck, and walked off.

Siham, the new teacher, seemed to be getting on well with the children and they appeared to be at ease with her, paying at the same time attention to what she was saying or doing. She had a wide spectrum of little individuals to take care of: the attention-seekers, the unengaged, the disruptive ones, and the heavy-eyed ones with their leader Smaeil who will turn three in September, 2014. The boy, well-behaved, quiet, and rather slow in learning was often falling asleep in the classroom. Having had a very poor family that was supporting itself through selling sheep meat, Smaeil was a lucky one to have had a sponsor. Aya, was the opposite to Smaeil, a very demanding child that was constantly seeking attention by asking Siham to do her hair, or unzip her jacket, and if the jacket was unzipped then to zip it back. She bossed the children around during games or even in the classroom. The children that were unengaged in lessons were simply occupied in finding a nook in a table or playing with their pens.

Samira and I were invited over to Siham's for the afternoon tea. Her house, two minutes away from the school, was a decent one floor dwelling with very colourful orangey yellow and blue walls on which were displayed pictures of her younger mum. We sat down in the living room awaiting tea, but instead we were pleasantly surprised when a plate of tagine was brought to the table along with salad and olives. The whole time I was there, I was expecting to meet the dictator but it wasn't my lucky day. Only his mum and sister were with us, and later on, we were joined by the two Mohameds from our Association.

On the way back to Khénifra, I stopped by a café and was joined by Mohamed who continued to be subdued. As giving up smoking wasn't an option, I gave him a list of natural ingredients that could enhance his mood. "Eat bananas, as my friend Sheldon used to say, they are good for depression; sunflower seeds, protein-rich food like turkey, chicken, milk. And think about giving up smoking, please," I was nagging this poor man.

******

It was the day for distributing clothes amongst our children. Once a year they were allowed to go to the allocated souk in the medina to choose from a variety of clothes and shoes. The Association received a significant discount from a particular merchant, a Moroccan guy who spent a number of years in Italy, in Bologna. "Allora, parliamo Italiano." What a flashback I had to my Florentine period! Over a chat, I got to drink a cup of strong Italian coffee made by the precious Italian coffee machine that was installed in his shop. The shop was packed out with children who were trying things on and returning them back to Mohamed or Mustapha who were both controlling the whole operation. *"Ciao bella, ci vediamo dopo,"* he concluded.

Anyhow, the day of distributing clothes was chaotic and not everything was given away as some children or their parents did not turn up. However, most of them were seen in front of the school at least two hours before. "What are you waiting for? You know there is no French lesson today." They responded with the usual wildness, laughter, and "madam, madam" heckle. Malak, the beautiful one, took me over to hers and introduced me to her two cows that were grazing in front of the school, one was called Hassan and the other one - Samira; that was her little chore to keep an eye on them. Just before 3.00pm they started to barricade the front door pushing and pulling each other while posing for some photos. Some of them were allowed to get in and waited quietly until the distribution commenced. It began straight after 3.00pm when some trustees turned up to monitor the distribution and to check that fingerprints were taken. One pregnant girl with a baby on her back drew my attention. "Who is this girl?" I asked Mohamed. "Malika Azziz and Meryam, a single mother, no one knows who the father is, she is also mentally retarded and there are some health problems with Meryam, she apparently cannot walk." "She looks pregnant to me?" "She is pregnant." "Who is the father?" "No one knows."

One hour later the clothes were distributed and we were to sit for tea and boucheyar brought by Siham. There were a few people that I had never met before; one of them, a man, invited me over to his place for Friday's couscous. I accepted; I accepted almost everything; I didn't want to let people down. In the meantime, I was asked to serve tea. Usually it was down to the oldest, but today I was honoured to do the ritual; to begin with, one has to pour the first glass and return it straight back to the teapot, secondly, into the same glass pour tiny bit to taste, if the tea is not sweet enough then add more sugar and repeat the whole ritual; if the taste is right, carry on pouring the tea for everybody else without touching or moving the glasses. In spite of all the glass manoeuvres, I had passed the test and was allowed to leave.

The taxi that pulled out in front of me was empty. The driver couldn't speak a word of French but kept asking questions in Arabic and I kept responding in French assuming he was asking about the work and the purpose of being here. The conversation felt weird and funny; it was like a monologue between two people who anticipated questions and responses at the same time. The taxi stopped twice: once it picked up a man, the second time three large women; one of them, too large perhaps, couldn't fit on the back seat of the taxi, so instead, she settled next to me in the front. Making herself comfortable, by taking over the whole seat and pushing me on to the gearbox, she made it difficult for the driver. *"Salam ali-koum.""Wa'ali-koum salam."* My response revealed the extent of my Arabic. "Desolée, mais je ne parle pas Arabic." She mumbled something, then gave me a very disapproving look, and started shouting in my ear. The whole taxi was buzzing with some kind of argument and she kept yelling, gesticulating, and glancing at me. "Why don't you just shut up?" I gave her that kind of look. I didn't know what the argument was about, but the taxi driver, a man in his 50's who was not interested in getting involved, kept looking at me and smiling making me feel like he was on my side, if he had to take one. I had no idea what was going on and what had stirred her aggressive behaviour; I was polite and gave her the whole space she needed. She was clearly the fat, smelly, arrogant, argumentative, ignorant racist, the type that would spit on me and throw stones, without a doubt. I was relieved when we reached Khénifra and I could get off. *Bslama.*

I went out to get some water. My friend's boutique was opened so I stopped there. He treated me to coffee, tea, and home-made yogurt on the house, asking me out. "Maybe one day but it's not a promise," I responded.

While walking back home, I bumped into my friend, the one that could speak French and English. "Tu me manques," he said. Simo must have been nineteen or maybe twenty years old, handsome with a distinctive stubble, his trendy clothes suggested that he might come from a rather well off Moroccan family.

******

The next day I met Simo at the "Omega" café. He came with his friend for a chat, drink and a spontaneous invitation for the New Year's Eve party with him and his friends. Simo had some family in Paris and was thinking of going there to continue his studies. "Young people want to get out of here," he said. "I agree with you, there is nothing to do. I'm probably the only attraction in this place," he laughed.

"I'm jealous of you," he said. "Why?" "Because you speak four languages," "And you speak three," "No, I don't. My English and French are not brilliant." "Mine too; keep practising them and you will become very fluent. I'm sure you have got many talents. "Not like you," he carried on. "Listen, if everyone was good at the same thing then nothing else would be functioning properly." Our conversation reminded me of what Albert Einstein once said: "We are all geniuses; but if you judge the fish on its ability to climb a tree it would grow thinking it's stupid." "Do you understand?" He claimed he did. I had to go home, it was getting dark and I did not want my family to worry about me. "Call me if you need me, or if you want to take coffee," he added.

On the way home I stopped at Mina's to say hello. Ali was also at home and they both were extremely pleased to see me. "Where were you? We missed you." I explained the busy weekend in the mountains and my work in El Borj. Mina was lying on the sofa wrapped up in a blanket watching TV. Her face was shining with good health. "*Hammam*," she said. The hard-scrubbing really worked well making the skin look healthy, supple, smooth and the wrinkles almost disappeared. She treated me to a spicy coffee with milk and sugar and home-made biscuits. "*Koul! Koul!*" Delicious as usual.

While I was showing photographs from the weekend in the mountains, Mina had suddenly vanished somewhere. A few minutes later she turned up with three djellabas. "Which one would you like?" I refused to take any of them but she insisted. The first of a grey colour was long and little bit too big. I liked it. The second one was light-pink, smaller size but too short. I didn't like it. The third one, the light-pink with some shiny elements was voted the best one for me. I liked it. Her spontaneous act of giving did not stop with the djellaba; she then took off her headscarf pressing me to take it. "I can't accept it, it's too much," I shouted but there was no way that she would let me go without accepting it. "Don't tell Hakima it was from me. Tell her that you bought it in the medina." "How much would that cost?" "150DH."

The following day was my outing with Ali and Mohamed. I was feeling under the weather and desperately needed a shower, but found the perfect alternative: some aspirin and a headscarf. Our regular get-together fed me with new concepts giving a broader picture of their culture and Islam, the domineering subject so far in our daily discussions. They kept showing me videos of Muslims praying in mosques and the Immam who was leading the whole proceedings. I was also introduced to some pop-culture represented by Moroccan and Algerian singers, including Kadem Sahir-Irak, Cheb Khaled, Cheb Bilal, Cheb Mami. "Let me guess," I said, "they sing about love don't they?" Indeed, they were singing about love; in fact love has been a leading subject in any Arabic songs. However, the man who impressed me most was the Moroccan legend, the king of the *loutar*, *Mohamed Rouicha*, with his *"Inas, Inas"* song: *"Inas, inas, mayrigh, Adas gghi zmane?..."* (Tell him what I can do to this life?...").

As Ali was pressed for time, I was invited over to Mohamed's to join a small celebration, the circumcision dinner of her sister's one-year-old son. When walking back home, we talked about life and the circumstances that brought us here. I derived a great deal of pleasure from our philosophical conversations; the strangest thing was that although our cultures and upbringing were miles apart, we seemed to have understood each other surprisingly well. "If you travel all the time you don't have time to settle down and have family, do you?" "That is probably right but the point of settling down is to find the right man to grow old with." I recalled a few boyfriend stories and made him laugh. "It's pure and simple coincidence that they all had different nationalities," I said. "Every single one had a real impact on me, and what I have now realised was that in the whole process of getting to know each other, I was doing nothing but rediscovering myself. In the end I had to ask myself an honest question: do I like myself when I'm with that man? Do I have enough respect for myself when I'm with that man? If the answers were no, the relationship was doomed and not worth continuing." "It's difficult to be happy," said Mohamed. "I disagree, the difficulty comes when we struggle to embrace a happiness that is different to our own. It's all relative." I also disagreed on that polar issue. How could the differences between people possibly unite them? Perhaps it could all be fun at the start with the infatuation stage, but spending one's whole life looking for a compromise and forgetting about one's own happiness has never sounded like fun to me. We mentioned Sartre in our discussion and back at home he recited me few lines from *"Huis Clos."* "Je ne peux pas supporter qu'on attende quelque chose de moi. Ça me donne tout de suite envie de faire le contraire." "This is about you," he added and continued with another one: "Je ne compte pas? Mais, petit oiseau, petite aluette, il y a beau temps que tu as à l'abri dans mon cœur. N'aie pas peur, je te regarderai sans répit, sans un battement de paupières. Tu vivras dans mon regard comme une paillette dans un rayon de soleil." "And that could be your ex-boyfriend talking," concluded Mohamed.

We joined the small gathering: his mum, dad, and the family of his sister's Suad. Over a big plate of tagine, I shared my stories with Suad's husband, the only one who could speak French, and he shared his, much more interesting army stories. For many years he had been serving in the Moroccan army. First, in the parachute division and now, defending borders with Mauritania where they have been stationed. I got excited. "Can I pay you a visit?" "The civilians are not allowed." "Can I obtain a pass as I writer?" He had no idea but his "maybe in the future...." answer was not convincing.

The baby was finally fast asleep; the two hour cry after the circumcision operation and the painkillers he was given made him exhausted. "It must be extremely painful. Why do you do that?" I asked. Despite all the pain that the baby had to go through, they all were in favour of the circumcision without stressing any particular reason other than religious.

Mohamed and I went for a short walk along the river continuing our discussion regarding liberty in a relationship. "Have you ever been in love?" It was a perfect moment for me to ask. He thought he was, in his cousin, but he could not imagine committing to her owing to the differences. "Dear Lord," I thought, "I would point out many other reasons … but differences." In the end it was not my business; things that were allowed or prohibited here were making my eyebrows raised, whereas for him the way I have lived seemed, at times, bizarre or even unacceptable.

I came back home feeling feverish and quickly had a good wash, took some tablets and went to bed. Two hours later I came downstairs to sit by the fire and listen to a story recalled by Lahcen. It was a story about *Baba* who some time ago had decided on a second wife. "He needed more than Halima could give him," joked Lahcen. Apparently, he had found a woman, married her, lived with her and everybody else in the same house, but one day he changed his mind. According to Lahcen, the marriage survived four weeks, according to Meryam - four months. "What happened?" "One day *Baba* opened the door and chased her away." "That's a Berber spirit," I commented.

******

I did not get out of bed before 10.00am as I wasn't feeling well. Meryam knocked at my door asking how I was and inviting me downstairs for breakfast. There was Itto, a woman from the mountains and *Äami* Lahcen who kept calling Hakima: "Hakima, eeeh, Hakima, Hakima, eeeh Hakima." This was nothing new for me or anybody else in the house as *Baba* was able to call Hakima even in the middle of the night and kept calling her name until she was there to see him. But this time she was out and *Baba's* grumpy persistence started annoying his wife - grandma Halima. Her reprimand did not sound very diplomatic especially when it all turned into shouting. They both kept the uproar until Halima's voice, fragile and taciturn at first, went into a very high jerky C sharp off the piano note; it was hilarious to observe them. When they calmed down, Halima went off to her bed, and as soon as she made herself comfortable, she beckoned me to come over to her. In this instance, it was not about her bottle or the plastic box, it was more serious; she put her fingers inside her mouth, a second later I understood her problem, but kept repeating this movement a few times. In case I wanted to escape, she was holding onto my hand. Then her upper body got possessed by a weird energy that kept her shoulders moving back and forward and it was followed by her forcing me to touch her stomach while she was raising the layers of her pyjamas. As I was getting more and more confused, I was glad that the rescue came with a visitor, one of Bahssa's daughters, very much like Suad but older; the same smile, same face, same pleasant and loving character. Zahra was in her twenties and had already been divorced, and lived in Khénifra. Because she grew up in the mountains like her younger siblings, her face unveiled some damage by the constant sun exposure and lack of sun protection. She was gazing at me smiling, making me feel like I was coming from a different sphere. "I want a photograph with you," she handed her mobile phone to Meryam. *"Zwina, zwina,"* she kept repeating but wanted few more. *"Zwina, zwina, chokrane."*

As I was familiar with the stuff in the "Omega" café and they were familiar with me, I had the tendency to spend most of the time after work sitting there creating files, updating, replying to emails, reading and taking advantage of the internet connection. I even became more adventurous with drinks, not only did I have teas and coffee crème tire, but also a fresh orange juice and avocado milk shake which was a real delight taking into account its freshness, thickness, and size. This time, Zouhir, the waiter, was taking care of me by serving a magic drink that was supposed to cure the sore throat problem: a glass of hot milk with the teabag of vervain and sugar, leaving me with a peculiar taste in my mouth. Zouhir made this place alive; he would come up to people grinning and spreading a positive attitude on them, unlike the second waiter Simo who appeared nice but dishonest. "Madam or Mademoiselle?" he stank like a bee when repetitively asking this question.

On the way home I was greeted by a few people and stopped by one man. "Je voudrais bien faire ta connaissance" and then added, "I speak English." "Good," I responded. "Are you on vacation here?" "No." "Do you have a number?" "No," he understood the pointlessness of this conversation and left me alone.

Mohamed, Ali's father, was sitting in his garage doing his usual; when noticing me coming, he jumped up, opened the door to his house, and showed me in. Mina was making *boucheyar* and invited me to watch her doing it and then try it myself. I formed two and got one to eat, heavenly tasty, crispy, light and just right with some honey on top. She was joking about opening a restaurant in Europe with me and Ali. ""Mina's *boucheyar*" - that would probably bring some profit; we would be rich," I joked. I was also treated to a cup of tea and extra spoonful of honey for my sore throat. When I was about to leave she hugged me and said: "Je t'aime, Je t'aime Zahra, Je t'aime." I was touched. "One more thing, don't mention to Hakima that you have eaten here. It's better that way," she said.

The whole aspect of hiding or lying was bothering me. I wanted to share my experience with those whom I loved rather than concealing it. If they are accustomed to falseness or secrecy, to what extent are they real? What is genuine in their behaviour? Where is the truth and where is the hiding part? How do they build honest long term relationships or friendships if their very construction is so feeble? I was sitting in my room contemplating and at the same time being strangled by smoke coming from the malfunctioning *forno*; air wasn't circulating and tears were running down my face; thirty minutes on and smoke was still coming in; to be able to breathe I put a scarf around my face and spent another hour in such position until the smoke was gone. The windows downstairs were wide open. "This is not healthy, you have to fix it or stop using it," I said. "It's good for your eyes," Papa Mohamed repeated his well-known phrase. "How come?" "It makes you cry and tears are good for your eyes." "Not if they are caused by smoke that sooner or later will give you real health problems." I very much was against his theory but no one else seemed to be bothered by either smoke or by the drivel that Papa Mohamed was spreading.

******

When this morning a taxi driver stopped to give instructions to a passing by car, I was nicely surprised by the language he used. "Lei parla Italiano?" I switched to my Italian. "Si, si, I spent ten years in Italy." "Dove?" "In Savona." As he could no longer keep his job as a chef in a restaurant called "Pasta et Basta," he was forced to return home one year ago. "I was a chef for ten years. I was making pasta." "What about pizza?" "No, only pasta." That certainly explained the name of this place. He described Morocco as a "disastro" where people have no jobs and the country instead of going uphill goes downhill. However, he called himself a lucky man as he was able to get employed by the taxi corporation. Although his two brothers were still living in Italy, where he could always go for a short visit, it would no longer be possible for him to obtain a working visa. With great passion he talked about his job as a chef; he loved the whole experience, the possibilities of travelling, making friends, simply having the freedom that Italy gave him and that Morocco took away. He also took the opportunity of learning Italian; the eight months free of charge Italian language course that the local government had offered him, made a real difference to all those years he had spent there. *"Morroco e bello ma non c'e lavoro qui,"* he concluded by giving me his phone number and was keen on seeing me again over coffee. He was brave to leave Morocco, pick up a new language, find a job, embrace the new conditions, environment, mentality, culture, and start something from scratch. I believed many of them would do the same if they had the opportunity.

The school today was cold and quiet. I sat down on the rooftop waiting for the break while Mohamed was polishing the floor. Straight after the break the children came up to play and interact with each other and the teachers. When the school was over Siham, Samira and Mohamed were waiting for me downstairs. "What about the couscous invitation?" "That's where we are going." Now I got it. The man who invited me for couscous was the nasty dictator, the bully, the man who smiles at you and stabs you in the back - father of Siham. O boy! Here we go! Straight into the mouth of the oppressor! The despot wasn't at home when we came in, instead her mum and sister sat with us at the table; we all shared olives, salad, bread, simple conversation and lots of laughter. But the atmosphere was about to change and it was not the couscous that disturbed the air but the presence of a man who for a reason was called the bully, the nasty, the tricky, the revengeful. The anxiety was seen on the face of Siham, all of a sudden the liveliness was gone, the goofy laugher was replaced with the modest one, and answers to some questions appeared to have been more thoughtful. The respect was distinguished but clearly led by fear; there was some sort of chill that immobilised her and her speech when he was around. I observed his presence carefully over a plate of couscous without making him feel uncomfortable; based on a simple principle that every human being makes a mistake and is forgiven, I pretended that I knew nothing of his affairs with our Association. I sympathised with him - the weak one, the defeated, the powerless who was convinced of his strength when confronting the weakest, the more venerable than himself, those who had to obey him on a simple principle of a social or cultural imperative. "Does he call himself a man? Is he worth the title?" I waited for some sort of interaction, a question, a statement that would prove me wrong, a change that he underwent, or a transformation he was yearning for. "I'm a better person now and I'm sorry for what I've done in the past, by the way, thank you for giving a chance to my daughter." Those long-anticipated words had never come. What was the point of inviting me over for dinner? There was nothing in his behaviour that suggested he was interested in getting to know me. Was that a form of bribe or perhaps intimidation? I give you couscous from time to time and you give my daughter the teaching position. The ocean of speculated thoughts were waved off and sunk a few weeks after when her performance was evaluated and rewarded with the employment contract.

******

On a global scale, *hammam* was a blessing; on a micro scale, it could turn into a hell if one chose the wrong venue. The one that I promised to go to with Hayat, the younger sister of Mohamed, used to be prison and was still recognisable as one by the heavy metal fences around it. The first lesson was not to go to the *hammam* on weekends, the second – it was better to go alone, the third – the cheaper it was, the worse it got. This was not like entering the prison but something between purgatory and hell and the one that I was thinking of was Dante's Hell. I felt as lost and assailed by the wild, naked bodies as the poet himself when he got lost in dark woods in front of the mountains and was attacked by some beasts. I was unable to find a "dritta via" to salvation and was conscious as Dante himself was that I was ruining myself and falling into a low place, "basso loco" where the sun was silent, "I sol tace." Unlike Dante I was rescued by nobody and the punishment, the "contrapasso," was as symbolic as it was real. And when I was passing through the gates of the *hammam* I *"abandoned all hope."* The very first souls that I came across there were as Dante described them: "uncommitted," neither good nor evil but oblivious. They were scrubbing and washing, washing and scrubbing, repeating it calmly, obediently as if they were neither there nor anywhere else. The second room revealed more perturbed souls who were closer to hell but not yet there. They seemed to be punished by their own indecisiveness which I noticed when my leading charon unlike Dante's was pushing me inside hell, straight into the third circle where the gluttony meets greed and the violence steps in. The cold and selfish deprived of their sensuality, charm and elegance bodies were spreading themselves wherever they could without any consideration of personal space or aesthetic principles.

"Here no pleasure when body bends and face to face meets its ends,

For now and forever, hides it-self for the grace that the nature place."

They were too absorbed in their activities that nothing but lack of water could wake those arrogant and greedy souls and drag them to the spring where they nagged and jostled to get what they wanted.

"I saw multitudes

To every side of me; their howls were loud

While, wheeling weights, they used their chest to push.

They stuck against each other; at that point

Each turned around and, wheeling back those weights

Cried out. Why do you hoard? Why do you squander?"

After two and half hours I managed to escape; I was strong enough to say: "Enough! I have seen enough, I want out, I don't want to be touched again and I don't want to eat mandarins, they don't have a different taste to the usual ones, as I was told. I'm clean but feel dirty when looking around. I want out! Please let me out!"

The distance from hell to paradise was short, about five minutes on foot. "How was it?" asked Mohamed, "Unique," I responded while drying my hair. Then we both sat in the kitchen and shared tagine when the "sex" subject came about. "Why are there so many sex scenes in your films?" "Because sex is part of anyone's life." I responded. "So, if anyone knows it so well why do film makers have to show it? For what reason?" Those questions arose after him watching "Love in the time of Cholera." "Didn't you like the film?" "Why did he have sex with all those women?" "It was his therapy to try to forget the love of his life." To understand our world one has to be born or live there at least. Here, the body's exposure in public is considered evil, immoral, and sinful. "Your body is a temple and only your wife or husband should see it," they kept repeating. I do understand, however, what is more sinful: hiding your sins in every corner of the street, or exposing them publicly? The naked body in our Western world does not equal perversion. Not everybody wants to kill his father and sleep with his mother; there is a difference between pornography and lovemaking scenes. Perhaps my puzzling question as to why there is so much indecent behaviour here in Morocco was just answered: they have no control over their sexual desire as it has simply been repressed; the only way it could come out would be either through marriage or masturbation which may not be the case because masturbation is regarded as sinful. So why do men chase after women? Do they straight away think about marriage? I doubt it. The oppressed sexual desire runs after those poor souls hoping to be freed, but would rarely see the daylight purely because it's regarded as immoral to have sex before marriage. In my opinion, the system here, which punishes any form of public affection, has created far more harm to the society than good.

Our conversation was spiced up when the film *"Casanegra"* was mentioned. It was the first Moroccan film that showed sex and masturbation. "What was the point of if?" "I don't know, I have not seen it. Perhaps it was unveiling the reality?"

Some people and critics described it as a masterpiece:

"Violence, language, sex – never a Moroccan film has been so far. "Casanegra," the second feature film from director Lakhmari Noureddine, 44, is becoming a social phenomenon in Morocco (…) the rooms, where the film is projected, are often full. Young, old, rich, poor, veiled women."

Likewise, the heavy criticism that was referring to the chocking and vulgar language, pathetic and unreliable characters, miserable, disappointing and ridicule was heard. "The film, giving very American tunes, is actually quite pretentious, probably depicts well the reality, but the style is so awkward and so heavy that the film becomes even towards the end - annoying," one observer commented. I watched the film and agreed with Mohamed and other people who had described the film as mediocre, and the whole masturbation scene that lasted five seconds as utterly pointless. The lovemaking scene was nothing of love and nothing of a scene. I was also not convinced as to the characters and the violence it presented.

However, I was still not able to respond to Mohamed's concerns regarding sex and masturbation but I wanted to look for the answers. "Where can I find answers to such a trivial but yet troublesome subject?" I was asking myself. I remembered what Ali once told me: "If you have any doubts or don't know the answer go to the Quran, there you will find the answer to everything." I was electronically leafing through the Quran, almost thousand pages, and Hadith, seeking the ripostes and thinking I would never find anything on subject of sex and very unlikely on subject of masturbation. And here it was. In a brief but beautiful expression, the Quran refers to "clothes" when describing the relation between husbands and wives: *They are your garments and you are their garments."*

The prophet, Sahim Muslim, explained that the sexual union between husband and wife was more than seeking a relief from the urge of desire but was referring to one of charities in Islam. He gives us a parable:

"And when the one of you makes love (has sex) it is a rewarding charity. His companions were surprised and asked him: How come the one of us answers the urge of his desire and out of this gets the reward of a charity? To which the prophet answered: Don't you see that if he does the same but in a forbidden situation it would be counted against him as a sin. And so if he does it in legitimacy it is counted for him as a charity."

The discourse went even further referring to a very special relation between spouses and the privacy that it deserved. It is not befitting that either of them divulges this aspect of their life to anyone. The prophet, Abu Said Bahadur Khan, raises questions:

"Would it be that the one of you locks his door and draws his curtains and seeks his need (sex) from his consort, and later when he goes out he talks to his friends about it? He then turned to the women and said: Would it be that the one of you locks her door and draws her curtains and seeks her need from her consort, and later when she goes out she talks to her women friends about it? There was an air of admitting silence and a woman said: It happens, apostle of God. The prophet said: Never do that or it would be like a male devil who encountered a female devil and copulated with her out in the middle of the road and then left her and went away."

The very surprising passages came from the prophet Anas ibn Malik who fourteen centuries ago recognised women's right to attain sexual satiety out of sexual intercourse, the prophet says: "If any of you has sex with his wife let he be true to her. If he attains his pleasure before her then he shouldn't hurry her away until she also attains her pleasure." Wasn't it thoughtful? He continues: "Let not the one of you fall upon his wife like a beast (camel) falls. It is more appropriate to set a messenger before the act." What is the messenger here? Looking for the explanation I reminded myself that everything written here was not modern - it was apparently written down fourteen centuries ago. The messenger was a simple "foreplay" which was rather well explained in the following article:

"Standard writings in sexology over the past few decades have described the physiological human sexual response and classified it into the four phases of excitation, plateau, orgasm, and resolution. Ideally these phases should coincide in both partners, otherwise there will be sexual disharmony, often due to the man getting his orgasm while the woman is still eagerly awaiting with inflamed desire, to also achieve her orgasm. As orgasm is followed by resolution where the male organ gets flaccid and the man enters into a refractory period after his sexual desire has been satiated through orgasm, the conclusion of the act at that stage would be unfair to the woman having been aroused but not satisfied, and that is what the prophet warns against. The man should not just turn his back and go away or go to sleep, leaving his wife frustrated. The coital exercise should proceed until she is satisfied. An effective method of correcting this form of disharmony is to spend time enjoying their intimacy and helping themselves to one another's bodies in totality, before moving on to genital intercourse. The pleasures of sex spread themselves over a much wider area than the genital region, as manifest in kissing, embracing and caressing the body especially over the erogenous zones of the female physique. This indeed is the normal and commendable approach to sex. It adds to the mechanistic element of sex, the emotional dimension of tender love and mutual affection beautifully portrayed in the Quran as: "They are your garments, and they are yours." It also ensures that by the time the couple move on to genital introduction, the woman would have been aroused over a sufficient period of time and become so excited that she is already quite near her orgasm. In modern medical jargon this prelude is called the "foreplay", but again long before it was dreamt in the rest of the world of such women's rights, the prophet of Islam gave the same guidance, politely referring to foreplay as the "messenger."

The couple's sensitivity to each other's needs, limitations, and ups and downs was also mentioned amongst the good sexual ethics. Even a virtuous excuse like deep involvement in worship was not accepted if the man forgot or ignored his wife's rights. In such a case, it was the woman's right to protest. History reported the woman who went to Umar ibn al-Khattab, second caliph, consulting him: "My husband fasts by day and prays all night and I feel embarrassed to complain seeing that he spends his time worshipping God." The man was summoned for a hearing. The final verdict was to have three nights for his own worship and to heed the needs of his wife during the rest of the week. Similarly, a woman should be responsive to her husband's call. Seeing that men are more prone to sexual arousal by a variety of visual stimuli as they move about all day, the prophet's advice was that the wife should always answer her husband's call: "The right of the husband is that when he calls his wife to sex she should not deny him herself," says prophet Abu Dawud Tialisi. The prophet also advised that whenever a man sees something that arouses his sexual desire, he should go and have sex with his wife.

The Quran even talks about situations like the unannounced return of a husband. Honey, I'm back! This would not be right, according to some prophets. He should never take his wife by surprise as she has to have time to beautify herself before meeting her husband. "If you are in a journey do not enter your home all of a sudden so that the tuggy hair would comb and the unprepared get ready."

I was surprised by the outcome of my further research on masturbation issue. The view on masturbation was divided between scholars; some of them put masturbation under the list of the forbidden categories of sexual fulfilment. "Those who guard their sexual organs except with their spouses or those whom their right hands possess, for (with regard to them) they are without blame. But those who crave something beyond that are transgressors." They call masturbation a deviation and that is enough to condemn it. However, there are some exceptions recalled by the followers of Shari'ah; if someone is afraid that he would commit a greater sin like *zina*, unlawful sexual intercourse, or he will be harmed by some psychological disorders, then the ban on masturbation would be relaxed just to remove the hardship, based on the Shari'ah principle that states that necessity is judged according to the circumstances that warrant it. They are two more conditions that may turn the "transgressor" into a "lawman:" the difficulty of getting married and the inability to fast.

****

The next couple of days I would describe as a crisis on a global scale; perhaps the sheer thought of spending Christmas here made me feel more sensitive, hence prone to negative energy or to be frustrated with small things, for example, the malfunctioning *forno* and smoke that we were still inhaling, or grandma Halima who was forcing me to eat even when I was consuming in front of her, or her everlasting persistence of giving away the tiny pieces of food from her own plate which was not only driving me crazy but everyone else in the house. Today, she wanted me to bring her some water, so I went to fetch her some water. "No, I want hot water," I got her the hot water. "This is too hot," she complained putting her fingers inside the cup. "Ulalala," I responded irritably but still smiling. "Grandma, you wanted some hot water and I brought you some."

This was the time when I could get easily upset with Meryam and her hurtful comments. As much as I tried to learn some Arabic, I wasn't devoted to it and the judgement that was coming with a response to a question, "does she speak Arabic?" was making me feel upset; perhaps, because it was coming from a person who could hardly formulate a sentence in French confirming what I pondered as the truth: the less you know the more you think you know, and the more you know the more you doubt.

The fact that I was still feeling under the weather might have been a significant factor in my ill-being. The challenging moment came when Meryam and I had to go over to Hannah's, a young daughter of Alla, to help Monsif, her son, with French. The boy was only nine years old and could already hold a conversation in French. He was a clever boy and the pleasure in helping him was huge. The real challenge was his own energy; being easily disrupted by absolutely everything was making lessons a real test. His little sister Selma, a walking, demanding disturbance, wasn't helping at all. *"Chouf! Chouf!"* she was jolting him and getting hysterical when neither Monsif nor his mum were giving her enough attention. On two occasions, I witnessed a brutal and vicious attack on her own mum. Her little arms seemed to have been possessed by some nasty energy that was assaulting Hannah's face; she was hitting her repeatedly and getting more vicious when being pushed away. Although she was hysterical and in tears when it all started, soon after, as being focused on slapping Hannah's face, she even forgot to cry. What followed next was tough to watch; her mum did the same, like in some sort of revenge she was hitting her little face until it all went red and the tears were streaming down her face.

This evening, however, passed without hysteria. The lesson was about 'nom propre et nom commun.' The ocean wasn't a problem, the Atlantic was, but with some thorough explanation followed by more examples, we could move on to conjugation which Hannah was obsessed with. "He is very good at it, give him some credit." "Not that good," she responded. "You should really be more encouraging," I commented. Meryam was pressing me to leave and Hannah was pressing me to stay and carry on reading with Monsif. "Two minutes and I'm done. Wait for me, please." She didn't. She shot off with Leila to the medina. "We'll be back in thirty minutes." "No, please wait. I'm coming with you." When we finished reading, Hannah's obsession with conjugation was getting on my nerves. "Sorry, I have to go." "Stay, stay, just one more time. You can't walk home by yourself." "Of course I can." "When can we come next? Wednesday?" "Any day but Wednesday." "So we come Wednesday evening," she added.

When strolling back home, I had to put up with constant: "Bonjour, ça va? Comment vas-tu? I can marry you and go to France." Why can't they just leave me alone? J'en ai mare de ça!

******

I don't think I know my vocation but I'm certain that it is not teaching; just observing the children was making me feel tired. They were incredibly demanding today, quickly bored, fidgeting and uninterested in most of the things that were taught by Siham. The majority were four and five years old; the youngest, two girls, were two years old; one of them was always bursting into tears every time she saw me, whereas the rest were very responsive to my silliness. At 12.30pm the children were picked up by their parents; the few that were living in the village had an easy walk, but many who were coming from far away were carried by mules; those children had real difficulties to get to the school each day. We discussed this problem with Mohamed and Mustapha and came to a conclusion that a small school bus would be a good solution. The only problem was money as 20.000DH was not obtainable.

Today's extra French lesson was extra stressful. Mohamed, completely took it over as the children were not able to understand simple commands. The "avoir" and "être" were applied in simple sentences and grilled over and over again until the children lost their confidence. "No! You idiot! Once again! Now! What did I say?" shouted Mohamed. Most of them were guessing, some - thinking. This was supposed to be fun both, for me and the children, but instead it was turning into a camp that trained the children to become soldiers. Now! Attack! Wrong! Once again! Idiot! This is not my vocation, I was honestly looking at myself; this is too stressful; how can one enjoy teaching? It's madness! I need a decent glass of wine to be able to function afterwards.

That day I did not get back home until very late. I sent a message to Meryam: "No reason to worry about me, I'm safe with Ali and Mohamed." We spent the whole evening in the café "Martil," next to the "Omega," with a few friends of Ali who joined us later on. Over *shiba* and *boucheyar* I shared with Mohamed the disturbing facts regarding Malika Azziz and Hannah's advice to look into it properly. My plan was to interview her and I needed a woman who would do all the translation from Amazigh to French. He had a friend who spoke Amazigh and English and was happy to meet up with me the next morning around 10.00am.

"What about a glass of wine and a film?" I was delighted. It was possible. We went off to a room that was rented by three or four people and the total cost of 120DH per month was split between them. The purpose of that room was to have fun and to feel free. Although the hiding place was tiny, three meters by one if not less, and had only a single mattress, a small table, shisha, and a pair of loudspeakers, it served the purpose. The first thing that hit me when walking in was smoke; luckily there was a window. Ali got a bottle of Cabernet Sauvignon du Medoc, 12%, Le vin de Cépage which we drunk from a tiny glass, one by one quickly, without making anyone wait too long. The leftovers of whisky Smith's were found in the room and swiftly, straight from the bottle, went down Mohamed's throat. The rushing part, I guessed, was down to the two major factors; the first one was to get drunk as soon as possible: "alcohol is for getting drunk," as simple as that, said my friend; the second one was more psychological; because deeply inside they knew that alcohol was prohibited and drinking it was considered shameful, the whole ritual of gulping it had nothing to do with fun, enjoyment or relaxation as such; as it tasted good and was doing something to the head, it had to be consumed quickly to wash away the guilt and the social unacceptance.

It was vividly portrayed in one of Abu Nouass' poems in which he was highlighting the sensual and carnal pleasures of life, asking his host to "serve him wine and call it nectar by name, and not serve it secretly when he can do in public." My friends could only consume this nectar clandestinely turning the pleasure into a sour necessity, "we drink until we get drunk otherwise there is no point of drinking," and, as explained in the following verses of the poem, a pleasure cannot be appreciated in the secret and shame, but must be displayed and proclaimed. The poet's remark on the hypocrisy that surrounds alcohol sounds as real now as it was centuries ago. There has always been a huge gap within Muslim society, between reality and social norms; an example of Morocco by the decree of 1967, where "every farmer has been banned (...) to sell or offer free alcoholic beverages to Muslim Moroccans," was a clear and unequivocal prohibition. But, if one looked a little on the figures, another reality appeared: according to reported by the national press data for the year 2012 alone, "more than 131 million litres of alcohol were sold in Morocco, so 400 million bottles of beer and 38 million of wine. However, if consumption was only reserved for foreign visitors, every tourist, including children, elderly and pregnant women would have drunk, on average, 50 cans of beer and 5 bottles of wine. Imagine, a little hangover from our tourists at the time of return," concluded a journalist.

Another article gave me three different stories with three characters that have illustrated the reports of the Arabs with alcohol before and after the advent of Islam. The first was of a certain Abu Ghabshan, a great dignitary of Khoza'a tribe who had the honourable position to protect and maintain the Kaaba, the Meccan's shrine, the place of pilgrimage revered by the Arabs. During an evening, well-watered, Abou Ghabshan, did the unthinkable: when drunk, he sold the keys of the Kaaba and gave them to a Qossay, the leader of a rival tribe, which henceforth became the protector of the Holy Place. Since this episode, "the Abu Ghabshan contract" means in Arabic a pact or a part that is fooled and loses the bet.

The second story involved a mythical figure adorned with all virtues and considered a hero of Islam: Hamza, the uncle of the Prophet Muhammad. After a very animated night, the drunken Hamza left his house and came across his nephew Ali, son of the Prophet and future caliph. Without reasonable grounds, Hamza insulted Ali and mutilated two of his camels. Alerted by the witnesses, the prophet Muhammad moved quickly to the place of altercation and took his drunken uncle away. According to some historians and compilers of Hadith, this incident was one of the reasons for Islam imposing more restrictions on alcohol.

The third example illustrated Al Walid ibn Yazid, a caliph Umayyad, known for his libertinism and promiscuous manners, but also for his poetic talent. In love with his servant and singer Leila, the caliph who was intoxicated by the voice and beauty of his concubine, but also a good amount of wine, asked her to replace him in a collective prayer of dawn - *al Fajr*. Leila then got the Al Walid's clothes, hiding her face like it was the custom of the princes at the time and ranked just behind the *Immam*, among men who thought it was caliph who came to fulfil his morning prayer.

Although my friend's relationship with alcohol was, with a few exceptions, more moderate than in the above examples, it was still against the law of Islam. And not only did we have wine, but also shisha which was also on the "interdiction list." It was popular in Morocco for people to frequent shisha cafés in order to socialise and to share water pipes with their friends. However, the Moroccan authorities had banned smoking pipe tobacco in cafés as the inhabitants of neighbouring properties had often complained about the odours caused by the shisha smoke. In addition, these shisha cafés were under the pressure to close as the tobacco used in these shisha cafés was laced with other drugs, specifically hashish.

The shisha we had today was pure, not spiked with any other drugs, but did not taste as good as it was on the Sahara Desert when I smoked it; perhaps it lacked the magic; the sky, the stars, the stillness of the scenery, the unspoiled soundless night. Perhaps, I should place the experience in the "unique" box and try not to replicate it as it will never taste the same. Here, it only scratched my throat and made my head spin unpleasantly. Certainly, the magic was not there. I was trying to introduce them to a few films but the linguistic problems with English and some sex episodes evoked nothing but slight embarrassment followed by indifference. Although the experimental "night out" was not something that I would like to repeat on a regular basis, the evening was pleasant; there was joy, conversation, singing and laughter, to a certain extent, it was relaxing. It was about 9.00pm and time for me to walk back home. "Here it is, eat it." I was given a tiny sachet with written: 'alsa-sucre arome vanilla.' "Why do I have to eat it?" "Because it disguises the smell of wine." It was hilarious. I had no more than one decent glass of wine and I had to disguise the smell of pleasure by eating vanilla sugar, a pack of crisps, and chewing gum. Who would have thought that a thirty-six-year-old woman would have to pretend to be sixteen again?

******

I sat down at the café, ordered the usual crème tiré, and waited for Sanae. She turned up on time, sat down and listened. The whole explanation took no longer than five minutes. "Would you be able to help me, please?" "Ok. Text me." She gave me two mobile numbers and said, "Can I go now?" "Do you want to have coffee with me?" "No" "Then go." The peculiar essence of the morning encounter extended over the afternoon, the French class in El Borj. I wondered what was running through the head of that chubby, slow to learn boy who had turned up in the class that day. His French was non-existent, his lack of respect - evident; he was sitting at the far end of the classroom shouting: *"Aji! Aji!"* adding more disorder to the current one. I managed to engage him in writing down the alphabet, every single letter, line by line, repeatedly until he got it right, and every time he finished a letter, he would shout: *"Aji! Aji!"* Although there were some well-behaved children, the agonisingly unsettled ones were failing to obey the rules in which they knew they would make me lose my temper. I got the better of them keeping my cool by taking long deep breaths and mostly concentrating on those who were paying attention to the actual exercises, like the chubby boy who did the alphabet to the letter.

Straight after leaving the school my immediate attention was drawn by a couple sheets of paper abandoned on the pavement, and an elderly man who walked passed, turned around and picked them up. To my disappointment, it was the alphabet, written letter by letter by the chubby boy; it wasn't even crumpled, left there unattached in the lurch, a lurch now reflected by a figure, a figure with a name, perhaps Mohamed or Abraham, old, sixty or seventy maybe, and as indifferent as the boy whose writing had filled the pages. The piece of paper turned into a culprit who kept slapping me in the face over and over again until I got humiliated publicly, in the open air, by that man who had not known what that piece of paper meant to me, what value it carried, what effort was written down on it. The man in the street was equally ignorant; he took it, looked at it and threw it back. It was nothing but rubbish amongst all the scattered junk and debris. I knew he would come up closer to me and would try to talk; what I did not anticipate was the action that followed: he grabbed me by my arm and kept showing me the way. "I'm not going with you," I said. He did not understand so a young man from across the street who was observing us, came to the rescue and took me off the hook. However harmless the old man was and whatever intentions he had, I always had to take note of one thing: be aware of the crazy ones. As soon as I articulated the "crazy" word in my mind, I was approached by another one, a black pregnant woman who did not look right in her head; usually she was sitting outside of one of those scantly-looking shelters, or was lying down on bare soil few meters away from the school. If only I had known what she was mumbling, I could probably have comprehended the creepy look she was giving me. She walked past me muttering and turning her head around. Having come across some individuals that were not to be trusted, I knew I had to be careful. However, there were many people here who would protect me and chase the crazy ones away, so I did not worry or feel threatened by anybody.

Back at home, my family and I had a very relaxing evening. This time the wood-burning stove was working properly emanating nothing but warmth. I was carrying on with teaching French to Achraf, Hamza - son of Fadma, and Moad, and making it more enjoyable by drawing pictures and words on a plastic board, simple exercises but challenging enough for them. Owing to the fact that Moad's biggest hobby was drawing, he particularly enjoyed our exercises. He impressed me with a few of his previous pen drawings which I shared with Papa Mohamed. "Look!" I was placing them in front of him. "He should be going to an art school, he is talented and he loves it." Papa Mohamed scrutinised all of them, and then agreed to pose for Moad for a quick portrait sketch. The drawing exercises found Papa Mohamed interested in sketching on my little board; he drew a long bus, trees, a few tiny people, and a footpath that led to the bus. It was a drawing of a five-year-old, simple, operated by well-known symbols but it was somehow therapeutic and calming not only for him, but also for all of us who were watching him doing it. Mustapha took over and drew faces until Papa Mohamed got hold off it once again and drew a *djaja* in a bag; the bird in the bag amused us all and led to something more ridiculous; Papa and I went into arm wrestling competition. *"Tandi! Tandi!"* the word invented by Papa meant only one thing: get down. I got on my front bracing hard my legs against the wall and defeating Papa. We carried on with those exercises for a while, cheating, trying to tickle one another. It was contagious, everyone got involved, from one armpit to another, from one foot to belly, every single person was looking for the weakest spot on each other's body. Now Hakima and I were working as a team attacking Papa Mohamed and giving him proper body spasms that were producing hysterical laughter. We all were in stitches except for Meryam. It was not the first time when as soon as I initiated some form of exercise, appreciated by everybody, Meryam was out of the room. It was her choice, in the end, how she wanted to spend time, but it did not pull us closer together, it was doing rather the opposite, creating more and more distance that was tricky to diminish.

******

Straight after breakfast Papa Mohamed, Mustapha and I went to the Amelou district to pick up a package that Hannah and Hmad had sent me, and to my surprise we took our *camion*. The translation of a *camion* as a simple van or lorry was not really the right description. The *camion* here did not resemble a van or lorry as such; it was a very hard-working truck with an open trailer prone to punctures, and it was impossible to buy a new tyre; according to Papa Mohamed, one tyre could cost around 2.000DH. Every time it happened, and it happened daily, somehow, without taking it to the garage, they managed to fix it. Owing to the fact that the ignition was broken, to start the engine required nothing more than to connect a couple of wires. In the little cabin that fitted three people, including a driver, one could also find a cassette recorder, so as soon as we sat down the music was on: I was dancing, they were both singing, and all three of us were laughing. The *camion* was a real trooper; when it was going through all the bumpy roads it felt like at any moment it would fall apart, and yet, it was keeping itself together in one piece and giving me a real sense of adventure. I loved that truck!

Mustapha was referring to the well-known and repeated subject: the photo of Dieu: "Margarena, regardez photo de Dieu?" "No." "Il y a beaucoup de photos de Dieu." Then, he took a piece of paper and wrote down a name Kamala. "Who is Kamala?" I asked "Une femme," "Is this your femme?" "Mustapha pas de femme; Maroc is not good, tout le monde regarde. Mustapha drinks whisky." "I know." "But everyone is talking, there is loads of blablabla. One day you come with me to El Borj to my grandfather and we will drink whisky there." "*Wakha*," I said.

He was recalling a story when once upon a time he had tried to escape to Spain: "Espagne est bonne, *mezyana*," he kept repeating. "I went to the harbour and looked for the boat. Police stopped me and asked: "Visa?" "No" "Passport?" "No." They grabbed him, took to the police station, questioned him, and soon after he was at large again. He was laughing out loud when reminiscing the story. "Europa beaucoup d'intelligence. Maroc - no; Margarena - intelligent, restez au Maroc."

At the post office I handed in the post notification but had no documents on me. "Passeport?" "I'm sorry I forgot." "No documents?" "No, I totally forgot." This was the moment that I knew I had to lie. "I can give you my passport number." He looked at me, picked up his pen and started writing the made up on spot combination: AD 5434782. I signed, picked up the package, and went out.

Hannah sent me two pair of Christmassy socks and some sweets; so charming of her. It was a second reminder this week, after my mum's message, that there was only one week left to Christmas. "I don't have energy to do anything because I know you won't be here for Christmas," she wrote. Indeed, it was to be the first time without a Christmas tree, presents, the beetroot soup, carp, cakes, *pierogi*, the midnight mass, family dinners, friends, walks to the forest or Christmas carols. I would miss it all but there was no tragedy. I had to swallow the longing and look forward to the next Christmas.

After coming back from the café, I took a nap fallowed by the usual 4.00/5.00pm tea at home. Because my room had this strong stench of smoke and the sun was shining, I wanted desperately to go out. "I'm going crazy, I have to go out," I said in English. I took "Huit Clos" with me and went out. Reading and listening to the music while walking, was the simplest way to ignore all those "dragueurs." However, when I was crossing the street a fancy 4x4 car was gradually slowing down; the passenger, a young man, stuck his head through the window, then the car pulled out and they both kept observing, and I kept ignoring them. They drove into a side street and parked there. This young man, handsome, and well-dressed approached me. "Do you speak Arabic?" "Not really, French, English, Italian, Polish?" "Aaahh, no, a little bit of French," he responded. He accompanied me to the garden asking the standard questions, whereupon he wanted to get my number. "I'm sorry I don't have one." "I give you mine." "I don't have a pen." "I'll come back with my number. You will be here, right?" "Yes, I'll be here." Five minutes later Yassin reappeared handing in his business card. "Here is my dad's association and my number. I'll wait the invitation," he said. "Do you mean my phone call?" "Yes." "*Inchallah*," I said. "I'm sorry to have bothered you," he added and walked away.

I carried on reading while walking towards a small park just outside the medina. I sat down on a bench and there was someone repeating my name. I looked up and saw the young Ayoub, the one who once wanted to become my brother. "Ayoub? What a surprise, how are you?" "My mum à l'hôpital." "I'm sorry, what happened?" He was pulling his skin. "Has she got a skin problem?" "No" "But, she is seriously ill?" "Yes" "Do you have dad?" He made "dormir" gesture and then kept pointing to the sky. "Is he dead?" "Yes" "I'm really sorry." Ayoub had got two older brothers and they all lived in the mountains. "Can we have tea?" "I don't have money on me." "No, it's me, I invite you, please, please." He was so enthusiastic. We sat down in a café where he seemed to know many people. "Do you like football?" he asked. "I don't, sorry." "My favourite is Ronaldo, he is great!" It was not easy to communicate with Ayoub as his French was difficult to understand. "I take coffee with milk, please." "I take black coffee," he said, "I don't like milk; we have a cow, I have to milk it," he was pulling cows' udders. "Voilà, you could drink it straight from the udder! How many cows do you have?" Un, deux, trois," he counted. "Any sheep?" "No, one mule," he said. "Please visit me, please, please, you and I will milk the cow. My mum will come back from the hospital tomorrow; my dad will be there." "So, is he not dead?" "No, he is sick; my brother speaks very good French, will you come?" "Ok, I will." "When?" "Tomorrow?" "What time?" "At midday?" "Twelve? ... un, deux, trois, quatre, ..." he counted to twelve. "Ok, ... aah, there is a football match tomorrow." "No problem. We can do it next week," I said. "Wait! Wait! No! We'll see each other tomorrow at 12.00pm." "Ok, if you have time." "Great!" He was so excited. "Would you like to eat?" "No, thank you, I'm not hungry." "With Ayoub, one boucheyar, please, please." "*Wakha*; I can have a little piece." "And some tea?" "It's fine, I have some coffee left." He went off to order some tea.

"Can I read French?" "Of course, if you want." There was no full stop or comma; everything was read on the same breath. "*Je ..... Je pense qu'à la longue ..... on doit ...... s'habituer aux meubles.*" "What is it?" "Try to imagine you are in a room with nothing but some furniture ... and you have to stay in this room for a long time ... but this is actually a metaphor." "What's metaphor?" "Nothing serious," "Français de Ayoub bon, no?" "Well, you just have to carry on practising it."

The sheer excitement of our rendez-vous tomorrow was written down on his face, his mouth was repeating the number twelve, whereas his smiling eyes were disbelieving saying: "Did I get the time right?" As he couldn't miss out on the chance of meeting me tomorrow, he left the table and came back with a man who confirmed the time and the place. "Correct; now I better go home," I said. "Do children bother you?" "Everyone bothers me," I laughed looking at him. "I will take you home and if someone tries to touch you I will protect you." His face went very serious and the fists he was showing were ready to punch. Ayoub was maybe 155cm tall; had got very dark hair, dark eyes and equally dark skin, but his external darkness was disappearing under his bright vivid smile and positive attitude.

We left the café. "You don't take your bicycle with you?" "Oh, I forgot." "How long does it take to get to your place?" "Marcher - about one hour, vélo - thirty minutes." He kept repeating the time and the day along with another line. "Don't forget, you are like my frère." "No," I corrected him, "like your sœur."

******

After four days of not having a shower I finally went off to the *hammam* and just to avoid the crowd, I set off straight after 8.00am. As only two women were occupying the first room leaving me alone in the hottest area and with easy access to water, I felt elated and relaxed. The single thing that was making this place crowded was their very strongly reverberated conversation which did not bother me at all. I left feeling rejuvenated and well-rested.

It did not surprise me that Ayoub was waiting with his bicycle just outside La Scierie, looking very sporty in his Ronaldo number 7 shirt, football socks and football boots. I felt a sudden predicament, perhaps his desultory conversation and scattered energy were making me feel like I was being pushed to something that I knew I would not enjoy. His sweetness was bewildering and his energy - wearing. He was bouncing off his little legs phrasing sentences that were implying a deep relationship between us. "Papa dit, Magdalena et Ayoub, je t'aime, mais no papa, amis, amis, mais papa dit: Ayoub, je t'aime Magdalena," he was recalling last night's conversations with his father. "I'm glad you made it clear." "Ayoub, Magdalena ma sœur," he added and carried on with his "je t'aime" phrase. "Ma maman est très heureuse voir Magdalena." "How is your mum and dad?" "*Mezyan, mezyan*," he said. "I want to buy something for them. Can we stop here?" I pointed at a local shop. "No, papa attend, il conduit taxi, Magdalena et Ayoub à la maison." In fact, his father was a taxi driver and was waiting for us in front of the café where we were supposed to meet today. His father did not look ill at all, on the contrary, he looked healthy and very cheerful. My nationality clearly confused Ayoub. "Je t'aime France." "I'm not French." "No? Where do you come from?" "Pologne … where is Pologne, in Europe?" "Yes, in Europe, we are bordered by Germany, Czech Republic, Belarus,…" He seemed a little bit disappointed, so his father joined in the conversation. "Will you stay over?" he asked. "No, no, I have to go back home." "But, one day you will come back and spend a night with us?" he continued. "*Inchallah*," I responded. "Ayoub, has to go to work at 2.00pm for two hours, you will stay with us, won't you?" "Actually, I have to get some work done too." I was happy with the sudden turn of events. "Will you come back tomorrow?" "Tomorrow may be impossible, I have to work."

We stopped by a local, well-stocked shop, picked up some yoghurts, milk and tea. Ayoub was terribly grateful and surprised that I spent 50DH on the shopping. We reached our destination within five minutes. When he was describing the location, I had in mind some distance, walking, hiking, some physical challenge similar to the mountaineering adventure that I had had with my family. Although we were further away from the centre of Khénifra, we still were closer to the city than to the mountains. The area where Ayoub lived was regarded poor and dangerous to walk at night as some nasty acts of aggression had been taking place there. "This is the house of my mum, regard," Ayoub was ecstatic. "Maman, maman, here is Magdalena." Two girls, three or four years old, were greeting us, and his mum with a few women invited us inside a very smoky room where a barbecue was on. When I was about to undo my laces, one of those little girls came up to help me. Scarcely had we undone my laces, when there was time to put my shoes back on. "Do you want to see the mountains? Do you want to see the little baby? Do you want to see my dog?" Ayoub was bombarding me with questions.

He took me to the second floor where the wife of his brother, who a short time ago had had baby, was sitting in a room breastfeeding. According to Ayoub, the baby was three days old, in fact, it was seventeen days old. No sooner had I said hello to the baby than I realised we were on the rooftop. "Here are the mountains," his remark sounded almost like the mountains were invisible all that time and only to Ayoub's command were lifting themselves up showing breath-taking beauty. "Here is my dog - Morri," he was pointing at a tiny dog on the ground. "Do you want to go and see him, or would you prefer to sit in the salon on the first floor?" "I will be happy to see the dog," I said smiling. The dog was rather timid and the way he was approaching us, hesitantly with his tail tucked in, insinuated distrust and fear towards the humans. Generally, dogs were not considered pets and furthermore they were not allowed inside the house as the old paraphrased proverb says: "When dogs are at home, the angels won't come in."

Everything he told me yesterday sounded like a misunderstanding: his mum looked rather well, his dad wasn't dead nor was he ill, he wasn't the youngest of his two brothers but the middle one; he wasn't living in the mountains and the destination wasn't as far away as he was describing it. The whole story was a little fishy to me and his brotherly intentions were clearer than ever. We went back home and sat down in the living room with a television that was turned on almost immediately. While he was setting the French channel, he put all his videos and CDs in front of me. "I love this man. Do you know him?" I had no idea who the man was, and honestly, I wasn't even interested in following it up. "I can give you those videos." "No, thank you, you keep them, I look him up on the internet," I added politely.

His mum brought some barbecued meat, a plate of very watery tagine, some Moroccan sweets and cake. It was extremely kind of her and a little bit too extravagant as neither she nor her children were sitting with us at the table. *"Koul! Koul!* Do you want some Fanta?" Ayoub was pouring himself a glass and at the same time placing a piece of meat and a cake in front of me. Hardly had I sat down at the table, hardly had I put anything into my mouth when it was time to leave. "Do you want to go now and see the cows?"

All that rush was strangely irritating but I was making all the effort to engage myself fully into that visit which soon turned into a show with a red carpet that was leading me to people's houses, cows' sheds and fields with working mules. Ayoub and his aunt led me inside the barn where the cows that were supposed to be milked were standing and being fully co-operative when the photo session with Ayoub and his aunt took place there. Then we carried on strolling through the village until we reached a field where one of his friends was ploughing the soil using his two mules. "It's a hard work, isn't it?" "No. I like it," he spoke a little English. "I like English; I go to school every night to practise it. My brother is in the United States, in New Hampshire, I want to go there one day," he said. "Good luck. I hope your dreams will come true one day."

On the way back to the village we walked across some muddy fields. He was pointing at every single moving object, couple of dogs, birds, cows, mules, cats, and then the mountains, trees, fields, each time shouting: *"Chouf! Chouf!"* I was not sure what was in the head of that boy, but presenting me to every single animal or a puddle, a mountain or a field, the sun or rain, felt like I was born on a different planet, where the animals, fields, the sun or rain did not exist. As much as I tried enjoying it, I had the impression that I got lumbered with his boring company of my own free will. I was sure he was a good-hearted boy, but I had my niggling suspicion as to why he was doing it. In the nick of the time, his father and his taxi appeared on the horizon. I thanked the family for the hospitality and quickly took a place in a car, at the back seat with Ayoub. "Ça fait?" Ayoub sounded clearly disappointed. "I don't have a phone number," I said. "What about Facebook?" "You can give me yours, if you want." As much as I tried to remember the "Facebook" name he was reciting while arguing with his father, the minute they dropped me off at La Scierie, the name was gone forever. I got off the taxi with breathless relief. This experimental outing had no particular sense to me, and sadly, the company of my young friend, who called himself my brother, was neither amusing nor stimulating and would have been false to continue.

Reading, napping, writing and fighting off the flu with another aspirin, rutinoscorbin and sachet of Lemsip Max Cold and Flu was on the afternoon's agenda but to my horror, a cloud of smoke was yet again coming in slowly invading the room and disturbing my afternoon plans. "This had been going on far too long," I was thinking out loud when shooting off downstairs. The smoke that took over the whole place was certainly responsible. Everyone, without exception, was squinting, rubbing their eyes and coughing. "You have to stop this, I repeat, this is not healthy!" "It will be cold," said Papa Mohamed. "I prefer to sit in a cold room with oxygen than without oxygen in a hot room. We will have to put more layers on and we will survive." Papa Mohamed looked unhappy with my idea, but when Hakima started creating more smoke by pumping in more air through the *rabouz*, he finally reacted. "Hakima, what are you doing? Look at the ceiling!" I could hardly breathe. I went out to get some fresh air but as soon as I walked inside I was suffocating in that heavy cloud.

Soon after dinner I left the room as not only the smoke but also Moad's stinking feet were bothering me. "Magdalena, are you ok?" asked Lahcen. "Are you malade?" "No, I'm not malade, but I cannot breathe and I have a headache." "There is plenty of oxygen," he said. "Really? Maybe for you but not enough for me." "Reste! Reste!" shouted Lahcen. "Sorry I need some fresh air." I left the room and hid in mine, put the scarf over my face, and used the air freshener hoping it would help, but it didn't, it was only making me feel sick. Lahcen was knocking at my door. "Are you ok?" "I'm ok but I can't breathe." "Why not? There is no smoke," he was looking around my room. "Are you an idiot? The whole house is full of smoke. Can't you smell it?" "Un peu," he said. He walked out and called me again. "Magdalena, here is the problem." Looking at the pipes and all those chinks through which smoke was leaking, he thought he recognised the problem. "I'm going to fix it." "Good luck, Lahcen."

******

I woke up with a splitting headache and painfully swollen eyes. While walking downstairs, I could smell *boucheyar*. Everybody looked tired, most of all Papa Mohamed who was lying down with a scarf around his head. "Très mal, très mal, fumée, pas bonne," he said it and I felt relieved, not because he suffered a headache but because he might have realised the long-term consequences of living with smoke. The atmosphere at the breakfast table was as heavy and suffocating as the day before's smoke so I quickly finished it off, and ran off to the café for my first Arabic lesson with Mohamed. It wasn't easy as the pronunciation of different k and h was really challenging. Here are some notes that I made in my notebook that day: H like Hannah, almost normal sound, e.g. *Smhli* (sorry); *Hayat* (life and name); KH – dirty H pronounced without moving the tongue, e.g. *Khalid* (name); *khatar* (dangerous), *khlini tranquille* (leave me alone); and Ĥ – deep sound that needs to be spat out, e.g. *maĥmtch* (I don't understand).

Here are some phrases that I learned: *Ma fyach jouâ* (I'm not hungry); *Wa déjà klit* (I have already eaten); *Jmâo rouskoum!* (Be quiet! impolite); *Skt! Skto!* (Be quiet!); *Smhli, maĥmtch ach tatgoul* (I'm sorry, I don't understand what you are saying); *Ach briti?* (What do you want?); *Ach mn saâa?* (At what time?); *Mâayach?* (When?); *Tan na koul* (I'm eating).

All the sentences that I was eager to learn reflected my daily struggles: how to get rid of dragueurs, what to tell children if they misbehaved, or how to respond to being constant asked to 'eat more.'

In fact, if one leafed through all my notebooks with words that I was intensively studying for the past fifteen years, disregarding language itself, one could easily draw a psychological portrait of me based on type of words that I was brushing up. All those linguistic diaries, as I call them, have been packed with verbs, nouns, adverbs, adjectives, phrasal verbs, idioms that were recalling page by page the important events in my life, situations in which I was feeling vulnerable (pose a threat, opt out, be in a quandary, conniving, mendacious, smite, recrimination); the deep sadness of losing friends (mourn, mournful, emphysema, pancreas, indelible, hereditary); my weakness (succumb, implicate myself in something), or simple happiness expresses (sublime, rapture, over the moon, life-enhancing). There were numerous quotations, references to books and names: Kant, Woody Allan, James Dean, Audrey Hepburn, Nijinsky or Nietzsche; I used to translate everything, word for word. Through my own persistent studying, I was able to observe my own mental and emotional development, the inevitable change and the impact that the foreign language had on me. I believed, and still believe in Sapir-Whorf's hypothesis that the language that we speak has an important effect on the way we think. For example, the common words like "thank you" or "sorry" which I had struggled to say in my native language, have been embedded in my head in English through the most precious of all dictionaries, the living and walking one, my ex-partner. "Why don't you say thank you or sorry?" he asked me once. "I do, but not as often as you," I responded. The implication of his remark was vital to me; I sounded arrogant to him, and perhaps I was. Moreover, I might have abused the language by not speaking it properly, meaning being insensitive to the linguistic norms that have required certain attitude, elegance or politeness. It's a real challenge for a foreigner to sound honest or apologetic, in spite of all the honesty and apology carried, if the linguistic rules of the spoken language are not fully understood. What did annoy me so much was when Moroccans abused the French language by repeating continually the phrase: "Do you understand?" In every day polite conversation an average speaking French Moroccan, unintentionally, sounded arrogant, e.g. "I don't have a job, do you understand? Or this cost 12DH, do you understand? Or I can't see you today but I'll see you tomorrow, do you understand?" At first, I wasn't sure what they meant by it; did they question my ability to understand French as such, or my ability to understand their French? I soon discovered it was neither of those two; it was a simple comma which they took it from their native language, *"fhmtchi?"* also overused, not having a slightest idea of the effect that it had on a listener. On the contrary, "I'm sorry" was very much underused or non-existent, and "thank you" much more popular but wasn't required, and I could easily recall situations where I was asked why I used *"chokrane"* so often.

Going back to my Arabic lesson, the two hours were sufficient. "Here you are, you have been working hard," I gave him some money. He refused. He didn't want it. "Don't be silly, you need the money and you are a brilliant teacher." He eventually took it, but his first refusal astonished me a great deal. As much as I wanted to get a grasp of Arabic, I most of all wanted to help him, support his rather difficult financial situation, and besides, I would never abuse friendship that way. I knew he had nothing but a great deal of honesty and pride.

As Hakima was waiting for me at home with couscous I had to rush back. After lunch Papa Mohamed, Mustapha, and I went off to the medina for coffee. We took the *camion* and parked just outside the centre. Mustapha was yet again referring to the photo of Dieu and the European system which has allowed people to be more free in other words, he, most of the time, felt watched and judged by everyone here. The café that offered internet access also gave me the opportunity to share my European experience with Mustapha by showing some of my photos. He very much wanted to see my family and friends, different cities, climates, my life in Europe in general. I remember vividly the café, the exact seat we took, the package of cigarettes that he went to get, the one coffee too many that he ordered that evening which made Papa Mohamed cross with him, and the sandwiches - sausages with spicy tomato sauce in pitta bread that we had in the medina when we had left the café.

Back at home we were yet again stunned. The smoke! It permeated the house. "Impossible!" I commented. Hakima and Meryam were trying to fix it; they disassembled the whole chimney, cleaned all the pipes but still something wasn't working. The *forno* was taken outside, then back inside again, then it still wasn't functioning, so the whole action of taking it out and then inside was repeated. And this is when the miracle happened. I could not believe it when I saw joyfully dancing flames and no smoke coming inside the hose. It was worthy of celebration with *louiza* and some popcorn.

******

Notes:

1 (p. 65) Amen, in Amazigh, water.

2 (p. 66) Idren, in Amazigh, acorns.

3 (p. 71) Ciao bella, ci vediamo dopo – Hello, pretty, we will see each other later.

4 (p. 72) Bslama, in Darija, goodbye.

5 (p. 73) Loutar is a name that derives from classical Arabic "Al-Watar" and in Darija means "rope". It is an instrument from the lute family; the body is made of a piece of cedar wood, hollow, pear-shaped or rounded, covered with a skin felted sheep and mounted with two or three strings. It has nylon strings and is mainly used in the Amazigh music of the Middle Atlas. The instrument was improved by Mohamed Rouicha, by adding a fourth string.

6 (p. 73) Mohamed Rouicha (1 January 1950 - 17 January 17, 2012 in Khénifra) was a Moroccan Berber singer, a specialist in playing loutar. In 1964, only fourteen years old Rouicha produced his first album in collaboration with the Moroccan channel RTV. His lyrics evoke a purely traditional folk style, love, nature, justice (whether in the secular world or religious), politics, life and death.

7 (p. 74) "Huis Clos suivi Les Mouches," Jean-Paul Sartre, 1979, p.37.

8 (p. 74) Ibid., p.71.

9 (p. 75) Zwina, in Darija, beautiful.

10 (p. 77) Morocco is beautiful but there is no work.

11 (p. 78) Lasciate ogne speranca, voi ch'intrate," "Abandon all hope ye who enter here," Inferno, John Ciardi, (1954).

12 (p. 78) This is a piece of my little poem on hammam.

13 (p. 78) Inferno, Canto VII, lines 25–30, Mandelbaum translation.

14 (p. 79) Casanegra, Moroccan film by NourEddine Lakhmari that came out in 2008 and was officially chosen to represent Morocco for the Oscar in category of Best Foreign films.

15 (p. 80) Quran (2:187).

16 (p. 80) "Sex Ethics, Islamic awareness."

17 (p. 80) Ibid.

18 (p. 81) Sex and Islam. Sexual Ethics.

19 (p. 82) Ibid.

20 (p. 82) Quran (18:470).

21 (p. 85) Zamane, L'Historie du Maroc, "Hypocrisie Quand Tu Nous tiens!" December, 2013, N.37. p.42.

22 (p. 85) Ibid. p.43.

23 (p. 88) Djaja, in Darija, bag.

24 (p. 90) "Huis Clos suivi Les Mouches," Jean-Paul Sartre, 1979, p. 13.

25 (p. 94) Rabouz, Moroccan artisanal air blower, very useful to fan the fire or simply for decoration.

End of Part Three

In Medina with Fadma, Fadma and Meryma.

Part Four

"You should go to London to study English," I said to Mohamed. "How?" "I shall help you to find a school. I'm sure we could find something affordable and of a good quality." When I was leafing through some online offers on English language courses, I could not believe the prices. "What!" I was stunned. I understood they must have gone up since I was studying there thirteen years ago but not by 500%! Instead of £800 per whole academic year they were now asking for up to £4000. The most affordable were fifteen hour courses per week for over £2000 for the whole academic year. I understand profit and competition but this surpasses any form of social organization. This is a rip off, a clear abuse of power that puts the poor-clever into a real predicament, a real quandary of how to afford it, where to get the money from? If only it was part of the higher education system, if only it could give a proper degree, maybe then borrowing the money or putting yourself in debt would be worth the pain, as French say. However, I am inclined to share Noam Chomsky's opinion on the whole scam of a loan. He basically sees a trap in all of that, the disciplinary technique that controls people.

"People have to be passive and apathetic and obedient. This is coming from liberals incidentally, not from the right wing. And part of this, right about that time (he is referring to the 1960s in the United States) student debt started going up. Whatever the purpose is, it is a way of trapping people. Once you have a big debt, you can't do things you might have wanted to do. Like, you might have wanted to graduate from law school and do public interest law, but if you have a $100,000 debt to pay off, you're going to have to go into a corporate law firm. Once you get into it, you're trapped by the culture and forget about public interest law. (…)The whole reward system is set up so as to make the system worse and worse."

Calculating and adding up all the hidden costs in all aspects of living and studying in London, we ended up with one plain, genuine question. "What about going to the medina?" It was a great idea as the centre had never been emptier. A one single reason that kept men far away from the medina and its souks was a football match. Today, ninety-eight per cent of men were occupying cafés and their own TV screens. Notwithstanding the fact that the match was due to start at 9.00pm, the cafés were already packed out with football fans that soon were hoping to be sharing in a victory by their wholeheartedly supported and loved team – Raja Casablanca. They were hoping to beat the Germans, FC Bayern Munich, and a defeat wasn't even considered. Therefore, the shops were closing earlier, the mobile companies were sending presents to their clients – fifty extra free messages, and even those who weren't keen on football, few and far between, were to support this memorable event. Just as Mohamed who belonged to the minority was thinking about joining the majority in a café. First however, he agreed to help me run some errands. Having seen

Mina struggling with her "on its last leg" mobile, I was keen on buying her a new one for Christmas. Remarkably, we found a shop that was still open and a mobile phone that met our expectations: simple, durable, with an option of using either one or two sim-cards. That simple Nokia phone cost 230DH after my negotiation which saved me 20DH for three greeting cards, two coffees, a pot of tea, some cake and some sunflower seeds. To find a seat in any café around 6.00pm was a hopeless task. Therefore, Mohamed suggested going to his uncle Aziz adding: "He is the intellectual one in our family, you will like him."

Uncle Aziz was a teacher in primary school and also a sociology student. He seemed to be fulfilled not only professionally, but also on a personal level. He loved his job and had a great deal of time to devote to his wife and two little boys. As soon as we sat down, the topic of teaching came up. I was explaining the predicament with my disobedient children pointing out the evident lack of respect for foreign teachers. "From the onset, I was the subordinate because they knew that punishment would not come." Uncle Aziz was trying to make me understand the simplicity of the Moroccan system. "We apply the traditional method. They have to fear us; they have to know who the boss is. If they keep misbehaving we are allowed to spank them. Unfortunately, this is the only method that they know of from their upbringing and they don't respond to anything else, and this attitude demonstrates itself at schools. We have to be strict with them as their parents expect us to be that way. I give you an example; one day a father of a boy who I teach, came up to me and asked if I hit him. No, I don't. Why not? He was bewildered as if I was doing something wrong."

If I had to describe uncle Aziz I would use a sentence that one of my disabled patients, Allan, used to repeat: "You are soft and warm and cuddly like a teddy bear." And uncle Aziz was like a teddy bear, a wonderfully warm person who wouldn't hurt a fly, so the question was how he could apply the traditional method of teaching if it didn't go along with his persona? This rather controversial, in my opinion, subject of implementing the traditional method of teaching has been studied, analysed and compared with the non-traditional methods by Stanford University, and the outcome was presented at "The worldwide Education Revolution 2012" conference. The findings were no real surprise: "Drawing on a conceptual framework developed from social constructivism and a review of previous literature and exploring the relationship between teaching methods and student achievements in Morocco, the non-traditional methods are more effective than traditional methods in increasing students' test scores."

We carried on talking until his wife came back home and made some tagine for us. Then the TV was turned on and I had no choice but to watch the football match. "Are you a football fan?" I asked uncle Aziz. "Not at all. I just watch it for social reasons. I know that tomorrow everybody will be talking about it, and I will have to participate in the conversation." Perhaps, there was not much of a conversation given the sad defeat by two goals to nil to the Germans.

We left his place late. Although my family had been informed, I was a little bit anxious, so the long forty minutes' walk got shortened to twenty minutes' run. The area where uncle Aziz lived was rather dodgy and "no one should walk it alone," I was told; the strange vibes were felt when we walked past some groups of men that were giving me a real fright. We got home safely though, and if there was any anxiety that my family felt, and I had anticipated, it was scrupulously hidden and nothing but a cheerful smile welcomed me home.

******

Today, together with Sanae and Mohamed, I went to El Borj to talk to Malika and her family; Mohamed, the vice-president, had agreed to take us there. Unfortunately, they didn't live in the village as such, and although the distance wasn't too far-off when looking from the main street, it still took us a good thirty minutes to reach the place in the mountains. It was a hot day so when we got to the top we were punting, puffing, sweating and trying to catch our breaths. The family house and their land were fenced with some spiky bushes and guarded by two or three malnourished barking dogs. The truly appalling condition of the house reflected the desperate poverty that was widespread across this area. We were greeted by Malika's mum and her younger sister, as Malika herself was keeping an eye on a grazing herd of sheep, somewhere in the mountains. "Go and get her," shouted Mohamed who was still out of breath. Having said that, his physical condition was not bad at all taking into account the amount of cigarettes that he had smoked for over twenty-five years. We waited for about fifteen minutes but there was no sign of Malika, and no matter how furious Mohamed felt, we had no choice but to descend. I was kept in the dark because apparently her case was well-known to everybody and everybody knew who the father of little Meryam was. "How come you never said anything? Is this the same man who got her pregnant again?" He claimed he did not know.

Five of us wanted to catch a taxi to Khénifra and Mohamed, for some reason, insisted that we all get into the same one. It took us thirty minutes at least to stop a taxi which already had two passengers inside. Sanae and I took the front seat and five grown-up men sat at back packed like sardines. When the taxi was approaching Khénifra and the well-known police spot control, Mohamed jumped out of the taxi, walked past the police check point and got back inside at the petrol station, where the taxi was waiting for him.

I invited Sanae and Mohamed for lunch "A chez Youssef," it was very much like an English fish and chips shop but instead of fish it served greasy sausages and barbecued pieces of chicken. When I mentioned Christmas tomorrow, Sanae took pity on me and invited me over to hers for lunch, which I accepted. After lunch, we bid her farewell and did our usual: a chat with some music over coffee, in our favourite café in the medina. How very much I loved those moments! Our little ponderings, philosophical reflections, the meaningful chats that always led to a decent exchange of literature and music were unforgettable. Sometime I got scared of how much I enjoyed it and how much more I still wanted. Something wasn't right. "I shouldn't have so much in common with a man who has represented different set of values shaped strongly by a culture and religion that I had little in common with. It should divide us rather than bring us together? Is this some kind of test?" I was asking myself. The "future" word was called into our conversation again, making me feel wistful and melancholic; I have been moving from country to country, building solid friendships and leading a decent life, but at the same time I have had this terrible urge to move, to experience more, to devour more of the world that was still a mystery to me. "You must have gipsy's blood running through your veins," I was told on a few occasions. Whatever was responsible for my unsettled soul, I knew I had to stop running one day. "Stay here," said Mohamed. "Perhaps you'll come to Europe with me?" I suggested. I would very much like to share my little nest of comfort with him, to give him freedom of choice, a better standard of life, something that could bring his struggle to a grinding halt and give him more opportunities. We talked about that too and he expressed his willingness; we needed to draw up a plan, a good-working, practical plan. However, the future planning was put aside as there was a present moment to be cherished and Majida El Roumi with her "Chicagoesque" song "Eaatazalt El Gharam" was embellishing it.

******

It all started on Christmas Eve. I woke up late, looked at my mobile phone that displayed "Christmas Eve all day today" message, got sentimental and had a real pang on missing home and my family. "Stay positive," I said to myself while rushing to meet Sanae in fifteen minutes. I explained to my family what the rush was about and left. It took us about forty minutes to get to her place and plenty of time to cover briefly several topics, the choice of wearing a veil or getting employed, the ridiculous harassment by men in public life on the streets and choice of accepting the right marriage offer. "There is a man who proposed to me. He now lives in France," said Sanae. "That's great! Is he nice, handsome?" "He is and he doesn't smoke." "Did you accept it?" "My mum didn't, she said it was too far away." "What is too far away?" "France." "Do you want me to talk to your mum?" I joked but at same time I was rather serious. My straightforward way of thinking was leading me to envisage a better, more secure life not only for her, but also for her own family. "No, I first have to finish my studies and find a job." She didn't like the idea of leaving her beloved mum and going abroad. Out of her own choice, she wouldn't go to Europe to live there, it would have to be temporary, meaning holidays only. Her way of perceiving the world was confirming a certain discrepancy in thinking between young men and young women. Perhaps it was still down to the very clear higher status of men above women. That is to say that, men bring home the bacon and women remain in private domestic places and are looked after. Perhaps, her religious beliefs and fatalism drove her to thinking of remaining here, or perhaps she was one of those single-minded individuals who would strive to change the corruptive, weak and inept system of justice. I didn't see any other sensible explanation as to why one would choose to carry on suffering if change was possible.

When we finally got to her place I was introduced to her family, mum, sisters and her cousin - a thirty-year-old woman with five children. I was seated in a room that had a computer and the internet access. Her mum kept bringing in food: olives, bread, tagine, sweets and tea, and almost the whole time Sanae was showing me her photographs; one particular photo stuck in my head. It was a photo of her on a beach in a loose, summery dress with her hair down. "Where was that and when?" "That is a photo-shopped image," she said. "Would you like to go to the beach one day and look like on this photo?" "Not really," she sounded unconvincing. What would be the whole point of saving and showing me her photo-shopped image if deep down inside she was not dreaming of going to the seaside, wearing a summary dress and having her hair down? I wanted to say that there was nothing wrong with desiring such a thing but I knew that my argument would be pointless, and I would never force my way of thinking on anyone. In general, I was sure that whatever she was going to do with her life it would always reflect her religious and moral standards. Sadly, we had no chance to develop friendship; the official reason was that the young women in general, had portrayed a very different set of values to mine and I had been struggling to embrace the mentality of the conservative and strictly religious people. The unofficial, I keep to myself. To everybody's horror, this young woman will soon be stricken by immense grief, a sudden and shocking loss of her father, the accident that left everyone paralysed. I bow my head in front of everyone from that family.

I returned home for five minutes just to explain to Meryam the fact that I was to spend the whole day with Ali and Mohamed. I started off by sending online Christmas greetings; then the news from home made me cry; my grandma wasn't well: "I hope I'll see you before I die. I'm only waiting for you," she told me on the phone. My brother's wife was due to give birth and I was longing to be with all of them. Oh, how lost I felt that day! Then, Ali came to the café and we exchanged presents, some chocolates and a bracelet with an adorable greeting card for some money, I thought he would need them more than chocolates. I couldn't wait to see Mohamed because we had all planned to go to his place and cook tagine together. And so we did. While he was giving private tuition to some children in his room downstairs, I was preparing chips, while Ali and Hayat were preparing the tagine. Blissful time! How I needed such an evening! If only my family had understood that feeling, the following events wouldn't have taken place. It was about 8.00pm when Ali received a first phone call from his mum saying that Maryam had come over to Mina's asking where I was. This phone call poisoned our meal leaving us not only baffled, but also obliged to walk back to La Scierie. As Mina understood the importance of Christmas Eve, she had baked a cake for me which we all were to have it. It was 9.30pm when furious Maryam walked into Mina's house and without saying a word pointed at the clock. "What time is it?" she shouted. The whole unexpected and unnecessary drama made me furious. Although I tried to explain the meaning of Christmas and the significance of this evening's gathering with my friends, I felt like I was hitting my head against a brick wall. Nothing of what I said was understood because her own righteousness wasn't absorbing any logical and sensible points that I was making. She knew that I did not deserve to be treated in this way as I had done nothing to merit such harshness and criticism. It was unacceptable. When she left, tears came running down my face. Mina cuddled me and assured that everything would be fine. I felt weak and didn't want to carry on fighting because I had no idea what I was fighting against? Was it just Meryam or the whole society? I couldn't possibly sacrifice more than I already had. They wanted me to be completely obedient, to be who they were, forgetting that I was representing a completely different set of values, almost the opposite to those that they represented. Feeling powerless, exhausted, and lost, I still had to defend myself.

When I entered the house everybody but Abdellah was sitting around the *forno*. "Why are you so angry with me all the time?" I asked Meryam. "Pas de toujours," she responded. "What is wrong with you? Why are you so against me and my friends? What do you want me to do?" She had nothing against my friends but ordained a curfew. "You have to be back at home by 6.00pm." *"La! La! La!"* I raised my voice. "I'm safe because my friends taking care of me." "People are looking at you," she said. "What people? I have to stay at home because people are looking at me?" Papa Mohamed and Abdellah who joined the conversation were trying to explain the same thing in more intimidating manner: "Someone was killed couple of days ago and his head was found today." They believed it may happen to me. "If something were to happen to me it could happen any time. I feel more vulnerable during the daytime than after the dusk because none of my friends is there to protect me. I will not stay at home because someone was killed. Do you know the crime rate in England? Almost every day someone is killed, or there are numerous of accidents, every day something happens but it doesn't stop people from living." I strongly expressed what I felt and showed my gratitude for such overbearing care, but I could not allow them to make my life miserable by putting the curfew on my life. This predominant feeling of solitude that evening made me burst into tears again. Meryam came up to me, hugged me, and apologised. So did Papa Mohamed who insisted that I stayed with them by the *forno*. I did and stubbornly kept announcing the most essential message that evening which sadly was escaping their attention: "It's Christmas Eve today!"

The following day went along without any problems until the evening when Mustapha came to say hello to me, mentioned whisky while mumbling something incomprehensible and left. I was lying in my bed completely exhausted as yesterday's events had made me sleepless, when all of a sudden, arguing voices were heard downstairs; it was Mustapha contra papa Mohamed and the rest. When the argument stopped and the door got slammed I was called to come downstairs for dinner and soon after went straight back to my room to carry on working on Malika's case. There was a rumour heard again, with some lusty exclamations, clear panic and a thundering slammed door, a real drama called Mustapha. I did not want to see it or hear it; I was going through my own hell with my father who was an alcoholic, so if I could stay away from drunken, dangerous lunatics, I chose to do so. A few minutes later the drama finally reached its climax of which I was informed by Lahcen who came to my room reporting on Mustapha's heavy fighting, his cut-opened forehead and the pool of blood downstairs. Apparently, they took the *camion* and drove him to the hospital.

The following morning I met Mohamed and Ali for coffee. "Did you hear what happened yesterday?" Ali did not want to talk. "You do, don't you? You must tell me," I insisted. "And you must promise not to tell anything to your family," he emphasised. That night, a very drunk Mustapha came to the billiards' room in La Scierie looking for Ali who had been there playing the pool. He came up to him as soon as he saw him and started spitting out some threats and complete nonsense that he should stay away from me, that our friendship should not be continued and by all means never should he touch me adding that he was expressing the feelings of the whole family. He was ready to pick up a fight with him when someone else, equally intoxicated by alcohol, walked into that room. Mustapha took the bottle of whisky and hit that man in his head, and then the attacked man picked up a piece of that broken bottle and stuck it into his forehead. It was lucky for Ali who had left the room in time. Heavily bleeding Mustapha was looking for him running around La Scierie and then breaking into Mina's house, shouting and going nuts. Soon after, he was caught and taken to the hospital. Apparently, the whole family believed that it was Ali who had attacked Mustapha.

I couldn't hide the upset and shock that this story gave me. If my presence stirs such problems perhaps I should not be here? What shall I do now? Shall I have a civilised and honest chat with my family and move out? The whole morning three of us were pondering different possibilities when Ali received a phone call from his mum. She was reporting on a visit that Maryam, Hakima and Mustapha had paid her this afternoon and apologised for what happened yesterday. Because they had expressed a sincere apology, neither Mina nor Ali wanted me to get involved in all of that. "It will be better if you carry on pretending that you know nothing."

I ought to share my concern with Hannah: "You know that I like and respect the family very much, but if this is going to continue I will look for an alternative place to live. I'm safe as much as I can be, my friends protect me and if anybody attacks my friends or threatens them I will not hesitate to report them to the police." Hannah and Hmad were very disturbed by the latest turn of events. I was informed then that some authorities had paid my family a visit asking questions about me, who I was, what I was doing here, and why I was staying with them? Apparently, the foreigners make them nervous as if something happened to them while in Morocco, nothing but the Moroccan image would suffer most. On the other hand, it was a way to keep control of people. In Hannah's words: "If anything happened to you, the people responsible for you, and that would also go for us, would be put in prison, supposedly to answer questions but before even beginning making any enquiries or asking any questions they can be left in prison from six months to over a year. This appears to be part of the reason that the family is over controlling." I was explained and advised to think about looking for an alternative dwelling. "You have another three months to cope and it is not fair on you, your friends or Hmad who is in the middle of it. They cannot treat you like this, even if they are afraid, it is being used to control you," Hannah expressed her sympathy. I was also asked to write and sign an agreement which would state that I would take all responsibility for my own safety here, so no one else would be incriminated if something happened to me.

The whole story brought up to the surface another issue, some men who I had refused to be friends with kept making rather stupid remarks towards Mohamed and the particular individual he was referring to was Simo, the waiter from the "Omega" café.

On the 25th of December I was also emotionally charged by disturbing facts heard during an interview with Malika, the twenty-one-year-old physically abused, vulnerable, mentally retarded woman with one child and another on its way. She agreed to come to the school and answer to some questions. It turned out that the first abuse took place in the mountains and it was eventually reported to the police. The man had denied the paternity and had paid the family 3500DH to keep quiet. The father of the second baby, that was due in May 2014, whose name was brought up during the interview, stirred anger in Mohamed, our vice president who in the middle of the interview was called in to confirm his existence. It was apparently a young man who was living in this village and studying in Khénifra. She knew his name and could point him out on the street. Allegedly, she was forced to have sex with him in front of the school at night. "What were you doing at night time here in the village?" I expressed my bewilderment. "I was visiting someone and got attacked on the way back."

Everybody from the Association knew this man very well and they were defending his innocence, saying that this young man would not be capable of such act. In their opinion, Malika was lying, and in my opinion, it was a mistake to call Mohamed in, not only was she intimidated, but she also changed the story; this time the second attack took place in the mountains. The inconsistency of the story made me believe in three possibilities: first she may be confused, second she may be lying, or last she may be telling the truth, whatever it was, it needed to be followed up. I recorded the whole interview, so that I could pass it over onto an organization that has been helping abused women, and the same day I made a report and searched for an association, but with no luck. Mohamed came to the rescue. It turned out that one of his former professors was volunteering for the Human Rights Organization that had its branch here in Khénifra. We decided to go and find him in his house and seek help immediately. He was more than happy to report the case to all the members of the Association and work with us on this case.

****

This morning I found myself in another hostile situation, silly, mediocre, almost embarrassing to mention which was provoked by a woman in the *hammam*, who disrespected me utterly. She turned the tap with cold water on so the whole basin got overflown and mixed up with the hot water making it lukewarm. The whole joy of spending time in the *hammam* was the heat and hot water that was making the place hot. For some reason, however, I believed she forgot to turn the tap off, so without hesitation, I did it for her. To my surprise, she got up a minute later and turned the tap on again. "Excuse me," I said, "The hot water is becoming cold. If it's still too hot for you can you simply add more cold water to your bucket, please?" She looked perplexed, confused and ready to pick up a verbal fight with me. Trying to be polite, I carried on humiliating myself by demonstrating "the mixing part" in my own bucket. Perhaps she did not understand my polite request? If I were her I would be hugely embarrassed and apologetic, instead she bristled at me and did exactly the opposite by turning the tap on once again. I was at the end of my tether but had no intentions to argue with her, nor fight, nor spend any more time in her company. Having had a quick wash in lukewarm water, I left "the rude one" to herself and her arrogance.

The professor set up a meeting for us with a woman called *Saida*. She was expecting us in the unemployment office where she was working at 11.30am. The short figure, perhaps 150cm tall, gave me the impression of being feisty, determined, and willing, but half way through the explanation of a case instead of searching for a solution she was showing us her credentials. The only solution she could come up with was reporting everything to the police, and if this wasn't of any help, she suggested using media, radio and newspaper to publicise it. "Is this really how it works?" I was asking myself. "The only statement we have is the recording, which you should listen to before making any judgment or sending the police over. We need to establish the truth first as what we have got here cannot be used as evidence. What I'd like you to do first is to take this recording, listen to it and share it with your colleges. In the meantime I'll do the second interview with Malika to confirm her previous statement. What about that?" She agreed and straight away picked up the phone and made a phone call informing someone of our visit, stressing how much she would love to work with us - the British Association. The recording was impossible to copy on to her computer; it had a virus which unfortunately affected my own USB key. We had to burn the recording on CD as neither via email nor in any other way was possible to transfer it. It was 27th of December 2013. "I'd like to invite you to the celebration of the Woman's Day," said Saida. "Do you mean March the 8th? "Yes." *"Inchallah."* "Would you like to come over to mine for couscous?" she continued. We kindly refused. I left her office feeling a little bit confused. As much as I wanted to believe in an easy and straightforward solution to the problem I didn't know what to think about her competence. Perhaps my instinct was wrong and she was the most capable person to lead the investigation taking into account how much she lived and breathed our visit.

We found a perfect substitute for the couscous: greasy, cheap and tasty sausages with chips and salad "A chez Youssef." As much as I loved tagine and couscous, I occasionally needed a change of diet and Youssef was nearly fulfilling my cravings. Then the usual coffee and discussion, this time, about Voltaire's "Candide" took place. We looked at the reasoning behind his "everyone has to look after his own garden," statement. It was crucial to realise that only we could fully be responsible for our lives by "cultivating our own gardens" through making the right decisions, and fate or luck had little to do with it. However, we both agreed that the need to believe in God, the Universe, something greater than us humans was helping in "nurturing one's garden." This conversation led me to ponder the ever-present *"fatalism"* in this country. *"Inchallah"* – "if God wills," was not a simple saying but it carried a strong message which was even subjected to a discussion at the Hoover Institution by someone interrupting a lecture about the war in Iraq. He has raised his hand and asked:

"What are we going to do about the fatalism in the Middle East? A while ago I was in Jordan, and I took a ride with this taxi cab. The driver drove the car at breakneck speed. I told him to slow down, but instead of doing it, he just said *'Inchallah'* - if God wills it, we will still be alive tomorrow.' So I want to know: what is to be done about all this fatalism?"

The Edward Said's book "Orientalism" had corrected the notion of the childlike Arab who sat under a palm tree, fanned himself, and waited for God do to his job. However, from the Islamic view, the events of the world take place within Allah's knowledge and will. Because the when, where, and how of those events were fixed by Allah's plan, e.g.:

"No misfortune can happen on earth or in your souls but is recorded in a decree before We (Allah). That is truly easy for Allah. In order that you may neither despair over matters that pass you by nor exult over favours bestowed upon you. For Allah loves not any vain glorious boaster."

The doctrine that all events are predetermined by fate and are therefore unalterable, or no matter what we do it is bound to happen, is strongly presented amongst Muslims. Having said that, the Islamic concept of *"qadaa"* and *"qadar"* to which the fatalism is usually referred to, differs from this doctrine. In Arabic, the words *"qadaa"* and *"qadar"* are often used for predetermination and destiny. The word "qada" (as from *"qadaa")* as a verb means to decide, to settle, or to judge. The word *"qadi"* as a noun is a judge who decides a matter between disputants. The word *"qadar"* as a verb means to measure, to assess, and to determine. This word has been used in the Quran frequently and was proving that any human's activities were separated from activities of God. e.g. "Whatever misfortune happens to you is because on the things your hands have wrought, and for many (of them) He grants forgiveness." So in Islam, there is no contradiction between belief in divine preordainment on the one hand, and the freedom of humans on the other, because Allah's will and plan are universal in scope, within which there is provision for a free and active role for humans, enabling them to consciously fashion their own destiny: "We have shown the path to humans, and they are free to choose the right path and be thankful or to choose the path of ingratitude."

To Muslims, salvation and damnation arise from the deeds and motives of people, not from matters that lie beyond their will or from natural phenomena. Neither environmental and hereditary factors nor the natural capacities present in people have any effect on people's salvation or damnation. The critics of Islam imagine that the Islamic belief in *"qadaa"* and *"qadar"* causes stagnation and inactivity in society. They may point to the social decline and backwardness in some Muslim countries as evidence. Nothing could be farther from the truth. First, social decline and backwardness are present in several non-Muslim societies too. Second, their causes, if analysed, can be seen to have nothing to do with the Muslims religious beliefs. And above all, the Islamic belief in *"qadar"* does not prevent people from striving to reach their goals in life. "Anyone who studies Islam can clearly see that there is nothing in Islam that encourages passivity and inaction," commented prof. Shahul Hameed.

Going back to our conversation, I also shared my opinion on the hypocrisy that I have observed in the Catholic Church, and how much it has bothered me. However, no matter what religion or beliefs we both have represented, we agreed on one important thing: love. We both talked about love as a superior and uncompromising feeling that has ruled and nothing could ever replace that. In this part of the world, however, it was rather difficult to observe "love" between people. Simple gestures like holding hands or embracing each other; natural and completely inoffensive ways to be together in public could not be seen. God forbids kissing publicly! In November 2013 three teenagers were arrested for posting a kissing picture of themselves on Facebook. Because of the lack of naturally developed connections between men and women, they gave me the harsh impression of being totally indifferent towards each other, and the most obvious connecting link between them seemed to be children. My spontaneous nature was to hug my friends or walk with them holding onto their arms, and on a few occasions I forget myself and was reprimanded by Ali. While walking home with him, and being freezing cold, I grabbed onto his arm. "You can't do that. People will see us and they'll talk." It wasn't him who didn't like it, the people, the society, the system that have controlled everybody giving only a permission to engaged or married couples to show such affection publicly. Do people notice or feel lack of love? Where is the closeness between men and women? Everything had this slight tinge of business and marriage was one of them.

Mohamed shared with me the rather sad story of his parents; his mum now forty-four years old, was born and raised in the mountains, she had not had the opportunity to go to school, make friends, and desperately wanted to get out of the mountains, moving to the city or even a village. When she was sixteen years old, she accepted a marriage proposal from his father as an obvious way of escaping home; just acceptance, no love. Until the present moment there was not much love seen between his parents, and what was worse, Mohamed suspected that his mum hated his father and his rather mucky hobby which was repairing his old car. The question is, in what lies the core of a problem here? Why have there been so many married couples like Mohamed's parents and so many divorced? Perhaps lack of love and controlling system that has ruled out the jolly important "getting to know each other" stage?

Tonight was the first time since the incident that I saw Mustapha. He was sitting behind the *forno* trying, at first, to hide his abused, worn out, heavily bruised face with his conspicuous black-eye. The heavy fighting of that night was seen through the stitches, a couple around the forehead and the biggest one running from the top of his nose down to the eye area. For the first five minutes he looked a little bit embarrassed avoiding my eyesight and sitting in the corner of the room. I wasn't encouraging him to any discussion so as not to provoke unnecessary argument. They all were convinced that I knew nothing of what took place that night. However, his embarrassment quickly disappeared and a conversation of what had developed that night was initiated by Mustapha himself. Everything was recalled in jest. "I was attacked by the Arab. He just went for me." As he never mentioned Ali or Mina in his story, his reckless act of aggression did not evoke my sympathy.

******

Each day brought a new story and with the new story came a sudden and unexpected turn of events, like today.

After breakfast I turned up at Ali's as planned for a second breakfast. However, he was still in bed and Mohamed didn't turn up either. Mina served me a small piece of pizza and some tea which I shared with his dad. Mohamed, Mina's husband, was much older than Mina. He had been divorced twice before making the third commitment to Mina. His first marriage happened at a very early age and did not last long owing to the very sad fact that his wife was unable to conceive, but she made him a decent proposal in the form of a second woman in the house who could give him a child. Her wise remark was accepted and a second wife soon appeared in the house. However, his first wife was far too jealous and her hysteria was producing constant arguments and disharmony in the family. One day Mohamed woke up and found no wives at home and no breakfast. The lack of breakfast on the table was the final straw.... he decided to divorce them both. When Mina married Mohamed she was only fourteen years old and they have been happily married ever since for about forty years.

When I sat in the café I found Hanna's letter in my mail box. She was telling me not to take the blame for what had happened over the Christmas period explaining the combination of circumstances including the controlling and fearful Moroccan authorities that have been making its citizens live in fear and the family who were dysfunctional and did not have a clue how to handle things. Although Hmad was born and raised in Khénifra, and although Hannah has been coming to Morocco for the past seventeen years, they both couldn't have predicted such a turn of events. "We thought staying with the family would be the best place for you. We are so sorry it has turned out the way it has. I wish I was closer that I might support you more. You have given so much for us and the charity and the last thing we wanted was for all this to happen," wrote Hannah.

She told me how much the family loved me and how they would be devastated to see me go and felt shame that they cursed me to go away. However, I was advised to look for alternative place to live. "They have to know that there are consequences and they cannot treat people like that."

The message was anticipated but still, in that particular moment, I found myself in a very vulnerable position realising the big change I was facing: to find a new place and live there by myself it wasn't something I desired. Where and how was I going to find it? What options did I have? This was one of Kafka's scenarios: people watch and follow asking questions then the authorities come to the house, interrogate the family, spread fear, I write my own statement that in case if something happens to me… madness… and now I had to find a place and live by myself. It was three days before New Year's Eve and we had already planned going off to Meknès. I had to get my act together and start looking for a new dwelling. Ali and Mohamed joined me. "I really need you now, please help me," I was begging them. The internet was the fastest and the only option for me to find a new place. The first house that I came across, at bikhir.ma, was a 120m2 house with a cosy-looking photograph, but some rather ambiguous details. The price was 1.500DH per month, in the centre and within my budget. In fact, it was the only one that I could afford. We called the number and set up an immediate meeting. Indeed, the location was great, across the bridge with a view on the Oum Er-Rbia river; unfortunately that was the only advantage of living in this house. The house was uninhabitable. It was an empty two-floor house in the shape and form of riad, with two open-space rooms and an open-space kitchen. I was stunned by housing conditions of that place when looking around and seeing and feeling the bare, naked, freezing-cold space that was called an apartment, and 1500DH stated in the online offer went up to 2000DH. I was brutally honest with a landlord. "It's nothing in here, no water, no bed, no electricity." "I can bring you a mattress," he said. "No, thank you very much. I'm no longer interested." I left disappointed. And what now? We wandered around the medina hoping to come across an offer, a sign, an advertisement, an estate agent. "Will you come with me to La Scierie and do the translation? I asked Mohamed "I don't want you to move out," said Ali. "It's not good to live by yourself." He was right and I didn't want to live by myself. They often referred to people who lived by themselves in Muslim society as "mentally troubled" or disinherited from their own families. The family bonding was priceless, but as a result, it put enormous pressure on those who lived in this country by themselves, and there were cases of such individuals who put a tragic end to their lives.

We went home through the Amelou district crossing through a friendly neighbourhood and thinking of stumbling across a house for rent. We stopped a man in the street, and he advised us to go to a local hairdresser. The hairdresser knew someone who had a house to rent. He made a phone call and ten minutes later a landlady turned up. She was not happy at all to see a foreigner wanting to rent the house, moreover the three months' contract made her even more oblivious to me. I could see the "am I bothered?" attitude written on her face. If the house had electricity and water, it would have been a charming little place to live in, taking into account its location and quite nice layout. However, yet again, there was nothing in that place and the landlady wasn't the nicest of all landladies I have met.

The fiasco of today's search made us all exhausted; on top of that I still had to go through a serious chat with my family. Hakima, Meryam, Fadma and Zahra were all sitting outside sieving grains. When I apologised for everything that happened lately and announced moving out Hakima burst into tears. "I don't want you to move out." "But it may be better for us all," I said choking on my own tears and at the same time feeling relived that they didn't want me out of the house. "Please stay, we are sorry for what happened," Hakima hugged me. "You really want me to stay?" "Of course, we love you." This was an extremely emotional moment for us all, but I knew I had to remind them of one important thing: to stop being paranoid and let me live. It was also a perfect moment to announce my New Year's Eve plans. "I need a break from Khénifra. I'm going to Meknès and Raba for a few days." They understood. We apologised, cried, hugged; it was cathartic; I felt lighter as I finally spoke the truth.

The three of us went off to the "Omega" café and sat there feeling relived. It was an extremely emotional period and we deserved a little break. "Where in Meknès are we going to stay?" I asked Mohamed. He had a few good friends there who were studying law at the university. "One of them will put us up, don't worry."

The strong foundation of Islam that had been instilled in Ali was yet again displayed. He was one of those individuals who could constantly talk about his religion but wasn't even practising it, and although our conversations were stimulating, I had this feeling of being "pushed" on to their side. It started off with a video of a converted to Islam woman on "You Tube." "Would you like to see it?" "Of course" I was curious when the name Queen Nicola in "They choose Islam" video popped out on the screen. It was an interview with a young woman who was not happy with her life, the consumerism, her job, the culture and she was yearning to find a "better purpose" to live for. Nicola was complaining that her whole life felt like a party and the more she was becoming familiar with Islam the more she felt in peace with herself. Her point of view, a woman who was spiritual and Islam was the perfect religion for her was flawlessly fine with me.

However, the only thing that puzzled me a little in that video was the constant complaint of binge drinking. "Do they have to drink, if they are not happy with drinking, or do they have to go to nightclubs, if the pleasure is not there?" I asked. "Do we have to convert to any religion to become truthful with ourselves and others?" In other words, she said she would offend her God if she went out drinking. "Ali, you don't have to convert to Islam to stop drinking. However, if religion makes you become a better person then you certainly should do that; If only religion makes you stop drinking you should become religious, if believing in God makes you stronger then you should not hesitate and become religious."

"Do you believe in Jesus?" asked Ali. "I'm religious." "But do you believe that Jesus was killed and he is the Son of God?" "I do believe in greater power than us humans and in a strong spiritual energy that protects me and my life is a proof. If you ask me about a concrete person, I can't answer yes or no because it is something that goes beyond the intellectual tangible reasoning. I suppose my religious beliefs cannot be labelled, however, I call myself a Christian."

Muslims don't believe that Jesus is the Son of God. Moreover, he wasn't killed but pretended to his killers that they killed him. God raised him to heaven, and he will come back at the end of the time to rule the world in the ultimate and final message of God. Also, they don't believe in the creation of three people in the same person and these two points strongly divide Christians and Muslims. I had nothing against Ali's or Muslims' or anybody's beliefs, if such beliefs don't harm anybody. However, knowing the historic past and shredded blood in many religious wars I would advise them to reach some sort of compromise. People, no matter of what race and religion, should be allowed to have faith, but at the same time respect each other's beliefs without making a big fuss about that because religion is nothing else than a direction of the heart:

"Religion is something infinitely simple, simple-minded. It is not knowledge, not the content of our emotion (for all possible content has been granted already from the beginning wherever a human being engages with life). It is neither duty nor renunciation; it is not limitation, but in the perfect expanse of the universe it is a direction of the heart. How a human being might go and err towards the right and towards the left, and knock himself and fall and get up, and committing injustice here and suffer injustice there, and be abused here and elsewhere wish others ill, and how he might abuse and misunderstand: all this is transferred into the great religion and there maintains and enriches the god that is there cantered. And man living still at the farthest periphery of this circle, belongs to this powerful centre even if he had turned his countenance toward it only once, perhaps while dying. That at specific hour the Arab turns to face the East and prostrates himself, that is religion. It is hardly "belief." It has no opposite. It is a natural movement within a human being through which god's wind sweeps three times a day if we are at least this: limber."

From there, we moved on to discuss a rather trivial subject: jeans. "Why do women wear tight jeans?" asked Ali and then explained. "When they do that, every single man looks at their bottoms." "Don't you think that the whole problem lies not in jeans but in men?" The problem here was very obvious: men were not used to women wearing jeans, it was still a novelty. "If you had hundreds of bottoms in tight jeans walking down the streets every single day would that still excite you? Would you still turn your head round each time when you see them, or would this rather become reality? You would finally get accustomed to seeing women in tight jeans, don't you think?"

The next question was a little bit shocking. "Do you think women should swim?" If they want to swim they should swim." "But they are in swimming costumes?" "Do you want them to swim in their djellabas?" "I think only husband should be allowed to see her wife's body," said Ali. "Do you want to deprive your wife of a pleasure like swimming only because you think that you have possessed the right to see her more exposed? And why you men are allowed to swim and take your clothes off and expose your body in front of other women, shouldn't this be equal? This is not logical."

"You want to go to Europe, is that right?" I continued. "Do you want to marry someone from Europe or would you rather have a Moroccan woman?" "I could pay for a marriage but that would only give me the opportunity to escape Morocco." My previous thought of being a passport for them was again confirmed. "If you were married here in Morocco, you would expect you wife to follow the rules of Islam, is that right? Would you also expect your wife to tolerate your weakness for alcohol and cigarettes? It is very much against Islam." Ali and seventy per cent of Muslims Moroccans were a big puzzle for me. They would never be against Islam or wouldn't dare to criticise it, but at the same time they would disobey its rules. From word to word we moved to discussion about control. "We are not controlled by Islam." "You are not? The rules that are imposed on you in any religion are to control people, an easy example, Islam forbids drinking and smoking, so if you smoke or drink you cannot practise Islam. If you not follow the rules of

Islam you out of it, is that right?" "But I have a choice, either I practise Islam or not." "We are not talking about that; we are talking about the people who practise Islam. You are not free to do what you want to do. If there is any form of restriction of your freedom there is some form of control."

"You are both real puzzles to me," I said to Mohamed and Ali. "You talk about Islam, you recite the Quran, you believe in God, you believe in the whole creation of God and yet you are out of it, you praise your religion and at the same time you disrespect it, simply because you take pleasure from drinking and smoking and…." I knew I had to shut up. "I pray every day to God to forgive me," said Ali. "That's beautiful, but don't you think it's pointless to ask him for forgiveness every day, if you don't change anything about your behaviour? Or perhaps you are not ready to change?"

******

I have never seriously pondered God in the context of a different religion. In other words, I have always believed that we had the same God but of different names. Here was Allah, God of love and forgiveness who did not search for vengeance. He was patient. He waited. He answered questions. He found solutions to any problem. He helped those who loved Him and explained things to those who didn't love Him waiting for them to come. Our God, the Christian's God seemed for them a little bit less patient and less forgiving, and if we looked at Him in the context of Stendhal's *"Le Rouge et le Noir,"* their suspicions were confirmed:

"Ce bon prêtre nous parlerait de Dieu. Mais quel Dieu? Non celui de la Bible, petit despote cruel et plein de la soif de se venger... mais le Dieu de Voltaire, juste, bon, infin ...."

There was another reference to our Christian's God.

"Si je trouve le Dieu de Chrétiens, je suis perdu: c'est un despote, et, comme tel, il est rempli d'idées de vengeance: sa Bible ne parle que de punitions atroces. Le ne l'ai jamais aimé; je n'ai même jamais voulu croire qu'on l'aimât sincèrement. Il est sans pitié (et il se rappela plusieurs passages de la Bible). Il me punira d'une manière abominable.... Mais si je trouve le Dieu de Fénelon! Il me dira peut-être: il te sera beaucoup pardonné, parce que tu as beaucoup aimé ..."

The question was why we should fear God if God was love. "If I do wrong I should fear myself or a punishment but not God," I said to Mohammed adding in jest: "My God is not angry with me if I enjoy a glass of wine with my friends. Why should he be angry with me? I have a good time, I don't hurt anybody, and I treasure such moments."

As the afternoon was approaching, I had to head back home. Hakima, Meryam, and Fadma were planning a little medina outing in order to buy a New Year's present for me and my mum, a pair of *babushki* each. The shop that sold mainly *babushki* was inevitably packed out with *babushki* of all sorts: plain simple, more sophisticated with emblazoned flowers, of a different shapes and colours: flat, pointy, furry, for both men and women, and children, and they choose for me two pairs of black pointy ones. We were strolling around stands with fabrics, then stopped by a cosmetics' shop and I bought us all pairs of earrings, simple, shiny, diamond-resembling studs. On the way home we went to a local patisserie for home-made yoghurt and some cake. Our honest conversation the other day helped ease the tension making the whole time spent together extremely enjoyable. Then there was another surprise waiting for me: *henna*. We all gathered around *forno* while Meryam was preparing the mixture.

The henna mixture contains substances called *baraka* and is believed to infuse the body with positive healing energy. It is applied during rite-of-passage ceremonies that typically include blood flow, such as male circumcision or the loss of female virginity during a wedding ceremony - both feet and both hands of the female, and a small, rather symbolic henna tattoo on the palm of a man. Pollution categories in Islam are based on the idea that the inner and outer bodies are separated into discrete, mutually exclusive elements that must be kept apart. However, certain substances can cross from the outer physical body to the inner spiritual body and purify the inner body, especially those substances containing *baraka*. It is not coincidental that Moroccan women chose to tattoo their bodies with substances containing *baraka* to symbolically enhance their bodies after first menstruation, a crucial moment in the life cycle. Through performing *henna* on a stranger like me, they were expressing deep affection and welcoming me in their house.

When the mixture was ready, Meryam started off by painting a few flower patterns on the palms of my hands and then on the outside. When that was finished, she moved on to my feet, covering the whole sole of the foot, moving up to the nails and then painting other flowery patters across the top of the feet. It took about two hours to finish it off and between one to two hours to dry it off. I was comfortably sitting around *forno* with legs up on the pillow and was being sweetly looked after by everybody. When dinner came I could not use my fingers, so instead Hakima was feeding me, giving me tiny pieces of bread soaked up in tagine and few pieces of meat. How I loved that woman!

In the meantime, a mixture of tea and sugar was applied all over the drying henna for the long-lasting effect. When it was dry, I was advised to put socks on and go to bed without scrubbing it off.

******

The next morning, the residues of henna were soaked up in olive oil for longer-lasting colour. I scrubbed the rest off, and indeed, the colour became more intense, more orange.

Mohamed, Ali and I went to the bus station to find out the timetable for tomorrow's journey to Meknès. There was no direct bus, so instead we were advised to take a bus to Ifrane and change there for Meknès. It came as no surprise that two different information points at the same bus station gave us two different prices. The first man that saw three of us together asked for 40DH, whereas the second one who saw only Mohamed asked for 30DH. "The first price was European," commented Mohamed. "We will have to hide you next time."

Over coffee I was told that none of his friends in Meknès wanted to put us up. The landlord of the first friend did not agree to the European woman staying with them, saying that he did not want to have any problems. The second friend kept changing his mind but in the end he also refused, and the reason was rather obvious. Our initial plan was to stay two nights in Meknès and from there go off to Raba. "We have no choice but to search for a riad for New Year's Eve, and if we won't be able to stay for the second night we will have to come back home," I said and started my research. Another problem arose after I booked the riad, a problem called "Two Moroccan boys and one European girl in the same room." "We may not be able to stay in the same room. According to the law we cannot spend a night in the same room with a woman unless we show the marriage certificate." "Don't worry, we will have separate beds, and if someone asked for an explanation I would give them," I tried to cheer them up and keep my positive attitude.

******

The New Year's adventure started around 6.30am with heating up some water and giving myself a good scrub, so I could embrace the impending voyage with all the freshness that it deserved. In fact, everybody at home had woken early today: Papa Mohamed, Mustapha and Moad were getting organised for the daily grind of loading and reloading the camion, Abdellah had his driving theory exam at 8.00am and Hakima did not have a choice but to get breakfast ready for everybody. Ali, Mohamed and I set off earlier, around 8.30am; Ali took his djellaba and box of Mina's cakes, Mohamed carried a second box with boucheyar, eggs and some cookies that her mum had prepared. My contribution, however, was rather miserable. It was a flask of tea, but not sweet, and not even Moroccan, so when it came down to drinking it, we mixed it up with some sugar and milk finding the taste even more disgusting. As snow was reported in the higher parts of the mountains, the breeze of that morning felt particularly cold, but despite its sharpness that kept us on our adventurous toes, we felt nothing but the sheer excitement of the day's escapade.

The Moroccan system of public transport was simple: no pre-booking, or buying tickets in advance; if the bus came and there were some seats left we would be on that bus, if not, hmm… there would be another one… in a few hours. That morning, we sat down in a café and were observing every bus that drove into the station looking out for one with the Italian flag on it; it was supposed to be our vehicle. Our New Year's celebration started off with something greater than coffee and cakes; it was a fête of Mohamed's resolution to quit smoking. While sipping his coffee and putting down the butt, he had enough stamina to say: "It's my last cigarette!" Finally my nagging, jostling, hustling, shoving… whatever force I used seemed to have worked. He was wholeheartedly supported by me, and I bet, his exasperated lungs which might have craved for a clean breath more than I had. Our trip was still up in the air; it was already 10.00am and no sign of a bus. When coffees were drunk, the cakes consumed, the last cigarette smoked it was a time to go and verify the thirty minutes' delay. As soon as we walked into the station we heard a man's voice shouting "Ifrane! Ifrane!" We knew the bus was coming but we still had no idea if there were spare seats left for us.

The energy at the bus station seemed chaotic to me; men who were selling tickets, were outshouting each other "Marrakesh! Ifrane! Raba!" and passengers were running around like headless chickens looking for the right bus. Our "Italian" bus finally arrived; from the outside it looked as if it had smoked countless packs of cigarettes or it might have suffered a heavy case of hyperthermia watching the rear hatch widely opened. But never judge a bus by its cover, right? Or... perhaps do. When we had finally managed to squeeze ourselves through the crowd of jostling travellers and took our seats, I was stunned by amount of litter everywhere, with used tickets, some sweets, food leftovers and chewing gum in almost every nook and cranny of the bus. The smell was repulsive, and on top of everything there was no ventilation whatsoever; hence, I started predicting the worse: a sudden and inevitable stomach movement. I was tapping my belly and wishing it good luck while firstly, hearing, then seeing, and then smelling a few other victims of that "comfort," and Ali was one of them. In time he took a plastic bag and moved up to the front hiding on the staircase. The staircase seemed to have been the only "asylum" for those who were brave enough to run fast, not many had succeeded though. Despite a few casualties, the bus driver refused to break announcing the next stopover in fifteen minutes. Although the combination of heat and smell was making me burp, my stomach was remarkably brave and survived the whole journey. The bus finally pulled out and we were able to get off and get some fresh air. "Can we go to the toilet?" My bladder was ready to explode. It was impossible; the bus was running late and longer stopovers weren't planned. "Bugger!"

When the bus stopped again, we were told that we would be arriving in the centre of Ifrane in ten minutes, but ten minutes later there was still no sign of a village on the horizon, only winding roads and rocky surroundings. "Where is Ifrane?" "We passed it already," responded the ticket inspector. "Why didn't you say anything? We were supposed to get off in Ifrane." The attitude of that man outraged us and made my friends angry. "You have to stop the bus, we want to get off!" "The driver cannot stop it here!" he was shouting and blaming us for all the trouble. We got other travellers' support and their opinions to go to the nearest village, but with no connecting buses to Meknès we ignored their advice. About twelve kilometres from Ifrane and circa one kilometre from a lake the bus finally stopped. "We should have lunch at the lake and then go back to Ifrane." I suggested. As we were walking towards it, a car pulled out offering a lift. "It's easy to travel with you; you are our visa to everything; people will stop when they see you," said Mohammed.

The lake, *Dayet Aoua,* was beautiful and calm; a few people could be seen on the other side of the lake and a few others in a boat. The weather was stunning: warm and sunny with a slight chill of winter but with no wind. I remember that particular moment very well; I felt that life was good giving us such abundance of freedom and forcing us to embrace it, to breathe it in, to inhale and exhale without any fear of losing it. I was familiar with this feeling, my friends, however, a little less, so in order to articulate the overwhelming joy we shouted *"wyih, wyih!"* and behaved like teenagers who had managed to escape very strict parents, and now were completely plunging themselves into the lavishness of independence, and no one could take it away. The ordinary breakfast: eggs, boucheyar, the cake and the horrible mixture of milk, sugar and green tea was even tastier than usual as it was flavoured with the most essential ingredient: a feeling of liberation, and… the company of hungry dogs.

"How good life is. How fair, how incorruptible, how impossible to deceive: not even by strength, not even by willpower, and not even by courage. How everything remains what it is and has only this choice: to come true, or to exaggerate and push too far…."

We then walked back to the main road to hitchhike; Mohamed was right, it wasn't difficult. A car with a young driver pulled out and agreed to give us a lift to Ifrane. The young man turned out to have worked as a mechanic in Italy, but was coming back often to Morocco for holidays. The music was on and it played well-known tunes: "On va s'aimer, on va dancer, c'est la vie, lalalala" that we sang it out loud expressing the feeling of ecstasy. At first, Karim appeared distant and very quiet; perhaps we gave him a wrong impression of being some lunatics, but after a short while he accepted our outlandishness and was becoming friendlier and friendlier. Not only did he stop by a magnificent place just outside *Azrou* to look at a splendid place guarded by two enormous pots of tea facing each other, but also wanted to drive us to *Ifrane* to have coffee together.

When we got to Ifrane, we were told that the bus station was further away from the centre than we had anticipated, so our coffee and the whole sightseeing trip had to be cut short. Ifrane was such a disappointment for me. I really did not expect to see a European ski resort town in this part of the world. Everything seemed European: the architecture, the panorama, tourists and the prices. For something of a terribly low quality, like lukewarm milk with a pinch of Nescafe, we paid 12DH instead of the expected 6DH. We took a few photographs of a fountain to memorise our short visit here and were trying to photograph the lion, a symbol of Ifrane, but failed terribly. The Lion was intolerably occupied with all those gatherers and although there was no sign of life in him, he was touched, rubbed, and talked to. We were considering doing the same, in case of some magic or happy powers he was emanating, but waiting to touch a piece of stone seemed like a waste of time and we were happy to get back on the road. Karim, all of a sudden, suggested driving us to El Hajeb in order to catch a bus to Meknès. "He must have enjoyed our company," I thought. We got in the car, he rolled his hashish-cigarette, smoked, shared with Ali and drove. Luckily, we arrived in El Hajeb in one piece, exchanged emails, and left. "Is this yours?" he shouted showing me a piece of rubber while I was getting off. "I don't think so." "Isn't that a sole of you shoe?" Indeed, it was a sole of my shoe. How bizarre! The temporary solution was applied and my boot had its "soul" put back on.

In El Hajeb we pondered our good fortune regarding a small adventure with Karim and now with a swift bus connection to Meknès. However, after one hour of sitting in the bus and waiting for it to move we were turning the good fortune into a possibility of spending a New Year's Eve in that bus as we still were waiting for more passengers. Here would be my advice: when travelling in Morocco embrace yourself for a long journey, never travel on a full stomach, or indulge yourself in drinking as you would only risk the pain and embarrassment of searching for a toilet. Finally, after one and half hours the driver turned the engine on; we were on the move again.

The time in the bus passed quickly while chatting and listening to music; then we couldn't take our eyes off the sunset when approaching Meknès; the magnificent red-orange-blue that was covering a huge part of the sky was slowly setting giving us the impression of fire, a burning desire painted on the sky. With that visual pleasure came relief; we were finally entering Meknès - the medieval city, the busy, vibrant suburbs, the noise that pleased me a little, the noise that I missed a little, the people, the sound of life.

At the station we were greeted by friends of Mohamed - the students of law, and their friend - a guy with a car. He agreed to take us to our riad; apparently, he knew this city like the back of his hand owing to the time he had passed here. However, disregarding all those years he had lived in Meknès, his knowledge of the medieval part was down to a level of a freshman. The medieval medina was a maze, attractive and vibrant which was seducing us to go inside and get lost. The winding, short, sometimes dead-end streets were making our heads spin and the more directions we were given the more we went round in circles. We had circled around the medina for some time but in the end we managed to find our riad. "Bad Berdaine" Riad was announcing its medieval character through a stunning, massive medieval wooden door with a metal door knocker that was staring at us with its fixed majestic gaze.

The owner of this riad wasn't Moroccan for sure; apparently his "h" in a word *"shari"* in Arabic means "street" was betraying his origin. He was a rather strange breed: with the djellaba and a hood on - he looked Moroccan, with the djellaba and a hood on and trainers - he looked less Moroccan, with his djellaba and no hood on and trainers - he resembled a Buddhist to me, a monk who was spreading a remarkable calm and peace and this was the last thing we were looking for tonight. However, three of us signed in without responding to any personal questions that could query our relationship.

The room was on the ground floor right next to the reception and the dining room where a few foreigners were spotted sitting and sipping wine. It was a good sign. "Can we have music on?" I asked. "There are children on this floor, so better keep quiet," the monk just proved my suspicions. "Do you celebrate the New Year's Eve at all?" "Not really but if you want to go to a restaurant with music, I can show you where it is. It's only three hundred meters from here." "Ok, but when we come back; our friends are waiting for us," I responded.

There were two questions: first, how to get a bottle of wine and second, where to spend the New Year's Eve. The first question was answered by our friends. "We are going to drive you to a shop where you can get some wine." In order to get to the shop, we had to cross the whole town. "Are we still in Meknès?" I joked. It was a supermarket on the suburbs of Meknès with a security guy and a heavy flapping plastic mat that was barricading the main entrance; it was difficult to get through; perhaps, it was to stop shoplifters? I tried to take some photos but the security guard reacted quickly reprimanding me and my friend. When I walked into the shop I was struck by two things: the arrangement of products, and men; it was like walking into a harem. Men were everywhere! Later I spotted only two women in that shop. As far as I remembered, usually the very first section straight after entering the shop was the section with bread, pastry, or vegetables; here however, the very first section was exposing the product that one would not expect to be so visible - the ever prohibited alcohol, and every man in that sector was stocking himself with vodka or whisky. I choose a bottle of Bordeaux, my friends - one litre of whisky, with two litres of Coca-Cola and a pack of crisps. We paid and drove off.

It was about time to start a real New Year's celebration. The first step was mixing up whisky and Coca-Cola in Karim's car while driving as it seemed the safest place to do it. However, there was one exception: Karim was not supposed to see or find out that we were drinking in his car, so the second step was to hide the bottles away from Karim. With hindsight, I understand his apprehension; If we were stopped by police, we all would go to jail, and I must say we were very lucky that evening. He may or may not have seen Mohamed making the mixture but everybody, including him, was pretending that nothing was going on. The proportions of that drink surpassed my expectations: instead of the usual 20% whisky and 80% Coca-Cola here the proportions were reversed: 80% whisky and 20 % Coca-Cola gave my head a real roll after taking a tiny sip. Hang on there, Maggie! It's just beginning!

Karim was the son of a wealthy man who ran a restaurant in Meknès and he invited us all to his dad's place for dinner. "Do we want to go?" asked Mohamed. "Oh yes, please!" I was starving. He took a table out and laid it with an exquisite meal for five persons with grilled pieces of meat, sausages, olives and bread. The generosity of that young man towards us strangers was impressive. Moreover, he offered to take us back to our riad. "Perhaps we all could spend New Year's Eve together?" I proposed. As the owner of a café that was open until late today, Karim had to go back to work; and Mohamed, the student of law, was not particularly interested in celebrating New Year, or perhaps he was not particularly keen on celebrating it in my company. For some reason, my presence stirred a little bit of anxiety amongst them. Not only the landlord, who refused to have me overnight, described "the European girl presence as a *mochkila*, but also some another friends who short while ago had invited Mohamed to his house party, this time said 'no' to having us over at his place; apparently, his girlfriend was jealous of the European girl and that was his excuse.

There was no choice but to look for an alternative plan and here was my mine: go back to the riad, refresh ourselves, have a glass of wine and go out. It was about 10.00pm when we returned to the riad. The place was lifeless and the landlord seemed to have taken a nap already which was indicated by length of time that took him to open the door. "We don't want to disturb you but we want to go out later on, so how could we get back in?" I asked. "I can give you the key to the main door." And so he did, and we felt relieved.

Our room was outstanding. It had one double bed which we all agreed was for me and two single beds ideal for Mohamed and Ali. However, one defect of that place was lack of bedding, only the double bed had a proper one, whereas the single beds were left with blankets. Apart from that the conditions were incredible; a spacious and stylish room with a massive bathroom and a fantastic shower. The pleasure that it gave me, after two months of not having a shower, was immense, and it consumed at least half hour of our precious time, and while I was pampering myself, my friends were getting drunk. When we all finished with indulging ourselves under the shower, we decided to go out and look for that restaurant that was supposed to play music tonight. To my surprise, the place was already closed, we were told by a passing by man who knew where it was. "Let's go somewhere else," I suggested. "It's dangerous," they replied. "You don't want to spend a New Year's Eve inside the ghostly riad, do you?" They didn't, but at the same time they were worried about my safety. I decided to take responsibility for myself and walked to Karim's café, outside the centre. It was decided. Meknès was a dead city that night; there was hardly anybody seen on the streets and only in few cafés that we walked past some men were spotted. I did not see a single woman that evening!

Karim's café was occupied by young men; I was introduced to a bunch of them, youthful students of law in their twenties, adorable and kind. However, sitting with ten heavy-smokers around the table wasn't an easy task, nor particularly enjoyable for my lungs; cigarettes and hashish were rolled and devoured by them, one by one as some kind of chain reaction was happening that even sucked up Mohamed's New Year's resolution. Then an obvious subject was brought up to the table: Islam, and to this day I cannot comprehend their religious presence in Islam. If they were devoted followers I could understand the urge of wanting to share such conviction. However, talking constantly about their religion wasn't making them in my eyes the true followers of Islam, and why, on every possible occasion, was the subject of Islam always discussed with me? Anyhow, a TV screen was showing a football match. "Can you change the channel so we could watch the New Year's celebration?" I asked Karim. He laughed. "Why can't you do that? Is this also prohibited?"

The celebration of the New Year was not prohibited absolutely but was not to be given special treatment by the Muslims as it is a pagan Roman festival associated with Janus – the two headed deity who symbolised change and the circumcision of Jesus. The Muslims have their own *Hijri* calendar that has been in constant use for 1400 years. The calendar has been initiated by *Sahaaba Umar*; it is based purely on *lunar cycles* and is marked by the incident of the immigration of the Muslims from Makkah to Madinah. According to the *Hijri* calendar the New Year actually begins on the first of Muharram. "New Year's Eve, there is nothing to celebrate," claim one of the Muslims living in England, and he calls the New Year's celebration "a total cut off from the reality" making a rather peculiar comparison with the two important religious celebration in the Muslims world, like *Eid al-Fitr* celebrated at the end of Ramadan and *Eid al-Adha* - the sheep slaughter. And he continues: "By adopting the celebrations of others, we are not harmlessly saying a few words or just enjoying ourselves. We are opening the door to disappearing within the dominant culture, to a future in which our children may have Muslim names, but are otherwise indistinguishable from non-Muslims in their habits, customs and appearances."

However, I have been accustomed to such a pointless celebration and have even been enjoying it. "Happy New Year to all of you! Let's raise our coffee cups!" I made a toast. However pleasant the evening was, the long adventurous day started to fatigue me and around 2.00am we all decided to go home. "We will walk you back to the riad, it will be safer." As the spirit of that night was still alive and singing was in the air; not only walking with six young men felt safer but also more amusing.

"Ya Laila, kif h'Alek lyoum. Ya mama bla bik majani noum noum ..... Rani ki Imhboul. Ya hyati ya mon amour, Rani ki Imjnoun yaaaa Lailaaaa..... Je suis fou de ton amour, ton corps, ta peau de velours, plus en plus fou sien que sourd, ya Lila mon seul amour…."

The singing went on until we stumbled upon a few drunk men who stopped us on the pavement wanting to know how I was and where we all lived. When we walked past them politely wishing a Happy New Year, they shouted back. "Stop! Stop!" We had to stop and the two Mohameds went to talk to them; fortunately they were too drunk to pick up a fight and let us go in peace. "You look after your woman!" their words were heard in no far off distance.

It was around 2.30am when we ended up safely in our room. There was still a significant amount of wine left, and following the Moroccan principle that nothing can get wasted, it was quickly finished off. After 3.30am I was in bed falling asleep instantly. However, Ali and Mohamed were continuing the New Year's celebration in our exquisite bathroom. Around 5.00am not only the heavy smoke woke me up but also the continuous whispering. "What is going on? You can't smoke in here! Besides, can you just shut up and get some sleep!" "Magda, you don't sleep?" asked Mohamed. "I try, but with you gossiping women it's not easy." "Magda, Magda,…" drunk Mohamed was nagging me. "Darling, can you just shut up?" "Désolé, je vais." And he did. The morning was cut short as another wake-up call happened at 8.00am. The children and their parents were up and sitting in the dining room outside our room. "Do I hear Mohamed and Ali with them? How come? Are they up?" I was hearing Mohamed's voice, but there was someone else sounding very much like him. "Bloody, noisy tourists!" The chat was adding to my headache; I was starving and I needed a shower. Soon after me, Mohamed and Ali dragged themselves out of bed. "Let's find out the price of breakfast. Perhaps we could eat something here?" Luckily, the breakfast was included and boucheyar, yogurts, eggs, orange juice, coffee and tea perfectly satisfied our hunger taking the half of the headache away.

We checked out and soon found ourselves in another café awaiting our friends; Mohamed turned up first and agreed to put us up for one night which meant we could go and do some sightseeing. He took our bags and promised to join me and Mohamed in a short while. Meknès was a stunning place; It is said that the origin of the name "Meknès" comes with a Berber tribe called *Miknasa* that had settled there in the 9th century. However, there is another version, less well-known, that explains the origins of Meknès through *"Makat annas,"* that means the "Mecca of people," signifying a cross-road for the travellers.

The main square was less busy than Jamaa el-Fnaa in Marrakesh but equally dangerous with all the performers who followed and forced one to participate in snaky-slippery around one's neck games; the well-trained monkey that cuddled you and jumped on one's head was equally trained to demand some dirham. The enticing music spectacles were seducing and then possessing one's soul in the whole "putting a spell on you" phenomena that was pushing one to move, to express, and the same happened to me; in my musical, dancing ecstasy I created a little "dance stop" or rather "happy-hips movement spot" and received some straight response from some passers-by who were encouraging me to continue by putting their thumbs up. "Perhaps I could earn some money here," I said in jest. "You really make people happy," responded Mohamed. "Thank you, I just move my hips."

We were then joined by the two Mohameds and Ali and started our little escapade around Meknès paying a visit to a museum that was showing some abstract paintings, then admiring "Baba Mansour," the largest and most stunning of the cities' gates, and visiting the "Mousolem of *Moulay Ismail.*" Then we took a walk towards the underground prison that was installed under the old city by Moulay Ismail. Unfortunately, we didn't go inside but here is a fascinating story told by a visitor of that prison:

"A guide took us underground into a series of vaults covering 7 hectares, and lit only by light from holes in the square above. This prison was built on orders of Sultan Ishmail. During his time there were about 80,000 prisoners living underground. There was an area for political prisoners like the Berber Moroccans and the Portuguese Christians, and then there was the area for the dangerous criminals. In the area for the dangerous prisoners were the torture pillars. We could still see the hole in the pillar where the poor souls were chained to the pillar with their neck and arms out to the side. The prisoners were forced to dig a tunnel on orders of the sultan from the prison to the outside of Meknes. This tunnel served as an underground route to supply the

Romans with supplies in Volubilis and take stuff back through a second tunnel. The tunnel is 13km long we were told. It is closed now as it is too dangerous for people to be in it."

As the sun was slowly setting down we had to rush to get the better view from *Sahrij Swani*, another Moulay Ismail place. The story of this lake was told by the Meknès historian - Ibn Zaydan:

"Mulay Isma'il had an ornamental lake, large enough to sail pleasure boats on, built inside the Kasbah. In fact, the 'Alawid prince, a contemporary of Louis XIV, had this lake constructed to guarantee the supply of water, in times of siege or drought, to the palaces and mosques of the town, as well as to the public baths, homes, gardens and the orchards that surrounded the town and provided for its daily fruit and vegetable requirements.

The masterpiece of the complex known as Hri Swani, the Basin of the Norias, Sahrij Swani, is an artificial lake notable for its size (148.75 m by 319 m with a depth of 3.20 m). Three tall crenelated walls that stood around the lake have today been reduced to an isolated section of rampart located on the southwest side towards the Bani Ahmad district and the remains of the base of an enclosure wall more than 2 m thick.

The size of the lake is reminiscent of the lakes of the Middle Atlas Mountains located to the south of the town. The lake was filled from two sources: Water from the ten wells dug near the Sahrij, below the silo, brought up using tennoria sand ceramic channels. Water from the wells was used at times of trouble (war, etc.) and drought. The second source, water from the Wadi Bufekrane which descends from the Middle Atlas Mountains, crosses the southern part of Meknès and feeds the lake and part of the town of Meknès."

Before reaching *Sahrij Swani* we had walked along a rather endless street. "What is this building?" "A Kings' place," said Mohamed. I believed it was the Royal Palace - *"Dar El Makhzen"* as more than a few guards were keeping an eye on it, and on us too. When we got to Sahrij Swani, we were joined by a very young man, perhaps eighteen years old or even less. The sun was already set and the guys were rolling another hashish cigarette looking for more secluded place to smoke it, and the medieval walls with its staircase were a perfect place for that. The luck was on our side as two minutes after the cigarette was put down, a couple of guards that had observed us while we were walking, came to say hello. We all kept our cool. "Where is the hashish and alcohol?" they asked first. "We don't have it." They started searching us, looking around the ground and sniffing the empty bottle of water. "You are coming with us" they told me. "Why? What did I do? We are just sitting here and having a relaxing time." We stepped down and carried on being interrogated. Passport, nationality, what are you doing here, where do you live, what is your relationship with those men…etc. "I'm just visiting Meknès and they are my friends. I'm sorry I left my passport at home." They were big and intimidating and the fact they spoke mainly Arabic with Ali and Mohamed was adding more anxiety to this bizarre interruption. "What do they want?" I whispered to Mohamed while they were on the "walkie-talkie" with someone. "They want to take us to the police station." "Why?" We all were very confused as to what they actually wanted. They called up the police. "Why do I have to go to the police station?" I asked. "We have to verify your identity." "I can get home and bring you my passport, that's not a problem." They did not agree and while we were awaiting a police van, they were making rather inappropriate comments, *"zwina, zwina,"* they looked at me and smiled. In the meantime, they found and confiscated hashish from that young man who had joined us but let him go, a very unequivocal act. The police van arrived in about ten minutes. They asked me the same questions but in a rather different, more professional manner, but still, three of us were invited to come with them to the police station. As those two policemen seemed approachable we tried to talk to them. Apparently, the two other police guards did not report on the hashish that they had confiscated and only "the European girl" seemed to have been a problem. When they talked between each other we heard the word "idiots" when referring to those who had stopped us. We were driven to the police station and were left there, waiting outside for my passport which Mohamed was supposed to deliver. There were some heavy fights going on that evening, and a very young, heavily bleeding victim turned up with his mum who was hysterical while reporting on a vicious attack on her son. We were observing, commenting, singing, and waiting. Finally, our friend Karim came with Mohamed and my passport. The police officer verified my identity and apologised for such silly incident. "Whenever you go, you should always go to the tourist police station to sign in; it's for your safety," he advised me when we were going away.

I apologised to my friends for all the trouble. "Better if we go home and cook dinner," suggested Mohamed. At his place we started off with some tea and music. Soon, some other friends arrived and we sat around an electric fire and were discussing, from the law point of view, mixed-race marriages and other topics in the same field, a part of preparation for the exam. Mohamed who was in charge of cooking chicken tagine asked me to help him, while another Mohamed was pretending to be a camera man and registering everything that we were doing. Then he took my camera and started recording an utterance of every single friend who was welcoming me in the house and their country. But in the meantime, we were keeping an eye on our tagine. Here was our menu: for a starter - tea plus hashish, dinner - chicken tagine, desert – more hashish. Mohamed, the cook, smoked hashish every single day without exceptions. Over dinner he was becoming spaced out and rather unsociable, subdued, slurping words making long pauses and seeming a little bit down. However, it was an immensely enjoyable and stimulating gathering that stopped around 1.00am. Mohamed, Ali, and I were sleeping in the same room where the temperature did not exceed a few degrees. The thin mattress and two blankets weren't sufficient; I could not sleep as it was so cold. By chance, I woke Mohamed up while searching for my winter jacket. "Sorry, I'm freezing, I'm looking for my jacket… and socks… well, trousers too."

The next morning we were nicely surprised by breakfast that Mohamed had prepared for us all. "We should get going if we want to catch a bus to Raba." We were supposed to go to Raba but, all of a sudden, they changed their minds not wanting to tell me the reason, just hinting that we won't have a place to stay. "In that case, we should go home." Before we did, we arranged lunch with Ali's sister, Fatima Zahra, a fine person who was doing her last year at university before becoming a doctor. She was twenty-five years old and already married to a man who was working in Spain. She took us to a place frequented by many people who had praised the high quality of food, but to me this restaurant looked and felt like a fast-food place; there was no time for a personal chit-chat as there were people already waiting to be seated. I was very unlucky with my meal too. Because I craved for some cheese, I decided on a meal that was absolutely horrendous: a fried piece of chicken covered with cheese. So ugly and tasteless!

All the guys were waiting for us in Karim's café studying hard for the upcoming exam. A few of them kept me company showing some videos on "You Tube," with an Israeli singer called Sarit Hadad who amazingly played darbuka and "Formidable" (ceci c'est pas une leçon) clip of a young Belgian singer-songwriter called Stromae. There was so much joy and laughter in all of this, so when it was a time to leave we all were struck by sadness and melancholy. Ali and Mohamed were "hashed up," but this time it was Mohamed who wasn't feeling well. "You know you've smoked too much but there is nothing to be done about that now, so just take a deep breath and relax, get the dictionary out and we'll play our game." We were guessing the words by choosing the page and the column and reading out loud a definition; we liked that game. Here, one of us had to guess a word that was described by: "A cultural modification of an individual, group, or people by adapting to or borrowing traits from another culture; also a merging of cultures as a result of prolonged contacts." In French it is called *"acculturation."* It was actually hilarious that we, the living example of that word, had stumbled upon it. "You are changing and I'm changing, we both involving into a funny hybrid, aren't we?" I commented. "I don't know what is happening? I can't breathe," said Mohamed. "Of course you can, just talk to me." There was something happening between us and we both felt it strongly but the hunger for more was subdued by the social and cultural predicament, and we both knew that very well. So we went quiet, pensive and nostalgic, but after a while we started pondering our time in Meknès. "You really brought so much happiness into our gathering; there was never so much joy and laughter." "Call it crazy European nature, but thank you, I'm happy." We looked thought the window and were observing the sky literally stuffed with shining starts and nature that was slowly disappearing into the darkness. One of us said: "Le ciel me manque" and that was it, we were first writing it in our heads, and then quickly putting our thoughts on a piece of paper:

"Le ciel qui me manque"

Quand je suis ivre

et sur la route

je chasse mes doutes

en faisant le dance

pour le ciel qui me manque.

Je couvre mes yeux

je touche les étoiles

qui ôtent le voile

sur tout le noir

pour moi ce soir.

Aujourd'hui je voyage

sans bagage

pour faire le mariage

la terre me soutient

pour aller loin

et me dit "Tiens!"

Bon courage!

Le ciel me parle de soif

et me sert un verre

cher

de pluie qui me libera

"Tu passes trop vite"

me dit le bon temps

et pour te rejoindre

j'emprunte le vent.

Our first poem was not finished as it was a time to get off in Khénifra. However, when we met up with uncle Aziz the next day and asked him to comment on it, he wrote down: "C'est un style entre deux monde, c'est un style qui met en evidence de l'acculturation."

Back at home, there was a family from Casablanca, a sister of Papa Mohamed, Itto, and her nineteen-year-old son Omar who studied in Canada. Omar was complaining about how much he hated Canada, Toronto, and how much he would love to be back home. "People are cold, they don't understand what sharing means and they are racists," he said. He was an extremely kind and happy, but he was doing nothing but complaining. "Do you know how lucky you are?" I asked. "I know, I know, but…" There was always "but". "Do you have friends there or a girlfriend?" he looked at his mum and smiled. "Yes, I have a girlfriend but I won't stay with her, I want a Moroccan girlfriend." "Does she know that?" "No, I can't really leave her now, she is in love with me, so I don't want to hurt her." "When are you going to tell her?" "After my studies, when I come back home." I expressed what I felt but it didn't change anything. In his mind, he was right. His mum was listening but did not comment much. The conversation between me and her felt a little bit uneasy, perhaps this was all down to the linguistics and the way she used English as there was a disharmony between what she wanted to find out and the way she was expressing it. However, I agreed with her on one major subject: "I don't like when Muslims mix religion with no religion. If you believe in Islam you should follow Islam, there is no other way, either you live Islam or leave Islam. You cannot chose which part of Islam you are going to follow and which not," she made that clear.

******

In the morning I went to the *hammam* and straight after that to "Omega" café for my Arabic lesson. This time I had to focus my attention on the Arabic alphabet and the countless combinations of each letter and its sound, and how would that change the primary letter. For example: written (ba) as an isolated letter looks like that: ب   However, its shape would depend on a contextual form, where is actually positioned; the initial letter would like that: ب the medial would present something like this :ب   and the final letter would look like that: ب   It does look logical and is possible to master it. However, with ba comes bu, bi, baa, buu, bii, ben, bun, bin and be, and as one can imagine those symbols, they don't resemble ba at all. The most tricky part comes when the twenty-eight letters of the alphabet have to be written down the same way like ca, cu, ci, or da, du, di and they all have to make sense, meaning to create something that is called a word. Here is my name, Magdalena:ماغدالينا   and here is the isolated "mim" M:م and "alif" A: ا; when "mim" and "alif" are joined together they give a symbol which looks like that: ما. It is an extremely fascinating process to watch and to be able to understand. However, it is not easy by all means, it requires effort and time.

"How do I express the future tense?" "Mostly we use present tense or we adding *"sa"* or *"sawfa."* In order to express a future action, one has to put the verb in the present tense and then use the prefix *"sa"* or *"sawfa,"* for example, a verb *"yalaab"* which means "play," adding *"sa"* or *"sawfa"* will create a future tense: *"syalalba"* - "will play," he asks - *"ħwa yasaal"* will become *"ħwa syasaal"* or *"ħwa sawfa yasaal."*

I wondered if the lack of a future tense had something to do with their "living in the present moment" attitude. Could it be possible that the lack of it influenced people's existence, in a sense that they did seem to live day by day without any constructive plan for the future and with a total acceptance of the present moment? Or perhaps the "living in the present moment" attitude, which I had observed, had nothing to do with securing the future moment, and depended totally on economic or social status? I was much surprised by the findings that I had come across that actually proved my way of thinking to be wrong. In 2013, the economist Keith Chen released a working paper suggesting that "speakers of languages without strong future tenses tended to be more responsible about planning for the future."

This fascinating subject and its findings were discussed in this article:

"Chen wondered whether languages with weak future tenses would be more thoughtful about the future because they consider it, grammatically, equivalent to the present. He mapped stronger and weak future-tense languages across Europe and correlated the data with future-oriented behaviours like saving, smoking, and using condoms. Remarkably, he discovered that speakers with weak future tenses (e.g. German, Finnish and Estonian) were 30 per cent more likely to save money, 24 per cent more likely to avoid smoking, 29 per cent more likely to exercise regularly, and 13 per cent less likely to be obese, than speakers of languages with strong future tenses, like English. He found the same results: Speakers with weak future tenses demonstrated dramatically, and statistically significantly, more responsible future-oriented behaviours even within countries like Switzerland, which are a motley blend of strong-future languages (like French) and weak-future languages (like German). "One important issue in interpreting these results is the possibility that language is not causing but rather reflecting deeper differences that drive savings behaviour," Chen concluded. Languages map to large groups of people, but so does religion, culture, family values, and a common history. Are Germans frugal because their language protects them from hyperbolic discounting, or is it just that, well, they're Germans?"

However, not only in my opinion, but in the opinion of many readers, the English language, should be classified as one of the languages with weak future tenses as what the "will" expresses in English is exactly what *"sa"* or *"sawfa"* in Arabic articulates. I was not convinced by the findings expecting firstly, to come across a study of countries that speak Arabic and secondly, believing to find a link between religion and language so to confirm or reject the belief of ever-existing fatalism in their culture expressed through language.

In the evening we met again in a café where we were joined by uncle Aziz who invited us over to his place in order to discuss an essay; it was a part of his preparation for an exam. We sat comfortably on a sofa, wrapped up in blankets and read out loud line by line a rather difficult essay in French written by *Lutz Raphael*. The social and cultural aspect of migration brought up to the surface "the double absence" and "the double presence" that we both were familiar with and could easily identify the product of it in our own lives, for example, the young generation, or perhaps the wide spectrum of individuals who were making a clear double presence in this country by acting verbally as Muslims, but performing more as Westerners. A very good example was demonstrated by a Muslim who lived in England, and had his little alcohol licenced shop but refused to sell alcohol to his Muslim brothers.

However stimulating the article was and what discussions it led us to, the linguistics aspect of it drained our energy. The plate of chicken tagine regenerated our batteries until it was time to go home. Uncle Aziz walked us through a dodgy part of this neighbourhood. Although walking along the main road felt safer, a few men who walked behind us gave me a panic attack. "What is going on? This is not the first time that you look behind and panic." "There is something from the past that haunts me." "You must tell me." "I was attacked once and was badly beaten up…." I couldn't tell him the whole story of a black bag, a ditch, rape, and my head that did not resemble a head afterwards. "I'm a little bit sensitive, that's all; don't worry, I know you'll protect me."

******

Mme Saida Mohamadi from The Human Rights Organization requested a formal document signed by Malika or her father in order to commence the investigation. On this specific document that we wrote, she requested the word "two" (duex) to be substituted by "few" (plusieurs), so instead of "I was abused by two men" which was clearly said and recorded in the previous interview, we supposed to write down: "I was abused by a few men."

I could not agree with her statement so in order to clarify this ambiguity, Mohamed and I paid another visit to the family of Azziz. I was a little bit apprehensive knowing that her father expressed his strong opinions on that matter and forbade Malika to come to the Association for the second interview which was supposed to take place yesterday. He said he didn't want a scandal in the village adding that the baby that was due in May was to be given away. They clearly couldn't understand the fact that it was not about getting rid of the baby, but to protect her daughter from reoccurring sexual abuses.

We went off to her place and were greeted warmly by her mum as her father was not present and Malika kept her distance sitting on a rock further away and was observing us. My suspicions as to how they perceived the case were confirmed in a dialogue with her mum. "We have already spoken to a nurse in the village about the birth control." "It's not only about that, we don't want to create any scandal but to protect your child in the future, do you understand?" We called Malika to come closer in order to confirm her previous statement. Here was the puzzle: while we were discussing the abuser in front of her mum she was referring to the same man with whom she had Meryam and the unborn baby. However, when her mum was asked to step aside, Malika suddenly changed her story referring to two abusers: Jamal and Abrachim and confirming two different fathers.

Perhaps, she was intimidated by her parents? Perhaps it would be better to take her to Khénifra, interview her in a presence of Saida and ask her to fingerprint the document there as without hers or her parents' signature we could not start the formal investigation. She then suddenly walked away and demanded 5DH from us just to come closer. When her mum had agreed on signing the document and giving her identity card, Malika shouted: "I'll tell everything to dad." "Are you sure you want to sign the document?" I asked. She confirmed. "In that case, we will come back tomorrow to take you with us to the office in El Borj." *"Inchallah,"* she said.

******

Notes:

1 (p. 99) "Noam Chomsky on the callous system of student debt and the structure of the "free market,'" Breakwater review, issue 10, 3013.

2 (p. 107) Saida, in Darija, happiness.

3 (p. 108) "Commentary are Arabs fatalists?" Nivien Saleh, University of St. Thomas, Houston, 2008, p.1.

4 (p. 108) Al-Hadid 57:22-23.

5 (p. 108) "Muslim Fatalism and its Consequences." 30-Days Muslim Prayer Focus, 2007.

6 (p. 109) As-Shura 42:30.

7 (p. 109) Al-Insan 76:3.

8 (p. 109) "Is Islam Religion of Fatalism?" Shahul Hameed in Islam Awarness.

9 (p. 113) "Letters on life", Rainer Maria Rilke, The Modern Library, 2006, p.163.

10 (p. 115) Stendhal "Le rouge et le Noir. Chronique du XIX siècle", 1990, p. 558 (This good priest talked to us about God. But what God? Not the one that comes from the Bible, the little cruel despot thirsty of the vengeance but the God of Voltaire, good, infinite).

11 (p. 115) Op. cit., p. 542 (If I find God of Christians, I'm lost: it's a despot, and, as such, He is filled with ideas of revenge. His Bible only speaks of atrocious punishments. I have never loved him; I have never wanted to believe that we are loved by Him sincerely. He is without mercy (he recalled several passages from the Bible). He will punish me in

an abominable manner... But when I found the God of Fenelon, he perhaps will tell me: you will be forgiven a lot because you are loved a lot).

12 (p. 116) Baraka has many meanings in Morocco, but it is principally the positive power of the saints. It is a source of inspiration among most Moroccan artisans. Baraka permeates all things to varying degrees; not only can it exist in jewellery, talismans and other manufactured objects, such as ceramics and textiles, it is also thought to suffuse plants, such as henna and oleander, and incenses, such as sandalwood and myrrh. This power is transferred to objects and textiles by the use of a particular artistic vocabulary of symbols, designs, motifs, colours and techniques that protect the object, creator and consumer. Baraka is sought and used to deal with the darker forces of life, curing illnesses and protecting oneself against the evil jnoun (spirits-the source of the English word "genie") and the evil eye. (The Culture of Arts of Morocco and the Berbers. The spiritual dimension in Berber design, p19).

13 (p. 119) Dayet Aoua lake is situated in the Middle Atlas in Morocco at 1460m altitude. The lake is surrounded by a massive oaks' forest and Cedrus Atlantica. Just look it up on "You Tube" or simply go there.

14 (p. 119) Wyih! It's an expression of "yes" in Amazigh but more joyful than "wakha"; it could simply be translated into "yeey!"

15 (p. 119) "Letter on life," Rainer Maria Rilke, the Modern Library New York, 2006, p. 23.

16 (p. 119) Cheb Khaled "C'est la vie."

17 (p. 119) Azrou, situated 89km from Fès in the region of Meknès-Tafilalet. Azrou, in Amazigh, means "rock, stone."

18 (p. 119) Ifrane - established by the French during the protectorate era, Ifrane is a town and a ski resort in the Middle Atlas. If one comes to Morocco to experience its authenticity, Ifrane should be at the bottom of "most wanted to be seen" places.

19 (p. 122) Mochkila, in Darija, problem.

20 (p. 123) 4 Reasons Why Muslims Shouldn't Celebrate New Year's, Muhammad Wajid Akhter, December 28, 2012 in Featured, Integration and Interactions, Islam Society.

21 (p. 123) The Islamic year consists of twelve, purely lunar, months. They are: Muharram, Safar, Rabi'ul Awwal, Rabi'uth Thani, Jumada al-Awwal, Jumada ath-Thani, Rajab, Sha'ban, Ramadhan, Shawwal, Thul Qi'dah, and THUL HIJJAH. Some of the most important dates in the Islamic year are: 1 Muharram (Islamic New Year); 1 Ramadhan (first day of fasting); 1 Shawwal (Eidul Fitr); 8-10 Thul Hijjah (the Hajj to Makkah); and 10 Thul Hijjah (Eidul Adh-ha). (From Islamic Calendar, History and Motivation, Waleed Muhanna, www.alinaam.org.za).

22 (p. 123) Sahaab Umar, belonged to the Umar family, a relative of Umar ibn al-Khattab, who was a companion of the Islamic prophet Muhammad.

23 (p. 123) Islamic Calendar - History and Motivation, Waleed Muhanna, www.alinaam.org.za.

24 (p. 123) 4 Reasons Why Muslims Shouldn't Celebrate New Year's, Muhammad Wajid Akhter, December 28, 2012 in Featured, Integration and Interactions, Islam Society.

25 (p. 123) Cheb Khaled – Laila Feat Marwan.

26 (p. 125) Despite his extreme brutality, Moulay Ismail is highly revered by Moroccans themselves so much that his mausoleum is ranked as an Islamic sight. Although only parts of it are open to non-Muslims, it is the only one in

Morocco that accepts this category of visitors. The parts that anyone can enter are fortunately highly rewarding aesthetically, the three brightly decorated courts, a mosque, and the tombs of the sultan. However, his family ethics may be a different issue although helped by the passing of time; thousands of people died at the brutal hand of the regime of Moulay Ismail simply for being non-Muslims. Being a shrine, local women frequent the place seeking divine blessings, Baraka, by touching predefined spots.

27 (p. 125) "Magical Meknes, my trip-journey.com."

28 (p. 125) Source: http://www.discoverislamicart.org.

29 (p. 128) An encyclopaedia Britannica, Merriam Webster.

30 (p. 128) "The sky that I miss." When I'm drunk/ and on the road/ I cast my doubts/doing the dance/ for heaven I lack. I cover my eyes/I touch the stars /which remove the veil/ all black/ for me tonight. Today I travel /without baggage /for marriage/earth supports me /to go far /and said "Hey!" /Good luck! The sky tells me thirsty /and serves me a glass /expensive /of rain that liberates me/"You go too fast"/said the good time /and to join you /I borrow the wind.

31 (p. 131) "Can Your Language Influence Your Spending, Eating, and Smoking Habits?" An absurd-sounding claim leads to a surprising finding, 2013.

32 (p. 131) "La théorie du Champ social et le migratoire by Lutz Rapahel, in "La migration méditerranéenne en Europe occidentale après 1945," volume 7, 2008.

End of Part Four

On the way to Azlal with grandma Rkia and Meryam.

Part Five

"Inchallah" could mean either she would change her mind or she would still be willing to help us. We trekked up that rough path to get to the top and found her standing outside the house waving at us. "Does it mean you are coming with us?" She was. This was a good start. She was certainly sensible enough to chase away all the speculations over a scandal, which they were so afraid of, and had her daughter's well-being in mind. Itto really liked us. In spite of all her struggles with pronouncing my name, she felt comfortable enough to keep asking questions about my life in Europe. At a certain point, she was convinced that my rucksack was filled with money. "What did she say?" I asked Mohamed to translate. "That you must have a lot of money in your backpack." "What is she saying now?" "She is complementing you a lot; she said she liked you scarf and your hair." "My hair? What is so nice about my hair?" Itto explained that every single woman from where I come from had a very strange yellow hair and that she didn't like it. "Yes, some people's hair is too yellow."

While descending, we spotted someone on a mule approaching us. "That's my husband," she said. Having heard his previous strong negative reaction to what we were trying to do, I was bracing myself for a nasty welcome, a spat of harmful opinions, and an invalid burden of words, a Berber curse in French translation of "mind your own business." Here however, a tiny man on a mule stopped to salute us warmly, articulating nothing but *chokrane* that was echoed from a distance when he disappeared behind the hill. I wondered what made him change his mind, and also why his daughter, who had both her parents support, had refused to co-operate with us? Perhaps she was lying and wasn't as innocent as we thought she was? Perhaps there was a question of swindling money from another person? I was pondering all sorts of possibilities; nevertheless I was convinced that we were doing the right thing; whether she was lying or not, she desperately needed some help. In the local office, oddly enough, they did not require a fingerprint but a simple mark; apparently it was sufficient as the document was also signed by the officials. I recall one particular moment from that office when a civil servant had greeted us with a cup of tea. It was a nice gesture, however with that nice gesture came a pretty revolting insolence; while she was serving tea for us, Itto, who stood next to us, was simply ignored; she was denied a cup of tea based on what, I wondered? Was she too poor or too stupid, or didn't they serve tea to illiterates? Whatever the reason was, certainly, in her mind's eye, she did not deserve a drink, and her grinding teeth, when she saw me giving Itto my cup, were confirming her rude attitude. It's curious how each of us had developed remarkably different level of sensitivity to minuscule gestures like serving someone poor tea and by pure and simple ignorance was making a clear social division.

I promised Itto to come back to see little Meryam and inform her of any development in her daughter's case. We then went to Saida's office to deliver the signed document. She took it, assured us to give it to the president and to schedule a meeting with other members as soon as possible. "Madam or Mademoiselle?" she asked me." "Still Mademoiselle," I responded. She took her handbag searching for something frantically and then placed a photograph in front of me. "Here is my son. I want you to marry him, ça ye? Il est bon garçon, no?" I looked at Mohamed, he looked at me, and we both looked at Mme Saida with disbelief, slight perplexity, lost for words, uncomfortable. If only she was joking! But this woman had serious intentions to get her son, not older than nineteen years old, to marry me. In that moment I questioned her professionalism, in fact we both did, and when we left the office, still a little bit shocked, we had to cool ourselves with coffee. "Is this normal?" I asked Mohamed. "I never came across anything like this. This is weird." "Do you think people in Morocco believe in love?"

I don't remember his response but I have a vivid memory of what was said next, over coffee. "I don't want you to go back to Europe." "The Europe subject" was haunting us both and often frequented our discussions, it was accompanying us to the medina, drinking coffees and teas with us and was sulking itself into the ocean of questions commenced by what, where, when, how, and why. To escape the "Europe" subject we were developing in our heads an alternative plan, a business plan that could work here, in Morocco. "I'd like people from Europe to experience what I've been experiencing, to give them a chance to see how the real people live and to support them through that income. What do you think?" "How do we do that?" "Good-working website, good competitive prices, offering more for less; this could work; the only question is how to get the money to set it up?" We scribbled our ideas on a piece of paper. It wouldn't be about taking tourists to the Sahara Desert or Marrakesh but to engage people into learning about such a different world by experiencing it through a simple exchange of thoughts, intellectual stimulus supported by some form of adventure. Renting out a house, making it beautiful, so we could not only accommodate our guests, but also organise some cultural events, for example, poetry evenings, intellectual deliberations, some sort of mental exercises to understand each other more, to bring us closer together, to diminish the culture clash, to stop the sweeping generalizations that we all tend to make.

There are many Moroccans that see Westerners as a visa, as a simple way to escape from their own misery. No matter how much it had irritated me, I very much sympathised with them and understood the origins as in a simple struggle for existence one would be prepared to do almost anything. Why did I hear young people saying that they would be willing to pay for a marriage just to escape their country? Why do young women take into account three essential elements when considering marrying someone: job, appearance and lack of addictions? Perhaps it's easier to fall in love with someone who could provide, give them adorable-looking children, and be mentally stable. Or perhaps, it was all down to the survival. In that sense, I empathised with women who needed to make this life-time decision on a partner. Two examples from my family: Mustapha and Meryam. Mustapha had no chance for a marriage: with his addiction to alcohol and cigarettes, and no money, he was too much of a risk to take, and he was aware of that. Meryam had given up school when she was fifteen years old in order to look after *Baba*. It has been ten years since she completely devoted herself to the family, and each marriage proposal was refused, partly down to her own choice but also *Baba's* who had not agreed on any of the suitors. She was a beautiful, strong, family oriented woman, and no matter what had happened between me and her, I could say that her moral standards and devotion to her own family were impeccable. She was a tough hard-working character and deserved someone good. At a certain point I gave her a business card of one of those charming characters that had approached me on the street. "Send him a message, he is wealthy and good-looking." She did send him a message but I never found out how the story developed, or if the story developed. It took me long time to understand how vital it was for them to secure their future, how to make their existence better and put the issue of love in a shadow. I'd like to see her own family and to know that they manage. In the meantime, I kept accepting numbers and business cards thinking about her; nonetheless, I also knew she would survive as she was a strong organism in the whole natural process of selection. She would make someone a happy man, if only she could find the right type with similar set of moral and religious values. I could not only talk about her moral criteria but also her practical skills, like cooking, as she was a good cook. That late afternoon when I came back home, she had prepared some *boucheyar*. I think it is about time that I share the recipe:

Boucheyar/Mssemen/Msemmen

400 g flour

100 g fine semolina

1 tbs salt

½ tbs yeast

5 g melted butter and some olive oil.

Take the flour, semolina, salt, yeast, a glass of water and make the dough. Cover the whole dough with the melted butter and oil mixture, and then divide it into small balls. While flatting the pancake, use more of the mixture of butter and oil and make the pancake as thin as possible. Sprinkle the very thin pancake with a tiny bit of semolina; this will keep the layers separated. Then fold the pancake to make a square.

Do the same with the second ball of *boucheyar* making it as thin as possible and then put the first folded pancake in the middle of the second one and form another square. Then once again make the whole folded pancake flat by using your fingers. Place the *boucheyar* in the pan and fry it turning over several times until golden and brown and make sure that the centre is cooked. It takes three to four minutes for both sides.

Then grab the fried pancake and squash it in your hands so the layers will becoming more separated. Serve with honey or jam. Bon appetite!

******

"He who knows nothing, loves nothing. He who can do nothing understands nothing. He who understands nothing is worthless. But he who understands also loves, notices, sees …. The more knowledge is inherent in a thing, the greater the love…. Anyone who imagines that all fruits ripen at the same time as the strawberries knows nothing about grapes."

Ah, love and marriage! Does it really go like horse and carriage? What make one work and another fail? Is there any antidote to a happy ending? I don't know; I'm not married. However, here and there I mentioned love, a subject that puzzles me, and a feeling that rips me apart when it gets me. A nagging desire, an overpowering impulse, a sheer excitement that turns into a compulsion, a need, a want, a must, and a question: what should be done? How to approach it? How to act on it? Is it only a biological urge or more mystical phenomena? How to control the sexual drive? How not to lose oneself in case of a failure? Is it possible though? What entices us to love one type and to be repulsed about another? Is it better to resist, and if so how?

"He himself was surprised. He had acted against his principles. Ten years earlier, when he had divorced his wife, he celebrated the event the way others celebrate a marriage. He understood he was not born to live side by side with any woman and could be fully himself only as a bachelor. He tried to design his life in such way that no woman could move in with a suitcase. That was why he had only one bed. Even though it was wide enough, Tomas would tell his mistress that he was unable to fall asleep with anyone next to him, and drive them home after midnight. And so it was not the flu that kept him from sleeping with Tereza on her first visit. The first night he had slept in his armchair, and the rest of that week he drove each night to the hospital, where he had a cot in his office. But this time he fell asleep by her side. When he woke up the next morning, he found Tereza, who was still asleep, holding his hand. Could they have been hand in hand all night? It was hard to believe."

The feeling of love possesses us all; remarkably, it functions as an eraser; it wipes off scrupulously written down past agonies, anguish, unbearable suffering, overreactions, indecent acts, accusations, and engraves the Love Tabula Rasa with newly-embellished forms of agony and suffering, milder, but still destructive acts of indecencies and accusations, torment that would keep you awake and despair that would lull you back into a sleep, into what was before, the beginning, the stage that was ignited by irrepressible desire, burning sexual necessity that had welded two-in-love beings into one screaming hedonistic ecstasy; the juice, the wetness, the act of possession, two human beings with entangled bodies that were desperate to become one and create one; dehydrated, exhausted, malnourished as the only nourishment they would get would be the juice produced by their own bodies passed from mouth to mouth, from touch to touch, from smell to smell. The fluid, which fed the ecstasy, was already flavoured with torment, an eternal and reoccurring torture to the souls and the bodies, but aroused by curiosity of discovered pleasure it was drowning, with all senses, in one bouquet of strongly scented roses with petals that caressed until made you soul cry with pleasure; you felt as if you couldn't stand more but you wanted more, you couldn't resist the touch, the feel, and the smell, and the look; you wanted to be penetrated by that smell, that gaze, and that touch, and those lips. The body permeated by the smell, the gaze and the touch would turn the soft cushion of the petals into a spiky bed of torture and the more pleasure you would gain, the more suffering your soul would have to endure; you were in paradise then but with one leg already in hell, and there was no exit, not even emergency doors. "You are stuck, my friend," you heard the destiny laughing out loud at you. You felt the bliss in that moment but you knew that the pain would come, not now, not tomorrow, in the future, in the solitude of two forms joined together who would live separate lives, and yet be desperate to be reunited. *"God Dammit!! I miss you….you are terribly missing. Come back."*

If we stripped love of its emotions, passions, desires, ridiculous acts of jealousy, what would we become? Is something out there like mature love that could be applied to any age, any conditions, between people of any ethnic groups on any continents? And if so, how to sustain passions, emotions, and desires? Would we still be the same fanatical creatures that burn, penetrate, and please? Do we predict a fiasco though, and do we know when we fail?

"Assume man as man, and his relationship to the world as a human one; you can exchange love only for love, confidence for confidence, etc. If you wish to enjoy art, you must be an artistically trained person, if you wish to have influence over people, you must be a person who has a really stimulating and furthering influence on other people. Every one of your relationships to man and to nature must be a definite expression of your real, individual life corresponding to the object of your will. If you love without calling forth love, that is, if your love as such does not produce love, if by means of an expression of life as a loving person you do not make of yourself a loved person, then your love is impotent, a misfortune."

To one philosopher: "Love is a decision, it is a judgment, it is a promise. If love were only a feeling, there would be no basis for the promise to love each other forever. A feeling comes and it may go. How can I judge that it will stay forever, when my act does not involve judgment and decision?" Another one sheds love off its romance and treats it more like a profession that one must to study.

"To take love seriously, to endure it, and to learn it the way one learns a profession – that is what young people need to do. People have misunderstood the role of love in life like so much else. They have turned love into a game and pleasant distraction because they thought that games and distractions are more blissful than work; but nothing is filled with greater joy and happiness than work, and love, exactly because it is the most extreme joy and happiness, can be nothing but work. A person in love thus has to try to behave as if he had to accomplish a major task: he has to spend a lot of time alone, reflect and think, collect himself and hold on to himself; he has to work; he has to become something!"

Once we made that decision, I suppose the horse would be ready to move the carriage, but... what if the horse or the carriage would not fit together, meaning such decision was forced upon someone? What if one didn't have a choice? It is exactly what has been happening in Morocco, and although the Moroccan society has been changing, the tradition and religion has still been a dominant factor, which excluded any romantic involvement before the marriage. Such rule was set and passed from one generation to another and has been regarded normal.

However, for the ordinary Westerner who had visited the country and fallen in love with it, such imperative might be difficult to comprehend. Knowing how easily it was to lose oneself in its beauty, disregarding poverty and suffering, this country with its attractive people has been regarded as highly romantic, it was difficult not to fall in love either in the country or a man or both, but to lose one's heart here meant to suffer or to take a risk. The question is what are the odds of a successful and happy marriage between two-in-love beings that have portrayed a different set of values throughout the whole moral, emotional and spiritual spectrum?

It's curious how easily one can stumble upon numerous websites entitled: "Should I marry a Moroccan?" or "Love stories or tragedies from Morocco." How many times did I hear: "Do not marry a Moroccan," and wondered why? What about Germans, English, Poles, Americans, Italians? Why all those romantic stories that might be equally tragic are not considered as catastrophic as Moroccan-European coupling? Well, the Westerners tend to be a bit more apprehensive and there are reasons for it; here for example, a Moroccan man presented his point of view, a little bit exaggerated in my opinion, on marrying a Moroccan:

"Before you marry a Moroccan you need to know few things: first of all you have no rights to say how to run home or family; you have to give up your job to look after home and your husband; you have to learn Moroccan and respect his culture and family values; you won't smoke or drink alcohol in front of your in-laws; you have to give up your friends, partying, going out to night clubs, staying up late, drinking with your friends as your husband is your priority; he comes even before your children! You will have no control over your money, even if you work (with his permission), you have to give him your wages and you'll have convert to Islam otherwise it will be hard for him to introduce you to his family and be accepted, and they will marry him to a seventeen-year-old virgin Moroccan Muslim and you can't do nothing about it as we have the rights to marry four women if we can afford."

His point of view is a little bit radical, but unfortunately very much accurate; it obviously depends on a man and his family, but even fellow Moroccans judge harshly their Moroccan brothers pointing their conservatism, strong religious beliefs that lead to overprotectiveness of their

134

culture, blaming narrow-mindedness for it. "As a Moroccan man I would like to say that Moroccan men are very different from each other, but it's a bit true that the majority of them are still conservative and more protective of their culture, especially if they are religious, but some, unfortunately very few, are very open to other cultures. For example, with friends and family pressure I had married this young Moroccan virgin in an arranged marriage, and while I was back in London trying to get all papers ready to bring her to this country, I met a woman from Slovakia whom I felt in love with at first sight."

How can anyone be denied such pleasure like love? To fall in or fall out, but always out of free will. The same man continues: "She smokes and drinks but I don't mind that at all, as I like having a drink myself, so I found it even better to share a nice bottle of wine with someone I love rather than finding a friend to go to a pub with." He made a pretty simple statement but this statement would outrage many Muslim families.

Here is another positive outlook on a cultural and emotional criss-cross:

"I'm a Moroccan myself and I have lived in the UK with a European lady whom I felt in love with and got married eight years ago and our marriage is doing fine. My wife is an atheist and it has never bothered me as I'm not into a religion myself. She drinks sometimes and so do I, and I found it very convenient, as we can do almost everything together. Since I have lived in the UK, I have had a problem to make Moroccan friends, as they would start to get involved in my relationship, and criticise my marriage pointing out the fact that we both drink and are not very religious, and because of that we were regarded sinful. Moroccans like the rest differ from person to person, but the majority is tricky and difficult to get on with and very influenced by religion."

Oddly, each happy love story that I read has highlighted strongly the equality and the importance of sharing between a man and a woman, something that is still in the bud in Morocco, and religion that proved to be the pivotal point in any criss-crossed cultural debates. "At the beginning we used to have arguments about religion and history, and some silly discussions like which nation was better, but later on we settled on the fact that we've come from different backgrounds and that surely would have a big influence on our lives. So we agreed to talk more about each matter freely without getting angry or offended. Since then, somehow, we managed to cope and find the happiness in our marriage."

Here I was. An anglophile, nearly thirty-seven-year-old Polish woman, raised in a Catholic family, an adventurous traveller who no longer knew to what part of Europe or to which continent she belonged to, or who she was representing, or what her identity was; a woman of a colourful romantic past, spoiled by her luck, pampered by pleasure, consequent and determined; she knew what she wanted from life. The world of the same woman had slowly been crumpled; her legs were becoming elastic and the gaze - fixed; her organs were slowly devoured by a diminishing distance between her and the object that she wanted to possess, but firstly, it was gulping her thoughts, then her dreams, and then reality. It was as real as tangible, but frustrating, and exhausting. She had to hide it, and her thoughts had to become sane, plain, straight and open to possibilities that should chase away the unplanned, imaginary happy end to her life. However, the obsession to turn the prohibited into a happy incident was occupying her thoughts and was mapping out the odds.

Would anyone describe the blissful feeling of love as a tragedy? If it wasn't mutual then it would certainly be a misfortune. However, I knew I was loved back, and yet I fretted. I was in a wrong country… I knew I would not be able to control myself, as how to control something much bigger than myself? How to conceal it and why? The frustration that this situation was creating was eating us both, we were becoming angrier with each other and with ourselves. That week we hardly talked; the words, if pronounced, would not express the truth, we were trapped in conventions, pacts, law, principles, formulas, theories that were deceptive as were disagreeing with our feelings. We didn't even see each other for two days, which was considered abnormal, as for the past one and a half months, a day would not pass without a salut, a word, a story, some advice or help. The abnormality was causing discomfort and pain; the suffering that was supposed to came later on, entered our lives a little bit too early; I had not even opened the door yet, but this emotional torment managed to squeeze itself through a gap, sneaked in during my absence. "How dare you to come uninvited and destroy the calm, the happiness!" I was yelling.

We met on Friday as good friends, a little bit chattier, but still feeling a great deal of discomfort. We talked about work; the professor had passed a message about the meeting with the Human Rights Organization for the forthcoming Sunday, and Mohamed invited me to his uncle Aziz for dinner tomorrow evening. I accepted the invitation but nothing else was planned for tomorrow; and when tomorrow came we still did not talk much, and during the family gathering at uncle's Aziz we were taciturn avoiding each other's eyes. "What's wrong with you Mohamed?" asked uncle Aziz. "I didn't sleep well," he responded and carried on his meditation. The more women were coming in, the more I felt subdued; it was the first time that I was not interested in any of the stories that were told, in tagine that was shared, in tea that was poured. We left the place quickly making excuses as tomorrow three of us, Mohamed, Khalid - a friend of ours, and I were supposed to get up early and go to a big souk in the centre of Khénifra, the biggest of all in this area, to sell and make some money.

******

I woke up at 6.20am and within twenty minutes was ready to go out when the text message arrived: "Bonjour, est-ce qu'on peut renccnter à 7.30, ok?" What a cruel note that was considering the early hour and the chilling temperature both: in my room and outside.

"Never do that again. Don't you think I wished to have slept a little bit longer too?" It was freezing cold and we both were jumping and rubbing our hands while waiting for Khalid, who was also running late. "Great. You guys do piss me off sometimes." "I had a terrible dream," said Mohamed. "What did you dream about?" "You were pregnant and were leaving me; I was terrified." "Pregnant? What were you terrified of?" "That you were going away." Whatever was unspoken between us was coming out in dreams. "I'm still here, but Khalid is not," I said in jest, "let's go and get him." The morning haze and the stunning rising sun gave us some energy but the unspoken feelings were still keeping us subdued.

I needed to distance myself in order to reflect, but the agony of the unexpressed wasn't allowing me to create that space. Anyhow, my philosophy was always to make things work, first - in my head, then - in the reality, and so far my mere existence functioned well shifting itself between "a brother-chicken" and "an egg-collector." "One man goes to a doctor. Doc, my brother is crazy. He thinks he is a chicken. So, why don't you turn him in? I would but I need an egg."

Khalid was placing bags with clothes into his *brwita* not even giving any apologies for the one hour delete. "Did you sleep well?" I tried to be horrible but he only laughed. The trolley was packed with clothes and we were ready for a half hour walk. The area, where the souk was taking place, was close to the Central Bus Station. To find a good spot to display our merchandise at this time, it was about 9.00am, was a bit tricky. "Some of the merchants had started as early as 6.00am," I was told, so to get a decent, more central spot, required an early start, between 7.00 and 8.00am, at least. Once you found yourself a space, you were charged 4DH, money that was collected by a man who walked around the souk. Having said that, even if the space seemed to have been secured, meaning all the goods were spread around and the place was paid for, you could have been easily kicked out of it by a neighbouring merchant, same as you, who would claim this particular spot as his. He could have turned up at 9.00am and chased you away by using a very simple prerogative: "This spot was always mine." And you had three choices, either you could argue with him and stay were you were, or you could move somewhere else, or you could argue with the one who took your space based on the same claim: "This spot was always mine."

Mohamed decided on staying calm and moving on to the other side "confiscating" someone else's piece of land, who, fortunately, was willing to share it with us. Our merchandise, compared with Khalid's, was minuscule, but still attractive, and when we set it up, placing babies' clothes and shoes, jackets, trousers, tops, pyjamas, belts on the ground we were able to go and search for breakfast – *boucheyar* and tea as coffee could not to be found in any of those souks' cafés. I have to admit that I have never seen a place like this one in my entire life. It could offer everything, from second hand goods to enormous stands with shoes, clothes, window frames, electronics, mattresses, tea pots, tools, metal pieces, cosmetics, buckets, spices, vegetables, fruits, piles of dyed wool, carpets, sacks, animals....everything! The prices varied but here the negotiation skills were very much required. "People instead of looking at my goods, they are looking at you," said Mohamed. This was certainly an advantage and by combining my femininity with cleverness, I was attracting men to our stand. "You like this jacket. Try it on." The two young men might have been interested in this leather jacket and I was pushing them to buy it. The biggest disadvantage was the language as they did not speak French. *"Zwin, zwin,"* I used some well-known Darija words instead and was pushing him even further: "You are a very attractive man with this jacket on." I wasn't lying, he was attractive, but... I did push. The price was 100DH. He wanted to get it for 40DH. *"La, la, la,* a leather jacket for 40DH, that's crazy, a brand-new cost 240DH." He walked away but he knew he would come back. "So how much do you offer now?" "50DH." *"La!* Our last price is 70DH." He walked away again and came back one more time. "I'll take it." Although he accepted 70DH, he gave Mohamed only 60DH. *"La, la, la,* take the money back or give me 10DH more." Sold for 70DH. It was our biggest sell. We managed to trade a few other bits and pieces, including a portable two hob gas oven for 40DH and some tops. Overall, we earned around 150DH and that was considered a good day. Having said that, I was annoyed that the half of the money Mohamed made from selling the items had to be paid back to the people that had supplied him.

In the meantime, I strolled around some of the larger stalls being curious as to what they were selling, when a man, a popular type, started getting on my nerves by walking behind me and repeating *"zwina"* followed by more unintelligible slurs. I stopped. "You are kind but leave me alone." He did not comprehend but backed off a little reading the frustration on my face. I walked around for a bit when out of blue the same man reappeared behind me and once again was trying to make contact with me. Infuriated, I stopped, turned around, and said: "Vaffanculo, cretino!" The well-memorised Italian curse seemed to have worked as he disappeared as quickly as he had appeared. When I went back to our stand, I was sweetly surprised by *chfnj* – the delicious donut rings and tea prepared by Mohamed's mum. As my throat wasn't any better and the dry, painful cough was starting to sound like a jerky old truck, I pondered the idea of becoming unsociable and try some garlic – the natural antibiotic. The old nanny's way of eating raw garlic with bread and solid salted butter seemed to me the perfect antidote to my throbbing lungs, and Mohamed's mum agreed to get me some.

"How much do I owe you?" "Nothing at all." "Out of curiosity, how much does a glove of garlic cost?" "2DH." To be aware of prices given to the locals was vital as the well-observed practice of salesmen emptying the European pockets of their valuable dirhams was very much on the agenda.

Here is some useful information on product prices:

1kg of tomatoes – 4/5DH, 1kg of potatoes – 2/3DH, onions – 3/4DH for the same amount; the price of pumpkins usually eaten with couscous varied between 3 to 10DH per kg; carrots were the cheapest offering with a more or less stable price of 2DH for 1kg. The price of chicken was 14DH for 1 kg, whereas one egg could cost between 0.80 – 1DH. Although there were a great number of mouths to be fed in my family, I was the tenth, we were lucky as most of the time we had meat to share between us.

We packed the unsold items and at around 1.00pm were ready to stroll back home. "Where is your father?" The shopping that his mum was carrying weighed tonnes! "He went home," said Mohamed. "Why didn't he take anything with him?" The fact was that he didn't and instead his mum had to pay a couple of dirhams to a boy with *carozza* to drop everything off at the bus station. "I will see you at 3.00pm," I said and rushed home to get something to eat, *hrira* and tagine at Fadma's, and I dashed back to a café for the scheduled meeting with all the members of the Human Rights Organization.

The café where we were supposed to meet was considered a student's place. With the rooftop space overlooking the mountains and a spacious first floor, the place was attracting the young ones who were still living in Khénifra, organizing special events for them with writers, poets or scientists. Mohamed and I sat down at the rooftop waiting for Saida and the professor. "Listen, we should talk," I said. "I was thinking about that too." "There are some feelings…, and I know what it is but I don't know if it's right or wrong. Perhaps we should just be friends as we are now." I was struggling to express what I really felt being fretted by the possibility of losing a dear friend. Although Saida and the rest were running late, we did not manage to make any sense out of what had been said and the discussion was left open to be continued another time.

It was 4.20pm when Saida came in with her daughter, I breathed with relief that it wasn't her son, considering her delay as normal, adding, "If I had known they were coming late, I would have stayed in the *hammam* longer." "What a nice and honest remark," I thought. Forty minutes later the other members of that group, with its president, turned up ready to tackle the case; out of eight people only two young men expressed the willingness to help us, highlighting how much they were touched and distressed by the reported abuse; however, they were not fully acquainted with the case but promised to listen to the recording. The face of that president looked blind; he had no idea how to deal with this case or any other similar ones. I pondered his position in this organization; perhaps he was well-connected and for that reason was chosen to represent them.

My faith in that group or their competence was slight, but having been given a promise to look into it with all the seriousness it deserved, I had to stay patient and wait for their next move: a promised phone call.

Afterwards I was invited for tea at Mohamed's. "Perhaps we should stop seeing each other," Mohamed started. "What about all our plans to travel and to work together? Is this the end of our friendship?" "It would do us good," he said. "Right. Let's have tea and then go on separate holidays." And then we took tea. "Would you like to go for a walk or shall I go home?" "Before you go home I want to give you something." He took a piece of paper out. "I wrote this last night, I couldn't sleep."

The letter talked about his feelings and dreams. "Pour t'écrire je dois chasser mes doutes or ils ne sont chasses que quand ensemble, toi et moi, nous les chassons." He then referred to "un sentiment singulier" that he felt for me not knowing the nature or the essence of it; he looked for a safe place calling it "le paradis" where we could be happy together, and at the same time making the social and economic pressure very transparent, saying that only through dreams that did not demand any actions or *"flouss"* we could find our happiness. "Nous allons construire cette maison dans la montagne et tu seras forte, nous allons voyager et tu seras forte, nous allons écrire des poèmes et tu seras forte, nous allons imaginer et tu seras forte, nous allons luter et tu seras forte, nous allons renoncer à tout et tu seras forte et nous allons rencontrer notre Dieu et tu seras tellement forte. Le rêve n'exige rien, on peut pratiquer sans *"flouss."*"

I remember the feeling of disappointment, sadness, and relief; I was glad it was spelt out but I wasn't sure what this letter meant. Was it an invitation to start something or to end it?

"Do I see you tomorrow, or are you taking a holiday?" I asked. "See you tomorrow," he said adding, "I received a message from a friend and he invited us both to his place for a weekend." "Can we travel next weekend?" I asked. "I'll ask him. He wants to meet you."

******

This morning the employment contract was signed by Siham and some options, of how to spend £270 that was donated to our Association last month, were discussed. As the children had never been given the opportunity to go on an excursion, it was decided to organise a trip to a place like Aglmam where they could paddle in the water and see some monkeys.

The series of tests that little Meryam had undergone produced a pile of prescriptions and written diagnoses that I was eager to consult with a doctor, ideally a paediatrician, in a local hospital that we both visited that afternoon, around 2.00pm. Walking from unit to unit we finally found a nurse who told us to come back in the morning. "There are no doctors in the afternoon," we heard him saying.

"Would you like to go for a run today?" I asked. "Shall we take advantage of that beautiful afternoon?" After tea in the medina I went home to get changed and ran back to Mohamed's. The lack of physical exertion that I missed wasn't a fault of the controlling society but rather the lack of a shower. Today, however, I was happy to wait for the *hammam* until the next morning.

I met Mohamed in Pisana and from there we ran through wild and empty fields passing only two houses with a few people sitting in front of them. Our legs were taking us to a wilder, more isolated space closer to the mountains. Being surrounded only by the wild, burned-orange fields of Khénifra, we allowed ourselves to become fully immersed in some physical exertion combined with rather childish behaviour. We were so happy playing simple and innocent games like fighting, joking and dancing. We ran to the very far end of that hill, or the very beginning of a new one that was slowly emerging, and came across a man meditating there. All of a sudden, there was a rapid and unexpected change of the air. We looked back and saw the very dark sky swiftly masking the mountains, painting an emerging dark-blue over the burnt-orange and turning the landscape into mad-looking, almost psychotic. In that epidemic scenery the light suddenly darkened and massive drops of rain fell with thunder heard in the far distance. Perhaps it was time for us to go back. As we turned, the sky turned with us giving us the impression of being chased by the gloomy clouds and the lightning. The sky's heavy crying was heard and felt, drop by drop, becoming more and more forceful on our skin. Lightning split the sky and thunder sent a warning. The power of it made me realise one thing: we were in the open space, completely in hands of Mother Nature. I felt vulnerable. "I don't want to die from the lightning," I said, "that would be pathetic." So I grabbed Mohamed's hand and we both ran, like in some sort of action film in which having the wind and heavy rain against us, we were being raced by the sinister clouds and the lightning. "Nooooo, we… don't… want… to… die!" We were hysterical. "Can you imagine if we were hit by the lightning? That would make some headlines." We were soaking wet when we reached the town and there was still a good ten minutes for me to run back home.

Fortunately, the wood-burning stove was working, and after vigorously wringing out my wet clothes, I was able to get cosy and they were able to get dry. My body was weirdly energised and hungry; I was waiting with anticipation for tagine to fill up my rumbling stomach. The goat tagine which we had that evening, was mouth-watering, and Papa and I got a solid bone to gnaw. The meat was eaten and all the possible juices were sucked in. To me, it seemed that there was nothing else left for consumption. I was wrong. Papa took my bone, placed it on a wooden block, then took another one and with the strong and decisive move he managed to get the bone marrow closer to the edge of my bone. I tried to suck it in but it was stuck. Yet again, Papa offered his helping hand: he took the bone and was hitting it repeatedly against that wooden block giving it real whacks until the mass of marrow ended up on that dirty wooden block. He scrapped everything off with his hands and said: *"Koul! Koul!"* I gagged but I ate.

I was observing something extraordinary at home; when my free-spirited being started having an impact on my family, I kept noticing a growing desire within Hakima to travel, for example when I was sharing the exciting news of going away for the weekend, her facial expression became abruptly distorted; she looked dismayed and quickly suggested a trip to Agadir with me. "Perhaps we could visit Raba together." I said. "When my mum feels better," responded Hakima. *"Wakha."* Since our mountaineering escapade Rkia's health had deteriorated a great deal, she was no longer the marching warrior but the inactive and weary-looking conqueror. "When are you going back home?" carried on Hakima. "In April." "Don't go, stay with us, you are one of us, you are Magdalena Naatit now." Her utterance made me emotional. "Magdalena Naatit, *wyih*, no Pologne, restez ici," add Mustapha. "I'll have to go back, but *Ichallah*, I may come back." "No, no, rester, Mustapha veux réaliser panser fin de l'amour avec toi, mais retard." It was his first official declaration of rather tragic, one-sided love for me and I was very much hoping that he was aware of his misfortune. When I was ready for bed, he came to my room expressing more "l'amour for Margarena" telling me how fidèle he would stay. "Margarena – maman – w$y$ih!"

******

"*Sbahlkhir*, are you ready for our little holiday?" "*Wyih!*" he responded. In fact, we both were, so we set off early by taking a bus to Beni Mellal which cost us only 70DH, and a two and a half hours journey. All seats were taken apart from two at the far back, so we squeezed in there. Two adults and a child were sitting next to us; the girl was no older than five years, and due to a lack of seats, she was sitting on a plastic stool. The bus was of no higher quality than the one we took to Ifrane, and as the day progressed and it was getting hotter, we suffered a similar problem to the one we had had on the way to Ifrane: lack of fresh air. Although there was a small rooftop window opened, the supply of fresh air as soon as it had reached us was quickly cut off by an annoying passenger who didn't like the breeze coming in. The smell of that collective odour was unbearable and it might have added to the little girl's problem. "*Mika, mika,*" it was announced by her mum. The bag did not make on time and that poor child vomited all over her mum's hands and her own clothes, and when the plastic bag finally was passed over to her, she was struggling to separate it; then another pair of hands grabbed that covered in vomit bag making it ready for another round. "Oh, yuk! Have some water and use this gel," I squeezed out a significant amount of antibacterial gel hoping it would quickly help to wipe off the memory of this incident. The girl's face looked uneven: one half seemed to have relaxed but the other half was still tortured by the motion sickness which was confirmed by her blurred eyes and fixed, motionless gaze. "I think she hasn't finished yet," and as soon as I articulated it, her ugly symphony of the queasiness was played again, however this time the notes were cushioned inside the bag. The stuffiness, the vomit, no fresh air … history repeated itself. The girl vomited once again, and when her face was cleaned, her mum's hand landed hard on it. "*La! La! La!*" We reacted angrily when she started crying. "That was very cruel," I thought, poor girl, not only was she sick, but also punished for being sick. I observed the whole story with astonishment and disgust and felt relieved when they got off at the next bus stop.

In the meantime the bus was making strange noises, and it felt as if it was leaning slightly more towards the right. "I think we got a flat tire," I said. The next stop did not detect any problem with the bus, but it offered us a short break with possibility of inhaling some fresh air. Having said that, the short stopovers would always make me feel a little bit on edge as all those heroic acts with people jumping inside buses while they are on the move, were never my cup of tea. Anyhow, I could not understand that phenomena: the buses were always running late and the passengers were always forced to jump in while they were in motion, as if that one minute would radically change the one hour delay.

"Please, tell the bus driver to open the rooftop window," I implored. "I have already asked him." We moved another few meters and the bus was at a standstill again: the flat tyre had to be replaced, and while one man was lifting and changing it, others were gathering around and watching him doing it. For us, it felt like a perfect moment to read a little. We took out Maupassant *"Boule de Suif"* and read out loud my favourite chapter called "La chevelure," a beautifully sensual piece of writing; a story about a man who felt in love with a lock of hair that he had found in XVII century Italian piece of furniture bought in Paris. The whole story began with :

"Jusqu'à l'âge de trente-deux ans, je vécus tranquille, sans amour. La vie m'apparaissait très simple, très bonne et très facile. J'étais riche. J'avais du gout pour tant de choses que je ne pouvais éprouver de passion pour rien. C'est bon de vivre. Je me réveillais heureux, chaque jour pour faire des choses qui me plaisaient, et je me couchais satisfait, avec l'espérance paisible du lendemain et de l'avenir sans souci, " and it continued, "Une énorme natte de cheveux blonde, presque roux (...) je demeurai stupéfait, tremblant, troublé (...) Je la pris, doucement, presque religieusement. (...) Qui les avait coupes? Un amant, un jour d'adieu? Un mari, un jour de vengeance? Ou bien celle qui les avait portes sur son front, un jour de désespoir? "

This exciting piece of writing poured over me a great deal of sensual pleasure; I felt a little bit drunk, dizzy, almost aroused, and I started to desire the man next to me. I felt thrilled that he and not anybody else was sitting close to me. Perhaps, one day I would express my feelings for him in a way that this necrophile had described his affection for the lock of hair.

"Ne me regard pas comme ça, " said Mohamed. "Pourquoi?" "Parce que tu me donne ce sensation." "Vraiment?" The gaze was doing something, whether it was causing an internal turmoil, or was steadier creating excitement, the sensation was felt and was gently touching his organs. In normal circumstance it would be the most desirable feeling to share, here however, it was unwanted as not suitable for this country. In the meantime the tyre got fixed and we would count another thirty minutes before reaching Beni Mellal from where we would have to take a taxi to Fkih Ben Salah. We arrived in Beni Mellal hungry and thirsty and the first thing we were looking for was some food.

The unusually steep road that we took, somehow reminded me of Los Angeles; however, spread out all over the pavement second-hand clothes, electronics, shoes, and odds and ends, rang more Moroccan than American bell. And the smell that was coming from a smoky boutique was tempting us to buy a pitta bread sandwich stuffed with some greasy meat that perfectly satisfied my hunger. When we walked down the same steep road back to a taxi stand, Mohamed had surprised me by taking my hand and behaving like my boyfriend. I guessed, it was safe in this part of Morocco as no one knew who we were, no one would question our relationship or the nature of it, whether we were married, engaged, lovers, friends, they should not care much. He confused me but I liked that confusion, and I accepted it. After buying something symbolic for the family of Mehdi, some mandarins and bananas, we got into a taxi that charged us 14DH per person. "This is a European price," stated Mohamed. We shared the first seat and were joined together by his arm that was put around me. It felt good, natural, and normal.

After about thirty minutes we arrived in *Fkih Ben Salah*, the Arab town, modern-looking, busy, the first impression – not very attractive. His friend, tall, handsome, with beard, dark hair, a beaming smile, who was wearing nothing but black, came to pick us up. He read English at university hence we were able to communicate in English. He took us to his home, where his mum and sister were waiting for us with a very late lunch. That modern house with all its commodities felt more like home to me than any other house that I had so far been to. It was a place of middle class well-off Arabs, inhabited by two generations: our friend Mehdi, his sister and parents, each occupied their own floor space. Every single room was equipped with sofas and proper tables and the same was applied to the fully furnished kitchen with a table, cooker, and a big fridge giving a real homely feeling. His sister Samira was practising law and his father was a lawyer in the local Court of Justice. Although the family was rather cheerful, welcoming and was sending a positive energy, their faces looked troubled, sad, and old.

The meal that they had prepared for us confirmed their generous nature; it was *lahmiss*, a massive plate of lentils mixed up with pieces of *lamsamen* soaked in a creamy sauce. Exquisite. They were curious as to whom I was, what I was doing here, and what my life was like back in Europe, expressing at the same time their sympathy for my situation: far away from home and with a job that didn't pay a penny. His mum felt like an angel to me; a beautiful woman who emanated calm energy, the energy that might have been a combination of her natural grace and men's oppression as no matter how loveable her character was it felt strongly tinged with obedience, submission, and the duty to be a good wife and the mother.

The area between the Middle and the High Atlas Mountains was called the Tadla – Azilal plateau or the Central High Atlas with *Beni Mellal* as its capital. The province, Fkih Ben Salah, situated two hundred kilometres from Casablanca has been a home to the regional office for the promotion of agriculture since the 1940s. The city wasn't the type I liked; it neither felt old nor modern, so after a short walk around the centre we happily sat down in a café. Mehdi was a particular individual, a typical twenty-something student with a very serious broken heart problem. This particular story called Sarah started few years back and no matter how many times they broke up and restarted it, it had never seen a happy end. He seemed to have suffered, but his suffering was a mixture of self-inflicted anguish and hedonism, a plot of happy coincidences which names and numbers I quickly lost count of, approximately three or four at that time, and from different parts of Morocco, one was from Raba, the other one was from Casablanca, the third one, could have been from Agadir, I don't remember, but what I do recall is the countless phone calls, the hours he had spent on responding to their calls, and the unceasing messages in between them. "Let me guess, Casablanca?" "Good guess," he responded laughing. "Which one do you love?" "I don't know, probably neither of them." Those unfortunate young girls were certainly attracted by his charm, his welfare and a promising future job after university, and who could have blamed them for trying? Mehdi took us to his secret place called Laveta. I never asked, but I believed it was a name of a district, where his past tragic love affair, Sarah, had lived and where they used to meet. I expected to see something more romantic than just buildings, at least a fountain or a café, or a secret place that was only known for them. Here, however, was just another zone, another area of Fkih Ben Salah where his romantic past was bottle up and buried, and no one but him would ever understand its significance. I was convinced, at a certain point, that his self-inflicted sorrow served its purpose: an escape from his luxurious easy life, a narrative that could embellish his existence, as firstly, he was making everything up in his head as romantic as possible, and then, in reality, he was acting more as a destructor trying to turn the whole story upside down making this poor girl suffer.

The dusk reminded us of soon closing shops hence we rushed to buy a hugely desired bottle of wine; but after a short walk Mehdi realised that the shops had closed early due to a celebration - the prophet Muhammad's birthday.

We were then introduced to a drug dealer, a Moroccan man who spent some years in Italy and who joined us for coffee, in a safe place where they could do the transaction. As the standard set of questions was asked and the conversation wasn't flowing, I proposed to change the place for somewhere more sheltered, warmer, more amiable, more normal. And the change of place occurred but it was swapped for somewhere even more bizarre: an open-up space that offered pool billiards and more young men who were either playing pool or watching others doing it. While we were waiting for something else, a young man of quite unusual eyes was keeping us company, rolling something and putting under his upper lip. "Goodness me, what is he doing that for? What drugs does he use?" I was told that he was using some tobacco powder, I presumed, it was *nafha*; firstly, he was placing some amount on a leaf and then twisting it until it had a proper form of a ball to put under his upper lip "to get higher" much quicker, as that particular part was more supplied with blood. He looked absolutely comical with his puffed up upper lip sticking out quite prominently. Surprisingly, such particular use of *nafha* has a name and it's called *kala*. Apparently, the 'kala' guy was also asked to deliver some L'eau de Vie to Mehdi's house, the alcohol that had almost killed Ali.

In the meantime two other characters had joined us, whom I believed were not only drug dealers. When I looked at them the sheer chill ran down my spine; the way they walked, with their hands and legs separated from their bodies, some sort of Moroccan cowboys, the way they introduced themselves and observed us was indicating a very dangerous type, stripped of any human feelings, guys who looked as vicious as brainless, the type of people that would perhaps be involved in a gang and would not hesitate to shoot. I knew this type very well as where I grew up, their presence had strongly been felt, seen, and marked by their horrendous acts. "I want to know who those guys are." I asked Mehdi. "I don't really know them but don't worry," his vague response and whispering did not make me feel at ease. "Listen, I don't like those guys, I don't want to spend the evening in their company and you should stay away from them," I said. "They will walk with us for a while and then we will go separate ways," he reassured me.

Here was my evening with Mohamed and Mehdi, his mafia acquaintances, and the drug dealer. Brilliant. Mohamed and I outran them and as we did not pay attention to how fast we walked, we lost sight of them and had to turn back. The drug dealer was the first one we spotted. "Do you want to try some snails?" he beaconed us first and then ordered a small cup for each of us. The outside portable *carozza* with two enormous pans of snails and broth was surrounded by quite a gathering of young men. The small cup of snails with two cups of spicy comforting broth was delicious.

Although it was around 9.00pm, there was not a single woman on the street. The women's absence, or the heavy presence of men, gave me the feeling of social injustice, it was unnatural, it did not correspond with a picture what the world should look like. They were too oppressed, too controlled, and treated, with some exceptions, as domestic slaves, some kind of *"Stepford wives."* "I heard that Moroccan men don't like to be married to clever women. Is that true?" "Sadly, yes, it is the truth. They feel threatened by educated women," said Mohamed. "Is it because they wouldn't be able to control them?" "Yes, they like simple women," he continued. "What about Moroccan's intellectuals? Do they also feel threatened by them?" "Even they have problems with accepting women with good working brains." "The compatibility here is a bit off, don't you think? And the men sound like chauvinists to me."

In the central part of Fkih Ben Salah we were introduced to Mehdi's friend, the owner of a grocery store who treated us to some fruits; and while Mehdi and I kept talking in English, his friend astonished me with his comment that was translated from Arabic as: "This is the first time that I hear something like this, usually I see two people speaking English only in films." Well, we were ready for take two: home.

At home his mum anticipated our arrival with spaghetti, but before we joined her for dinner, we went over to Mehdi's second house, the next door one, with his friend - the 'kala' man who was waiting for us in front of his house with L'eau de Vie. The drug dealer, the 'kala' man, Mohamed and I were invited to sit in the leaving room. We hardly spoke. Everyone was taciturn as if there was something wrong with this party, as if it was doomed to failure from the very onset. As I had no energy to ask the same questions all over again and they didn't ask any, I wasn't bothered to make conversation. This whole gathering felt almost wrong, forbidden, false, young, too young for me.

The drug dealer took his pipe out. "This is a very handsome pipe," I commented, "what do you smoke?" "Pure, organic hashish," he explained. It was a sweet smell, light and fresh, in contrast to the 'kala' boy who had the third class hashish, which was inorganic and had no particular smell. They had both been smoking hashish since they were fifteen years old, and apparently that was the "fault" of the deceased King Hassan II, the father of the ruling King Mohammed VI, who had smoked hashish and not only had announced it publicly but also had encouraged his citizens to smoke hashish and not cigarettes in order to support the domestic industry that has been generating a healthy income for the public sector in Morocco.

As they hardly spoke French, I might have misunderstood them. In my research, the countless articles that I have read regarding this matter, I did not come across anything that could prove such claim.

The issue has been politically sensitive because relations between Rabat and the Rif, the region where the vast plantations of cannabis are, have always been strained. Going back to 1921-1925 period, Riffian leader, Abdelkrim al Khattabi, temporarily proclaimed the independence of its region which was under Spanish rule at that time. Then, in 1950s King Mohamed V who reigned from 1927 until 1961 sent anti-cannabis military forces into the Rif however, in 1956, as Morocco became independent from France, King Mohammed V, promised the Rif people who had staged important guerrilla actions against the French that they could keep growing cannabis to generate an income, creating a parallel economy. This concession may also be perceived as a personal revenge, as his son, Hassan II deliberately excluded the region from any economic development. Until today, literacy rate in the Rif is the lowest in the country and basic infrastructure has yet to match that of the rest of the country. Indicatively, during his reign from 1961 to 1999, Hassan II never visited the region and had declared a "war on drugs" in 1992. He was described as a very perilous King: "Hassan was a very dangerous king; he was a big friend of the USA; the USA put its army and spies here. He saw Morocco as his company, with us as his employees. In the 1980's, when the Riffies got too strong, he sent in helicopters to shoot them and take others to prison. He hit almost all the major hashish people at the same time. Ever since, the royal policy is, 'Don't hurt the Riffies too much or they will hurt you, but don't let them get too wealthy and powerful, because they will take over the country.' His son, Mohammed VI, is rumoured to be a kif smoker and he has mostly left us alone. Lucky for him that he has."

It was not King Hassan II who smoked kif but the ruling King Mohamed VI. Since he became king, he has launched several projects to develop the Rif region that has suffered from extremely difficult climatic conditions and offered very little earning opportunities for its people. "This is everything I own: I use it to buy grains, wheat, oil, soap, school books, pay for electricity," said Abdelouaret El Bohidi, a farmer, pointing to a bag of marijuana. "If they take this from me, I will lose my mind. I won't have anything left to feed my children."

A port was built in Tangier and another one in the eastern city of Nador to make the north of the country more economically attractive.

The Rif is a spectacular geologic feature, stripped bare of its natural vegetation by centuries of overpopulation and irrational land use practices, so that the raw undulations of stone, peaks, valleys and cliffs are seen with stark clarity. Riffies grow, process and transfer cannabis products to other Moroccans and to Europeans who are largely responsible for getting Moroccan cannabis resin, otherwise known as hashish, across the water to Europe. It takes place in a forbidden mountain region near Ketama, a seedy city notorious as the capital of the Moroccan hash trade.

Morocco, the world's leading producer and exporter of kif: the dried bud of the female marijuana plant, according to the United Nations, has for decades tolerated the illegal production of cannabis that allows an entire region to survive. "I'd be a lot happier if the state leaves us alone, stops the arrests and lets us grow the herb," said Tahiri, a father of seven whose house in the village of Beni Gmil was raided by anti-drug security forces last year. He said he'd be willing to sell his cannabis resin for 7,500DH per kilo, about half of what he is now getting from middlemen.

More than seventy per cent of European countries in 2008 claimed that Morocco was their prime source of cannabis - either directly, or via Spain, or the Netherlands - according to the most recent figures from the United Nations Office on Drugs and Crime. These countries have pressured Morocco to take action to significantly reduce its production of the drug.

The Government in Rabat says it will begin a big crop substitution programme for the Rif cannabis farmers and has asked Europe to help pay for it. But whatever different crops they grow, farmers will have to take a huge cut in income.

In the past few years, the country has started to crack down on production of the crop and has invested millions in not only burning the fields but also helping farmers cultivate other kinds of crops. Since 2003, Morocco has received €28 million ($38 million) from the European Union to eradicate the cultivation of cannabis and signed several treaties pledging to do so. In addition, the United States donated $43 million to help farmers find new crops to replace hashish. In theory, such a plan should work. In reality though, it has faced many challenges and experts say it is likely to fail in the long run.

The shift in approach to drug policy comes after the authorities waged a campaign against cannabis farmers prior to the 2011 Arab Spring uprisings; areas growing cannabis were drastically reduced from 137,000 hectares in 2003 to just 47,000 hectares at the end of the campaign. The authorities encouraged farmers to plant orchards and grow olives and almonds. Typically, these sell for between 70 and 100DH a kilo; annual sales of marijuana in Morocco are estimated to at $10 billion. For farmers trying to make a living and provide for their families and communities, it is easy to see why many - an estimated 800,000 - choose to cultivate cannabis instead.

The attempts to wipe out production have also affected the lives of others, namely consumers. The price of hashish has doubled even tripled over the past few years depending on quality.

"Five years ago, the best quality hashish was from Ketama - it was $30 for 12.5 grams - and now the price has doubled and it's hard to find it," explained Salim, a regular hashish buyer. "Even bad quality hash has become expensive. "Farkhacha," a mixed product used to be only 10DH and is now 60 or 70DH."As a result, many drugs dealers have stopped selling hashish and have turned to more profitable sources of income: harder drugs.

In 2013 there was an attempt to legalise cannabis in Morocco that has been cultivated since the fifteen century with the official right to grow it in the Rif Mountains in the nineteenth century. The bill however, was rejected.

The whole process of the Morocco's modern hash making methodology was explained in another article.

"Making hashish involves placing marijuana plants on top of sieves, pieces of cloth, or other materials that have very small pore sizes, covering the cannabis with heavy plastic, and then shaking or pounding the cannabis so that resin glands fall through the pores.

Sometimes, cannabis is placed inside a bag made of mesh fabric such as nylon. The bag is placed inside a bucket and the top of the bucket is sealed with plastic and then laid on its side. The bucket is hit with a rubber mallet or piece of wood for a few minutes so that only the heaviest resin glands detach and fall through the mesh.

The bucket, opened and emptied of the mesh bag containing cannabis, is coated with a fine dust that is mostly mature cannabis glands and a small amount of soil dust. This type of first-run, carefully-made resin powder, when derived from fully mature plants that possess superior genetics, is pressed into top-ranked, pale gold-colored traditional hashish that is often called "double zero," "primero," or "supreme."

When processors want more profits, they beat the cannabis harder and use larger pore sizes, so crushed leaves and other plant material fall through and add to extract volume. This product is inferior to double zero, is darker in color, and is often sold in Dutch coffee shops as "Honey Maroc," or "Golden Maroc."

Farmers use chemical fertilizers because they could not easily find manures and other natural fertilizers to augment the soil, which was especially lacking in phosphorus and nitrogen.

Immature plants are cut down and stored in the sun or indoors in high temperatures; sunlight and heat break down cannabinoids into inferior, degraded products that produce sedative effects rather than a euphoric "up" high."

The very high top hashish is ironically called "King Hassan." It is described as medium brown, soft and velvety with cookie dough interior; it bends before breaking and it cracks open resembling "dried riverbed" earth. It has a smell of soft chocolate-mint; sweet and candy-like, and has a really lovely floating high, which match the taste.

I believed that our friend, the drug dealer might have smoked kif, and the pipe that he used was the one described as a *"sebsi,"* a long-stemmed pipe, fragile and often made from the hollowed stalk of a marijuana plant, with a tiny bowl on the end that would be big enough to hold an amount of cannabis slightly larger than the size of a pea.

He was stuffing the pipe with kif and at the same time the 'kala' friend and Mohamed were rolling joints made out of the lower class hashish. The 'kala' guy did not smoke cigarettes though. "I don't like the smell of cigarettes and the smoke really bothers me," he explained. Mohamed, however, was alternating joints with cigarettes, same went for the drug dealer. Not for me, thank you very much; once I inhaled the hashish in Arougou, I had never desired it ever since; this however, wasn't resolving a problem of itchy, irritated skin and the more it was exposed to smoke the more itchy, tired, irritated and wrinkled it felt.

The 'kala' guy took a plastic bag out of his pocket. "What's this?" L'eau de Vie. "Why is in the plastic bag?" "It's home-made and it is safer to carry it." "What is it made of?" "It is made of figs; we put the very ripe figs into water to boil them; then it is left for fermentation followed by distillation." That was how they made it, and here is professionals' approach:

"To start distilling at home, you'll need some technical knowledge about the equipment, process and how to handle the delicious results. Make sure your still is clean."

Once you followed all the steps to set up your still for a distillation run, you then start the process of distillation.

Foreshots: The first alcohol to come out is called the foreshots. The foreshots are heavily contaminated with acetone and methyl alcohol. The still does not create these alcohols, but it concentrates them. In quantity, acetone and methyl (wood) alcohol are poisonous. They also smell horrible. Learn this smell. You cannot go too slowly at this stage. The foreshots are thrown away.

Heads: The heads contain a mix of the undesirable alcohols and an increasing percentage of ethyl acetate, which is one of the important flavour compounds in grape wine, and methanol. Most commercial distillers save the heads to run through the still a second and third time. You may want to save them, toss them, or add at least some to the hearts. There is no fixed rule.

Hearts: The hearts is the main run of ethanol. The smell is bright and fresh and is strongly evocative of the underlying fruit or herb in fruit wines and fruit and herbal macerations. As you maintain the still at a steady slow drip you will find that you are slowly increasing the temperature of the still. One drop every second, or even every two or three seconds is what you are looking for from a small still. Collect in small glasses, like shot glasses.

Tails: At some point the flavour changes, becoming more dilute and the smell is less pleasant. At that point you are sliding into the tails. The tails contain a high percentage of water mixed with ethanol and fusel alcohols.

And so on…

As keen as I was on trying this intoxicant, hoping to drink only hearts, I had to wait after we get back from dinner. Samira had prepared a big plate of spaghetti Bolognese. "Do you like it?" she asked. "I do, thank you, it's delicious." It was really tasty, but the only thing I opposed to was Fanta; it simply didn't go well with spaghetti, and I was excused.

After a quick dinner we went back to the party finding the 'kala' guy and the drug dealer sitting in the same position as how we had left them, silent and completely mesmerised by a film they were watching, looking like zombies.

I sat down and waited. "Can someone serve me a drink, please?" If I didn't ask I wouldn't be served anything. "Do you want to taste it first?" asked the 'kala' guy and poured me a tiny bit in a glass. The liquid was of a blurred white-light-blue colour and tasted like soap flavoured with a soft, sweetly nutty, almond aroma. "I can't drink it pure; I have to mix it with something." "Try with Coca-Cola," they suggested. "Can I get my own glass, though, please? I'd rather sip it than gulp it." I fetched my own glass and made myself a drink.

Generally, the whole evening was a bit mind-numbing as when the drug theme was exhausted, we went back to the square one: silence. The 'kala' guy and the drug dealer both left around 11.00pm leaving us to ourselves and the L'eau de Vie that was drunk by Mohamed like water. He could not control himself nor the countless cigarettes and joints that he smoked, so around 3.00am I decided to confiscate L'eau de Vie and all the leftovers of hashish. His eyes were red and words indistinct, but he still was keen on drinking and smoking and begged me to give it back, and I begged him to stop. "Please give me my whisky and hashish." "No way. I will give you back tomorrow." He was roaring like a wounded lion but I was merciless. Then he hugged me. "This is not going to work, sorry." It was time to open a window to bring some fresh air, it was time to rest; I begged them to stop smoking in this room where we were supposed to sleep. I was cold. I asked for more blankets. Then I felt feverish; my skin was burning and I could only blame the post-effect of smoke that restfully settled under it.

I was woken at around 8.00am, feeling awful, like after a heavy night of drinking, whereas the only drink I had had was the one I had prepared myself. My face was very red, the smoke was still inside me, and I was hungry too. We all got up and went off to his parents for breakfast. The table was laden with some cake, *boucheyar*, eggs, cheese, bread, coffee, tea, milk; those thick poured with melted salty butter boucheyar were exquisite and the one on the far bottom, which was paddling itself in that greasy saltiness was certainly a winner. What a breakfast!

It was one week ago when Mehdi crashed utterly a rented car. He was high on drugs, alcohol and was speeding, so when he was approaching the city, he had lost control over the vehicle. He and his friend survived, and both had managed to escape the place before the police arrived. Today, however, he intended to borrow his father's car to take us places. He lingered being hesitant, not knowing how to approach his father, a man who seemed pleasant but not warm, respected but not much loved, and superior to every other being in this household. The father - son relationship seemed jittery to me; perhaps it was temporary; perhaps the 11.000DH that their insurance company had to pay for that crashed car was responsible for his current aloofness. However, Mehdi was allowed to take his father's car. I believed the condition was to bring with us his sister Samira and another relative before dropping off his mum in Beni Mellal. Samira was in control of Mehdi's speeding shouting "Slow down! Slow down!" even when he wasn't speeding. We were taken to Beni Mellal's stunning castle called *El Kasbah Ain* to walk around it and admire the view. To my astonishment, all these Arab's places that I had so for been to or pass through had one thing in common: tidiness. The rubbish here as opposed to any place inhabited by the Berbères, was where it belonged: in a rubbish bin.

When we left Beni Mellal, we headed south toward *Bin El Widan*. It was a stunning drive mostly through uninhabited Atlas with occasional shops which had offered minerals, and cafés that were cooling one's thirst. That gorgeous milieu forced me to shout out loud: *"Beauty! Beauty!"* and pushed some passengers to call me "crazy." And although we still felt drowsy from last night, there was still some energy left to sing and dance.

The location of the lake couldn't have been better; it was surrounded by the Atlas Mountains and copiousness of olive trees that were embedded into lavishes of stones, pebbles, rocks - the domineering aspect of that landscape. A small bark, which was left grounded on the shore, was ready to take people for a ride any minute; the splendid, breath-taking blue colour of the water was becoming transparent when was hit by the sunbeams that were revealing what was under: the life of flora and fauna. "When the heat strikes the swimming here becomes a habit," I was told. Now, one could only admire it.

When we were ready to drive back, we then realised how late it was and that we would not be able to catch the last bus to Khénifa; left with no choice, we had to spend the night here and travel home early morning tomorrow. I sent a couple of messages to Meryam informing my family of a sudden change of plans, so they would not worry about me. Mohamed wasn't talking to me and I didn't know why; I gave him back the confiscated hashish, but he kept being taciturn and a little bit offish. When we stopped in Beni Mellal to pick up Mehdi's mum we had time to talk. "What is wrong?" "Nothing." I knew well that nothing; in nothing there was always something. "You have been behaving like my boyfriend and now you are like a distant friend." "I don't want this to be one night." "Me too." "But you are going to leave." "Maybe, it all depends, it's hard to say what I'm going to do in two months, and you know that."

When we left Beni Mellal, we all went to Mehdi's for tagine, and then to another place. Again, Mehdi took his father's car and drove us out of the town. "What's here?" "A friend lives here." The pitch black suburbs were not utterly inviting to get out of the car, but I wasn't willing to stay inside it either. We pulled out in front of a house which was surrounded by meadows and shrubs. He knocked at a window and soon a head appeared in there, then two men came out of the house. Their faces and shapes lit by their mobile phones emerged from the darkness. Almost instantly, I was given some short videos and photographs to look at. "Are you both hunters?" I asked. "Yes, look at this video." That video-film showed dogs fetching dead pheasants and chasing after a rabbit. "Do you want to come and see the dogs?" "With pleasure." In order to get to the back of that yard, we had to creep through some tall bushes and meadows, so as not to make dogs nervous. The three German Shorthaired Pointers were beautiful but frightened of strangers, so after a brief look, we left them in peace. The subsequent video-films I watched and the stories they shared exposed the quite hedonistic life they were living. I believed they were also selling drugs otherwise our short visit there would not have made sense.

That evening another friend of Mehdi kept us company until around midnight. "I'll walk you back home," said Mehdi when his friend was ready to leave. Mohamed and I were left alone. "Listen, I'm tired, I'm going to bed." I was taking off my trousers hiding under the blanket and only by chance he saw my naked limb. "Cover your leg," I was reprimanded. "It's just a leg, haven't you seen a naked woman before, you are such a shy and innocent boy." "Do you want me to switch off the lights?" he asked. "If you don't mind." "I'm going upstairs, I will sleep there," he said. "Alright. Good night then." He turned the lights off and disappeared. The house was silent and cold but only for two minutes as it was interrupted by reappearing Mohamed. The comeback was sudden and unexpected, warned by him repeating my name twice and shot off with energy that only a passionate lover, or a husband not yet stripped of his passions could carry, a force that could only permeate, a force that was gentle but felt hard, a force that energised and weakened at the same time, a force that penetrated all the senses that were ready to be touched, felt, smelled, and tasted. The persuasive lips couldn't have been more succulent, and the more I felt them, the more I kept my eyes closed, in case if I was dreaming. The kiss was embedded; if only the first kiss had such passionate and sensual qualities, maybe then I would remember it. All of a sudden, we heard Mehdi's steps. It was time to wipe pleasure off our faces. "Good night," said Mehdi, "I'm going to sleep upstairs." Mohamed lay down on a sofa parallel to mine. "Come here," he said. "What if Mehdi comes down?" "He won't." "Not much room here." It wasn't a complaint. We had three hours left before the alarm would go off. We didn't sleep a wink. We talked a little.

******

The 6.00am bus left on time and within a second we found ourselves in Khénifra. We slept through that entire journey and when we woke up, we found ourselves in another world, a bit cruel, too controlling, too isolating; the world that separated us the minute we got off the bus. This place made us both suffer; we had to be friends here. "I don't like it," I said. "We have no choice." This world, in which everything including feelings had to be controlled, started to depress me. I couldn't stand the idea of having another relationship where I had to hide my feelings; I knew it could only create frustration and suffering.

Back at home I found Hakima and Meryam in the kitchen. "Did you have a good time? Where were you?" The question sounded a little bit odd to me taking into account that I had sent a couple of messages. "Didn't you get my messages?" "No," said Meryam a little bit perplexed. "Look, they both were delivered and the number is registered under your name." "That is not my number," she said. "Whose then? I'm so sorry, you must have been worried sick about me!" I felt dreadful as not only I had promised to send a message, but also to come back on Sunday evening. Whose number did I register under Meryam's name? Searching through messages and phone calls I figured it out - it was Ali's number. I felt let down by him and his careless attitude. If only he had sent a message back! If only he had passed it on to my family, he would have prevented them from unnecessary qualms. It was then that I realised that our friendship was fragile and based on nothing but some false promises. Ali had backed off; he now hardly ever got involved in trips together, daily outings, coffees and walks. He must have recognised that I wasn't interested in anything else but friendship, and no matter how much I loved his mum, we would never go beyond just being friends.

That afternoon I met Mohamed for coffee. "Look at your eyes! You are stoned, aren't you? Why did you smoke again?" "Because I wanted." "I thought we were supposed to have a serious discussion." He looked depressed, but more depressing subject came with his former professor. He joined us in the café and sucked up all the energy that we were left with. He was badmouthing Saida, the president of the Human Rights Organization and a few other members by presenting some formal documents which were proving corruption, malpractice, and lack of action. "Why are you saying all those things about your fellow-workers? I don't want to get involved in any of the personal problems. What I want from you and your colleagues is to help Malika." Ignoring what I said, he then wanted me to write a petition to a regional president of the same organization to fire the local one. I did not agree with him and didn't want to work with him either. When he left, we both sighed with relief.

And then something else had to be spelled out. "I don't want you to do modelling," said Mohamed. "I can't stand thinking that other people look at you." "What actually do you think about me?" I was very confused as to where this discussion was leading us. "You have to look at paintings to understand the complexity behind a naked figure." "I can't look at them." "This is not something that has been discovered recently, throughout the centuries artists were painting or drawing naked bodies," I tried to explain. "I don't want to have a woman who does this type of job."

Before I left for Morocco, I had spent a long time "life modelling." It kept me financially stable; I could afford to live in London or move to different countries and find employment there. No matter how odd this job was, and it always will be, I treated it as a profession and I was good at it. I was evolving into another human being by acquiring vital knowledge about myself, my body, and others - mainly artists. I had gained a great deal of confidence, and the work I was given, had made me realise that perhaps there was something unique about my face or my body, the way it moved or was being expressed. Artists loved the shapes and the dynamism that they were trying to capture in a drawing, painting or a sculpture. I loved my job and all those peculiar, sometimes even entertaining characters that I was meeting. However, as time went on, despite the success and popularity as life model, I was no longer satisfied; on the contrary, I felt less and less human. I was giving too much and getting hardly anything in return. It got to a certain point when I could not stop feeling, when attending private gatherings, that I was being looked upon as someone of a lower quality, "the model" who by definition could never be as good as the artist, and such thoughts were always stronger when surrounded by successful artists with money. Only during my Italian period did I feel more like a human being rather than "just a life model." The group of friends that I loved and worked with gave me enough confidence to say what I really wanted to say to those who couldn't and wouldn't treat me as an equal: who moves, breathes, and feels like them, those three human qualities that really counted.

"A model should never complain, even the best one; how dare she! We shall not call her back!" And they didn't. Models would stand still, straining their bodies for hours and gaining as little as 9 Euro per hour, but apparently they were privileged to work for an American academy that has trained people to draw like all the Italian Masters. What a sad existence in an equally sad place! I did learn that everything in this job was temporary, that the uniqueness of one model could quickly be substituted with another one, a new flesh, a new shape, and they would call it diversity. I kept my body and mind strong and I would go to a different phase of modelling where I would entertain them, and when the life drawing room turned into a stage I would push myself, I was hard on myself, I would even slip a disc once and repeat the same mistake all over again. Would they care? There were always individuals who had compassion but all those sentiments never lasted long. Finally, after losing a modelling job that was supposed to give me some income, and after arranging my voluntary work here, I was strong enough to say: "I'm quitting!" I no longer want to feel like a substitute or be slapped hard in the face.

Here however, I had to face another problem, more complex and more sensitive: Moroccan's mentality and their perception on nudity. He had never said that, but in his eyes I was a prostitute. And his remark hurt me a great deal. "You should have thought about that before you touched me," I said and left.

******

Today we were both supposed to go to the hospital to see the paediatrician. However, I did not desire the company of a man who felt false to me, hence I did this trip alone. A doctor was busy seeing patients, so I waited, trying to get my clothes dry as I had been caught in heavy rain. The unit looked very basic, and through opened doors I could see how rudimentary it was; rooms were exposing nothing but beds and respirators in a few of them. When the doctor, a young woman, was ready to see me, she firstly apologised to me for waiting which I thought that was extraordinary; I did not make an appointment, I turned up out of blue and she made an apology. When we settled in her consulting room, I showed her all the prescriptions, as here everything was written on a prescription paper. "Could you just read out loud this one for me, please? I can't read this writing." She did and then explained the results which I had studied at home before coming here. The doctor confirmed a very low level of red blood cells that had caused anaemia, and clarified that with medications it could quite easily be treated within two or three months, if it was absorbed well, if it wasn't a pathology. She talked about prenatal and postnatal suffering that could cause all sorts of problems including heart problems, coeliac disease and a couple of other aspects, medical terms that I did not absorb well in French.

Those tests, however, had nothing to do with Meryam not being able to walk. This was another matter and for that, a scan was scheduled for May. If she obtained the *medical card*, she would get the treatment for free, if not, she would have to pay and it would certainly be out of her pocket.

From the hospital, I went straight to Saida's office to find out if any progress was made in Malika's case as the promised phone call had never reached me. When she saw me, she became very enthusiastic and invited me over to the other building where one of her colleagues worked. Khalid, appeared to have had a very sensible attitude. "The president contacted the local authorities in El Borj and he will contact the jury in order to obtain a permission to start the legal action. In the meantime what we could do for Malika would be to move her to Casablanca, so she could live in a place for single mothers." he said. "That could be tricky to persuade her to move to Casablanca, I'm not sure what her parents would think. It would be easier if I could take Malika and her mum with me to Casablanca only to show them the place, and give them to decide. Would it be possible to contact that place and organise a meeting with them?" He was positive, and what was more, the place was already prepared for her. I was impressed. If it worked, if I could convince Malika to a better future for her and her baby, a bit far away from home though but still in a proper place where they would be looked after and she could learn a craft, if it worked, it would bring a smile to my face.

I reported back to Hannah and waited her response as I would never make such a decision single-handedly. In my mail box there was another uplifting message from Stuart, Hannah's son, who is also one of the UK trustee for the charity. It was a warm, encouraging and supporting email with fine concluding lines:

"I am sure that the school, children and family dramas are keeping you extremely busy, but I really hope you are finding time to enjoy yourself as much as possible, making new friends and seeing the sites that the area has to offer. I truly hope you are loving the experience. My mum showed me some of the recent Facebook photos, the one with the caption "they do keep a close eye on me" we all found particularly amusing! Thanks once again for all your fantastic help, volunteers like you are one of the main reasons why the charity is able to function and make a real long term difference to the kids' lives and their families lives."

Then I found a strange one line from Mustapha who was using someone else's email account; the message was short and written like this: "Salut sa va!! tu va bien? Où tu abandonner le père de l'enfant ... c'est Mostapha." First, I thought he was talking about my baby that I did not know of, but then I made a link to what he had mentioned the last time - Malika's baby. However, the message was still not clear to me as to why he would stick his nose into a case that was highly sensitive and private.

At home, Papa Mohamed suffered a splitting headache. It was then, when I made another link to a different story. I remember one day when I went off to the school with a scarf around my head, it wasn't the usual way they wore it, but more in my style, when I was asked by the both Mohameds if I had had a headache. I talked about fashion more than pain, but soon after I took it off: the scarf around a head was clearly associated with a headache. So, there was Papa Mohamed with a splitting headache and Hakima who was wrapping a scarf around his head, and I swore it couldn't have been tighter. "Is this supposed to cure your headache?" He nodded.

******

The fourth day of very heavy rain and strong winds here; it was raining almost nonstop looking as if it was never going to cease. To get out of the house meant to go across a "swimming pool" with its maximum depth just outside our door. "Something has to be done with it. I'll take some photographs." I took some non-action photographs, where only the camion and the paddle were exposed, and then the action shots with Meryam, Hakima and Fadma who were sweeping all that water away. This was not an ideal time to go out and considering a sad loss of my boot's sole and holes in every pair of my trainers, I suffered the constant "wet feet" problem, which might have added to the throat problem that I was still suffering from. Also, the Human Rights Organisation was at odds and the professor was waging a war with the president, but only verbal and behind his back.

Mohamed's apologies along with an invitation for breakfast at his place were accepted. His mum who was to travel today to see her own father wanted to share tea with me. The old man lived in the mountains and was in real need of a woman; he was actually desperate for a woman and was expressing it strongly through an emotional blackmail; "If you don't find me a woman I'll kill myself!" Her father was once married but sadly his wife had died long time ago; the second woman moved in a few years back, but according to Mohamed's mum, the second woman was old and couldn't even look after herself; she had also proved to be exceptionally unreliable by coming and going, and it was quite a while ago when she walked out on her father, leaving them with no choice but to look for another woman, ideally younger, prettier and more mobile who would agree to marry this old man and who would live with him in the mountains. However, the second one, the old one with rheumatism, the unreliable, the one with poor mobility moved back in a couple of weeks ago, while they were looking for a third woman. Although polygamy was lawful and was supposed to treat every single wife equally, no prettier, no smarter, no better, no worse, here it sounded more like a trading, like swapping the old one for a young one. No matter how equal they would want this to be, in practice it would never work that way, and that was even confirmed by the prophet An-Nissa: "You will never be able to do perfect justice between wives even if it is your ardent desire." Papa Mohamed was often pulling Hakima's leg saying: "Hakima

157

not zwina, Hakima not good, I need Madam X, Madam Toxo." And Madam Toxo was the living and breathing anecdote of many evenings spent together. I knew there was not a pinch of truth in Papa's joke; they struggled but they struggled together, they created a very loving and strong family, they were still affectionate and the flame was yet burning. Anyway, to find someone of Hakima's quality would not be an easy task.

However, what qualities are we talking about and why Islam has allowed such practice? Here is the verse most commonly referred to with the topic of polygamy: "If ye fear that ye shall not be able to deal justly with the orphans, marry women of your choice, Two or three or four; but if ye fear that ye shall not be able to deal justly (with them), then only one, or (a captive) that your right hands possess, that will be more suitable, to prevent you from doing injustice."

The study shows that forty-four per cent of the Moroccan population supports polygamy and that public opinion favouring polygamy is more significant in the educated classes than the non-educated classes.

In Morocco, polygamy is subject to a judge's authorization and to strict legal conditions. Few articles present a deep insight into polygamy:

Here is one man's point of view, a man who had two wives and was looking for the third one:

"To have many wives is the best way I have found to reconcile my compulsions with my Muslim faith. Let's not delude ourselves, it is not in man's nature to be faithful to one single woman. This is how it is all over the world. Some choose to take mistresses and carry out secret relationships, while others, like me, prefer transparency and get married."

What are the consequences of having more than one wife, and why would a man wanted to have more than one family? The answer is rather obvious: sex. "Imad, a professor of math with a physique of never-ending youth - a veritable macho man - commented nonchalantly, "Who doesn't dream of being a Don Juan, a Casanova. (…) Men who pretend otherwise are liars; deep inside we all fantasise of having a harem. Harems, however, are a privilege reserved for kings; polygamy is available to everyone.

Another comment affirmed in an equally laid-back, shameless manner: "It may seem a bit vulgar to you, but we cannot eat chicken every day. We need variety."

This oft-cited excuse by proponents of polygamy assumes that the desire for diversity of pleasures is only applicable to men, but never for women, as polyandry, which is a practice of a woman having more than one husband is not permitted. "Polygamy is prejudiced against women, but it also has dire consequences for children and society," sounded the president of the Democratic League For Women's Rights (LDDF).

It is all down to pleasure and bodies are only used as tools: "For us as men - instinctively hunters - marrying multiple women is the ideal solution that allows us to live out our pleasures and fantasies, but in a way that is *halal* and guilt free. This is because Islam condones these relations."

Another fellow humiliated his wife by stating: "When women feel they have competition or that they are in danger, they amp up their efforts to satisfy their husbands, to "win" him. They pay more attention to themselves, dress up for us…and it's amazing! Anything but difficult, having multiple wives gives a real sense of power."

The pleasure obviously came first, but paying for it wasn't something that they were in favour of: "This makes my housing budget close to 10,000DH each month for two separated apartments for two wives. This is no small amount. In my eyes, money is the only real obstacle that I see in taking another wife," lamented a polygamist, who had to buy a family home on the suburbs of Casablanca to put each of his two wives on a separate floor. He claimed to spend one night with one, and then the next with the other.

What do wives put the polygamist through? "Sometimes I feel well at home and spend a nice evening with the children. However, as soon as I get ready to leave to spend the night with the second wife, it is always the same. Often she shouts at me: 'Go, leave my house and see your tramp.' It is painful," and he continued, "I have to let everything go and escape by myself or with a friend to relax, especially morally. I am always tired, but I feel tenderness for both of my wives," A real headache … What do women actually think about polygamy? "When my husband told me he wanted to take another wife, my entire world collapsed. Overcome with anger, I tried to understand why this was happening to me, what on earth could I have done wrong, where did I fail, and how in the end did I prove myself to be incomplete in a way that has made him desire another? We had been married for ten years with two beautiful children. Certainly, like all couples, there are highs and lows, but nothing out of the ordinary, except for a marked distance that had grown between us over the past two years, mostly because of his travels for work. Learning that he wanted to take another wife was truly humiliating," recalls forty-three-year-old Sonia and an employee at a business.

The same article brings another story told by a thirty-five-year-old housewife. "It was a shock. I had an idea that my husband was a hound and that he had mistresses - *zehouani* - as we say, especially since the birth of our children. I just never imagined for an instant that the man with whom I had fallen in love, an educated and modern man, could go through with this and remarry." If there was so much suffering why did wives give their consent? "The pressure on these women is huge, and society has no pity for them. In Morocco, we always prefer for women to stay married, even if she is unhappy, rather than be subjected to the dishonour of divorce."

"Polygamy is a real psychological torture for women. This torture is perpetrated not only by the husbands who choose to take a second wife, but by the families of these women who, far from being supportive, have one single obsession in mind: avoid their daughters' divorce at all costs, above all to prevent their return to their parents' home," confirms a member of the Democratic League For Women's Rights.

"Sure, I could have refused and asked for a divorce. I have the material means to get by on my own, I have a good job. But I thought of my children, who I would have deprived of a father in the eyes of society. Also, as a forty-three-year-old divorcee with two children, how would I redo my life? What man would still want me? Thus I have resigned myself to give him my consent to remarry," and the same woman, according to this article was seeing a psychiatrist since then and was taking medication for chronic depression. This scenario is rather typical, according to a psychologist who specialises in couples issues. "When their husband takes another wife, women find themselves in grave distress or overtaken by feelings of guilt, often upheld by the attitude of those surrounding them and by society. This leaves them feeling that if their husband wants to remarry, it must mean that they were unable to satisfy, or "retain" them. This chagrin and disarray sometimes degrades into depression, the effects of which can by dramatic, even fatal.

This is the case of a woman who killed herself in 2008, with her two daughters in Mohammedia, after having learned that her husband had wanted to marry another woman since she had failed to give him any sons. In January 2014, a woman killed herself and this was brought to daylight by the head of the opposition Socialist Union of Popular Forces, Driss Lachgar that called for the ban to polygamy and was quickly accused of apostasy. The distress experienced by women is often shared by their children who inevitably bear the brunt of polygamy and the distortion of the nuclear family. "When a father gets married for a second time, it inevitably has extremely harmful consequences on the children. Following this, it is not uncommon to see delays or failures in school and psychological withdrawal."

The strong willingness to be on the top of that game pushes women to humiliate themselves by feeding men vanity. "Then, little by little, I brought out my real game: fine lingerie, I lost weight, started working out, updated my wardrobe and changed my attitude with my husband. The results did not take long. After having become almost totally absent from my home, he came around more often, was more attentive and even seemed to be in love. In contrast, he has not yet repudiated the other wife; however I expect I will succeed in this respect sooner or later."

Going back to the subject of grandpa; someone from Errachidia who was called the mediator, found a woman for him, a young one, almost my age, who agreed to tie the knot with the old man. "Why?" I asked? "Is he rich?" It was evident that either she might have pondered the possibility of a fat inheritance, or she was looking for a way to escape from her own family, and certainly she wasn't a virgin; ninety-nine percent she was divorced, which was slimming down profoundly the chances of getting remarried to someone closer her age. There would not be any other reason why a young woman would want to marry an old man and live in deep mountains with him. Mohamed's mum wanted to evaluate the situation and calm down her father by bringing the good news.

"Would you by chance adopt a dog? I changed the subject, "a beautiful, sweet, black and playful puppy that had followed me on the street." "Where would we keep it?" "At home?" "We cannot bring dogs home?" "Why not?" "If dogs are at home the angels cannot come in?" "What is this?" "Our prophet, Muhammad." "He must have hated dogs, mustn't he? You don't know what you are missing, they are beautiful creatures." "I had a dog when I was little." "At home?" "At home." "What about angels? Weren't they present when you were little?"

I did mention the dogs-angels beliefs before, however hearing something like this from my own boyfriend irritated me massively as it sounded naïve, so naïve that it almost led us to an argument.

Any closeness between unmarried man and woman was also forbidden by religion and yet ... I wondered if angels were at home when we were kissing, and if so, what would they be thinking? We desired each other because we were in love, and it was stronger that any instruction, advice, caution or admonishment. However, his house hardly allowed any intimacy; there were no doors and additionally his room had a very strange hole in a very strange place; it was overlooking the staircase creating little heaven for Peeping Toms; I wondered if the house was built that way deliberately, as a form of control; it was certainly reflecting his mum's over controlling character.

It was time for me to go home and get ready for a new born baby celebration with Hakima and Fadma, and lucky us - we got a lift from our neighbour whose wife was also asked to join in. On arrival we were greeted by a few women. The one who gave birth was lying in the bed, but there was no sign of a baby. After a quick 'hello' we were invited to join a few other women who were sitting around the table in the neighbouring room, a small one, with sofas that were put against walls and two separate big tables in the middle of the room; the space that we were left with was very limited and every time someone wanted to move or go out of the room, the tables had to be moved accordingly. Three of us sat in front of five women that were pleasantly and silently observing us; one of them, a bigger size than usual, was sharing her smile with me. Such taciturn attitude was baffling me a little and from time to time I was trying to express my consternation by looking at Fadma and Hakima who seemed not to have been interested in bonding with anybody, and neither was I. Finally, a woman who was sitting next to me broke the silence. Her story, rather short, told in very broken French, was that she was living in Paris for twenty eight years in the 13th zone.

Then a man in charge walked in and turned the music on: an upbeat Berber track but far too loud for such a small room; the CD's were quickly swapped, broken records were disposed of, and we could finally feel the blues in our hips. One of the women initiated clapping – a particular type of applause in which stiff and strained hands create claps that visually reminded me of the strenuous actions of catching an insect or something equally tireless. The same woman then pulled me to the dance floor. As tables were moved, providing more space to move in, and the "Rock on!" command was given, I did not linger but encouraged my hips to follow the particular chant which within a moment attracted the attentions of a young woman who first observed me dancing, then dressed me in her pyjama, and then tightened a scarf around my hips; the same young woman joined me in in order to demonstrate a movement of her hips which was not easy for me to copy.

Even though the women seemed to have been happy with my performance, I felt intimidated when encouraged to do more, as despite my improved shoulder movement, I was sure that I did not come close to their performing standards. But as soon as I sat down, another woman declared her willingness to dance with me and when I lingered, the large lady stood up and swept me off my feet. What a performance she gave! Her largely visible masses of fat were rolling itself under her djellaba with astonishing grace; she kept the eye-contact with me smiling when coming closer and closer as if she was trying to seduce me by performing her incredibly suggestive dance; she turned around offering the full view of her giant rear end that was looking very much in trans while shaking it and circling in an "S" shape. This woman knew how to dance! She was my diva, my heroine. "Bravo! Bravo!" I chanted.

When dinner was served we were treated to a grilled chicken in a sweetly caramelised onion sauce with some olives and spicy sauces that were put in a separate, tiny ceramic dishes placed on top of that chicken. After this delicious savoury treat we were ready for the one that fallowed: a tiny sweet pasta dish with some raisins sprinkled with cinnamon and custard. Delightful. To digest it all, the table was yet laden with some mandarins and bananas, and was finished off with a pot of *shiba* and yet again some sweets that we had to pack and take it home. We were simply not able to eat more. As I had praised the chef's talent, he came to see me handing in his number. In fact many people asked for it, saying that they wanted to come with me to France. "I'm not French." "Where do you come from?" "Poland." They were trying to locate it in their virtual maps but guesses were mostly wrong. "Is it close to Italy, right? So you share the bother with France." Someone even put Poland in Africa close to Kenya." However, in order to reassure themselves that getting to know me was worth the trouble, the question-statement: "Is it in Europe, right?" was always posed.

******

Notes:

1 (p. 140) Paracelsus.

2 (p. 140) The Unbearable Lightness of Being, Milan Kundera, Faber and Faber, 1984, p.9.

3 (p. 141) James Dean. The Mutant King, David Dalton, Plexus, London 1983, p. 141.

4 (p. 142) Economic & Philosophical Manuscripts of 1844, K. Marx, Progress Publishers, Moscow, 1959, p. 614.

5 (p. 142) The Art of Loving, Erich Fromm, Rebis, 2004, p.34.

6 (p. 142) Letters on life, Rainer Maria Rilke, The Modern Library New York, 2006, p.187.

7 (p. 145) Woody Allen, in "Annie Hall."

8 (p. 145) Brwita/carozza – trolley.

9 (p. 147) Chfnj/sfnj – donate ring.

10 (p. 148) In order to write I have to chase away my doubts, but when we are together, you and I, we chased them away.

11 (p. 148) Flouss, in Darija, money.

12 (p. 148) We are going to build a house in the mountains and you will be strong, we are going to travel and you will be strong, we are going to write poems and you will be strong, we are going to imagine and you will be strong, we are going to sing and you will be strong, we are going to give up everything and you will be strong, we are going to meet our God and will be so strong. The dream requires nothing, one can practise it without money.

13 (p. 150) Sbahlkhir, in Darija, good morning.

14 (p. 151) Mika, in Darija, bag.

15 (p. 152) "Until the age of thirty-two, I lived alone, without love. Life seemed to me very simple, very good and very easy. I was rich. I had the taste for so many things that I could not feel passion for anything. It is good to live. I woke up happy every day to do things that I liked and I went to bed satisfied with the quiet hope of tomorrow and the carefree future." (…) "A huge plait of blond hair, almost red (...) I was startled, trembling, disturbed (...) I took it gently, almost religiously. (...) Who had cut it? A lover, a day of farewell? A husband, a day of vengeance? Or one that had doors on his forehead, a day of despair?" ("Boule de suif," Guy de Maupassant, Albin Michel, 1984, p.111-116).

16 (p. 152) Fkih Ben Salah – literally, "a holy son of goodness."

17 (p. 153) Lamsamen – is made of flour and semolina, it does not contain yeast - the one ingredient that differentiate them from boucheyar.

18 (p. 153) Beni Mellal translate itself into Day, this city was, back in 1688, called Ismali, since Moulay Ismail, the second ruler of Moroccan Alaouite Dynasty, build the fortresses of Tadla. Beni Mellal is nestled in the heart of an immense orchard at the foot of the Atlas. Thanks to the dam of Bin-el-Ouidane and major irrigation works, the city and its region have developed vast tree areas. The Apricot and olive trees has been cultivated, and oranges have the best reputation in Morocco. The heat at summer time is unbearable. ("Le Routard, Maroc, 2013, p.394).

19 (p. 155) The Stepford Wives is a 1972 satirical thriller novel by Ira Levin. The story concerns Joanna Eberhart, a photographer and young mother who begins to suspect that the frighteningly submissive housewives in her new idyllic Connecticut neighbourhood may be robots created by their husbands. Two films of the same name have been adapted from the novel; the first starred Katharine Ross and was released in 1975, while a remake starring Nicole Kidman appeared in 2004. Edgar J. Scherick produced the 1975 version, all three sequels, and was posthumously credited as producer in the 2004 remake.

20 (p. 156-159) The "cannabis" part is supported by a few articles: "Morocco to legalise cannabis?" Jonathan Dibb, 2013; "Drug Trafficking in Northwest Africa: The Moroccan Gateway," Abdelkader Abderrahmane, 2013; "The green shoots of recovery? Morocco considers the legalisation of marijuana cultivation," Souhail Kamar, 2013; "Morocco: Cannabis fields touched, Aida Alami, 2011; "On the trail of Double Zero, deep in the heart of the Rif," Pete Brady, 2003; "King's Ire Brings Hashish Down From Its High," MARLISE SIMONS, 1996.

21 (p. 159) "Step-by-Step Home Distilling," William Rubel, 2012.

22 (p. 161) El Kasbah Ain, there is scarcely any information available on this monument, even "Le Routard. Maroc, 2013" guide does not provide with any knowledge. The Wikipedia says that it was made from stone and it is close to the spring of Ain Asserdoun. The Kasbah was believed to have been built in order to protect this spring and to protect the surrounding area.

23 (p. 161) Bin l'Widane (Bin el Ouidane Dam), a barrage around 60 km South from Beni Mellal.

24 (p. 161) From the film: "A room with a view," 1985, based on the novel by E. M. Forster.

25 (p. 155) The most needy in Morocco have access to a Medical Assistance Scheme (RAMED). This scheme is based on the principle of social welfare and national solidarity. It allows persons who are not paying into the AMO - the basic medical scheme that all Moroccan citizens are required to be members since 2005, to benefit from treatment dispensed in public medical centres as well as state-provided health services. (From: "The healthcare system in morocco,"2012).

26 (p. 167) Quran, Surat 4 An-Nisaa, Part 5, verse 129.

27 (p. 168) Quran, Surah 4 An-Nisa, Part 4, verse 3.

28 (p. 168-170) To present polygamy in all its light, I have reached for a few articles: "Morocco to probe Salafist over polygamy row," in Al Arabiya News, 2014; "Current Issues Polygamy, Women's Islamic Initiative In spirituality and Equality." "Polygamy and Sex in Morocco," Fadwa Islah and Hicham Oulmouddane, in: Al Monitor - The pulses of the Middle East, 2013.

End of Part Five

Fadma with Meryam in front of their house in the mountains.

Part Six

"Once upon a time there was a long beach where thousands upon thousands of starfish had been washed up and were dying because they couldn't get back into the water. A man was walking along the beach and he came across a young boy who was picking up starfish after starfish, and walking to the sea and throwing them back in, then another here and there. The man said to the boy quite mockingly. 'What do you think you are doing? This is useless; it is making no difference, look at all these starfish.' The boy picked up another one and went to the edge and threw it in; he then turned to the man and said. 'It made a difference to that one.' That is what we are doing - making a difference to just one here and there, but we are making a difference, so whenever you feel you are not doing enough, think of the starfish and the boy."

It was another wet and cold day. I was sitting inside the café "Martil" and had the pleasure to be joined by my boyfriend, known to everybody as my friend; there might have been some speculations going on but not a single question had ever been asked, not even by his close friend Ali. We kept our heart stories to ourselves knowing that sharing them with anybody would not be wise; to play an intelligent game here meant keeping things quiet without arousing any suspicions in order to avoid condemnation, badmouthing, or experiencing people's bad intentions.

"What shall we do? Are you going to tell your parents? I cannot even imagine their reaction." I was anxious whenever I pondered such scenario. "Would you like to marry me?" asked Mohamed. "I would like to marry you. What about you? Do you see yourself marrying Maggie?" "Yes I do. I'd be very happy. I'll talk to my parents." I was ecstatic in my head. I had finally found someone whom I wanted to marry, a man who fitted my description and who communicated the same feelings for me. Wasn't I lucky? In many aspects we were very similar, both passionate, active intellectuals who would always strive to be better and to do better, and we would have our dream house in the mountains, and we would spend hours there studying together, exchanging knowledge and experiences, and write our own books, and we would grow older together, and we would make love all the time. Perhaps I over romanticised my relationship, but my goals sounded very achievable for me. However, this time, my quixotic attitude, made me take my notebook out and I was eager to write: "Let's talk about issues on which we will have to compromise; tell me, what would be difficult for you to accept?" Wasn't that romantic? He started off with NUDITY, a sensitive subject that was discussed many times but it needed to be deliberated on one more time. "What about summer time in Europe?" I asked. "You know it won't be similar to what is here." After a hot debate we reached a compromise: we both would be swimming naked in some secluded places. The second one was also a bit tricky:

166

HOMOSEXUALITY. His tolerance for homosexuals was rather low. I wasn't really sure if it was down to the religion that eliminated and condemned homosexuals, or rather the opposite, but that was already established when I had asked his sexual preferences. "You know that my best friend is gay, and I love him to bits, and you will have to accept that." I was positive that he would, so then we went to the third point on our list which was peculiar: WINE. "But, you drink more than me." I commented. In fact, the wine point wasn't referring to wine as such, there was a hidden agenda of trust as it was not so much drinking the wine which occupied his head rather the effect of drinking, as in his mind, after a glass, I could easily be seduced or could be the seducer. "You have to get to know me a little bit better to feel more secure." He was also bothered by SALUTATIONS, the particular way I greeted men. It was then when I first learnt I should not salute men by pecking them on their cheeks, not even close friends, and certainly not married men. "Did you see confusion on my uncle's Aziz face when you kissed him?" "I'm sorry, I had no idea." Having said that, the second time that I saw uncle Aziz, it was him who had initiated this particular way of greeting; so it wasn't as terribly inappropriate as he thought. The last thing that had bothered him was: SHORT JUMPERS, meaning any type of top that wasn't covering the troublesome bottom.

My list concerned health issues: hashish, cigarettes and unimaginable amounts of alcohol. "That's easy," he said, "anything else?" "Yes, slurping, generally savoir vivre at the table." "I'm not that bad?" "Yes, you are bad, you slurp and smack your lips like a pig, sorry." "But it's difficult not to slurp when the tea is hot." I demonstrated the silent way of drinking whereupon he took a sip, a very unsuccessful one. "I'm not designed for silent drinking." "Bullshit, it is just a bad habit, that's all, we'll be practising it otherwise you will drive me crazy." He understood and promised to improve.

No matter how much I painted my future pink, there were moments of doubt in my solitude. I was thinking of how we would be able to overcome obstacles that were piling up and over which we had no control; it was society that was in control of us, the society that I struggled to understand and it bothered me because the sad fact was that I had nobody else in this country but Mohamed. My man would be my morning and the afternoon, and the very much desired evening and the night time; he would often say that I pumped some life back into him, and that would make him the starfish and I would be the boy in Hannah's story; but, there were moments where he would drift too far away from the shore leaving me feeling lonesome as depriving me of a morning coffee or an afternoon chat meant solitude. Although I would be with people, or surrounded by them all the time, I would still feel solitary because I craved for more than their physical presence; and in that sense, my man would also become my isolation as I would desire his far away existence in those moments; and he would also become my fear, the hundred times repeated in my head phrases when I would introduce him to my mum - the devoted Catholic. "Mum, I'm going to marry a Muslim man." No... "Mum, you wouldn't believe what happened? I'm going to get married," or... maybe, "Mum, you will be happy for me, won't you?" I went through countless possibilities, but somehow, in my head, she sounded unconvinced; she would tell me that I lost my mind that I should look for something more secure and easier. And how it looked for Mohamed? Probably very much the same as he was already losing friends and people were passing judgment on him. I needed to talk to someone just to get this burden off my shoulders; it felt too heavy for my body type. However, I sought a temporary solution and for the fifth time I watched "Beginners," the film which moved me particular deeply that evening, provoking some reflections and allowing me to dispose of a bucket of tears making me feel lighter, at least.

******

We had planned another trip for this weekend: a couple of days in the mountains with Mohamed's uncle, Mustapha, and I would be introduced to his grandfather - the one who was desperate for a woman.

Just before we took off Mohamed shared his news with me. "This morning I talked to my mum." "Did you? How did it go?" "She was very happy for us." "Really? Wasn't she angry, disappointed and furious with you?" "She likes you very much and besides she suspected something." This news brought upon me a mixture of feelings, it made me happy to be so easily accepted by his family but it also made me scared; I had to do the same, face my own demons, my own family.

The next step was to talk to his sister Suad and convince her of our plans. Although she seemed to have been keen on me, I was minded to believe that she would rather see her own brother with a Moroccan woman than with a crazy European with whom she could not even communicate. Suad lived in El Kebab, around fifty kilometres down south from Khénifra, with her two children and her step-mother; her husband was the one who was serving in the Moroccan Army hence his visits home were limited to only a couple per year. The taxi dropped us off in the centre of El Kebab, a place that I would recommend to anyone to visit. Behind the radical conservatism that was seen on the face of it, there was something mystical to the place. Perhaps, it was all down to the light and the brown-orangey mountains right behind those buildings that were making this place looked more supernatural, or the steep, narrow road that was uncovering endless shops and cafés with men sitting inside, and their mules parked just outside. We passed by the local butcher, fish and grocery shops, all-in-one shops, a high-fashion stand, a few stalls with tea, plants, sweets, and cigarettes. Everything looked rather mystical, strangely busy but not busy at all, just the whole layout was giving me that impression. We stopped to get some yogurts and chocolates for children, and half a kilogram of dates which in total cost us only 35DH.

Suad was busy cooking tagine and looking after her children, but after short greetings exchanged with her and her mother in law, we were invited to sit down, whereupon the whole marriage grilling was about to start. All the questions were very predictable and she commenced with the most obvious question: work. What would we do for work? "We will sort something out; we have a business plan in our heads, besides we could live in Europe." Religion was next; would our children be Muslims or Christians? "Honestly, I don't know, perhaps we'll ponder it when they come." My answer did not satisfy her; anyhow if I said I would prefer them to be Christians, she would perhaps protest, if not, I would probably be stating something that I was not yet prepared to admit. "Where would you live?" "We can live everywhere we want, in Europe, in Africa; we are free to choose a place where we want to settle down." Mohamed's sister, Hayat, who had come to Suad's for the weekend, congratulated us, but Suad's face was still contaminated with disbelief, doubt, and scepticism. She might have also questioned my sanity, why would a European girl, older, non-Muslim, with a colourful past, certainly not a virgin, like to marry a poor Moroccan man? I wasn't surprised by her scepticism; however, there was one utterance that took me aback; she stated that we would not be able to live with Mohamed's mum and that we should look for our own place. I found her remark offensive and discriminatory not because it wasn't her business, but because in Moroccan's culture a married woman, whether she wanted or not, had to live with her in-laws; I suppose this custom did not apply to Europeans. On the other hand, why would she be thinking that an independent, European woman would like to sacrifice her freedom to live and be controlled by her parents-in-law: I wasn't that mad.

We talked about responsibilities within a marriage, children's upbringing and a fair-share of work and money. "It must be very hard on you to bring up your children single-handedly?" She said it wasn't. "I have nothing else to do; it is my job to run a house and bring up my children." The Stepford wife called Suad did not convince me as to her reality of her happiness; didn't she desire her husband? Didn't she yearn for him to be at home when her children were growing up? Furthermore, didn't she have any dreams apart from moving to Khénifra where they were building a house?

It was time for us to get going as there was a long walk ahead of us. The steep hill that we trekked led us on to a steadier dirt path that would take us to Timdghass where we were supposed to stay overnight. "How many kilometres?" I asked. "Around five." "Shall we call your uncle in about half an hour to come and pick us up?" No matter how romantic this path was and what a stunning backdrop it was giving us, the distance felt too long to get there before the sunset. His uncle, Mustapha, was informed and turned up thirty minutes later in his three-wheeled motorbike that had a little trailer with blankets inside. The sunset, the drive, and those surroundings - words can hardly describe the feeling of that evening.

The house in the mountains, made of stones, was very basic; it provided one room which was treated as the living/sleeping space and a separate kitchen. The house next to it was of the same build but instead of two rooms it offered only one where his grandpa lived, and perhaps, would his future woman. It has to be said: to move into this space and to live with him would equal suicide, it would be a reckless act, an abnormal move, something incomprehensible as it was more like a barn than home, no light, no warmth, and the old man would not even come as a comfort; he was lying down on some carpets in the corner of that dark, cold room and did not even get up to greet his grandson. How on earth would he make a woman happy?

On the contrary, Mustapha seemed to have taken good care of his family. Fatima, his wife, was an extraordinary woman, beautiful, healthy, and happy looking; their children were even more adorable, and I very much felt in love with the youngest one - Meryam. This beautiful tiny adult in a body of a child, terribly composed, well-behaved, gave me the impression of being thoughtful and seeing a wider spectrum of life, or even comprehending the planet that wasn't pampering her at all. She had this little, skinny doll that she was carrying in her bag, and when she wasn't walking with her, she was dressing her instead with a piece of cloth that had a hole to go through her doll's head, and that was the fun part. What an amazing energy this child was emanating! I warned Mustapha and Fatima of my willingness to kidnap her, in case, if they would wonder where she was.

There was also a young woman with us, the twenty-one-year-old Mona, a charming and lovable girl, sadly, already divorced. She was living with her parents in the same area, fifteen minutes on foot from Mustapha's house, the only place that she was allowed to go to as her parents would fret about her safety, in other words, she was divorced so no longer a virgin, hence she could easily be used by other men. They were very protective of her beautiful, very trusting, and still naïve daughter. I was fond of her and she shared the same sympathy for me. "Madeleine, restez avec nous," she said when it was time to go home.

But before we went away, we had spent a pleasant time with them, sitting around *forno*, sharing tagine, and stories; in the evening, when everybody had fallen asleep, Mustapha was recalling his tales until very late; he was only thirty-eight years old but already complaining how old he felt. When his first wife didn't appreciate life in the mountains, he had to divorce her and then got remarried to Fatima. Although he had an opportunity to make big money, someone had offered him a job in the Riff with the drug industry, he had never accepted it. "I went there to see how everything functioned and I could never imagine myself living such life; always in danger; madness! I prefer to earn less and have a quiet life with my family." We brew tea on the wood-burning stove and carried on talking, and when I got exhausted, I wondered where I would sleep. "You'll stay here and Mohamed will go to the kitchen." "No, no, leave him here, there is enough space for all of us, he will freeze to death out there," I protested. He agreed but he moved him to the other corner of that room so the two of us could not sleep next to each other. The children, Mona, and Fadma occupied another corner and were also fast asleep, but when it came down to making beds for me and Mohamed, Mustapha, no matter how amiable he was, made his wife get up and prepare beds for us, this clearly wasn't his job. She laid a couple of woollen blankets on the floor and gave me a few to cover myself with, but despite having three layers on and three or four woollen blankets, I was still trembling. When the flames were down and the sudden chill entered the room, I was also concerned about Mohamed who had not been given as many covers as I had. It was a harsh environment and I wondered how they survived there. During the night I could hear the children coughing nonstop as if the lungs were to be coughed out; little Meryam was vomiting and Fatima did not get much sleep. What a tough life! No isolation, no beds, and no electricity, they were deprived of the basics to which every human being should be entitled.

"How can you not have electricity?" I asked the following morning. "If you are not "friends" with the local authorities you won't get it. There are more or less twenty houses that still don't have it, and no matter how many petitions we send, we never had any response back." "Bastards! On top of everything corrupted!" It is something unimaginable that we all have been living in the same XXI century, some of us were flying to the moon, reaching the stars, but others still didn't have electricity in their home. "I'd like to help you, perhaps we could work together," I suggested.

After breakfast we were sent off to the centre of Timdghass to fill up the empty bottles of gas, and to have a little wander around, and in order to do that we had to take the motorbike. "Have you ever ridden this before?" I asked Mohamed. "Never, I'm going to learn now." Mustapha showed him how to get the engine going, then how to change the gear, and that was the end of the lesson. We took with us two bottles of gas and drove along rough dirt road that challenged our little bike and its driver with larger than normal puddles in the middle of the path making us drown in the mud; some pebbles and stones were also throwing themselves under the wheels and nearly threw us overboard. "You must slow down, please, slow down, otherwise we will fall over!" We were so close to a collision but, somehow, taking the foot of the accelerator got us safely to the main road. We refilled the bottles and went for a little ride along the main road. "Ok, cowboy, you are doing great but remember to slow down; and if we see a side road pull out so we can go for a walk." It was no longer than five minutes when we spotted something interesting on the horizon. "Let's go there but… slow down, slow down, slow…." I shouted when the motorbike was turning into that side road far too fast, and it almost didn't make it; if Mohamed had not used his feet to keep balance we would certainly have crashed. Instead, we drove into a field and stopped the engine. "Do you know what, I think I'll go for a little walk," I was laughing but my legs were still trembling. "How would you back the motorbike?" "I will drive a little further and make a turn." And when he did, we decided that perhaps going home would be safer.

While Fatima and children were doing little chores at home, Mustapha was in the forest with his mule searching for a decent supply of wood for the *forno*. As we had promised to have lunch with them, we went for a little stroll around the fields resisting all sorts of temptation that had to do with our temperaments and being in isolation. However, even in the middle of nowhere, Mohamed's paranoia of being seen by people was creating unnecessary tension. He would always say, "I need to respect my society." Therefore, we obeyed society and went home to spend the last hour with the family, to observe a cow giving birth while grazing in the field, to share a mouth-watering tagine, and to drive back to the nearest place from where we could catch a taxi back to Khénifra. We got cosy on the back seat with a couple of other passengers, and two more at the front. All of a sudden, the taxi pulled out and a man who needed a ride jumped on the front and shared the seat with … the driver. Never had I seen eight people in the car before and certainly not two men behind the steering wheel!

******

I was going to get married. It was official. I was congratulated by the family of my future husband Mohamed. Their enthusiasm astonished me; his mum was pondering a small engagement party that consisted of reading the Quran, dressing me up in a traditional clothes and preparing a special dinner. His father beamed with joy. "Madeleine, Madeleine, bravo, you two are great together." His dad did like me; he would regularly, through Mohamed, invite me for tea at the house. "My dad is really fond of you and he loves your laughter," said Mohamed. "I'm pleased." When we chatted over tea, his mum asked me a question. "Is your mum happy for you?" "I don't know, she doesn't know anything," I felt a little bit embarrassed. "It would be great if your mum could come here for the wedding," she continued. "I'm not very sure; my mum is a wonderful woman but ... one day, *Inchallah*."

Soon after breakfast, we were on the way to the medina to the Office of Civil Status to find out what documents we would need to get married. The judge invited us to wait in his office until he had finished presiding over a wedding. His office was an open space room that was occupied by a few people and someone who looked like a secretary. The judge was swift and pleasant but the pile of documents he gave us was far from pleasant. "Are you French?" "No, I'm Polish." In that case, he took another list with documents written in Arabic; he then ticked all "musts" applicable to my nationality and came up with eleven requirements. "Is that all?" I mocked him looking at the list:

1) Application on behalf of the foreign would-be spouse from the head of the family.

2) Birth certificate.

3) Proof of residency.

4) Criminal record from my own country.

5) Proof of employment and salary.

6) Four recent photographs.

7) Copy of passport.

8) Legal copy of identity card.

9) Certificate of Legal Capacity to Contract Marriage from the Moroccan Embassy.

10) Criminal record from the Ministry of Justice in Rabat.

11) Medical certificate.

It's so damn easy to get married in Morocco! I didn't hide my surprise regarding a couple of documents. "What medical certificate do I need?" "That proves you are a virgin." "What about if

I wasn't?" "Then it needs to be approved by your future husband." "What about you? You don't need any medical certificate?" "No." "What fairness!" I commented. "Why do they need a proof of my employment and revenue?" "He said it was in case you had to take care of me while being abroad." "What about you? Do you have to prove to the state your financial responsibility towards me?" "No." Once again, what equality!

How do I obtain all those documents? My revenue is very much out of date and my profession... I know that I'm a freelancer but in what actually? The criminal record... in what country should I apply for it? Then all those documents from the court... This was a little bit depressing. "What shall we do?" I asked Mohamed. "I don't know." We felt deflated; all those unexpected obstacles killed off our enthusiasm and marriage did not look as romantic as I had anticipated. "Let's keep our spirits up," I said. "We shall find a solution. Now tell me all your romantic stories." "When I was fifteen years old...." "No! Did you?"... We made a fair exchange, his story for my story... one after another... and one too many. The honest exchange of past romantic accounts was not a brilliant idea as my future husband did get upset and wasn't accepting my follow up statements of how much I was looking forward to our life together. I loved his little weirdness, but to be jealous of the past was a bit too outlandish. Although there was lots of honesty in him and a great deal of kindness and fragility that I wanted to protect, today's disbeliefs and doubts chased me away home where I would chew on the marriage documents and ponder the future, and how to make it work.

When I returned home, Hakima and another lady from our street were working at the rooftop dying the wool to make blankets and carpets. They used a big pan with boiling water that was sitting on top of a burning charcoal and were putting big volumes of sheep skin into red and orange boiling pigment. The amount of steam that this action generated was adding more magic to it in which Hakima and her friend were performing some witchlike practices; ha ha ha... I could hear the witches laughing and saying: "Take two breaths of Moroccan's spirit, few notes of Mohamed Rouicha *Inas Inas,*" all those forbidden kisses and hugs, and use a wooden stick to mix it all up, and if the wool did not turn as bright as you wanted, put it back inside and spice it all up with the forbidden... ha ha ha ha... Mix it all up gently, and then say the spell... ha ha ha ha..." The spell worked, it magically turned all those volumes of dirty wool into bright orange, and red, and it was left to dry.

******

A couple of days ago I met Mohamed's cousin, Jamal, a young man who lived in El Kebab, and who, with few other fellows from the same town, seemed to have been willing to improve young people' lives in his town. He was trying to create an association that would mainly concentrate on young, neglected, uneducated girls, and he would give them opportunities to become creative, to motivate them to act and to actively participate in all those undertakings provided by Jamal and his friends. "Would you like to join us? It would be great if you both could come one day and share your ideas with us." We agreed. We had also been thinking to involve them in developing the road project between El Kebab and Timdghass, and try to help households that had no electricity.

In the meantime, I was concentrating on improving the drainage system in La Scierie by writing a petition to the local authorities in French and asking Mohamed to translate it into Arabic. Then, I would take as many signatures as possible, and to support the complaint - I would attach some photographs.

However, everything that I had done or intended to do felt like a drop in the ocean considering how much else needed to be done and how much time and energy everything was consuming as there was no quick solution to anything.

Khalid, from the Human Rights Organization, had done nothing so far to help to progress our case, and what was worse, nothing he had said last time was true. "I don't understand; you told me that the place was ready for her. Now you are saying there is a place in Fès but not suitable for Malika because it doesn't have a psychologist!" The conversation was disturbed by the appearance of the annoying professor, the persona non grata, who disregarded the privacy of this meeting and had no intention of leaving the office. They both frustrated me a great deal. "Why didn't you do anything and said that you had done?" "I'm resigning," he said. "I no longer want to work with them." "I don't care about any of your infighting in this organization. I'm so frustrated with all of you. Because of your empty-promises we have just wasted over one month, unbelievable! And now, you are just backing off." Try as I might, I couldn't express my upset and irritation. "Before you resign, can you give me the contact number of a competent person who could take it over?" My upset was even greater as a few days ago I had had a chance to talk to Malika's mum who did not oppose nor seemed to be shocked about the idea of moving her daughter to a place in Casablanca; she had appeared to have been rather sensible, and now the chances of putting such plan into effect went down to drain.

I felt powerless and was slowly cracking under the Moroccan system, I simply hated it. The methods they were using, the schemes they were trying to apply, the arrangements and the co-ordination, all of it had proved useless as instead of helping people it was creating more obstacles, more and more problems were emerging in which the corruption, bickering and ineptitude of individuals were playing a crucial part. I could no longer bottle up my worries as it was driving me nuts, so in one breath, I shared them with Hannah in one of my emails. Her opinion regarding the hugely frustrating Moroccan system was very much the same, but she encouraged me not to give up and stay strong, and Hannah could easily comprehend and relate to my love story as her husband was also Moroccan. "I know how it feels to have that connection with someone even though they are from such a different culture." She talked about problems, tension, and faith. "Do you realise that it will be expected of you to convert to Islam? Would Mohamed expect you to do Ramadan and could you do it? Marriage is a huge step and can never be taken lightly, but when you find the right person then you need to embrace your life and future; anyhow, whatever we do in life will always have an element of risk, if not, we can miss on what would enrich us and make us happy."

I shared her opinion regarding marriage as if I had taken it lightly, I would have been married a long time ago. In my mind, it was always sacred and for life, otherwise what would be the point of getting married, and even the fact that we both had nothing, no possessions, no place to live, no jobs, did not scare me at all.

I wasn't thinking about religion then, perhaps because I never believed that religion could become a problem; besides, I could never imagine myself being Muslim. Why would anyone like me to convert to Islam? It was not my faith, I liked my God and I wasn't ready to swap Him for Allah. As much as I respected their beliefs, I thought they would also respect mine, and it was confirmed by Mohamed. "You will not have to convert to Islam and I don't want you to do that." His family was also aware of it and they seemed not to have been bothered by my Christian roots. Instead, his mum had paid me a rather startling compliment the other day. "I couldn't even compare you to Moroccan girls but if I had to you would always win. You are the best of all of them and I couldn't have been happier." I wasn't sure what I did to deserve such complement, but indeed, it did make me feel content.

Sharing all my concerns with Hannah improved my well-being, at least I felt lighter; however, it wasn't long before my calm-being experienced another emotional upheaval caused by Rkia's illness; she was getting sicker and sicker and couple of weeks ago she had been moved to another house to be taken care of. It was far too much for Hakima as not only her mum, but also *Baba* and Halima needed her attention all the time. "Would you like to come with us to see her?" I wanted and I went.

Rkia was more ill than I had anticipated; she was lying down on a single bed in the living room where we all would gather, eat, and chat. Grandma had lost weight significantly: her face had never been skinner, one could clearly see the structure of her skull as the skin was wrapped around it tightly; her whole body became transparent because she hardly ate, two spoonfuls per meal, no more, only every ten minutes she would ask for water and take tiny sips. Rkia was well-looked after by her children and family who were always present there. It was heart-breaking for me to see her in such a state as I remembered nothing else but her heroism and strength during our mountaineering escapade, and now she couldn't even get up without help or go to the toilet by herself. This visit was emotionally and physically straining and one hour later I was prepared to go home as the lack of communication, constant coming and going of relatives, and a terrible child that was screaming and running around the house were making my head sore. I texted Mohamed: "I so want to get out of here, my head will explode soon, help." I got a straight answer back. "I wish I could help you, I would rather you were here." I was lying down but couldn't relax owing to the fact that the boy's behaviour was getting worse and worse, and when he refused to calm down and go to bed, his mum took a plastic racket that resembled a tennis one and hit him repeatedly. "What a nightmare! That must have hurt!" Fadma stood up for this boy, took him in her arms, and put him to bed. It was late when we had dinner - a beef tagine that did not go well with my stomach; somehow it wasn't digestible, it just landed heavily there and was ready to be taken out when we finally, around 11.00pm, reached our home.

******

When Mohamed and I paid Khalid one more visit in his office, he was ready to drive us to another place and introduce us to an alternative group that would take over Malika's case. He dropped us off and that was the end of our co-operation. Three guys invited us for coffee, while they were gathering necessary information about Malika. Those men were confirming success in similar cases they had been working on in the past, making a promise to take care of this one too. They sounded more competent than the previous group but I didn't want to get my hopes up too high, in case if they turned up to be of similar scams. They sounded positive about paying the family of Azziz a visit, but everything depended on the weather as it would not be fun trekking along that path while was pouring with rain. They took my number and promised to call.

"I'd like you to have a passport," I said to Mohamed. "Shall we go and get the papers ready?" We went to the office to find out what documents he needed. "Are you not from Khénifra?" asked the official looking at his identity card. "I am. I have lived here for a long time but I was born here" "You need to be registered here in Khénifra to obtain your passport here." In order to do that he would have to travel to Khouribga to get his birth certificate. What a nightmare. Another obstacle.

Fadma was keen on performing henna on me for quite some time and tonight it seemed to have been a perfect moment. She came in with the mixture already prepared, and spread it generously all over my feet and hands, no making any particular patterns, just simple and plain. The cold, rainy weather attracted more people to our house and gathered around the *forno*; there were: Fadma and her husband, another Fadma and her son Hamza, Lahcen, Mustapha, Papa Mohamed, Hakima, Meryam, Halima, *Baba*, and the children, so that the packed out room was oozing with life. While Fadma started covering the bottom of my foot, Mustapha decided to do his own henna tattoo on the palm of his hands; on his left he wrote: MAGDALENA, and on his right he drew a heart with an arrow cutting through it. He had never failed to surprise me; now he would demonstrate his affection for me in front of everybody, he would not only study particular words picked up from his French-Darija pocket dictionary that would indicate his devotion, but he would also come up to me and try to snuggle up. The drunken Mustapha would always give me a hug and kiss me on the forehead before everybody's eyes. Tonight, he was sitting next to me admiring my feet. "Quoi? Ça?" he asked when pointing at my scar. "Bottle… gas… phhuuu… school… auwww!!" He laughed. "It's not funny Mustapha, it was a terrible accident at school. When I was fifteen years old a massive cylinder bottle with gas slid down the stairs from the first floor and, unfortunately, hit my leg. I was lucky that the bottle did not explode and that my parents took me out of the hospital where they had wanted to amputate my leg." "Couper?" Now he looked terrified. "Yes, couper, but a different hospital saved it. I walked on crutches for months, I couldn't go to school, I lived with my relatives so the teachers could come and do their job, and when the plaster was taken off, my bone cracked again in the same place." I was trying to be as descriptive as possible so he could understand the whole story, and he got so into it that without even asking touched my leg. Meryam just looked at me and smiled when I had slapped his hand. "Get your hands off me." He laughed. "Mustapha fidèle, quoi fidèle?" He used to read words out loud and would always add "quoi?" "Mustapha sérieux, quoi sérieux? Margarena belle, généreuse, quoi généreuse? Mustapha donnez Margarena cœur, *wyih*, Margarena dans mon cœur toujours, quoi toujours?" "Tu es fou, Mustapha est complètement fou." "Margarena maman, maman… mariage… Margarena et Mustapha." "You know, that I won't marry you. Look for someone else; there are many wonderful women here." "Je veux photocopy de Margarena."

When Fadma had finished with my feet, she moved on to the palm of my hand, slowly and gently drawing the line around it and then filling in the white space with henna. Then it was time to get comfortable in front of the *forno* to get it all dried up and watch Meryam having her feet done. *Henna*, with its smell: light, sweet meadow-like which I loved especially the following day when it all get mixed up with olive oil, had some calming effect on me, and I started believing in the healing aspects of this herb too. I remembered, once, Papa Mohamed cut the palm of his hand quite deeply and was parading around like it was nothing; I managed to make him sit down to disinfect the wound and wrap a bandage around it. The bandage survived one night; the following morning it was taken off and henna was applied on that deep wound. Another time, henna was used on his toe that accidentally got squashed by something heavy at work, and it looked as if the nail was to come off. In both cases, the healing properties of henna seemed to have worked.

The next day my feet and hands were incredibly orange and flavoured with the scent of sweet, freshly cut grass. In fact, it might have been the first time that I fully appreciated the smell of my own feet.

A visit to a café brought some news from Hannah. She was wondering if I was staying in Morocco and if so, she would offer me a job with the Association doing exactly what I had been doing but with some regular income, and I seriously considered her offer. She was also informing me about a group of Scouts from the Central Yorkshire Scout Country that would be coming to El Borj in summer and camping on our land for three days. They had raised £2000 for our Association and wondered how the money could best be used.

From the same correspondence I also found out about another organization called Authentic Morocco that was willing to help us to develop and finance a project which proved to have been successfully run in different part of Morocco, in Skoura, in the region of Ouarzazate. The scheme was called "the goat project" and it would involve sourcing the more expensive milking goats to produce milk and cheese, and a billy goat of the same breed to make beautiful babies of pure race. The milky goats would be given to women, and not to their husbands, whereas the billy goat would be in rotation, he would go from one house to another, derive pleasure from meeting female goats and when babies would arrive, the second female baby would be given to another woman in the village to help keep the herd growing. They would require monthly reports and photos to keep the donations coming in.

In my opinion and the opinion of my colleagues the idea was brilliant and when we said yes to goats there was some work that needed to be done. Sarah, from the Sahara Children Foundation, who was also in charge of this project, required a full report back bombarding us with questions:

"Who are they? How do they live? What are their sources of revenue? What are their needs and struggles? What will they do with the goats? Do they have a local cooperative/women's association? Are other "donors" providing support to the same people/area? In what kind? Is there an action plan of what the women will do with the goats? How will the initial investment help bring in more and more sustainable revenue for the women? Do they know how to manage goats? Do they already have goats? Is this the main need/most useful investment? What other contributions could be useful, if any?"

In the meantime we were gathering information regarding prices and location, founding out that nearest place for milky goats was about two hundred kilometres from Khénifra, in a place called Sidi-Kacem.

In the report that I made, I shared my concerns regarding families that were surviving harsh winters here without any heating. It was something that occupied my head for a very long time and I was looking for a way to provide simple wood-burning stoves for, at least, some of the poorest families in El Borj. I wrote:

"The other most useful contribution would be providing families with wood-burning stoves or installing some kind of heating system that could keep them fairly warm during the winter time. Although days are warm, nights are very cold. The consequences of living permanently in freezing shelters lead inevitably to illnesses that most of the time are ignored as people just wait for the illness to pass. The people that I've spent time with suffer from: lung problems, respiration problems with children as young as one year old, circulation problems, rheumatism later in life, swollen hands, and frostbite. On the contrary, the families who own wood-burning stoves talk about social aspects of having one: it improves families/friends relationships (times spend together in front of the stove), helps children with concentration and with sleeping."

It was indeed a massive problem and children suffered a great deal. Suad's boy, over one year old, had to be rushed to the hospital the other day with a serious breathing problem - the consequence of living in freezing cold houses all the time. The little Meryam, the children of Mustapha, and many more were also the victims of such hash conditions, and when they felt ill, their parents were not able to provide the medical care due to lack of money. For example, when I took Meryam's prescriptions to the pharmacy in February, I found out that she had been prescribed antibiotics in December; the same went for the medicine for her anaemia. It did not surprise me considering that a tiny bottle of syrup cost 35DH and another 400ml of some liquid with a high dose of iron cost 84DH. The overall cost was obviously far too great to even consider buying.

Going back to the goats, the pure quality ones turned up to be more expensive than what was initially said; the quote I was given for a billy varied between 3000-4000DH each, and not 600DH, and the price for a milky goat that could give around four litres of milk per day, reached up 2500DH and not the expected 1500DH.

******

I often wondered why people would make things complicated, why out of their own free will they mess things up. Why can't they just settle with the idea of being jovial and carry on living in such state instead of doubting and disbelieving, making things up, and projecting all their insecurities onto others? What is about the SELF and the MAN that they don't get on well? Who is responsible for the doubt: you or your SELF? The universal doubt has many names and it spreads itself across continents giving philosophers opportunities to ponder:

"A part of a person is a manifest absurdity. When a man loses his state, his health, his strength, he is still the same person, and has lost nothing of his personality. If he has a leg or an arm cut off, he is still the same person he was before. The amputated member is no part of his person, otherwise it would have a right to part of his estate, and be liable for a part of his engagements. It would be entitled to a share of his merit and demerit, which is manifestly absurd. A person is something indivisible.... Many thoughts, and actions, and feelings change every moment; they have no continued, but a successive existence; but that self or I, to which they belong, is permanent, and has the same relation to all the succeeding thoughts, actions and feelings which I call mine."

The SELF is composite but the man is not. Theoretically, we would be the same, but we would not be seen the same, not only by the onlookers, but also by ourselves. If we had no limbs, or lost our estate, or lost our health how we would possibly be looking at ourselves the same way as we had looked at ourselves before. Whatever we gain or lose it always has an incredible effect on us and our personality; if we did not change, we would not grow.

However, there is tendency to be clinically unhappy and only momentarily exultant as if the high spirit would only accompany the occasion. I wish I understood people, I wish I understood my boyfriend, maybe then I would be able to help him. When he would cry, I would want to protect him, but I wouldn't know from what as he would not know why he would cry, or wouldn't want to share it with me. When he would get angry, I would not know why and the explanation would not come until few days later. However, I believed, I discovered a pattern as his emotional upheaval would always occur after smoking or drinking. It was easy to read him, I would sense and see the heavy curse of an intoxicated mind, and I would always ask myself what was the point of self-inflicted unhappiness. "Do you really want to marry such a poor boy?" he asked. "What has money got to do with love? If I wanted to marry someone rich I would have done it by now. Why are you so insecure? Let's go for a walk." It was a beautiful spring day and it was warmer outside than in Mohamed's place. That day he wasn't himself. "I want a kiss," I stated when we were in the middle of a field. "No!" "Just one kiss, please" "No!" "Why not?" "I have to respect my society," he repeated the embedded in his head phrase. "You are paranoid with your society, there is nobody around anyway." From one word to another I was called mental again, totally irresponsible, some hybrid that landed in Morocco and wanted to turn everything upside down. "What happened? You don't look particularly happy?" "Because you don't understand how difficult it is for me to be around you and to behave normally. And you are not helping me." "Same goes for you; you have no idea what it is to have lived with all the liberty given and here have it all taken away. It's unnatural for me to be dictated to as regards the time and the place where I can kiss you or touch you or hug you. You can't rule feelings in such way; this is madness, how is it possible to live that way? Be careful not to kill it in the bud. And by the way, I'm not trying to offend your society, but I'm not part of it either and I wouldn't like to be as it feels false to me." I said and added. "I have some work to do so I better go home. Would you still want to come with me to El Borj tomorrow? I need to give Itto medication for little Meryam. I would appreciate it if you could explain it all in Amazigh."

At home I sat down on the rooftop trying to read and write, doing everything to occupy my head and not get bogged down with Mohamed's emotional upheavals that had frequented our lives recently. Soon I was joined by Hakima, Papa Mohamed, and Mustapha. They were fencing the roof with some wire, and Mustapha would keep me company, and share a strange wood-like root that resembled a pineapple. He was peeling off all its layers just to get inside it to grab a tiny portion of the root which more or less tasted like a cabbage stump. Apparently, this peculiar thing was good for digestion.

All afternoon I was pampered by Mustapha who was serving me tea, bread, and keeping me company downstairs. Nowadays he tended to drink less, but it was the lack of money that kept him away from the bottle and not his conscious mind. The difficulty was to find a job in the rainy season and his dependency on Papa Mohamed and his camion wasn't helping either. They had both been out of work for quite a stretch of time. I believed the frustration of being jobless was particularly stressful for Papa Mohamed's stomach. He did suffer and when I mentioned taking him to the hospital he refused, claiming that someone from the family had promised to take care of him.

I loved this man and his peculiar way of seeing things. He would often come to my room and stand in the door and look around to see what I had in there. Like a curious child, he would scan in his head all the exhibited objects on my chest of drawers, and then he would nod and repeat slowly, *"mezyan, mezyan."* Papa would always be inquisitive about messages I received, or to whom I was sending them, and when we all gathered together, he would ask questions regarding my departure, whereupon he would take his hand and slowly count using his fingers saying: "Meryam, Abdellah, Moad, Acharf, Margarena, kif-kif." There was so much pressure on him to provide for the family that he would become stressed out, he would worry, he would recall past stories when they had money, when *Baba* sold all that land he had owned and had bought him and Alla the *camions*. He would show me photographs of his four children, still babies, and be staring at them and be proud. But the pressure was on him and unfortunately on his oldest son Abdellah who was struggling to keep up with the university. Although he had passed his first exams, his dad would force him to stop as five years sounded far too long for him. "You should support him, it may sound like a long time but this would be a great investment, if he finishes he would secure his future, and in the meantime, he could look for a job in Meknès." Papa Mohamed disagreed with me. "He needs to get a job now. Maybe Poland? Do they have *camions* there?" "They are very different from what you have it here, but I don't know anything about *camions* or jobs in Poland or anywhere else. I'm the worse person to ask; I wouldn't be able to find him a job. Besides, he neither speaks Polish nor English nor French." I could see how frustrating the lack of work was for Papa Mohamed and Abdellah, but it was beyond my scope, because as much as I wanted to help them, I felt equally powerless.

The following morning I waited for Mohamed at the taxi stand at 10.00am but he didn't turn up and his mobile was switched off. I decided to go there by myself hoping that Itto would understand my instructions in French. When I was trekking that rough path, I received a phone call from the new organization. "Are you in El Borj?" "Yes. I'm on my way to Malika." "We will be there in ten minutes." "Great. I'll wait for you then." I went back to the school and soon they arrived. The man turned up with his colleague, who, I later found out, was a journalist for a newspaper here, in Khénifra. I introduced them both to Mohamed, the caretaker, hoping that he would join us. "Will you come with us, please?" He agreed, but as soon as we walked past the bridge, he turned back saying: "I can't go with you, I have a fever." He didn't look particularly well, but I still wanted him to keep me company and not to be left alone with them. Willy-nilly I had no choice.

Those two men kept mocking each other. "You are too old for that. Look at you, you need a break," he teased the journalist while he was catching his breath resting on a rock. "This is an incredible morning and I have to thank you for that." "I'm glad you are enjoying it. Don't you go for walks?" I asked. "I haven't done anything like this for about twenty years. I should start doing some exercise. It does feel great." I was very content, and fortunately for us all, Malika and her mum were too. Itto brought out a large piece of plastic mat and spread it on the ground so that we could get comfortable. The interview, done in a very professional manner, was conducted in Amazigh, the only language that Malika spoke, but the way it was handled, made her feel calm while answering the questions. However, later on he acknowledged the difficulty that this case may bring quickly excluding the possibility of putting her into a single mothers dwelling. Those places were designed for single mothers who through learning some craft would gain confidence and leave the house ready to lead an independent life, and as Malika did appear to be mentally slow, in his opinion, she would not be even admitted to such place. What he promised was to have a meeting with a public prosecutor and a doctor. "Thank you for this." "Excuse me?" "Without you we would not be able to help her," he said. "No, this is me who should thank you. Let's hope she will get some help. What are you working on now?" "We had this woman, a very young one, whose father was abusing her physically and she was completely terrified of him to that extent that the abuse went on until her mum finally stood up for her and reported him to the police. It was a very difficult case because this man was rich and influential, but he was prosecuted." "Well done, it must be horrible to deal with cases like this one. Do you sometimes fear for your safety?" "Yes, they would try to blackmail me, but so far nothing serious had happened." They dropped me off in Khénifra. "We will be in touch." "Thank you very much. I shall call you next week."

"Are you still in bed?" I called up Mohamed. "Can you meet me in the "Martil"?" He joined me in the café. "Why didn't you come to El Borj with me? I really needed you today." "I overslept," he said. "I really don't believe you but it doesn't matter." "Would you contact Khalid, I'd like to buy some clothes for Malika's family, please." Khalid had quite a large collection of second-hand clothes and I thought he could also do with some money. His second hand possessions were kept at home in four massive bags that he would take to the souk in La Scierie on Wednesdays, then to a big souk in the centre, the one that I had already experienced, on Sundays, and also travelled to Mrirt, on Fridays. The collection was steadily growing as the minute he would trade, the same minute he would invest into something else. From the pile of clothes that he had showed me, I choose a few jumpers, a winter jacket and couple of tops for little Meryam. "How much do you want for this dressing-gown?" "80DH." "No way! Why is this twice as expensive as this jacket?" "Because it is cashmere." "Khalid, this is not cashmere and you must trust me on this one. Sorry, I won't buy it." I couldn't resist a long dark-blue coat though, very simple and stylish, thinking about Papa Mohamed, and it cost only 45DH. "So, how much would you charge me for all of them?" He counted 129DH and I gave him 150. "You deserve a bonus but don't tell me ever again that this is cashmere," he laughed and was happy with the trading.

I was struck by another idea supported and explained by my latest purchase: there must be rich people in Khénifra and they must have things that they no longer use; so if I could identify the "rich zone" I would certainly pay them a visit. "What do you think? Would you help me?" "Of course I'll help you," said Mohamed. "Where shall we go?" "There are a few rich areas, one of them is not far from where I live." And soon we would find ourselves knocking at people's doors and asking for second-hand clothes, toys, shoes, anything that they would consider giving away. The first house was rather generous and gave us a bag of clothes. It was a good start, but generally we were asked to come back either tomorrow or the following weekend, so they could get it prepared for us. And we waited, and would go back, and be stunned by some people's generosity and shocked by the attitude of others; for example, a young man who came out of his house and went back promising to look for some things, but instead he came back with 5DH saying: "Sorry I have to take a shower, I have just came back from running." There was another woman in her castle who was busy cooking, she opened the window and said to us: *"Layssahel;"*

this was a response that only beggars could get here. There was another man in his 4x4car wearing a type of djellaba that indicated his *Hajj* - the pilgrimage to Kaba, in Saudi Arabia. This man did not even get out of his car but pulled the window down, interrogated us, and then chased us away saying: "We have nothing to give you." Luckily for us, people like him were in the minority as the majority were extremely generous, and we ended up with quite a volume of clothes, shoes and a significant volume of baby clothes.

******

A few days ago Mohamed's mum invited us to stay over for a weekend with a family of her brother, in the vicinity of El Kebab. I happily accepted the invitation; not only did I fancy meeting Mohamed's extended family, but I also wanted to meet all those youngsters from Jamal's organization. Killing two birds with one stone, or killing the tension between me and Mohamed, however I looked at it, I felt as if I was killing something.

Jamal, who was waiting for us in El Kebab, took us to the community centre where all those teenagers had exercised their ideas by running a theatre group, some aerobic classes, and some dancing programmes. Around ten young people turned up that day and shared their notions about how to tackle the problem that we had presented, going straight away to confront local authorities. "In my opinion, it would be better to have some kind of evidence first, perhaps a petition with signatures, photos and videos, and then we could call up a meeting and make a decent presentation. I could also contact press from Khénifra. What do you think?" They agreed with me and were willing to help. "I'll write the petition and perhaps next week we will come back." Those young people were as keen as mustard, extremely positive and eager to act, driven and motivated, hence it was vital to act on their impulses; we scheduled another meeting for the next week hopping that a few days would not make any different to such enthusiasm. The meeting was over and we were on our way to Suad's for lunch with Jamal. "How did you learn English?" "At school." "Did you want to go away?" "I once applied for a place in a school in London and I was accepted." "Why didn't you go?" "My mum did not want me to go away; she insisted that I stayed at home with her." "And now you don't have a job, no money, no studies; if you had a second chance, would you go?" I asked. "My mum would not give me the money." "Do you have a chance to get a job here though?" "I have been looking for over a year, but still have not found anything." The reality was sad, and it looked as if it was often the parents who stopped children from growing.

After lunch we were ready to go to Lenda, called by Moroccans – London – a village from where we would walk to his uncle's place. Jamal accompanied us to the main road until a car pulled out and gave us a lift. Suad sat in between me and Mohamed and was strangely observing me. "You are very quiet today," she said. "Well, I have nothing to say, so I prefer to be silent than talk nonsense." When we arrived in "London" we were picked up by Mustapha who came on his motorbike, dropped us off, and headed back home to his wife and children. His uncle saluted us and invited inside his very modern house with a proper fire place and the big open-space kitchen, and a massive TV screen in the leaving room where some women were sitting and watching a film and others were preparing a meal. The atmosphere was extremely bizarre: no one talked to us and there was hardly any conversation made between them; only the children who were showing off with their French were asking questions. "Who is your favourite singer? Do you know this one?" Those children sounded as boring as they were wounded, almost not loved by their parents, and their parents seemed to have hated each other. At a certain point, I started wondering if it was my presence that stopped them from acting as a normal family, perhaps they knew about my relationship with Mohamed and disapproved of it; but then, what would be the point of inviting us over? His wife might have been a wonderful human being, but the fact was brutal: she was a very unattractive woman, and her attitude was even uglier, she did not make any effort, or a slightest attempt to communicate with us. She acted as she was clearly troubled by something. "Why don't people talk?" I whispered to Mohamed. "I don't know. Do you think it is us?" he also suspected the same thing. His sister Suad was actively observing me and Mohamed, his mum was helping with cooking, his uncle was preparing sheep skin for the open fire barbecue, and the rest were continuing watching TV. The dinner that was supposed to unite us did the opposite, whether it was intentional or not, it felt bizarre, as although we all were sitting in the same room, we did not share the same table, the Khénifra family occupied one table with me, the children and some kind of step-parents of his uncle who were equally taciturn, and the rest of them were comfortably sitting in front of the fireplace within two metres distance from us; and we would not talk but whisper. When the dinner was served I almost choked seeing a bowl of *hrira* in front of me. As Mohamed knew my secret, I looked at him begging to take it away from me. He understood. "Magdalena doesn't like *hrira*," he announced that publicly, adding, "don't eat it." "What a cheek!" I thought. All eyes were on me. "Mohamed!" I slurped his name slowly and wanted to kill him. "You don't like the soup?" the question arrived. "It's not about this soup, I bet it's delicious, it's in general ....I don't like *hrira*." I was sweating trying to be polite. A few minutes later, I sneaked out to the kitchen and put it back into the pan, no food wasting. Luckily for me and my stomach the next lentil-based dish was delicious. "Can we go for a walk now?" I was eager to get out." "Let's go." While we were getting ready to go out, we were stopped by his uncle. "Try this." I was given a stick with the barbecued meat - the lamb *organs* which were apparently eaten on a large scale with the celebration of *Eid al-Adha*, and I must admit: it wasn't my cup of tea. I knew that amongst all those pieces was one of sheep stomach, but the rest was a big fat question mark, too heavy and too greasy for me.

When we finally managed to leave the house, I couldn't keep my thoughts for myself. "Your family is weird and your uncle is a little bit simple, besides he struck me as a very unfaithful man. He may have an affair, or rather, another woman." Mohamed was also disappointed with him. "I haven't seen him for years and I expected to see a different man." We walked for a while, talked, and then he tried to kiss me. "Why do you do that now? Didn't you tell me off last time when I wanted one kiss from you?" "It's dark here." "So, it's not the desire but the convenience; sorry, I don't feel like kissing you right now, and I hope you will see the difference one day." When we were on the way back home, suddenly, a figure appeared on the horizon, and it was his mum. "Hurry up, we are going home," she said. "But, weren't we supposed to stay overnight?" we couldn't hide our surprise. "They said, they don't have enough blankets for us all." We took our bags, said goodnight, and were taken back to Khénifra by his uncle who did not say a word to us. They dropped me off at La Scierie and I rushed back home to join my family: normal, chatty, and smiling. Soon after, I received a phone call from Mohamed. "I'm sorry for this evening, but you were right, you are some kind of psycho, my uncle is in a relationship with another woman, she was there with us and that's why his wife was so upset."

******

"*Äami* Lahcen and Halima are very ill. Papa Mohamed insisted that I let you know," I wrote a message to Hannah. Indeed, something wasn't right with them. Firstly, it was Halima who suddenly felt ill, and now *Baba* was in a very bad condition. The family and friends were informed which meant the unequivocal: one had to be prepared for their sudden departure. Tonight the house was busy with constant visits of relatives, and even a young man from Raba, who I saw for the first time, came to see grandparents, and stayed overnight. With Rkia, who wasn't getting better, then, the constant absence of Hakima, and now, both, very ill grandparents, the house seemed darker than ever. That night, Meryam, who was sitting in the small room downstairs rolling up into a ball the dyed threads of wool, appeared to have been overwhelmed by everything. Halima looked extremely pale and her lying down position with her eyes and mouth opened aroused both: mine and Mustapha's suspicions. "Halima, Halima, *la bas*?" She made some noise and we felt relieved.

The following day looked very similar or even worse. *Baba's* cough deteriorated while he was sweating enormously having fever; and as he was not able to get up, he would get incontinent regularly. The struggle and suffering made Papa Mohamed cry. It was the first time I saw him in tears; he did not hide them, he was sitting with all of us watching his parents being in pain, and all of a sudden, he broke down and cried with tiredness, resignation, powerlessness, but also care, love and devotion to his family.

"How peculiar, the way life works. If this were not a bit arrogant, one would like to position oneself outside of it all, on the opposite side of everything that happens just in order not to miss anything at all - even there one would remain rooted in life's true center, maybe there even more so than elsewhere, there were all things come together without having a proper name. But ultimately we are quite attracted and taken in by names, by titles, by the pretext of life, because the whole is infinite and we recover from it only by naming it for a while with the name of one love, no matter how much this passionate delimitation then puts us in the wrong, makes us culpable, murders us…"

******

The Moroccan's temper was incredibly short, and almost immediately the tantrum, or whoever stood behind it, was ready to pick up a fight. Mohamed and I went to the town hall to deposit documents for the passport. The queue in front of that office was weirdly squeezed, and some people were standing too close to one another creating unnecessary tautness. Theoretically, there was still thirty minutes to the lunch hour; perhaps the fact that it was soon be closing made people become more aggressive and more irritated with each other. While I was sitting and filling out Mohamed's application, he was standing patiently in that queue. Suddenly, one man in front of that row raised his voice at a fellow behind him, who without doubt, was pushing him forward. The man behind did not hesitate and grabbed the man in front, and this was how the scuffle started. Fortunately, everybody reacted, and separated those two rather feisty characters; however, the verbal abuse was still going on and as soon as the man behind was released, he went once again for the man in front, this time with his fists. Neither the security guard nor the officers, who were sitting comfortably in the room, reacted to what had been going on. The fighting guys, once again, were separated out by the "fellow-queuers" and their temperaments were slightly cooled down by the lunch hour announcement; the whole gathering, at least twenty people, was dispersed. "Mohamed, what time is it?" I asked when we left the building. "It's 1.15pm." "Shouldn't the lunch hour start at 1.30pm?" "Yes, you are right, it should." "Let's go back there. You just need to stamp your application and they should still be at work," he agreed with me and we marched back. A couple of those officials were standing outside smoking. When Mohamed interrupted their earlier lunch hour break pointing out at the watch, firstly, they bristled, and then looked at me, the foreigner, and quickly went back to open the office to stamp Mohamed's application. "Good job, young man! Now we can go to the hospital."

The next task was as simple as the previous one: we had to get to the hospital to sign a document for his sister Suad. However, the only doctor who could do that was the one who worked in the emergency unit, and the emergency unit was as busy as the passport office. The bodyguard was controlling the crowd, but the crowd was too wild to be controlled. The first outburst of anger that we witnessed, broke out soon after we had sat down; it seemed as if two young men had been waiting far too long to be seen by the doctor and were annoyed by notoriously reappearing "queue-jumpers." While they were arguing with the bodyguard, Mohamed sneaked into the room to see the doctor, but he refused even to look at the document asking him to get in the queue. In the meantime, the bodyguard handed everybody a number which had irritated even more these two young men who were to be seen eleven and twelve. The queue did not move and half an hour later we decided to leave this crazy unit.

We sat in a café. "People are mad here," I said. "Don't you think that their explosive characters could have something to do with smoking hashish all the time, or perhaps even drinking? You know that liver is the seat of our emotions. That man's liver, the one from the town hall must be wrecked! He was insane!" "I know him, it's my neighbour. His children are little monsters, and he is stupid. In the past, I saw him running after his children with knife," recalled Mohamed. "What a terrible man! Someone should report him to the police; he is a lunatic and a real bully.

Anyhow, shall we listen to some music?" He found a video of a very famous Egyptian singer, Oum Kalthoum, with her playing orchestra-entourage as large as forty musicians, and spectacularly long, exceeding one hour performances. And Mohamed would always sing and his face would always bright up, his eyes would smile, and his whole spirit would lift itself up to perform. In such moments we would forget problems and draw ourselves in literature, more music, and more discussions. "What would you like to do in life?" "I'd like to become a writer, a famous writer," he said. "We would be writing together," I stated. "What are your dreams?" he asked. "I'd like to carry on helping, writing, and then I'd like to meet Kirsty Young on Desert Island Discs. And I would then paraphrase Jack Dee and say: "I know what is wrong with me, I'm a writer!" Honestly, it would be a very fulfilling life; and I'd like to have my little place with a juice-maker, and a coffee maker." "A juice-maker?" he repeated. "Yes, every morning I would squeeze all the juices out of it, pure health."

******

Apparently, last night, Papa Mohamed was promised a job. "Where has he gone?" I asked Mustapha. "Cherchez d'argent, 500DH" "How?" "Je ne sais pas, mais ça va." He was supposed to go away for a few days, but this morning I found him sitting in the cold room downstairs. He was a very proud man and despite mentioning lack of money now and then, he had never asked for any. "There is no more wood for the *forno*." Another obstacle and another worry for Papa. "Mustapha, shall we go and steal some wood? Where can we get it?" "Mustapha will bring it," he jumped up and went away. The milky soup for dinner that we had for the past couple of days, which was quite unusual, and frugal lunches, indicated some financial trouble that I wasn't even aware of. "*Baba* is going to the hospital, we just need to get him to the taxi," said Papa. When the taxi arrived, Mustapha, Papa, and Abdellah had to carry him in his arms as he was too weak to stand up; in the evening, poor *Baba* had fever that was controlled by Papa and Hakima with cold compresses put over his head, legs and back. In my opinion, it was a good sing, it meant that his body was fighting off the illness, but because we had no idea how high the temperature was, it might have been risky leaving this old man to his boiling body. The next morning, he was taken to the hospital in Meknès.

The atmosphere at home was very tense. Everyone looked tired of being poor and having nothing, tired of the struggle, misery, and misfortune. "Wishes! Desires! What does life know about them? Life urges and pushes forward and it has its mighty nature into which we stare with our waiting eyes."

******

Now I understand what it is to be hungry and to suffer; to have no money and eat bread dipped in olive oil every day; I understand the anger and frustration that come with lack of earnings when there are at least ten people to feed; I understand tears that come with resignation, hardship, agony, and anxiety, in one word: poverty; the illness that one cannot cure because there is no money to afford medication. I understand what it is to have no bed and to sleep on the floor all year round, have neither bathroom nor toilet, neither shower nor bath. I understand what it means to be cold, to sleep in a room with no windows and a constant circling breeze. I understand the blessing of the rain for the crops and the rain that comes inside the house. I understand the fragility of a man and his overprotection. I understand the lack of energy that comes with lack of nutrition. I understand love and happiness that come with smallest things. I understand the sacrifices the family is making and their mistrust towards anyone else. I understand.

******

I felt ill. For over two months I was struggling to get rid of the cough and now the pain moved to my chest. I believed I suffered from pneumonia. In pharmacy, I was given antibiotics, only three tablets, and some medication for the cold. It cost me 98DH. And how could the poor afford it? Besides, most of them believed it would pass by itself; if not the regular usage of *olive oil*, the natural healer, would come to help. Papa Mohamed would sit in front of the *forno* and have his body massaged with olive oil claiming its magical effect the following day.

The olive oil does have a magical effect on a body; it's recommended to rub it on the face and body after washing, and it does sooth a dry and irritated cough. However, my case was a little bit too advanced to be cured with some oil as in spite of all the regular intakes of oil olive everyone at home seemed to have suffered from the same problem.

The lack of nutrition in my daily diet was also responsible for my weak state. Although tagine and couscous were delicious, the overcooked vegetable couldn't keep much nutrition values. I also struggled to eat bread and I dreamed of a piece of steak and simple salad with a glass of red wine; and yesterday I had this craving for some hot chocolate. "Maybe we can have a feast?" I asked Mohamed. There was a shop in the medina that supplied us not only with Nesquik, but also with some milk and a tiny pack of some cereals that turned up to be biscuits. Along with those three things I bought a jar of Nescafé, salted almonds, and milk chocolate. This was actually the first time that I had spent money on such ridiculous products. The prices were not fixed and the salesman ripped me off badly. I was so shocked when he quoted 130DH. I couldn't believe that the jar of coffee, a tiny pack of almonds, chocolate, milk, Nesquik, and those biscuits could possibly add up to 130DH. As soon as I spent all that money, I felt guilty and that guilt killed off the pleasure of eating. "How could I be so carless?" I was asking myself when passing by all those hungry people on the street. "What a stupid idea it was! I spend 130DH on things that I could live without!" And although we made hot chocolate at Mohamed's that evening, the flavour of that guilt did not go away.

******

My body carried on fighting against that hideous illness that had attacked me quite badly producing tonnes of sweat preventing me from sleeping. While I was tossing and turning, my body would stick to the sleeping bag and I would yearn to be at home, in Europe, in my bed, inside a cosy house; and I would get up and sit in the warm kitchen sipping my morning coffee and eating a bowl of cereal, and for dinner - a hot bowl of chicken broth, it felt like a life-saver in my dreams. However, the reality was that I had to stay in bed for the three following days. As I had little to eat, my body could not consume bread, nor tagines, nor milky soups, and I had tonnes of raw garlic mixed with some tablets, my time spent with the family was limited to the very necessary: a quick lunch or dinner, as they would still call me over; the repulsive garlicky odour, my red-hot face, and my greasy and dishevelled hair kept me away from a mirror. I was weak like never before, and lonely, as the only company that I had, was the unattractive image of myself that was trapped in my head. On the third day of my crusade, I asked Mohamed to come round, and he did, and everybody was shocked, and they were talking about his visit over dinner. It was an extremely short visit though and was only extended by Meryam who came to my room with tea and some bread. "That was so nice of her," I commented. "Why do you still believe that my family hate you?"

******

The earlier hour of the *hammam* was beneficial for both: me and my family. I could actually sit over breakfast without feeling embarrassed about how I look or smell. The *boucheyar* gave me some energy to walk to the central souk where Mohamed was doing his commercial with the helping hands of his mum and dad. "Why didn't you come and see us?" "I was very ill. Mohamed didn't say anything?" Although my energy level was higher, the cough did not go away, and oddly, everything was getting on my nerves today. "Why does you mum sell things for so little? 5DH for a shirt? You won't earn anything." His mum was a very domineering and controlling person and most of the time she was convinced as to her righteousness; she wasn't progress-oriented being either; the lack of *forno* or unpainted walls in the house did not bother her in the slightest. At the very beginning of our friendship, I suggested painting the walls to give the house a more friendly and warm look. "You can't paint over those walls. They are not finished." "Have you just moved in?" "It was seven years ago," she responded. Some time ago, I suggested installing a wood-burning stove in their house. "This house is freezing cold and it would be good for the family to have one." She said it was unnecessary. Weirdly, his mum could not see the fact that her character, self-righteous and stubborn, did not help to bond the family which she complained about on a few occasions.

Anyhow, we left the souk soon after 1.00pm and went over to the café "Martil" wanting to finish writing our petition. "I started scribbling it down last night. How does it sound?"

189

"En tant qu'habitants de la rue11 à La Scierie, nous nous permettons d'attirer votre attention sur les problèmes du drainage bloqué que nous rencontrons dans ce quartier et particulièrement dans la rue 11…"

When the petition regarding drainage system problem was written, we started producing another one for Timdghass, but the sudden interruption of Mustapha, stopped our inspiration flowing. Although we both liked Mustapha, he was nothing but a character, his presence always created tension between me and Mohamed. Despite all his weirdness and aggressive behaviour after drinking, Mustapha was a terribly honest man. He would be open about his life, and would recall any details of his "adventurously drunken stories," including details of lives of others. There was not much hiding in him which I appreciated. He desperately wanted to communicate with me and his pocket Darija-French phrase book would always be with him. However, when Mohamed was with us, he would be relaying on him to do all the translation. "I'm going with Rashid tonight, we are going to Meknès." "You've got some work, that's good." "What about Papa Mohamed?" "He is too sick, he can't work, but he also doesn't want me to work with anybody else but him." "Why is that? Do you give the family some money? They feed you and give you the shelter; if you explain that you would support them financially, I'm sure he wouldn't mind." When he explained to me how little he earned, I was not surprised that every dirham went to his pocket or rather his throat. "He pays you 200DH for five days of work?" "But I like working with Rashid," he said. "His *camion* is much better, modern, and fast, and I don't have to work too hard compared to what I have to do with Mohamed. He would always say that he was sick and I had to do all that work." "Where do you sleep when you don't come back for a few days?" "In the *camion*," "That must be freezing and uncomfortable." He confirmed that it could get very cold and his body was sore afterwards. Mustapha would tell me everything. "What did he say about Rashid and hashish? Can you translate, please?" I asked Mohamed. "Rashid is a drug dealer; they use his *camion* to transport drugs." "This is the same guy I know?" "The same one," he confirmed. "Translate for me, please," Mohamed appeared extremely unhappy. "Rashid saved up 100.000DH and went off to Spain to work for a couple of years." Apparently, he lived and worked in Madrid but he never liked it, neither Spain nor Spanish people. He called them racists. "Do you know that in Madrid there is a bar that Moroccans cannot enter as it's written down: "No dogs and Moroccans."" "You must be joking?" "No. Rashid saw it and took a photograph."

In 2011 there were nearly one million Moroccan immigrants residing in Spain and the Moroccan government has aggressively been implementing "a strategy of great magnitude" to exert control over the religious and cultural beliefs and practices over them. "The strategy involved establishing a parallel Muslim society in Spain by discouraging Moroccans from integrating into their host country, and by encouraging them instead to live an Islamic lifestyle isolated from Spanish society." According to this article the constructions of hundreds of mosques in Spain has been financed by Raba and *Immams* were directly appointed by the Moroccan government. The

Moroccan state has also been able to control its citizens abroad by imposing Muslim religious instruction in Spanish public schools, and would pressure Moroccan families to remove their children from those schools if they failed to comply.

A separate CNI report about financing Jihad in Spain provides other examples of how the Moroccan government is using Islam for political ends. For example, in November 2008, "the Moroccan Minister of Islamic Affairs organised and paid for a meeting in Marrakesh which was attended by a considerable number of *Immams* and leaders of the Islamic communities in Spain," according to the CNI. At that meeting, the Moroccan government promised "financing for all religious associations and mosques that are prepared to submit to the control of the Moroccan regime and to adhere to its instructions." The keynote speaker at the meeting was Mohamed Yassine Mansouri, head of the Moroccan Secret Service (DGED). The CNI report also states: "The financing is having negative consequences for multicultural coexistence in Spain, such as the emergence of parallel societies and ghettos, Islamic courts and police that operate outside of Spanish jurisprudence, removing girls from schools or forced marriages."

******

The relationship with my Moroccan family had not always been easy but I grew to love them. Although I observed the hardship that they had been experiencing lately, I had no idea how bad the situation at home was until this evening when Allah took 500DH out of his pocket and forced Papa Mohamed to accept it; but no matter how badly he needed the money, his pride could not swallow this generous act of his brother. The following morning, I found Papa Mohamed sitting in the freezing cold room with *Baba* and Halima who, fortunately, were feeling much better. "How much would the wood cost?" I asked. He was showing 10DH and multiplying it until it got to around 145DH. It was the cost of hundred kilograms of wood. I run upstairs and fetched 200DH. "Please, take it." *"La! La! La!"* he was shouting while giving back to me. Finally, Maryam who was watching us fighting, in all fun of it, managed to convince Papa Mohamed to accept the money. His face really brightened up, and like my father, he pulled me to his arms, gave me a big hug, and kissed me on the forehead.

He straight away went to buy some wood and the room was warm again. How this brightened up my day! And how miraculously changed my existence! On the 23 February, 2014, after three and a half months of living in Morocco and experiencing all sorts of emotional dramas, I reported in my diary the irreversible change, and until today I would not know if it was the money or something else that drastically improved their attitude towards me. Perhaps they needed some sorts of reassurance that I did care for them and this small act convinced them of my unconditional love for them. The warmth of that evening was exceptional: both families of Boukmam and Naatit were in our house posing for photos, dancing, singing, sharing food, and then going into a fight… this time the weapon was: skin of consumed mandarins. The pieces of skin were scattered around the room, everybody, with exception of *Baba* and Halima, were participating in this bizarrely enjoyable "fight." It was that evening when *Baba* and Halima were feeling stronger and the family showed an exceptional bond.

The following day I took Mohamed with me to do the translation: "I'd like to take you and Hakima to see a doctor." "We cannot allow you to do that." "Why not?" "You are our child, we cannot accept any help from you." "If I'm your child then I want to take care of you, my parents, allow me to do it, please." *"Wakha,"* and they added, "you know that you have brought so much happiness to our lives, the atmosphere at home has changed, it's not the same home as it was before. You are Magdalena Naatit." Hakima gave me a big hug and Papa once again apologised for the Christmas palaver. "There is no need for that. I understood you wanted to protect me, it was just a big misunderstanding." "I will get you some medication first as you probably have an ulcer." The last time he went to see a doctor was in 1976 in Meknès. Papa praised his Polish doctor who cured the pain almost instantly. Then, some years later when the pain came back, he was given tablets by Hannah's brother, and he claimed that they had helped him. I found out the name and the pharmacy sold them for me. "If those tablets won't help you, and you must take them regularly, we will go to Casablanca to see a doctor," *"Chokrane,"* he reassured me that he would go.

******

I continued to be sick but stubbornly didn't want to go and see a doctor, sounding exactly like half of the nation of Moroccans. "It will pass, I'll get better in Europe," I said to Mohamed. Our relationship had been emotionally and morally tested. "I don't like it when you write things down, you are using your family to write your book," Mohamed accused me. "I'm not using anybody; I'm writing a book about them, so how else can I do it but by writing things down?" "I don't like it," he said angrily. "It seems like everything annoys you lately, but that is not my problem." While Mohamed and I were drifting apart, Mustapha was going through a phase of stealing people's mobiles during nights and sending messages to me. *"Wyih,* toi, tu es maman, ma maman, je t'aime Zahra, moi je fidèle, toujours." Amongst some nonsensical notions, and very much the same endlessly repeated messages, he was also reciting some poetry in Amazigh, and if he wasn't texting, he was inviting himself to my room, splashing handsomely my perfumes over his jumpers and repeating how much he desired to "dormir avec moi," adding, "Je suis malade avec amour pour toi, fatigué, Mustapha fatigué."

In the meantime, we had a visitor in our house; a sister of Papa Mohamed, Itto, who lived in Casablanca with her husband Mustapha and two children, Zechariah and Safwa, came to spend one week with us. It was then when I found out that it was Zechariah who was studying medicine and who was supposed to refer Papa Mohamed to the doctor at the Casablanca's hospital.

One evening, Itto, presented me with a fait accompli before the whole family. "You pay 100DH towards the petrol, I pay 100DH towards the petrol, and the rest will chip in towards food." Her very direct utterance surprised me a little. "Where are we going?" "We all are going to have a picnic in the forest of Ajdir. Are you ok with that?" "Yes, I'd be very happy." She took 100DH out of her purse and gave it to Alla who was supposed to drive us there. "I will give you the money tomorrow," I said and got an even more peculiar response. "No, because Alla has to get some petrol," "Well, I don't have it on me." "I can lend it to you if you want." I took a deep breath knowing that her linguistic "savoir-vivre" wasn't the best; however, what followed next gave me something to ponder about later on. She took another 100DH out of her purse and handed it to Alla, whereupon Alla looked at her, made a comment that allowed her to spit out something incomprehensible: "I trust her." Her response stunned me. I didn't know whether to treat it as a complement, she actually trusted me, or to get offended; the evident lack of her linguistic manners did bother me, but in the end, I treated it as philological faux-pas and I was looking forward to our trip tomorrow. "Who is going to stay with *Baba*?" I asked. "Meryam." "Perhaps we could call Khadeja and ask her to take care of *Baba*; it would be great for Meryam to get out of the house." They didn't, and while in the morning, Hakima was preparing boucheyar, Papa and I went to a local butcher to get two chickens. Then a bag of sardines, fruits, bread, teas, and the whole crew: Hakima, Achraf, Papa Mohamed, Mustapha, Fadma, and I were ready to climb up onto the trailer of Alla's camion, whereas Itto and another sister of Mohamed sat at the front. We drove past Arougou and stopped at Sources Oum Rabia to get some drinkable water. As soon as we entered the Ajdir forest, the landscape changed radically sharing with us patches of snow scattered all over that spectacular scenery and a cool breeze that was accompanying this sudden transformation. Driving right into the forest, picking a good spot in the sun, collecting some wood for the fire and plenty more to take home with us, frying *djeja* and *hut*, drinking tea, having the company of two dogs and sliding down a small snowy hill on a metal dish was all we were doing. The only downside was a freezing cold evening that whipped us and made us tremble on the way home; however, within that drawback there was a positive aspect of sitting in the open trailer - the sky that with its countless dazzling stars was cleanly gazing at us sharing its energy and glee that was simply expressed through *"Inas Inas"* song. What a joy it was coming home and drinking hot tea, and sharing all the stories and photographs with everybody! "Shall we do it again this week? This time Meryam would come with us and Khadeja will stay with grandparents. What do you think?" Itto agreed with me and we would plan another picnic in different place, further away from Khénifra. "I'll give you 200DH, and you Itto give 200DH, and that should be fine, no?" This time it was me who suggested it, trying to avoid further linguistic confusion.

The day of our second trip was bright and sunny, we all got up early, had breakfast, and were ready to set off. Seeing Khadeja who turned up that morning with her daughter and son, convinced me that Meryam would be coming with us; I hugged her and expressed my gratitude, but when we all were getting prepared, Meryam was making bread. "Why are you not ready yet?"

"I'm not coming with you," she said. "Why not? Khadeja is here and you need to get out of the house." "Khadeja wants to go with you," "Shall I talk to her?" "*La!* She will be very upset." The selfishness of Khadeja's attitude disturbed me and got me angry; they all knew how hard Meryam worked and how few opportunities she had to go out, and yet, no one from that large family was willing to sacrifice one day to let her go and have some fun. Instead, Khadeja's daughter, terribly miserable throughout the whole journey, joined us with her brother, the drug addict, who was doing nothing but either sleeping stretched across the truck trailer, or hurrying everyone to get back home when he got bored. Our destination sounded like Rhmad and was written down Lghmad by Mustapha, but my map reading gave me no name that would sound or be written in such or a similar way; however, the one confirmed destination was Assoul, and somewhere in between Khénifra and Assoul we had found our picnic place. On the way there the truck was buzzing with life as all the women and men, excluding Monsif, were making music holding on to plastic bottles or containers while chanting and performing a Berber dance. Most of the time spent in nature was composed of cooking, eating, walking and sliding down a much bigger snow-covered mountain hill, yet again on a metal plate that was taking us right to the bottom of that hill with unimaginable speed. After that, the open fire came as a great source of comfort especially for wet socks, freezing cold feet and hands. Then Mustapha who would call me "love of his life," was sharing with me more tales from his daring life. And before we headed back home, my family, flesh and blood Berber, had performed a dance called *Ahidouss*; they were lined up in a semi-circle with everything in their hands that was used as an instrument, and they were tapping, singing, and dancing for quite a stretch of time. Unforgettable. The way back home was yet again dark and cold, but although there were not enough blankets, we managed to sit close together and keep warm; it was a perfect moment for Mustapha who would take advantage of the situation and force his head on my lap while whispering: "Mon amour, mon amour, *habibi, wyih!*"

******

Notes:

1 (p. 188) Henna plant contains essential oils with high levels of monoterpene alcohols, such as tea tree, eucalyptus, cajeput or lavender, which explained the calming and healing effects. On the other hand, it is known to be dangerous to people with glucose-6-phosphate dehydrogenase deficiency, which is more common in males than females. The negative effects of natural henna paste, may cause occasional allergic reactions.

2 (p. 190) Think, Simon Blackburn, Oxford University Press, 1999, p. 123.

3 (p. 194) Layssahel, lit. God will ease you.

4 (p. 195) It's Moroccan tradition to prepare organ meats such as the liver and heart on the day of the slaughter. Subsequent days include more meat intensive dishes such as Mechoui which is traditionally prepared as a whole roasted lamb either on a spit over a fire or in a pit in the ground. The meat is eaten by hand with salt and cumin for dipping; steamed lamb and Mrouzia - a sweet and spicy Moroccan tagine; a key ingredient in Mrouzia is the Moroccan spice mix called Ras El Hanout - it may contain up to 30 different ingredients including cardamom, nutmeg, anise, mace, cinnamon, ginger, various peppers, and turmeric; saffron also contributes to Mrouzia's unique flavour. Moroccans tend to be very frugal, and there are special dishes which use the head, tail, intestines, stomach and feet.

Even the brains, fat and testicles don't go to waste. (From the articles: "Eid al-Adha in Morocco - Eid al-Kabir, Moroccan Food Traditions for the Festival of Sacrifice," Christine Benlafquih; "Ras El Hanout Recipe - Moroccan Spice Blend," Christine Benlafquih).

5 (p.197) Letters on life, Rainer Maria Rilke, The Modern Library New York, 2006, p.17.

6 (p. 199) Ibid., p. 8.

7 (p. 199) What is olive oil good for? Dry Skin: After exfoliating your body with white sugar on a wash cloth (in the shower, take a little olive oil (infused with a few drops of lavender, if you wish) and gently massage it all over your body. Result? Skin like velvet. If your facial skin is feeling especially dry, take one drop of olive oil in your hands, and very gently tap it all over your face, making sure it doesn't look slick. Take a tissue and blot your skin just a little. You'll have skin that's soft and moist, but not greasy. Extra-dry elbows and feet: First exfoliate both areas with white sugar. Then, massage a little extra virgin olive oil on your elbows and feet (especially the heels) every night. You will see an unbelievable transformation. Sun Burn, Rash, Wound or Insect Bites: Gently apply a light layer of olive oil and leave uncovered. It helps with the itching and speeds up the healing. It's great for diaper rash, too. Makeup Remover: This is the best and most gentle way to remove makeup from your face, even your eyes. Olive oil can remove the toughest waterproof mascara without harsh chemicals or soap that can irritate eyes. Allergic reactions to olive oil are practically non-existent. Cuticles: Soak your nails in a little tray of olive oil. This will soften cuticles, making them easier to push during a manicure. Avoid cutting cuticles as that could cause infection or irritation. Shaving: Whether shaving facial hair or your legs, putting a light layer of olive oil on damp skin first is a better option that shaving cream. Dandruff: Massage a light layer of olive oil onto your scalp and leave it there for a few hours before washing. If your baby has cradle cap, a very common skin condition on the scalp, apply a layer of olive oil every day until it disappears. Weight Loss: Many people, especially from the Mediterranean, drink ¼ cup of extra virgin olive oil every morning, followed by a small glass of warm water mixed with fresh lemon juice. This helps to cleanse the body, and jump-start the system. Women I met in Israel swear that drinking the olive oil each morning keeps hunger pangs away and has helped with weight loss and maintenance. Olive oil is also good for: Heart Disease and Stroke Prevention, Gallstone Reduction, Colon Cancer Prevention, Breast Cancer Prevention, Alzheimer's Disease, Diabetes. (From the article: The Healing Power Of Olive Oil, Barbara Hannah Grufferman).

8 (p. 201) As the residents of the street 11 in La Scierie, we would like to draw your attention to problems of the blocked drainage that we encounter in this area, and particularly on the street number 11.

9 (p. 202) Morocco Blocking Integration of Muslim Immigrants in Spain, Soeren Kern, 2011.

10 (p. 205) Hut, in Darija, fish.

11 (p. 206) Ahidouss, written also Ahidus, a collective Berber dance, next to Ahouach, is held by a number of performers from both men and women playing on the rhythms of drums while chanting. It is said that these dances begin with chanted prayer, and that the ritual music is also used as protection against evil spirit.

12 (p. 206) Habibi/Habeebi, in Arabic, my beloved, darling, also a friend.

End of Part Six

Washing sheep skin on the banks of Oum er-Rbia river with Hakima.

Part Seven

"Mum, I believe I have found a man with whom I'd like to spend my life. Isn't it odd that he is Moroccan? Please see the attached photograph." I tried to be gentle and not to scare my mum, or give her unnecessary palpitations. My mum's response was rather sensible and unexpected. "I don't want to be a bad mother and I will not stand in the way of your happiness, you have to do what your heart tells you." However, the final comment in that email, "it's not something that could be discussed over an email or a phone call," insinuated certain difficulties that my following announcement could bring about. I tried to highlight, first the positive aspects of meeting a man who was giving me the stimulus that was needed to build a successful relationship, and in the same breath underlying all the differences related to culture and religion, and how it was uniting instead of dividing us. I was also trying to justify that hasty decision of wanting to tie the knot by making relevant comparisons with my previous long-term failed relationships; I then asked my mum to look for my birth certificate and gather necessary information from the Office of Civil Status. The next message that came from her was brief, full of worries and shock. "Are you familiar with the law there? If something would not work out, what would happen to you?" adding that she wanted me to be happy, but regretfully, she would not go to any office and would advise me to postpone my decision. I could understand her concern and had I been her I would probably have reacted in the same way; however, with obstacles piling up, frustration and the lack of support from anyone, her opposition was the last thing I wanted to hear.

The difficulty was not with the waiting but pretending. I was getting tired of acting as if there was nothing between us, and the more fake situations I had to put myself though, the more frustrating arguments Mohamed and I had to face. Without doubt, to have a normal relationship in Morocco was simply impossible.

I listened to the followers of Islam, who would tell me that friendship between a man and a woman does not exist, and that a man's visit to the house must always be explained. "A man who comes to your house must have a motive," Itto, a devoted follower of Islam, explained. She recalled a story: "My sister in law is going to get married. All the formalities are done but the act of marriage. I cannot invite this man to my house despite the fact that I know they are going to get married. I need to see a marriage certificate." When I mentioned Mohamed's brief visit to our house while I was sick, her response was predictable but sounded equally abnormal for me: "If it was me, I would not have allowed him to enter the house. I would not tolerate his presence there." And she added: "If you follow Islam you are not supposed to: pick up girls, lie, smoke, drink alcohol, have intimate relationships before marriage, or show your feelings towards your spouse publicly." "Don't you think it's a little bit harsh?" "No, you are making a choice, either your follow Islam entirely, or you lead your life without Islam. This is what people do here, everyone follows the Ramadan but not everyone follows Islam. They choose what they want to follow and what they want to abandon, and that's wrong."

It seemed to me as if Moroccan society was divided into three groups; the first consisted of the devoted followers of Islam, the second was the mixed one with no dedicated followers but those who strongly proclaimed Islamic roots, and the third would be those who seemed not to obey any rules, including any moral etiquette. That group was represented by Simo, the waiter from the "Omega" café who purely by chance happened to talk to a man whom he was not supposed to talk: Mustapha.

One evening, Mustapha came to my room mumbling something incomprehensible. "What Simo are you talking about?" "Omega" café. "What is he saying?" "Dormir avec Margarena." "Are you asking me if I slept with him? Why would I do that? Who told you those things?" "Simo m'a dit quelque chose." No matter how badly he tried to get the message across, I failed to understand his story. However, the following day Mohamed and I bumped into him. "Can you explain your story to Mohamed, please?" He did, and it turned out that Simo, the waiter, who at the very beginning of my stay in Morocco was very keen on getting to know me but had been turned away, was now spreading some nasty lies amongst people from the "Omega" café. He claimed a rather successful evening in my company where he had got me drunk and then slept with me. I could not believe this nonsense. He wasn't even bad-mouthing me, he was damaging my reputation claiming that I was a drunken, easy slut. "He can't get away with those lies. Mustapha, will you come with me to the café?" His shifts at work were quite easily established and one evening three of us paid him a visit. We sat outside and waited for him to come out and take the order. "Hi Simo, could you remind me one thing?" I said. "When was that evening that you got me drunk and slept with me? My memory is like a sieve." He got uncomfortable and straight away accused Mustapha of lying. "You are crazy, you are insane," he said pointing at him and disappeared. "He will come back with our teas," I was calming Mustapha down. And he did. "Sit down, we need to talk," Mustapha placed a chair in front of him when he reappeared at our table. "I'm busy now but give me two minutes and I'll come back."

Simo was the guy who would constantly make spiteful remarks towards Mohamed, and would always stick his nose into my coffee with his "Madame or Mademoiselle" comment. His attitude and a sudden disappearance of Zouhir made me stop going to that café a long time ago.

This time Simo came back with a rather apologetic attitude. "So why did you say all things?" "I was only joking," he said. "This is not funny; you know that if I went to the police, you would be imprisoned." It was not only my remark that made him anxious, but also a "crazy" Mustapha who was observing him without saying a word. "If you carry on spreading lies you will lose your job." "Désolé, désolé, I didn't mean to upset you," he said. He was plain stupid and his face marked with quite a number of scars confirmed his dumbness, his brainless verbal and physical acts, his careless remarks, his dull presence. This story irritated Mustapha who was ready to punch him and add another scar to his collection. "I'll find out where he lives," he said. "Oh no, you stay calm, it's not worth fighting with him, you will just get into some trouble, don't do it." I said. "Margarena *mezyana*," he commented. "If he keeps spreading lies then we will tackle it in a different way." Later we also found out that he was married with two children.

******

I contacted the Human Rights Organization and heard some good news. The prosecutor looked into our case and sent the police over to Jamal's, but the man ran away. Also Meryam's medical condition was to be checked by a doctor. When I paid another visit to the family of Azziz delivering the clothes I had bought them, I was informed of the police visit to their house and Malika's willingness to co-operate with them. "Where is Malika?" I asked. "She is testifying at the police station," said Itto. When I heard the news I felt elated, happy for the family and proud that a small step towards the protection of a vulnerable human being was taken; it still felt like a small step but it was made and perhaps the second would be made too. I wanted to believe that with a little bit more persistence and patience we would win this battle and many more that would come. However, I would soon find out that my view on protecting Malika would not be shared or perceived the same way by everybody, but in fact it would provoke the opposite reaction by those who should never have got involved in the case.

I wanted to keep the positive energy and look at other cases that waited to be resolved, with the same optimism and confident drive. The petition regarding the drainage system in our street was deposited at the right office in Khénifra and another one was ready to be taken to Timdghass. The petition, ink and the camera were packed and we were on our way to El Kebab. "Where are your friends?" I was taken aback by seeing only Jamal at the bus stop. "Do they no longer want to help us?" "They got scared." said Jamal. "Scared of what?" "Theoretically, we haven't formed an association yet and they believe they could get into trouble with the authorities," he explained. "Do you have to be represented by an association to talk to people, take their signatures or make a video-film?" I asked bewildered. "I don't think so, but they will not help us." On the contrary, it was me who could have got into trouble with the Moroccan authorities, as by law, the smallest action that I was taking or helping with was considered unlawful and could be regarded as a political provocation.

Fortunately, the person that we depended on, uncle Mustapha, turned up thirty minutes later and drove us around the mountains in his three-wheeled motorbike. The houses with no electricity were scattered all over the mountains and some proved impossible to get to on that motorcycle. The most peculiar thing of all was that amongst the households that were deprived of electricity were families who weren't affected by the lack of it. In other words, one house with no access to electricity stood only twenty meters from the one that had it, which confirmed Mustapha's speculations about connections and corruption. When we stopped by one household to take signatures, we managed to interview a man who had signed up to the XXI century not a long time ago. Probably unconsciously, he revealed his links with the local authorities, stating that without connections there was nothing one could do. Another house with eight inhabitants was totally dependent on a singular solar panel, others were using gas to light up their homes. The last house cut-off from any electricity that we visited that day was Mona's and her parents.

"Madeleine, Madeleine," she was hugging me while repeating how happy she was to see me. We were asked to come inside for tea and while Mohamed was taking signatures, I explained something important to Mona. "This is not Mohamed, this is Jamal." Tracing the story back, after my very first visit in the mountains when I had met Mona, I came back with an idea of introducing her to Mohamed, the caretaker, thinking of them as a perfect match. When I first mentioned it to Mohamed he smiled, but on the second occasion his interest in meeting her was confirmed. "Mohamed, she is really wonderful, you will like her," I encouraged him to come with us to Timdghass one day and spend some time with Mona, warning him that she was divorced, hence no longer a virgin.

So when I saw her that day, she did appear a little bit nervous and was hiding in the kitchen for the first ten minutes of our visit, thus I owed her explanation. "We may come back next week or the following one." She was excited about the possibility of meeting Mohamed, and I wanted to be a good matchmaker. When our job was done, five short video-films were made, a number of photographs taken, and fingerprints collected, we headed back to El Kebab to catch a taxi. Not far from El Kebab we were pulled over by a car which we had overtaken that turned out to be the police. "Who are you? Where do you come from? What are you doing here? Where do you live etc.?" He kept asking and I kept responding without mentioning my unlawful activities. Fortunately, he did not require any documents and appeared to have been satisfied with my answers, letting us go and wishing me good luck.

The next visit at uncle's Mustapha happened only a few days later and in a company of Mohamed, the caretaker. "We will meet at 9.30am at the bus station," I texted him the day before. At 9.30am he wasn't there but informed us through a message about his delay. "I'm about to catch a taxi now." When another fifteen minutes passed and there was no sign of Mohamed, I picked up my phone. "Where are you?" "In El Borj," he said. "You are late, the bus is leaving in ten minutes, hurry up." I was a little bit irritated with him. "A guy who was running late for his first date wasn't a promising sign," I was thinking. Just after 10.00am Mohamed appeared on the horizon, and not one single *smhli* was given. The bus that we took was crammed full of passengers; we sat at the back, so when finally the ticket inspector got to us, we were quite a distance from Khénifra. "60DH for three," he said. "What?" We couldn't hide our surprise and were quickly calculating in our heads the startling difference between what we had paid to get to

El Kebab and what we had to pay now for a five kilometre longer journey. It was illogical and we were sniffing a swindle, an opportunity for this guy to make some money. Mohamed picked up his mobile and called a friend who had travelled to Timdghass one month ago and had only paid 12DH per ticket, which meant that this guy had in his pocket our 20DH. The second time, when the same ticket collector jostled his way forward to charge new passengers, Mohamed couldn't help but say to him: "The ticket doesn't cost 20DH, does it?" "Of course it does," he claimed. "Why did the same ticket cost 12DH one month ago? You should give us back our 20DH," carried on Mohamed. The ticket collector flew off the handle while giving us and other passenger who were actively listening and looking a real spectacle. He took money out of his pocket and threw 20DH and then another 20DH while articulating angrily some nonsense. This man was neither innocent nor was he honest and his irrational behaviour exposed nothing but his opportunistic character and transparent intentions. We confiscated the 20DH that he had stolen from us and gave him back the second banknote that he had carelessly abandoned.

Mona, in her glorious pyjama and perfect make-up, was ready to meet the suitor. She seemed nothing but excited, but the suitor showed no emotion whatsoever, there was neither positive nor negative emotion seen on his face but rather bland, unaffected reflection; his mouth was expressing nothing, he wasn't engaged in any conversation nor did he try to make any. On the contrary, Mona's face looked bright, her eyes were smiling and she was whispering in my ear: "*Chokrane*, Madeleine, *chokrane, zwin, zwin, chokrane*," indicating nothing but glee and arousal. I was pleased that she fancied him, but so far it was one-sided infatuation. I knew I had to provoke a situation that would allow them to interact. "Let's all go for a walk, Mona, Mohamed, get ready." They did look good together and I was hoping that Mohamed's indifference would soon be substituted with a promise or, at least, a smile. As there was no time to be wasted, Mohamed and I quickly left them in the middle of the field to themselves. "Mohamed, what do you think?" "They talk, that's a good sign," he said. We strolled around the fields but were actively observing every move of Mona and Mohamed. "They are still sitting and talking, I hope this matchmaking will work."

When they came back, Mohamed, the caretaker, suggested going home before lunch. "Oo, oo, that doesn't sound promising," I was thinking. "We will have lunch here first and then we will go. Do you want to come with us to see what's over there?" I pointed at the opposite side of the field. We sat down within a safe distance of the house. "So how did it go?" I was eager to hear the news. "You don't look particularly happy, don't you like Mona? Isn't she beautiful and sweet?" "Yes," he responded and went silent. "Yes what?" I was trying to pin him down. "She is very nice," he said. "Nice is not good, is it?" "She doesn't have a mobile, so it will be very difficult to communicate with her. She gave me Fatima's number though." Mohamed strongly disagreed. "If you don't like her, you should not contact her." "I suppose it's very difficult to make a decision right away, perhaps it would be worth them exchanging some messages. Why do you disagree with that?" I asked. "It's not the way that it should be done," he went on. "What you are saying is that he should make up his mind now?" I asked. "If he has intentions to marry her, he should come back and see her parents," he stated. "What do you think, Mohamed?" "I don't know," he said. "Where is that girl whose photos you showed me?" "In Spain," he said. "Ah, poor Mona has not a chance against a girl who lives in Spain," I joked meaningfully. He gently denied it, but it was a very sad truth. Yes, what man would choose a poor, divorced girl who lives in the mountains with her controlling parents over the possibility of travelling, or even living abroad with a more independent, single woman? We headed back home to have lunch. "*Chokrane* Madeleine, *chokrane*," Mona continued to thank me and I didn't dare to take this joy away. I can only say that I was a very unsuccessful matchmaker.

******

The sudden and unexpected disappearance of Khadeja and her daughter after our second family trip was considered abnormal by everyone at home. As soon as we arrived in La Scierie, very late in the evening, there was no sign of them and no one knew what had happened. The day after, however, we were invited to Khadeja's for lunch and yet again we took the camion. This time it was Maryam and Lahcen's father who came with us. There was a large quantity of food that I could hardly consume and what was served last and what I liked most was the home-made *elben* with couscous. It tasted so healthy but I had only found a tiny space in my stomach that fitted a small bowlful, no more than that. When we filled up our "bidons," Papa and I went out. "Do you want to drive the *camion*?" he asked me. "Can I?" "Let's go, I'll show you how it works." I wasn't sure if I would manage to drive this old truck but I was up for trying. Papa connected the necessary cables to get the engine running and explained the gear to me. "Three forward gears plus one reverse." "So, to reverse I need to pull it forward; got it." Off to pedals now. "Oh merde, that is tricky," I said laughing. "Maybe we should oil them?" I added. I succeeded in reversing the old truck and then had a little go with driving forward but I couldn't see myself continuing it on the main road. "You are certainly much better than me," I said to Papa. "However, I can proudly say that I drove the *camion* in Morocco; I can go home satisfied." Papa liked my little drive but was happy to take over.

Our next little stroll across the fields was taking us over to Mohamed's mum's house, where Meryam, Saida one of Khadeja's daughters and Lahcen's father were found sitting in a room with TV on, keeping Mohamed's mum company and helping her make boucheyar. The man who would start eating and always finish first would be Lahcen's father. Goodness me, this man was deprived of table manners or any manners at all, he was the simplest of all the people that I met: he would come to our house and wait until lunch or dinner was served and as soon as the plate was on the table, he would begin without waiting for the others. He was the worst of all the belchers, lip-smackers, slurpers, and devourers of food. His lack of manners would reach so far as to stretch over on to everybody else's side of the plate, raking the food in without any hesitation, concern, shame or embarrassment. And the moment he finished he would be gone. "He doesn't even contribute towards food," I was told by Itto. I did not trust this man and his arrogance disturbed me; however, I had no choice but simply tolerate him.

******

On the 3rd March, Mustapha was to celebrate his 30th birthday. As he had never had a birthday party before, I wanted to surprise him with a cake and a present. Mohamed agreed to accompany me to the medina to print off some photographs for him and to get a scarf. "You were right," he said. "About what?" "Controlled feelings. I understand it now and it drives me crazy." "May I give you a kiss?" I asked. "Yes." In fact it was our second public kiss, and oddly enough nothing happened, the public did not react and carried on with their lives as before, no one shouted or pointed at us, we neither got arrested nor dragged to the police station, we didn't offend anyone but perhaps only made them jealous by proclaiming our feelings publicly. And what is all the fuss about kissing in public? Here is the answer: kissing equals crime:

"In this world, where cultural and religious beliefs play a predominant role, public display of affection is not normal but is considered a crime punishable with varying punishments. In such countries, people are uncomfortable when affection is displayed in public even in a moderate level. In the Arab world, encompassing twenty-two countries in the Middle East and North Africa, Islam is the official religion in most of the countries. Such countries are governed by the Shari'ah Law (Islamic Law). Accordingly, couples, whether married or otherwise, are strictly prohibited from displaying affection in any form in public. The punishment for the offence ranges from flogging to imprisonment, to fine, and sometimes even deportation, in the case of expatriates."

Being alone with a woman or a man, looking at each other, kissing, hugging, touching are on the list of the forbidden in Muslim world as it could only tempt evil, the greater *zina*, which is adultery or fornication: "Allaah has decreed for every son of Adam his share of *zina*, which he will inevitably commit. The *zina* of the eyes is looking, the *zina* of the tongue is speaking, one may wish and desire, and the private parts confirm that or deny it." Allaah says: "Tell the believing men to lower their gaze (from looking at forbidden things), and protect their private parts (from illegal sexual acts). That is purer for them. Verily, Allaah is All Aware of what they do. And tell the believing women to lower their gaze (from looking at forbidden things), and protect their private parts (from illegal sexual acts)."

One article explains the gazing part:

"Allaah commands the believing men and women to lower their gaze and guard their chastity, which is because of the serious nature of *zina* and what it leads to of great corruption among the Muslims. Letting one's gaze wander freely is one of the causes of SICKNESS IN THE HEART and the occurrence of immoral actions, whereas lowering the gaze is one of the means of keeping oneself safe from that. Think about how Allaah connects the issue of lowering the gaze with the issue of protecting the private parts (guarding one's chastity) in these verses, and how lowering the gaze is mentioned first, before protecting the private parts, because the eye influences the heart."

Does "sickness in the heart" or "eye influences the heart" stand for LOVE? If so, to follow this way of thinking it would mean that Islam does not allow Muslims to fall in love before making a life-lasting commitment. I believe this may explain my reoccurring question as to why there is an equally high rate of marriages and divorces. "Allaah knows the fraud of the eyes, and all that the breasts conceal." But if Allah saw a growing pure love between two yet unmarried people would he condemn such feeling? The following passage not only dooms love before marriage but also spreads anxiety:

"The Muslim has to fear his Lord in secret and in public, and keep away from that which Allaah has forbidden of being alone with a member of the opposite sex, looking, shaking hands, kissing and other *haraam* (forbidden) actions which lead to the immoral action of *zina*."

The person who is behind those acts is instantly called a sinner:

"The sinner should not be deceived into thinking that he will not commit *zina* and that he will stop at these *haraam* actions and not go that far, for the Shaytaan will never leave him alone. There is no *hadd* punishment for these *haraam* actions, such as kissing etc., because the *hadd* punishment is only for intercourse *(zina)*, but the judge may punish him with a *ta'zeer* punishment to deter him and others like him from committing these sins."

Hadd punishment that makes the chill run down my spine, is a prescribed punishment in Islam for particular crimes. If guilt is established beyond doubt in a shari'ah court, then the punishment cannot be overturned, pardoned or changed. Specifically it is for the following crimes:

- Drinking alcohol, taking drugs or other intoxicants - 40 lashes for a first offence and 80 lashes for continuous offences.

- Giving false testimony e.g. accusing a woman of adultery/fornication without 4 trustworthy eyewitnesses - 80 lashes.

- For cutting the hand of the burglar that steals tangible non-perishable wealth (e.g. gold or silver but not food) of value above that of 1.0625g of gold from a hidden secure place without having any right to it and while there is no drought, famine, war etc.

- For unlawful sexual intercourse - 100 lashes for an unmarried man or woman and death by stoning for a married man or woman.

•   For apostasy without repenting - capital punishment, and treason by betraying and fighting against the Muslim nation.

Hadd does not apply to any other types of crime. On the other hand, *ta'zeer* is a punishment decided by the Shari'ah judge for other crimes and is always less than the *hadd* e.g. maximum of 39 lashes (i.e. less than the punishment of drinking alcohol). This could be a fine, it could be confiscation or it could be lashes.

The following passage explains:

"The Shari'ah provision nips the evil in the bud with a firm hand and puts down its foot strongly to stop mischief and to ensure peace to the society. Islamic punishments are, therefore, the most suited to bring about peace and peaceful conditions. Islam deals with the culprit rather heavily in the interest of his would-be victims."

Another chapter from a different article made me realise another important aspect of integrating with men. How many times had I raised the question: "Why do they talk about Islam with me all the time?" or stated: "Ali can just talk about Islam with me."

"To be clear, Islam does not forbid women and men from talking to one another, but asks that they practice modesty and remain within the limits that Shari'ah has set. In the case of talking, one should talk only when necessary about an important and relevant matter to a teacher, a co-worker, a relative, and neighbours as long as conditions are applied and are normal. It is permissible for men and women to mix for the purpose of medical treatment. Also, if THE PURPOSE OF MIXING IS TO LEARN ABOUT ISLAM or other education permitted by Shari'ah, THEN MIXING IS ALLOWED. In the case of family, in 'Silat ar-Rahm' which is to keep the ties of kinship or family ties, good relations between all members of the family and taking care of those who are in need is important. In this occasion, mixing is permitted as long as it is not done privately and not for the purpose of entertainment and socialising and is kept within limits. By following the guidelines of Islam, men and women can achieve positive relationships that incorporate respect and understanding. Muslims must develop a mutual understanding of the limits and rules, which apply to both men and women. The proper contact and cooperation between opposite sexes is nothing if not a test of faith."

To behave the lawful way meaning the *"halal"* way is to avoid desire - *"shahawat"* and doubts - *"shubuhat"* one of the reasons why dating is not allowed.

"The Shari'ah, or Islamic law, has set certain guidelines that should be followed by every male and female, old or young, married or single. These guidelines explain how to deal with any relationship, whether at work, school, with relatives, friends, or even in markets. There are rules in relation to how to speak, dress, and behave, as well as what to prevent from happening in case of contact with the opposite sex. Free mixing between members of the opposite sex is only allowed with permanently or blood-related Muslims, known as *'mahrams,'* i.e. people of the opposite sex who have reached puberty that a Muslim is not allowed to marry. *Mahrams* to women are the father, grandfather, great-grandfather, son, brother, grandson, great-grandson, father-in-law, son-in-law, uncle, stepson, stepfather, and *rada*, people who have become *mahrams* because of being nursed by the same mother. This also applies for *mahrams* to men, who would include their aunt, grandmother, sister and so on. If a Muslim or a Muslimah (a female Muslim) is a *non-mahram (ghayr mahram)*, not a relative within the prohibited degrees in seclusion, all the rules established by Shari'ah about separation of both sexes apply. All these rules apply when dealing with both Muslims and non-Muslims of the opposite sex. Islam directed that a man and a woman should avoid being alone with one another. The Prophet Mohammad said, "No man should be alone with a woman except when there is a *mahram* with her." (Sahih Muslim). This is of course to avoid any sin through action or thought."

I believe, I broke every single rule of Shari'ah by applying my own rules: I looked at people, I smiled at them, I was left alone with men, I kissed a man and that man even came to my house and my bedroom: "If a man or a woman are alone together in an isolated place, then the third is Satan." This is related to the concept of *'khulwa,'* which means seclusion—where a *non-mahram* man and woman are in a private place that requires permission to get in, such as a house or a bedroom. This is highly forbidden in Islam and goes against the rules of Shari'ah."

The religious standpoints of Islam are highly controversial. The case of a couple that was arrested for kissing publicly, or rather showing photographs on Facebook in December 2013, which I had already mentioned, brought out rather mixed feelings. While many were defending those teenagers in an organised public kissing protest, others were condemning them saying: "We are an Islamic country and kissing in public is forbidden. A simple kiss can lead to other things."

Another article brought to light somewhat harsh criticism:

"Love may be in the air, but it is not allowed in the world of Islam. Several recent cases of public kissing and hugging have caused such a stir, one would think something truly tragic must be happening. But no, it is nothing more than a string of cases where people just want to be friendly." And the same author continues: "Modesty and morality are fantastic traits to have, but the Islamic religious police have become so overzealous, what is called a "conservative culture" by the mainstream media, is really a stifling civilization fixated on suppressing any and every demonstration of love. This is apparently out of fear of contaminating their otherwise sparkling clean, healthy and moral society. Right? After all, rapes, tortures, honour killings, child marriages, female genital mutilation, slavery and constant human rights abuses in general, all point to a "moral and modest" society. Well, this is morality in a Muslim world."

We went from kissing to printing off quite a collection of photographs and buying a rather nice scarf – this time cashmere for sure. It was before 11.00pm when Mustapha came to my room to use my perfumes. "Margarena, demain anniversaire de Mustapha." "I know. In fact I have a present for you. As it's only one our left to your birthday I can give you now." My present, nicely wrapped up, evoked an extreme joy that led him to push me tightly towards him while hugging and lifting me up at the same time. "Insanity runs through your blood," I laughed. "*Wyih! Chokrane*, tu es généreuse, belle, *bzzaf, bzzaf, bzzaf.*" "It's nothing, it's just a small gift, I hope you will like it." He really did; he found a comfortable pocket for the photographs that he carried with him all the time, a pocket of the coat that I had initially bought for Papa Mohamed, and the scarf, disregarding the weather, sunny, rainy, cold or hot, was kept around his neck. The *torta* that I bought the following morning was swiftly consumed in the afternoon in the company of the two Fadmas, Meryam and Hakima.

Later that day, I took Mustapha to a café and afterwards accepted his invitation to walk around the medina with him. Incidentally, we came across a young man, a son of Alla, with whom we exchanged greetings, and then were attracted by the smell that was coming from a popcorn machine which I adored as it was popping out fresh, crunchy corns for as little as 1DH for a reasonable amount.

"There is another scandal in the family," said Mustapha. "What scandal?" "Alla's son, the one who we've just seen, is in love with an older woman." "Why is that a problem? Can't he love someone older than him?" Unfortunately, I didn't understand his explanation of the whole problem behind something that he had described as a scandal but I understood well another dilemma of his. "So you still don't have a mobile phone?" "I have this old one but I don't have a number," he said. "How do you look for work without a mobile?" "No work for Mustapha now, but *Inchallah*." "Let's go to the boutique and I'll get you that number. It doesn't cost that much does it?" "25DH." That evening he was able to make a few phone calls and managed to line up a few days of work. The only downside of getting him that number was his instant, persistent and constant message-sending pasting. Whether he would be away or sitting in the downstairs room, his messages would flow and his love expressed through them would keep him awake until the moment when he would get physically and emotionally exhausted. "Je suis fatigué avec l'amour pour toi." Then he would stop sending me messages for few hours and then start all over again with informing me about his whereabouts and his future dreams.

However, that evening threw a spanner in the works of going away with Hakima as Rkia who was moved to our house seemed to have been in rather a critical condition.

******

The relationship with my boyfriend wasn't the easiest of all. He would spend less and less time with me and the fifteen minutes over coffee would feel more like a sacrifice than a pleasure. The accusation of me taking advantage of my family to write the book was heard on more than one occasion; so when I would pose any question, he would get suspicious and hesitate to answer. As, from the very onset, he knew about my writing plans, it was difficult for me to understand such peculiar behaviour. It felt as if he was sabotaging the relationship as his criticism had no real basis, everyone else around me was keen on sharing their stories. "I want this story to be as authentic as possible and I want it to be read," I said, adding, "out of all people, I would have never expected to be judged or criticised by you." My point of view was barely understood. Perhaps I overestimated some of the European features that I had seen in him; but it wasn't even a question of his origin but his character, and in many arguments he had shown his self-righteousness, narrow-mindedness and lack of sensitivity. The mature Mohamed that I had known had turned into a spoilt, stubborn child who wouldn't listen but would provoke, and who wasn't even apologetic afterwards. It was hard to communicate, and the more we tried, the more we talked at cross purposes.

Anyhow, Mustapha, who talked repetitively about my generosity, love, and his desire to spend a night with me, was keeping more and more company with me at the café "Martil" "Let's run home," I said. "I'm hungry. I hope it won't be too late for lunch." Luckily, there were some leftovers left for us that were shared between me, Mustapha, and Zahra, Bahssa's daughter, who paid us a visit that afternoon. At the table, I overheard the word *epo* in the discussion between Meryam and Papa. I could feel the heavy weight of that word injected with a great deal of worries and grief. "How is Rkia?" I asked. "She is going to the hospital," they replied. "Can I come with you?" They all agreed. Within five minutes we were organised and ready to assist her. When the taxi arrived, the extremely fragile and immobile granny had to be carried by Mustapha, and together with Mina and other neighbour, she was taken to the emergency unit. "You will go with Papa Mohamed, Hakima, Fadma and Zahra. *Wakha*?" said Meryam. "*Wakha*. Why is Mina going with us?" "She knows some doctor." That was the sad Moroccan reality: connections counted even in the public health sector.

Papa Mohamed drove through the town and dropped us off in front of the hospital. The same emergency unit with more less the same number of sick people and the same chaos controlled by the same guard who recognised me and acknowledged my presence with a warm greeting. To enter the emergency unit with calm and quiet meant to get into the queue and wait for a long stretch of time as a number of spectacular and dramatic entries with sick people being carried in someone's arms and surrounded by a few who would create chaos by jostling through the crowd and shouting giving the feeling of an extreme sense of emergency, were always referred to a doctor first; and Rkia was the perfect example of it. We all waited patiently for the good news. When Mustapha appeared at the door to tell us that everything was going smoothly, the bodyguard invited me in. At first I refused, but after a short while I slipped through the crowd to get to another room with more sick people who were being seen by a couple of doctors, and then through the corridor to a bigger room with six beds lined up. It was a room for patients that were kept there for longer term observation.

Rkia's bed was the closest to the half-opened window protected by metal bars. As it was overlooking the front yard, there were large numbers of people who would stand in front of it and ask for information about the patients inside. Rkia was there with Hakima and Mina and a young doctor or a nurse who was inserting the drip. Her face looked extremely pale and her widely open and blunt eyes kept staring at a fixed point giving me a rather creepy feeling of her resignation. The only word she kept repeating every few minutes was *amen* that she always carried with her in a tiny bottle.

I will never forget that fixed gaze and fear seen in her stare and the strength with which she was holding my hand, and I let her squeeze it as hard as she wanted; it might have been her only comfort in that moment. All of a sudden, a young man sobbing loudly, entered the room carrying in his arms a torso and legs; no head was visible. The body, in some sort of convulsion, was placed on the closest to ours bed, and I finally could see a woman. Tortured by tremendous pain, her rapid, shallow and jerky breaths were forcing the ribcage out giving the sensation of being pushed out far too much; the extremity flattened the torso making it look like a box rather than a body. The young man's strong sobs made it clear to Mina that the woman was having a heart attack. The half scene that I could see from behind the screen, as Rkia was not letting go of my hand, showed not only the panic of that young man, but also two other individuals with him who weren't particularly bothered by his grief. On the contrary, they were standing in front of that dying woman talking to each other smiling. They seemed content. However, Mina's motherly instinct led her to hug this young man strickened by anguish and comfort him by saying that everything was going to be well. "Your mum will be fine, you will see," she kept repeating it making him feel calmer. If only I had been able to get up, I would have done the same; but grandma Rkia needed my hand and I couldn't take it away from her.

The doctor put the oxygen mask around her face but her breaths were still unbearably arrhythmic, out of control - perturbing and nerve-racking to watch. "Don't worry," I said to that boy on the first occasion I saw him, "your mum will be fine, they will rescue her." He gave me a smile but gigantic tears were streaming down his face. He went out, but not a minute would pass without him standing in front of the window looking anxious. "Come back inside, your mum is feeling better," I shared with him the good news. Not forty minutes had elapsed when the same woman stood up, said *bslama*, and walked away without even consulting the doctor.

In the meantime, when Rkia was on the second 500ml drip, a doctor came by. *"La bas? Chwiya?"* he asked. "Now we will stop the drip in order to take the blood pressure," he said. The blood pressure wasn't bad at all, 108/68, which was very close to the normal 120/80. The doctor left and he didn't return for a long while leaving us in limbo. "So what do we do now?" I asked Mina who was the only one there with me. "I don't know," she responded. "Do you think he forgot about the drip?" I continued. She was sure he did. "I'll turn it on, our grandma needs some strength," I added. The steady flow of the drip was put back on and fully monitored.

Not more than fifteen minutes after the lady with the heart attack had left the room, another woman in tears and total distress interrupted the silence. She put her daughter on a bed and was trying to calm her down while she was crawling in pain on that bed. This girl was only nine years old and was experiencing moments of irregular heartbeats causing her to freak out. "Mum, mum, I can't breathe, I can't breathe," Mina was explaining her agony. This girl was left to herself, her pain, and her mum. No doctor or nurse was there; so when she was going through another breathless moment that was hard to watch, I reacted, "where is the doctor?" and left the room to search for help. While I walked through the corridor sticking my head through each door, I finally came across a female doctor who was sitting in her cabinet. "Excuse me, a child needs your help." I said it in a rather irritated manner; but while I was expressing my annoyance with that medic, the mother and the girl had left the room in search for some help.

My curious nature found out it was rheumatic fever that this child suffered from, a potentially life-threatening disease, a complication of untreated strep throat caused by a bacteria called group 'A' streptococcus. An extremely dangerous disease that not only effects some parts of the body by making them become swollen, but also very seriously effects the nervous system, a disease called chorea known as St. Vitus' Dance, and most of all the heart.

"As pain often migrates from one joint to another, the greatest danger from the disease is the damage it can do to the heart. In more than half of all cases, rheumatic fever scars the valves of the heart, forcing this vital organ to work harder to pump blood. Over a period of months or even years - particularly if the disease strikes again - this damage to the heart can lead to a serious condition known as rheumatic heart disease, which can eventually cause the heart to fail."

"Rheumatic fever mainly affects children aged between five and fifteen years old," explains another article. "Boys and girls have the same risk of developing the disease; girls and women tend to have more severe symptoms. The disease is fairly rare in most developed nations, but is still common in many other parts of the world, particularly in sub-Saharan Africa, south central Asia, and the indigenous population of Australia and New Zealand. Before the widespread introduction of antibiotics and increased levels of public sanitation and living standards, rheumatic fever used to be one of the leading causes of acquired heart disease in developed nations."

The disease tends to strike most often in cool, damp weather during the winter and early spring. The same article places great emphasis on dealing with sore throat problems, especially in children, highlighting the importance of a visit to a doctor: "If your child has a severe sore throat without other cold symptoms, or a milder sore throat that persists for more than two or three days, see a doctor. It may be strep throat, which should be treated with antibiotics."

When reading this article, I still hear the children with whom I had spent some time coughing their lungs out throughout the whole period of winter and spring time.

To prevent the disease from developing, a throat culture test needs to be done. It involves "swabbing a sample of throat mucus for lab analysis. It usually takes twenty-four hours to grow and analyse the culture. Some doctors also use a rapid strep test that can give results in about five minutes, but it isn't as accurate as the culture."

Not only did lack of money stop them from taking any action to prevent the disease from spreading, but also the inept medical care and lack of equipment. According to an article published in 2013, the shortage of medical staff, lack of equipment and health insurance (less than thirty per cent of Moroccan are covered) are responsible for the high death rate, especially amongst infants.

"When a child comes in with meningitis, we must perform a lumbar puncture, but we can't because we don't have the equipment to do it," said a doctor who asked not to be identified by name because complaining might cost him his job. "So we try to use our instincts to guess if they're sick or not." A group of trainee doctors in the hallway were discussing a recent case of a baby with breathing problems. Lacking a respirator, all they had been able to do was rub his chest. The infant had died. "Monitors don't even work," said one of the doctors. "Once, the machine in paediatrics indicated 265 as a pulse, which doesn't even exist — and the baby was already dead. We didn't realise he was dead right away." Critics argue that the system is crippled by corruption, both large and small. The Central Commission for the Prevention of Corruption, a Moroccan governmental institution, published an investigation in 2011 on corruption in the health sector. Three people out of ten said they had resorted to bribery to receive health care "There is a lot of small corruption in these hospitals because doctors and nurses are not paid well," Dr. Naciri Bennani of the doctor's union said."

The same article gives us some insight to the figures:

"The Moroccan government spends more than $5 billion a year on healthcare. It allocated 3.2 per cent of its budget to health care this year, according to the Finance Ministry's 2013 budget documents. World Bank data published last year showed that Moroccan public health spending accounted for 6.5 percent of all public spending compared with 8.12 percent in Algeria and 6.2 percent in Tunisia. Annual spending per person averages $147 in Morocco, compared with $186 in Algeria and $246 in Tunisia, according to the bank's data. According to Health Ministry figures from the three countries, Morocco has one doctor per 1,600 inhabitants, compared with one for 800 people in Tunisia and one for 600 in Algeria."

Mina's presence in the hospital might have been a crucial factor in the care and attention Rkia received that afternoon, and the careless attitude towards the sick child may be explained as a simple lack of connections.

When the second drip was finished, Rkia asked for some food. *"Hubz, hubz,"* she whispered. "Mina, Rkia, *koul!*" No matter in how broken language I said it, I was elated to share this piece of information with her. *"Rkia brit hubz,"* I shouted through the window communicating Rkia's hunger with the family and close relatives that were gathered outside. They laughed but understood my utterance and quickly came back with a piece of cake and some drinkable yogurt.

Feeding her wasn't easy as she rejected each piece of cake I was putting into her mouth. The same went for the yogurt, she drunk only a tiny bit. "I'm tired and I want to sleep," she said. I called the nurse to inform him of the finished drip.

I believed that my presence might have also speeded up their responses and interest in the patient. The female doctor, the same one that had irritated me before, came in with another male nurse. *"La bas? Chwiya?"* the same questions were repeated. When not much response was coming from grandma, they decided to put her on a smaller portion of glucose. "When this drip is finished, you will able to take her back home," said the nurse walking away. "What is wrong with her?" I asked him. "I don't know," he answered. "Do you think she is going to get better?" "I hope so. If not, you can always bring her back here. *Malhababic.*" I couldn't believe everything what I was hearing. Firstly, he had not the slightest knowledge about his patient, nor was he willing to do any tests to find out, and on top of everything, he was welcoming us back.

I called Papa Mohamed to come and fetch her, and while he was taking Rkia in his arms, she continued to squeeze my hand hard. The difficulty and awkwardness of walking through the corridor was spotted by a nurse, who went to fetch the hospital bed; and although she looked more comfortable on that bed, it added more struggle for me to walk beside her. Bending forward over the bed while Papa was pushing it was the only solution to get through the door. The people looked at as with some bewilderment; considering that I was the only stranger in that unit and to that stranger's hand was attached the hand of the elderly sick Moroccan woman, we might have given them a story to talk about later on.

It was only Hakima who managed to open Rkia's tightly clenched fingers and let my hand go free. All the relatives and family went home either with Rkia in a taxi or on foot; only Papa Mohamed and I decided on going to our favourite place in the medina to have some *iben* and heavenly tasty avocado juice. This man kept astonishing me, not only did he refuse money from me, but also, without hesitation, ordered a home-made yogurt for a beggar who came in asking for some money.

******

In my overall report back to Hannah, I had described it as an excellent way to treat aggression, a therapy that could cure unnecessary tension, violence, or ferocity. I am talking about washing sheep skin on the banks of the river – a perfect solution to calm nerves down. Two solid bags filled with the wool, three wooden thick sticks, two plastic stools, some snacks, i.e. bread and mandarins, and some tea were packed on to the *carozza*. The weather was excellent; it gave all the children and teenagers an opportunity to come to the river, paddle in the water and for braver ones, a great occasion to swim. We had a superb spot and quickly a company of some other women who were doing the same. The dirty sheep skin was first put into a large basin with water and a generous amount of salt, then after a quick soak, a small portion of it was taken out, placed on flat stones that each of us had, and was beaten hard with the wooden stick until it looked fairly clean. I beat hard, as hard as I could, portion after portion until it all looked fine to me and my hands got wounded. It was hard to avoid blisters, but in my case it was even harder. My hands had not done any physical work for a long time, hence my blisters were not only immense but filled with blood. "Look at your hands," Hakima and Fadma looked terrified. "It's nothing, I will fix it," I said laughing. The beaten wool had to be washed once again in the clean waters of the river and then spread out on rocks that were part of the surroundings to get them all dried. Then, after a short break over snacks, the still wet wool had to be placed back inside the bags, then on to the trolley, and we were ready to head back home. No matter how badly my hands looked, I offered to help any time; I enjoyed the physical aspect of it and with pleasure would do this again. Having said that, if I had to do it on a regular basis as they do, I am not sure how much more joy I would derive from it.

I was worried about heavily pregnant Fadma, who had done enough physical exercise and this one seemed to be particularly straining, but on the other hand, I knew she was a tough cookie. I understood why she desired to have a girl instead of a third boy, who would become as useless with such tasks as her two boys who would not even consider helping their pregnant mum with any petty housework, not mentioning "beating the dirt out of the wool." They grow to become men.

******

That afternoon I was also invited over to Khadeja's with Hakima and Fadama; on that visit I hoped that I would see Rkia in a better physical condition; but no, she wasn't getting any better. She was as tired as she was weak, and those drips given to her yesterday in the hospital, had only made her vomit.

There were fourteen women counted that evening and a few more who were only passing by. Despite comprehending a little of their *Arbiya*, the more common and well-developed language used was sign language. After their brief "sniffing", they looked at me with a certain refinement that was explained through their gratitude and enthusiasm confirmed by endless *zwina* and *mezyan* words. Amongst all those women was one whose face I had already seen somewhere and that woman was particularly interested in finding out who I was. It turned out she was from El Borj and ninety-nine per cent related to the family of Boukmam, meaning Mustapha; so after Hakima's brief explanation of who I was and what I was doing here, she became terribly fond of me. When it was time for us to go home, she continued talking to me believing that I fully comprehended her soliloquy in which she expressed yet again her immense gratitude for my work here through her warm words, her look, and endless hugs. This complete stranger gave me the feeling that every step of my journey here, no matter how hard or frustrating, was worth living through.

There was another woman who was as cheerful and appreciative as the one from El Borj. When passing by an outdoor place with *chfnj*, run by an elderly couple, she grabbed me by the hand and forced me to follow her. "No *flouss*," I said to her. "No, I want to buy it for you," she responded while handing in one delicious *chfnj*. The simple, kind and well-meant gesture nicely surprised me; only rarely was I given something unconditionally. When we said goodbye to the ladies, Hakima and the two Fadmas were showing me another short-cut through a narrow street to get to the medina. A few children were playing football in the middle of that street, when out of blue, a man on a bicycle that wasn't even moving tried to get past them. The hilarious moment arrived with the same man who came to a sudden and rapid standstill, lost control and collapsed under his bicycle. We three looked at him, first with disbelief as to how it happened, and then with the slight smile that was hard to take off our faces. The way he felt down was as comical as was our hysterical laughter after he had managed to get back on his bike and cycled off.

******

I wanted to believe in the honesty of each individual that I allowed to get close to me; but inevitably that trust was challenged by doubt in the face of certain unexplained and sombre acts.

Once, 200DH disappeared from my purse but I blamed my own absent-mindedness for it and no one else. Today, however, I got rather suspicious; one of the keys to my suitcase locker, I believe I had two, had disappeared. "I'm losing my mind," I said to myself, but in case I wasn't, I changed the key locker for a spare with a code that I kept. I wrote down the combination, locked my room and left to the café "Martil." When I came back, I hesitantly looked at the locker and was shocked; the combination had been changed. I had my niggling suspicions as to whom it might be visiting my room but without catching him or her red-handed I would have never been able to support my worrying doubt.

On the other hand, Abdellah and Meryam came to ask for help. "The University has not yet paid me the grant," he was showing me his credit card adding, "can you lend me 300DH and I promise to give it back to you in two days." Of course I wanted to help him and of course I knew he would not have the money to pay me back, and it was confirmed five days later by Abdellah, who finally stopped avoiding me and had the courage to apologise for the delay. "Treat it as a present, it was my pleasure to help you." It was a weight off his mind and he was grateful. Lack of money did bother him a great deal. Sometimes he even sounded desperate. On the second day of our family picnic, I recalled a moment when Abdellah sat next to me and asked if I could possibly find him a girl abroad, slightly insinuating an easier option. "I can't marry you, and you know that, right?" "C'est bon, c'est bon," replied Abdellah. "Marriage doesn't work the same way as it works here. I don't think I'll be able to help you." It was rather awkward for him to bring up the subject of marriage, but I hoped he understood my impotence in resolving this matter.

Drunken Mustapha kept sending me messages and calling every fifteen minutes until I picked it up. This time I could hardly understand his slurs and the only intelligible sentence was: "Où es-tu, je veux te voir," repeated over and over again. I sensed some trouble but did not anticipate the following. When entering home in the late afternoon, I picked up another phone call from Mustapha. *"La bas, la bas,"* I repeated it in front of Abdellah and Meryam who were sitting in the living room downstairs and giving me some signals while whispering. "C'est Mustapha?" I nodded. They were waving their hands in the air saying: "No, no, no, he can't come here." So when he asked me where I was, I made up a story on the spot. "Actually, I have changed my mind and I won't be coming home until very late. Mohamed's mum invited me over at their place for dinner." He sounded furious with my response and put the phone down.

"What's going on?" I asked Meryam. There was nobody in the house apart from *Baba*, Halima, Meryam and Abdellah; Hakima was with her mum and Papa Mohamed on a job. "Il est ivre, très ivre, complètement fou, *mochkila*," his behaviour explained Abdellah in those few simple words. Meryam took me upstairs to look at the broken window. "Why was he aggressive?" "Il est fou, fou," she repeated it. The broken window was close to my room. As Meryam wasn't able to explain what had happened, I tried to link this story with his countless messages and phone calls today and the lack of my response to most of them; perhaps my absence when he came upstairs looking for me, might have stirred his violent behaviour.

That evening Mustapha did not cease calling me, but I kept ignoring his phone calls. Instead, I sat downstairs and kept Meryam company, when one hour later, drunken Mustapha was in front of the door banging. "Do you want me to go to my room?" I asked. "Yes, yes, hide in your room." I quietly sneaked up the stairs, locked the room and turned the light off in case he decided to come upstairs. However, he wasn't allowed to enter the house, so after a brief exchange of views between him and Meryam, he walked off and left us all in peace.

On the 9th of March he was officially banned from entering the house. The following day he met up with me and explained what had happened that evening and what story Meryam was spreading. It went that he came in drunk, tried to kiss her and proposed her marriage; and when his offer was turned down, he became furious, then broke the window and was chased away by Meryam.

However aggressive he might have been, it was hard for me to believe in her story. If he had had any feelings for Meryam, he would have had expressed them a long time ago as he had been given countless opportunities to get close to her; on the contrary, he was not displaying any affection towards her, but in front of everybody at home, including Meryam, was exposing his infatuation for me, on numerous occasions. My intuition was telling me that this was a perfect moment for Meryam to get rid of the troublemaker for good, there were no witnesses, and her story would make a perfect sense to everybody around: he was drunk, hence could act like a lunatic, which he had done on many instances in the past.

After coffee, he walked me back home. When Meryam unlocked the door, she did not allow him to come inside and gave me a creepy look as if it was me who had done something wrong. In the evening, I witnessed something rather horrible. Mustapha came in with his brother Youssef, a total opposite to Mustapha, and they both stayed over for dinner. Firstly, tea was served but one cup was missing. "Here you are, have some tea Mustapha," I gave him my cup pretending I wasn't thirsty. But what outraged me the most was the dinner time. When Meryam walked around with a kettle, everybody but Mustapha had their hands washed. It was the first time that I observed something like this. We all were sitting around a plate of tagine, whereas Mustapha was watching us eating. I felt uncomfortable and couldn't swallow. It upset me. It wasn't only Meryam's punishing attitude, but also everybody else's around that table. That evening I saw a flock of sheep consuming tagine, brainless with no particular ability to make an adequate judgement. I understood the punishment of banning him from coming to the house, but that evening he was sitting there watching us eating. It was like sitting in the medina in front of a restaurant and being watched by hungry beggars. On a couple of occasions, I had no choice but to give boucheyar away as no matter how hungry I was, I could never compare my cravings to their everlasting hunger. The second time, I was sitting outside a café, at the far back of it, surrounded by many people, and even then I was spotted by a passing by woman who stopped and starred. At first, I tried to ignore that distant gaze, but when she wasn't giving up, she made it difficult for me to bite and swallow it. It wasn't hard to give away my food, the hard part was to look into the eyes of hungry people.

And that evening I had difficulty eating. The fact that there was Lahcen's father devouring that food, made even more awkward for me. I did not trust this man for a minute, in my eyes he was a cunning and spurious user and if I had to bet on someone in the worst of all scenarios, I would bet on Mustapha and not on him. The following morning he would come again for lunch, proclaiming his opinion about Mustapha, "Mustapha, *La! La! La!*" pointing to the door, then shovelling the food down his throat, and without a single *"chokrane"* he would walk away.

I left the dinner table very quickly. I disagreed with all those satisfied guzzlers. There was no point pretending. Ah, you human beings, how I wished to have had thicker skin!

******

We apparently broke up. I had no idea that my *bslama* in one of my text messages was read as the forever "arrivederci," simple as that. But what was even more shocking came later that day. I went off to the cafe "Martil," sat outside as the weather was hot and beautiful, and was searching through the web, when my boyfriend passed by in front of me, without a greeting, any acknowledgment or hesitation. I felt ill in that moment and had a sudden pain in my stomach. This incredibly conniving act made me pick up my phone and sent him a text message to which he responded with a certain attitude, like there was nothing wrong with cutting me dead. Ten minutes later he was with me at the café.

His act was also noticed by Mustapha, the waiter, an amiable and decent character who came up to the table equally shocked. "What was that?" he said to Mohamed and continued reprimanding him. "You have just passed by without saying a word and you have come back? What is going on?" Mustapha's reaction took me aback. He was only a guy who served me coffee each day; smiling all the time, did not ask questions but my name, and that guy, clearly disturbed by such a devious act of ignorance was chastising his fellow-Moroccan; extraordinary; he stood up for me - the European. Mohamed did not find words, he was looking down listening. We chatted but even then I felt a strange tingling or numbness of the left side of my body. "What kind of man was he?" I was asking myself. "What kind of man could talk about love and show such ignorance? Do some people have natural aptitude to hurt intentionally, or is it down to a lack of experience? Perhaps the lack of deeper interaction with people is to blame for such attitude? How shall I treat such disappointment? Is it worth investing more energy in order to understand, or simply to treat it as a failure?" The questions were piling up but the answers were still in limbo.

******

I had courage to go to the hairdresser in La Scierie. I hesitated though as I have always been scared of them, and the more haircuts I had had, the more I was convinced by the simple statement: "Not a single hairdresser will ever make me or my hair happy." I always sit down in a chair with confidence. "Everything will be fine and I will look stunning," I'm talking to myself looking at the mirror. Then I can't look any longer but I still have confidence. However, when it comes down to the final stage of refining the style, I panic. I hear the scissors and I know that they are doing something hideous, undesirable, something that I was trying to avoid, and my internal scream expressed by an external "thank you" when looking at the finished "product," convinces me to the followed up statement: "It will grow back." And I would repeat this phrase again when looking at the ugly, thick strands of hair that I call "the wet chicken style" the exact opposite to what I always hoped to get.

That afternoon, both salons were closed. "Perhaps it was a sign," I said to myself, but my neighbour thought the opposite and went to look for *Sherifa* who a few minutes later came to open her salon. The small room contained a sofa, a mirror, and a chair, with the walls displaying pictures of hairstyles cut out from colourful magazines. Owing to the poor hygiene, my hair became brittle and difficult to comb. "Only the dry, damaged ends and a small fringe improvement, please." As the operation was very simple, she understood it well; however she read my request very literally. She grabbed a bottle with water, sprayed only the ends of the longest hair, combed it through, pull it tightly, and made a cut. It did not matter for her that the length of my hair differed, endings meant only the longest, the rest - had been left untouched. She grabbed my fringe and the scissors made a blunt noise. She asked in Arabic: "Who cut it, was it you?" "Yes, it's not easy to do it yourself." She laughed. She had a reason. It looked awful.

217

I put my trust into her blunt scissors. Five minutes had passed and we moved on to blow-drying my rather dry hair. The whole operation of cutting wasn't bad at all. I only panicked once when I had a quick look at the mirror at the end. I saw these uneven waves of single sharp strands of hair hanging down my forehead while she was trying to make it "nice" with her fingers. "It's great, thank you very much," I said, dishevelled it instantly, paid 25DH, and left.

The quick solution to uneven hair problem was applied: a black triangular Berber headscarf with shiny sequins sewn to one side of it was tight around my head; and to match up the style I slipped on my colourful pyjama that I had bought back from Hakima the other day. Exotic as I looked, I went out. The constant "*zwina*, what's your number, je veux prendre café avec toi" made me only realise that my style wasn't too close to Moroccan panache. In the medina, I looked for a stall that could repair my boot. It desperately needed the sole, and a very old, genuine-looking man did a great job with repairing it for as little as 10DH.

In two days I was to celebrate my 37th birthday. Meryam was planning on baking a *torta*, Fadma was to come with a second *torta* and another Fadma with a bottle of Coca-Cola and Fanta.

In the meantime, Mohamed apologised for his latest performance. "It's easy for you to be in a relationship as you have had a few. For me relationship means marriage," he tried to justify his actions. "I will never marry you if I don't feel a good connection between us. How can you talk about marriage and at the same time feel miserable in my company, disrespect me, disagree with what I do and accuse me all those indecencies. I'm sorry, I don't understand."

We walked towards the medina continuing with our discourse. *Baba* needed a bedpan and we had identified a pharmacy that was selling it. The day was hot and the medina look even more packed out with homeless people on the streets. A dirty bare-footed man walking down the street drew my attention and received a great deal of compassion. "What do you feel when you see all those homeless people in your country?" "I'm used to them, I was born here and grew up with them, it's normal for me," he responded. "So they became a part of the environment, nothing else; that is depressing," I commented adding, "perhaps it would be inappropriate to make such a comparison, but you are so bothered by women in tight jeans, but homeless people don't even distress you."

That day we passed by a small public office called, "Bureau d'écriture publique." It had never before crossed my mind to think that they exist, but it made perfect sense. The data shows that sixteen per cent of males and twenty-six per cent of females are unable to read or write. Papa and Hakima were also illiterate. Many times when Papa had to search through his little notebook for a phone number, it was always Meryam who went through pages reading out loud all the names found in there. Often when I sat down and read the "Psychology" magazine, Papa curiously was leafing through the content pointing at the pictures saying, "*mezyan*" or asking "France? France?" He was rather open about his illiteracy. "I can't read or write, I have no job, and here...," he was looking at something that he had found in the magazine, "... *mezyan*, Europe *mezyana*, Maroc no."

I agreed with him. The life was tough on him, and I betted, his stomach problem must have been adding to his emotional upheaval and the feeling of resignation.

I was sitting in my bed that late evening and heard Papa shouting, "Margarena, *la bas, bikhir*?" He was standing outside my room, *"Wyih,"* I responded, "come on in." He did his usual look around, sat at my bed and took his *nafha* out. "Can I try a little bit?" He placed a tiny bit of a fine black tobacco on my hand and instructed me how to use it. *"La, comme ça."* He demonstrated one swift "Pulp Fiction" sniff. *"Wakha,"* I said and gawkily sniffed some of it into my left nostril first, and then, a little bit clumsier, into the right one. Within a few seconds both my nostrils felt unblocked and clean, but my throat - irritated. "Is it ok that I feel it inside my throat?" *"La, la, la,* you are supposed to feel it in your nostril. Blow your nose," he advised me. Although a tiny bit of *nafha* came out, my throat still felt that funny scratch, and with that burning sensation compared to having a strong chilli pepper inside the nose, came a little head spin making me feel very light-headed. Five minutes later, the strange burning feeling was gone but the powder's residues were successively coming out with every nose-blow.

******

The next day after breakfast, Papa Mohamed announced his willingness to travel to Casablanca today to see a doctor. "Today? Did you get an appointment?" "No, no, it's not necessary. Zechariah works in the hospital," said Papa. I quickly went to the *hammam* and when I got undressed and was about to enter it, I got stopped by a woman. "Rkia, Rkia," she kept repeating. "I don't understand what you are saying? Are you talking about *epo* de Hakima?" She nodded and added, "ça fait, ça fait." She was probably referring to someone else and her message was a clear misunderstanding; but nevertheless, I was anxious to get back home; and yes there was no reason to panic.

Before I went away, Mohamed wanted to see me to give me a birthday present: a pen and a key ring. He once again apologised for his behaviour, and I once again highlighted how indifferent and volatile characters bothered me. "I'd like you to join me for a lecture, this afternoon." he replied. "If I don't go to Casablanca, I'll join you with pleasure."

It was around 3.15pm when Papa was ready to go to the bus station. "We don't even know if there will be a bus at this time," I said. "It will be, I'm sure," assured me clean and perfumed Papa. As soon as we left the house, it started pouring down, so Papa decided on taking a taxi which turned out to be a complete waste of money as there was no buses to Casablanca, two direct ones were leaving at the night time at 2.00am and 4.00am. We both decided to travel at 2.00am and in the meantime, I invited him for coffee and then ran to join Mohamed for the lecture.

Soaked wet, I reached the café and saw Mohamed sitting with his three "mute" friends: Sanae, her very depressed-looking girlfriend, and another guy. They were calculating some figures as a part of their homework forgetting any basic or more advanced manners, making me feel like a persona non grata. Even Sanae who knew me and with whom I had lunches, including a Christmas meal, did not pose a single question, not even on progress in Malika's case; and my instinct confirmed as to why she was trying to help me. "Dear Lord, Moroccan mentality drains me," I was talking to myself. The weirdest of all was my boyfriend's behaviour, he was neither talking to me nor was he giving me any attention. And the truth was, if it wasn't for him, I wouldn't have come here. However, I sat down, took a book and started reading, but the book I picked up in that café was as boring as the company of these people. "It's time for me to go home," I said after thirty silent minutes. In front of me, Sanae asked Mohamed a question in Arabic, "is she going home?" "Yes, she is going home," I responded. Some people clearly underestimate my understanding of some Arabic. "Do you want to change the table?" asked my boyfriend. "What lack of manners," I thought, "he invited me here, paid no attention to me whatsoever, and now when I decided to leave, he was asking me if I wanted to change the table.

"If your friends weren't with you, you would have asked me to stay, wouldn't you?" I quizzed him when we left the café. Something was extremely strange about him. The inconsistency of his behaviour, talking about love and respect and acting indifferent was wearing me out. "Leave me alone," I said, and he did.

At home, Meryam treated me, Papa, Alla and Mustapha's father to some barbecued meat and while we were sitting and enjoying our meal, Alla encouraged *Baba* to tell his story. He was vividly portraying some horse story while singing, reciting and using his walking stick to make it more real. I had no idea what the story was about, but oddly enough the following morning, when Papa Mohamed and I were sitting in a café in Casablanca, a programme on TV called *"Le dance de Baroud"* was shown. And this was exactly the story that *Baba* was recalling last night. Guys on horses were performing something rather special, and this rather special spectacle was called *"Lab el Baroud"* translated as "gunpowder game" or "horse play" know as *Fantasia*: different traditional horse shows simulating military assaults, mostly practised in North Africa. The performance is inspired by the historical wartime attacks of Berber and Arabian Desert riders. Nowadays, the fantasia is considered a cultural performance and a kind of martial art; it also symbolises a strong relationship between the man and the horse, as well as an attachment to tradition. The performance consists of a group of horse riders, all wearing traditional clothes, who charge along a straight path at the same speed so as to form a line, and then at the end of the charge (about two hundred meters) fire into the sky using old muskets or muzzle-loading rifles. The difficulty of the performance is in synchronising the movement of the horses during acceleration of the charge, and especially in firing the guns simultaneously so that one single shot is heard. The horse is referred to as a fantasia horse and is of the type called a Barb or Berber horse. It may also, depending on the region, be carried by camel or on foot.

Each region in Morocco has one or several fantasia groups, called Serba, totalling thousands of horse riders nationwide. Performances are usually during local seasonal, cultural or religious festivals, also called *"moussem"* – "season" in Arabic.

Eugène Delacroix portrayed Fantasia in one of his paintings called "Fantasia ou Jeu de la poudre devant la porte d'entrée de la ville de Méquinez," in 1832. It also became one of the favourite subjects of the most famous Orientalist painters such as Eugène Fromentin or Marià Fortuny.

******

Papa, dressed in his orange mucky coverall that he used for work, and I left home around 1.15am. We walked to the station and arrived there just on time. A single ticket to Casablanca cost 70DH and Papa insisted on paying. When we got inside the bus: cold, old, uncomfortable, I was observing and was amazed by what other passengers were able to pack inside the boot; there were: a motorbike, doors, and piles of long pieces of wood.

Papa left me for a better sit, at the back, where he was able to stretch out his long legs and get some sleep. When the bus left the station, I felt a strong draught coming from somewhere. At first I thought that the door was still opened but then I quickly realised that it was a fault of the rooftop window; it turned out that the window was broken; the solution to prevent the wind from coming in was certainly simple and practical, but unfortunately a jacket that was hanging down from that rooftop window did not resolve the problem, the breeze was still coming in. "Happy birthday!" I congratulated myself on gaining another year while sitting in the night bus to Casablanca curled up shivering. And while the harsh temperature and my grinding teeth kept me widely awake, someone else couldn't sleep. *"Aji! Aji!"* I heard someone talking to me. The lights were off but I could see a man's figure standing in the aisle. "Pourquoi?" I was surprised. *"Aji* at the front," he repeated. "Was he concerned about me, or was he trying to chat me up?" I was thinking. "Thanks, but I'm fine here," the ambiguity made me turn down the outgoing ticket inspector's offer.

Throughout the whole journey I was trembling, the cold was unbearable, and even the extra pair of socks and trousers that I had managed to put on, came as nothing but a little comfort.

After 7.00am, the sudden and unexpected *"aji!"* command coming this time from Papa Mohamed made me realise that we had arrived at the suburbs of Casablanca. "I'm so cold," I made one weak complaint to Papa. He looked at his coverall and responded proudly: "They kept me warm." We crossed a busy street and ended up in a café where we watched *"La dance de Baroud"* while sipping: coffee, hot chocolate with a piece of cake and a small bun with cream cheese that cost us 40DH, twice as expensive as in Khénifra. Neither of us liked the price.

It was before 8.00am when we reached our destination: the posh house of Itto, the school teacher, and her husband, Mustapha, the Director of the Factory Inspectors. Firstly, he welcomed us in his posh house, but instantly acted a little surprised with our plans of seeing a doctor this week. Over breakfast, served by his housemaid, he was lecturing us as how it should have been handled. "Yes, I do understand the word "appointment" very well. It is used in the part of the world that I come from; but Papa Mohamed claimed he did not need an appointment, so I believed it was discussed between you two."

He struck me as an arrogant buffoon and his children, Safwa and Zechariah, did not show much respect for him laughing their heads off when he was trying to speak English with me. His daughter, Safwa, was young and full of herself. She was so conceited that she left me with no choice but to dislike her. "Do you study?" I asked her. "Of course. I'm the youngest," she spat it out abruptly. "I don't know that, do I? I've just met you." Later on, when we sat down in the kitchen, she offered me some artichoke. "No, thank you, I'm not hungry," I said. "I don't eat because I'm hungry, I eat because I like it," she barked. "Well then, bonne appetite." In another conversation she asked me about my grandma. "She is fairly well, thank you, ninety-six this year." "That's young!" she said. "Are you crazy? This is almost a century. What is old for you then?" I couldn't stand this girl and her offish, incredibly irritating character.

On the contrary, Zechariah, was a nice, easy-going individual. The way he spoke about people suggested that the medicine was his vocation. "I'd like to have my little cabinet in a rural part of Morocco and treat the poor for nothing," he said. "That is a very noble idea and you will certainly make a very good doctor." He then talked about his passion for music. "I'm learning to play guitar." And then he added, "but I don't have a place to practise it." "Can't you do it at home?" "No, music is forbidden in our house." "Seriously?" "Yes, music is associated with fun, hence drinking and that is against Islam." "What a harsh environment to grow up in," I sympathised with him.

On the second day of our visit there, he shared with me his *sebsi* pipe stuffed with marihuana. "It is so strong! How can you smoke it so often?" My head was spinning and I felt nausea straight after the first puff. "It's the only thing that keeps me going, I don't think I would have gone through the medical school if I didn't smoke." "Had he had a little bit of amusement at home, he wouldn't have had to seek it anywhere else," I thought.

Going back to our breakfast. Mustapha left for work, Safwa for the university, and Papa and I were left to ourselves. We took the metro to the centre of Casablanca and strolled around it while feeling the last night's exhaustion. Casablanca was a very beautiful and modern city, crowded and expensive as any city is. However, despite being cosmopolitan, even here I experienced a few weird encounters. Today, there was a young man who was following me, first he heard me and Papa talking, and then I saw him behind us; and when we both sat down on a bench, he sat on the opposite one smiling and giving me a gesture of wanting to talk. Although every distant chat-up took place in front of me and Papa Mohamed, he chose not to see any of what was happening around him and I wondered why.

Papa was hungry and in pain. "I'm taking you to the restaurant for my birthday." As he did not understand the word "anniversaire," there was no particular reaction to my utterance. *"Hut?"* he asked. "Let's have some *hut*." He loved fish, and regularly, when there was money, he would deliver a significant amount and we would have barbecue at home.

The only fish restaurant that was open, offered us two massive plates of three varieties of fish, calamari and shrimp, bread with some tomato sauce and some water. Papa wasn't keen either on calamari or shrimp, hence we made an exchange: his calamari and shrimp for my fish, and when he ended up with six quite large pieces of fish on his plate, he first looked at me, then stretched his arms out, shrugged his shoulders and said: "LOOO!" I looked at him, made a face saying: "I don't know what you will do with all that fish," and we were both in stitches; this ridiculously funny moment made my day.

And we couldn't eat it all; therefore all the leftovers were made into three sandwiches and taken with us. The meal cost 144DH and it was considered very expensive by Papa. As we still had some time to kill, we wandered around Casablanca and then, when feeling more tired, we sat down on one of the benches by the main road. As we were sitting there longer than five minutes, Papa had fallen asleep drawing the attention of all those passers-by; but that little snooze gave him some energy to walk more, sniff *nafha*, spit everywhere and get on to a bus that was supposed to take us… somewhere. I was more than convinced that Papa knew where we were heading, but thirty minutes later when the bus drove through some industrial parts of Casablanca, I changed my mind: he didn't know where we were going. After a short visit to a supermarket, we went back to the bus stop that would take us back to where we had come from.

The bus was crammed full of people and we were both sandwiched between the driver's cabin and a few other passengers. All of a sudden, shouting broke out in the middle part of the bus and all those young men who had certainly not behaved in a gentlemanly like way, created tremendous disorder. "What is going on?" I asked Papa but he wasn't able to explain. From what I observed, the whole commotion evolved around a few ticket controllers and someone who was travelling without a ticket and a few others who either stood up for this boy who walked around the bus in search for the money to pay off the fine or who also travelled without a ticket. That boy was a very lucky one as a few passengers chipped in and he was able to pay the fine and walked away without any bruise on his face.

After this incident, we both decided to go home. I craved for a nap and a shower and managed to get both. Three hours later I got up. "Where is Papa?" I asked Itto. "He is sleeping upstairs." She said and invited me to the living room where her husband was watching football. "Would you like to watch BBC?" she asked me. "That would be very nice, I feel like I lost touch with reality," I responded. I sat down on the floor, but Itto's suggestion to change the channel was utterly ignored by Mustapha. Then when still watching football, we were joined by his friend, if I remembered it well, he was a professor of physics or mathematics at university. "You become whom you befriend," this simple proverb would describe how I felt about Mustapha and his friend, and I was sorry for Itto. If I had such an arrogant, full of himself, lecturing husband, I would have strangled him and left his body for vultures.

While we were having a meal, Itto explained to me her husband's wish. "Mustapha thinks that you should change the title of your book." "Take a deep breath Maggie, here is another lecture coming," I said to myself and waited for Mustapha's speech. "Berber has wrong connotation, people will think about barbaric," he said. "Yes I know about barbaric derivation, but they are two opposite words with two different spellings...." "No, no," he butt into my explanation and carried on with his own discourse. Willingly, I turned myself off as no matter what I would say, he would always claim his intellectual or moral superiority, and I bet the list of his supremacy would be even longer.

The Encyclopaedia Britannica, explains the origin of the world: "Berber," self-name Amazigh, plural *Imazighen*, any of the descendants of the pre-Arab inhabitants of North Africa; There are some variant of the word *i-Mazigh-en* (singular: a-*Mazigh*), possibly meaning "free people" or "free and noble men." The word has probably an ancient parallel in the Roman and Greek names for some of the Berbers, *"Mazices."*

The name Berber appeared for the first time after the end of the Roman Empire. The use of the term Berber spread in the period following the arrival of the Vandals during their major invasions. A history by a Roman consul in Africa made the first reference of the term "barbarian" to describe Numidia. Muslim historians, some time after, also mentioned the Berbers. The English term was introduced in the nineteenth century, replacing the earlier Barbary, a loan from Arabic. ITS ULTIMATE ETYMOLOGICAL IDENTITY WITH BARBARIAN IS UNCERTAIN.

It was the Arabs, who had enlisted Berber warriors for the conquest of Spain, who nevertheless gave those peoples a single name, turning barbarian (speakers of a language other than Greek and Latin) into Barbar, the name of a race descended from Noah. While unifying the indigenous groups under one rubric, the Arabs began their Islamisation.

Meanwhile, Berber merchants and nomads of the Sahara had initiated a trans-Saharan trade in gold and slaves that incorporated the lands of the Sudan into the Islamic world. Those achievements of the Berber were celebrated in a massive history of North Africa (Kitāb al-ʿIbār) by the 14th century Arab historian Ibn Khaldūn. By then, however, the Berbers were in retreat, subjected to Arabisation of two very different kinds. The predominance of written Arabic had ended the writing of Amazigh (Berber) languages in both the old Libyan and the new Arabic script, reducing its languages to folk languages. At the same time, an influx from the east of warrior Arab nomads from the 11th century onward was driving the Berbers off the plains and into the mountains and overrunning the desert. Together those factors were turning the population from Berber speakers into Arabic speakers, with a consequent loss of original identities. From the

16th century onward the process continued in the absence of Berber dynasties, which were replaced in Morocco by Arabs claiming descent from the Prophet and elsewhere by Turks at Algiers, Tunis, and Tripoli.

When the French conquered Algeria in the 19th century and Morocco in the 20th, they seized on the distinction between the Arab majority and the Berbers of the mountains. On the strength of Ibn Khaldūn's history, the latter were once again classified as a people under their modern name of Berbers. The identification and description of their language, the anthropological study of their society, and their geographical isolation all gave grounds for their separate administration as a people going back before the time of Islam to a pagan and Christian past. Those colonial studies and policies have determined much of the history of the Berbers down to the present but meanwhile have left a record of their manners and customs before the advent of modernity.

By the beginning of the 20th century, the Berber world had been reduced to enclaves of varying sizes. In Tripolitania and southern Tunisia they were chiefly formed by the hills of the Nafūsah Plateau and the island of Jerba, in eastern Algeria by the mountains of the Aurès and Kabylie, and in Morocco by the ranges of the Rif, the Middle and High Atlas, the Anti-Atlas, and the Saharan Atlas. In southern Morocco they consisted of the oases of the Drâa valley, and in the northern Sahara mainly those of the M'zab with those of Ghadāmis, Touggourt, and Gourara. In the central and southern Sahara was the vast area of the Ahaggar mountains and the desert to the south.

The economy was largely subsistence agriculture and pastoralism practiced by farmers, travellers, and nomads, coupled with weaving, pottery, metalwork, and leatherwork, and local and some long-distance trade. Dwellings varied from caves to pitched-roof houses to flat-roofed "castles" to tents. Whatever the dwelling, its construction was designed to create an interior ruled by the women of the family. Outside the home, women would gather at the fountain or well and at the tomb of the local saint, whereas men would meet at the mosque or in the street and square. In the case of the nomadic and matrilineal Tuareg of the central Sahara, the camp was largely controlled by the women, who chose their husbands and, with their songs, were central to social gatherings.

The dwelling was home to the nuclear, usually patrilineal family, which was the basic unit of a tribal group going under the name of a common ancestor, whose Ait, or people, they claimed to be. In principle all families and clans were equal, governed by codes of honour likely to give rise to feuds but also by a council of elders, the jamā'ah, who kept the peace by adjudication, rulings on compensation, and determination of punishments. In fact the various societies were not egalitarian. The village and the clan regularly admitted newcomers as inferiors, and the ruling elders came from leading families. If villages or clans went to war, as they frequently did, a chief might be chosen who on the strength of his prowess might attract clients, form his own army, and —like the lords of the High Atlas about 1900—establish his own dominion. The Tuareg of the Ahaggar and southern Sahara, also called Blue Men because of their indigo-dyed robes and face veils, were aristocratic nomads ruling over vassals, serfs, and slaves who cultivated the oases on their behalf; they in turn recognised supreme chiefs or kings, who were called amenukals. They had preserved a form of the old Libyan consonantal script under the name of Tifinagh, though most writing was in Arabic, by a class of Muslim scholars. Such saintly scholars were always considered figures of authority, and among the Ibadi Berbers of the M'zab they ruled the community.

While many of those features of Berber society have survived, they have been greatly modified by the economic and political pressures and opportunities that have built up since the early years of the 20th century. Beginning with the Kabyle of Algeria, emigration from the mountains in search of employment created permanent Berber communities in the cities of the Maghrib as well as in France and the rest of Western Europe. That emigration in turn has conveyed modern material and popular culture back into the homelands. The independence of Morocco, Algeria, Tunisia, Libya, Mauritania, Mali, and Niger meanwhile created a new political situation in which Berber nationalism made its appearance. That circumstance was largely a reaction to the policies of the new governments, which have frowned on a separate Berber identity as a relic of colonialism incompatible with national unity. In Morocco the monarchy felt threatened, first by the French use of Berbers to dethrone the sultan in 1953 and second by the role of Berber officers in the attempted assassinations of the king in 1971–72. In Algeria the rebellion in Kabylie in 1963–64 was further justification for a policy of Arabisation, resented by Berbers not least because many had been educated in French. Berber studies were forbidden or repressed in both Morocco and Algeria, but in Algeria in 1980–81 the cancellation of a lecture on Berber poetry set off a "Berber Spring" of demonstrations in Kabylie that were energized by popular Berber songs and singers.

The Berbers live in scattered communities across Morocco, Algeria, Tunisia, Libya, Egypt, Mali, Niger, and Mauretania. They speak various Amazigh languages belonging to the Afro-Asiatic family related to Ancient Egyptian. At the turn of the 21st century, there were perhaps 14 million in Morocco, 9 million in Algeria, and much smaller numbers in Tunisia, Libya, Egypt, and Mauretania; in the Sahara of southern Algeria and of Libya, Mali and Niger, the Berber Tuareg number about 1 million.

******

The Berber, Zechariah, who turned up late that evening, informed us of a doctor's appointment for tomorrow morning. "At what time should we get there?" I asked. "As early as possible," he said.

The following morning, I got up at 7.30, took a shower and was ready to go, but Papa and Zechariah were still in bed. "Sorry, to wake you up," I was knocking at his door. "It's after eight o'clock." The "as early as possible" turned out to be 10.00am. We went to the hospital and were ordered to wait for him in a student's café, but the doctor that Papa Mohamed was supposed to see, was not available. What a disappointment! "He is too busy," he said adding, "the next possible visit would be Monday."

For me the prospect of spending the weekend with Mustapha wasn't terribly alluring and as much as I wanted to see Casablanca with Zechariah, who begged us to stay, I was concerned about my already shattered emotions. However, I was prepared to stay until tomorrow and encouraged Papa to hang out here until the visit. He did not want to and I understood. He felt lost in Casablanca; it was far too big for him and far too expensive. Then he missed Hakima and the children, and as Rkia's condition wasn't improving, he felt the need to go home. "I have an appointment tomorrow," he said instead. "We will go home together, but you have to promise me that you will come back on Monday," I insisted. "*Wakha*, I promise." And he said, "Home today?" "Why not, we can travel today."

"Why don't you stay for the weekend? Mohamed can go home, but you don't have to. We will go to the sea tomorrow and go out and have a drink." I did not tell him the reason why I wanted to go home, but he understood that I was not staying. It was a shame, because I was certain that I would have had a good time with him, but I couldn't stand the idea of being lectured by his dad again. As they say, whoever laughs at his own jokes first is a very bad joker.

"Do you have to go back to the hospital?" "No, I took a day off thinking of spending it with you, and then I will play a football match," he said. "That's great! So take me to the place where the Casablanca film was made," I was keen on seeing it. "I'm not entirely sure, but we will find it." We walked across the city and then stopped in the park. Mohamed was in immense pain so he lay down on the grass while Zechariah was loading his *sebsi* pipe. "You both go to that place and I'll stay here," said Papa. "No, we can't leave you here. In fact, we don't need to go to that place," I stated, but Papa disagreed and got up. "It's fine, I'll come back another time." He was stubborn and walked with us in pain until we spotted a taxi. "This place is about thirty meters from here, but I'm not sure where exactly it is, let's take a taxi." The Casablanca taxi could only take four people and each one that had passed us had at least one passenger. I kept repeating that it was not worth the trouble, but Papa Mohamed insisted. Fifteen minutes later, a taxi that was going the opposite direction stopped and was willing to drive us there for... 100DH. "He was crazy! It should be 10DH," expressed his shock Zechariah. "That's the European price. We going home now," I decided, Papa agreed, and a taxi took us to Itto's house for 12DH.

We had some couscous and were driven by Itto to the bus stop hoping to get the 4.00pm bus. The bus was not direct and on top of that, there were no seats left. We were charged 100DH for two seats on the floor. Another rip off! The bus drove through villages and small towns, and went past Khouribga, a town where Mohamed was born. "This plaque is not from smoking, as everyone thinks, but it's from phosphate," he told me once.

Phosphate was discovered there during the French protectorate in early nineties, and now Morocco is considered to be the biggest phosphate exporter in the world. With several mines in the province of Khouribga, the reserve is estimated between 35 to 40 billion cubic meters which is ranked first at the national level.

Phosphate rock is radioactive and the recent studies showed the potential health problems associated with phosphate mining. "The mining process takes what is underground (soils and clays) and brings it to the surface. In doing so, some of the radioactive elements that were buried underground are exposed. There are two key areas of concern for impact on public health. The first is whether the radioactive elements can get into water supplies, be released to the air, absorbed into the skin or accumulated in fish or animals. The second concern is what happens when the radioactive particles, such as radium and thorium, are concentrated in the clay settling ponds. Most scientists recognize that exposure to radioactive particles in water or air can cause cancer."

We passed Khouribga and were headed towards our final stop, *Kasba Tadla*.

"Kasba Tadla was founded in 1687 by Sultan Moulay Ismail. Its citadel is one of the largest in Morocco. During colonization, the French turned this city into a military garrison housing two mosques. One of them keeps the Almohad style characterized by a diamond shape on the minaret. Another mosque in turn carries a Sahelian architecture with wooden stakes out of the minaret. Another monument of the city, the bridge that crosses the ten arches river Oum er-Rbia was also built by Sultan Moulay Ismail. To fully enjoy the beautiful view of the casbah of the city, visitors must go to the south of the city, on the small promontory dominated by an austere monument with four blades parallel concrete standing skyward."

It was around 8pm when we arrived at the Kasba Tadla bus station. It was dark and cold. At the information point we were told that there should be a bus to Khénifra in about half an hour but that could not be confirmed yet. "When?" "In twenty minutes," he said. "How much is the ticket 45DH. Papa could not believe the price and tried to argue with that man. "It's not worth it, I'll get the tickets; but what if the bus won't come? What will we do?" Although we sat down inside the station for tea, I did not feel particularly safe there as Papa did not pay any attention to the dodgy men who were circulating around like vultures winking and signalling. Then a young man came up to me and said that there was no bus to Khénifra tonight. "It can't be true," I said and kept my hopes up high.

Half an hour later we waited outside and looked at each bus that was coming in, when we heard a man shouting "Khénifra! Khénifra!" That was a happy moment for both of us: we were going to get home tonight. A young man dressed in his djellaba was selling tickets. "Do I know you from somewhere?" good chat-up line I thought, but responded: "I don't think so." "Where are you going?" "Khénifra, can I have two tickets, please." I wanted to give him the exact amount but took out 100DH. "Don't you have 70DH?" "I have 70DH." "That's enough, he said." "The other one wanted 90DH,"I told him. "That's kind of you, thank you." He went away to sell some tickets, but soon after came back to keep me company asking questions and recalling girlfriends' stories. "I had one from the UK but she wanted me to leave Morocco and I didn't want to live in the UK. The second one was from the USA; she was a liar, she had a husband back at home and I only discovered that by chance," he continued with his stories and I couldn't wait for the bus to arrive. "Maybe one day we can have coffee together," he said. "Sorry, I'm leaving in two weeks." "But here is my business card, if you ever come to Kasba, give me a ring." Rachid handed his "Location de Voiture Sans Chauffeur" card when it was time to leave Kasba Tadla.

When we got off the bus in Khénifra, there was a man standing just in front of it with a massive pot of snails and broth. Papa was keen on having a cup. "*Wakha.*" "C'est bon," said a young man who stood next to it drinking the broth. "This is our whisky," he added smiling. "*Malhababik à Khénifra*" said the same man and walked off while we were still sipping it. "How much is this?" I wanted to pay. "That man has paid for you. *Malhababik.*"

******

Notes:

1 (p. 213) Smhli, in Darija, I'm sorry.

2 (p. 214) Elben – sour milk.

3 (p. 215) Countries where Public Displays of Affection are Crimes, Afreen Ahamed, 2013.

4 (p. 215) Al-Bukhaari, 5889; Muslim, 2657.

5 (p. 215) Al-Noor 24:30-31.

6 (p. 216) Islam Question and Answer, Shaykh Muhammad Saalih al-Munajjid, 2014.

7 (p. 216) Ghaafir 40:19.

8 (p. 216) Islam Question and Answer, op.cit.

9 (p. 216) Ibid.

10 (p. 216) In law & legal issues, religion & spirituality, the difference between Haad and Tazeer.

11 (p. 217) Studying Islam, Islam philosophy of the Islamic concept of punishment, 2005.

12 (p. 217) Dating & Islam…to Me It's an Oxymoron, Dania Shahza, 2012.

13 (p. 218) Couple Arrested in Morocco for Kissing, December 11, 2013.

14 (p. 219) Islam: Love Is Not in the Air, Rachel Molschky.

15 (p. 219) Bzzaf, in Darija, very.

16 (p. 219) Torta, in Darija, cake.

17 (p. 220) Epo, in Amazigh, mother.

18 (p. 223) "Understanding Rheumatic Fever - the Basics," Varnada Karriem-Norwood, 2014; "What Is Rheumatic Fever? What Causes Rheumatic Fever?" 2010.

19 (p. 223) Ibid.

20 (p. 223) "Morocco's Health Care System in Distress," The New York Times, Aida Alami, 2013.

21 (p. 224) Hubz, in Darija, bread.

22 (p. 224) Malhababic, in Darija, welcome.

23 (p. 226) Arbiya, in Darija, Arabic.

24 (p. 230) Sherifa, it's a name, but also a title given to a respected, elderly woman, the same as "Äami" for men.

25 (p. 231) "Challenging Illiteracy in Morocco, a Bookseller Pursues Paradise," Hannah Rehak, 2014.

26 (p. 233) Fantasia: wikipedia.org.

27 (p. 237-240) Berber: Encyclopaedia Britannica.

28 (p. 241) Excessive Consumption Of Phosphate Is Harmful To Health, 2012.

29 (p. 242) Kasba Tadla: wikipedia.org.

End of Part Seven

Arougou café with me and Mohamed.

Part Eight

"Morocco is not the easiest place to live. You have been through a huge amount both physically and emotionally. Be prepared for a culture shock when you return to Europe. It will feel very different and your values will have changed. You will need time to adjust."

Four months have passed since my return and I still feel the need for a long holiday just to get my act together, to redefine my values and to make sense of what I have lost and gained. On no account could my brief journey be compared to that of a war but I feel like I fought a few battles and got heavily wounded. What do I do with the pain that not many around me comprehend? What do I do with this chapter in my life? What do I do with experience that feels undesirable when it hurts and like water when it appeases me. I can neither rewrite it nor erase it nor go back to who I was before. The before. The after. The consequences of living. The irreversible.

I gained the experience before gaining knowledge. Had I had the knowledge, would I have experienced it differently? I wonder. How much the "knowing" changes the "perceiving"? On a global scale, would a painter have evolved into the same one, if he had not been exposed to art before? Would a writer have established a different style if he had not been influenced by what he had read before? Who would he or she be? The before. The after. The consequences of thinking. The irreversible.

My wound feels still fresh, open, and no medic can stitch it up. "Try not to think too much," my alter ego tells me. Life goes on no matter where I am or how I feel. Morocco, Khénifra, La Scierie, café "Martil," Hay Haddon Nhlima, El Borj; with or without me they manage. The before. There may not be the after. The consequences of surviving. The reversible.

I hear people saying: "I want to change the world to live in a better, safer, more equal place." And I say: "You will be lucky if you change one single life. That is already a massive task to undertake but don't give up, keep trying."

There are too many visions of how the world should look like and too much arrogance and egotism to reach a compromise. While hundreds of people still sleep on the streets of Khénifra, building the first supermarket in La Scierie is called progress. While the rich sleep in rooms adorned with gold at the Mamounia Hotel in Marrakesh, nearby there are slums. Is this called progress? On my first visit to Marrakesh I had experienced both. First a guy who stopped me on the street was showing me around and taking me to his place where he was living with his family; the appalling conditions of that shelter unveiled something that should be banned by law as it takes away from human dignity. Then straight from the slums I went to the most expensive and extravagant Mamounia Hotel for dinner. Walking through the land of glory with grass that seemed to have been sprinkled with gold, swimming pools and tennis courts monitored 24/7 by guards in case nature scratched it with a leaf or a feather, straight to the hotel that was first a museum and then turned into five different cultural salons: French, Italian, Indian, English, and Moroccan. Each offered exquisite food and a live performance. I am very grateful for this experience but I struggle to find logic to the word "progress." And why a country that allows people to die on the streets, to live in disconcerting bareness and with hunger, the same country shows off with such ridiculous wealth? The before. The after. The consequence of greed. The irreversible.

******

It cost Mustapha 110DH to buy two bottles of whisky that went down his throat the night before that he had spent sitting by the river and gazing at the sky of El Borj pondering his solitary existence thrown at him with that irresistible bottle of whisky, one too many, that had broken the window in La Scierie and forced upon him the irrational behaviour. "There is something that I feel when I'm drunk that I cannot control," he explained. But before he had joined me and Mohamed at the café "Martil," I went out. Once again Mohamed and I talked through our problems, the cultural misunderstanding that gives us both a splitting headache.

I invited him out to have some fish as a part of my birthday celebration. In comparison to Casablanca's restaurant, here they served moderate portions and for less. "Why are you not eating?" "I'm not hungry," said Mohamed who consumed the better part, meaning calamari, and left all the fish. Where I grew up I had to eat whatever was on the table or consume it later. Here I learned to respect food even more, enjoying it or not, I always felt compulsion to eat as being fussy or making a complaint was simply inappropriate. Beggars can't be choosers, so I placed the fish on the bread and gave it away to a beggar at the next occasion.

At the café "Martil" Mustapha, the waiter, was strangely offish with me and punishing me with old, stale, undrinkable avocado shake that had to be remade twice. I wondered what it was that was bothering him. Mustapha turned up that day dressed in elegant trousers and a clean jumper and had his moustache shaved off. He looked so much better without his facial hair. "Look at you! What a transformation!" I commented. He came to wish me a happy birthday saying: "I had tried to steal a baby sheep at my father's farm to buy you a present, but my father caught me red-handed." "What a drama!" I said. "What happened next?" "My father was so good with me that gave me 200DH but I had spent it on alcohol and cigarettes," he admitted and added, "no cadeaux pour Margarena." He had been talking about giving me a present since Christmas time, but the temptation to swap dirhams for a present required a certain stamina that Mustapha was still lacking.

After our short encounter with Mustapha, Mohamed and I went to the river to have my birthday drink, when Mustapha kept calling me. "I'm not at home, I'm busy now," I said. "I want to see you in twenty minutes," he stated. "Not now, I'll see you in the evening and I'll give you that booklet." He was desperate for my little Darija-French dictionary and insisted on an immediate meeting with me. I met him in the evening outside La Scierie, went to fetch the booklet and came back with it. "Do you want to come and say hello to the family?" He was keen on seeing *Baba*, so we both walked and both witnessed something peculiar. When we entered the house, Papa Mohamed who was sitting in the leaving room, sprung to his feet, grabbed a video recorder and shouted in Mustapha's face. Mustapha, with extraordinary calm backed off saying, "ça fait, ça fait," and walked off. Through this weird behaviour Papa was apparently trying to make him realise the mistake he made with breaking the window. "You cannot come home, no matter how drunk, and destroy things," he said. "Of course, I agree with you." "I have nothing against him drinking alcohol but breaking things, causing trouble all the time it's out of order," he continued looking a little bit down. "Here is some money for you to go to Casablanca," I was hoping to cheer him up a little. "Are you travelling tonight, right?" "Yes, I'm going," he confirmed. "I hope everything will go well, fingers crossed."

The following day, over lunch, I was told that Papa saw a doctor and his problem was resolved. That night he come back home with a rather different energy, first he gave me a massive hug and then explained the whole operation with putting a tube through his mouth and pinching the ulcer, saying how much difference it made to his well-being. "I no longer vomit," he added. I was over the moon, took his prescription and ran off to the pharmacy. The cost, 110DH for twenty-eight soluble tablets, made me ponder Papa's consistency not only as regards buying them, but also taking them regularly. So far, he proved to have been an extremely irregular tablet taker. He would cease taking any medicine if after a few days he did not feel an immediate improvement claiming it wasn't beneficial enough.

However, it was a joy to see him happy and not in pain that evening. But the next day, the pain reappeared. "Why do you still vomit?" I asked. "Wasn't it supposed to stop?" It turned out that Papa's stories of a pinched ulcer was a total fabrication. There was a different story depended on who was telling it. Apparently, he did not allow the doctor to put a tube or a camera down his throat; but, according to the second tale the machine at the hospital had been broken. Whichever was the real story, the truth was that the tale I was told was untrue. I felt disappointed, not with the fact that he had not had it done, but with the lack of sincerity. In the end it was him who chose long-term suffering over a temporary pain. I did not mention anything to him nor to anybody else in the family. Instead I was trying to make him take those tables but the simplest instruction that it must be drunk twenty minutes before breakfast was understood neither by him nor by Meryam. "It's important that you do it that way, otherwise it won't work," a said on a few occasions when he wasn't drinking it or claiming that he had done it the night before.

******

Victoria from the Children of the Sahara Organization wrote back to us informing us of progress in the goat project:

"We are very touched by the honest and to the point explanation about the lives of the families and their struggles, especially the condition of their shelters, the issues with the cold nights and the lack of proper nutrition and revenue to support productive expenditures such as school and health care fees. We would like to propose to you that we can support a small project (could be one or more separate things) of about US $1500-2000. It is up to you to write a proposal how you would use the funds, who it will benefit, how it will be implemented, how it will be supervised, and what follow-up/reporting/monitoring you would like to do. Hence, since you highlight several needs, please put together a proposal/action plan and we will try to finance it. The one main requirement we have is that you provide us with a monthly update of the project and the outcomes it produces. If you can draft a proposal within the next week or two then we can comment on it if there is anything we would like more clarity on and then we can move forward."

It was such good news for the Association and the people who would benefit from it. I instantly responded and started writing the proposal and then presuming that we would receive the maximum $2000, I suggested dividing the funds into: goats and wood-burning stoves; and I received the confirmation that our proposal could have more than one activity. Calculating the cost of purchasing goats and wood-burning stoves, I recommended getting three female goats plus one billy and ten wood-stoves for the poorest in the village. The only concern regarding the *fornos* was the safety, given that stoves can cause accidents if not used properly. Hence, the proposal had to be very specific:

"We would like to see in your proposal what you would do to minimize this risk. Please describe the mitigation measures you will take to reduce risks of negative consequences. This could be to provide info/training to recipient families on the proper use and dangers of improper use. Highlighting the risks and mitigation measures is important to us as we do not want to be involved in a project which, while well meaning, could unintentionally have negative side effects."

I understood their concerns as observing my family for the past few months I gained vital knowledge as to how little they knew about safety and the consequences of living with smoke. Even I, by chance, burnt my arm by coming too close to the pipe that left me with a visible mark. Hakima did the same to herself a few times and *Baba* burnt his urine bottle by leaving it nearby.

The proposal, however, was quickly sent off and we waited with anticipation for their response.

Their response came a few days before my departure and after a period of a terrible sadness and an unexpected event introduced by Papa Mohamed. The organization needed further explanation regarding the cost of goats, a suggestion to buy less expensive goats of a lower quality but to raise the quantity, and details of how we would monitor the daily intake of milk by children.

I emphasised in the proposal the need for dairy products and how it would serve families especially with anaemic children and pregnant women. Then with a growing herd, I saw the possibility of bringing a healthy income to those households:

"Taking into account the location, El Borj is on the main road towards Meknès, Rabat and all the big cities, we could promote our project by offering home-made cheese and goats' milk (iben) to locals, passers-by, tourists that stop here at the local café and at the fossils' shop. The women could offer *iben* and *elben.*" I also saw a clear opportunity to promote both charities by creating a piece of information that could be given away with every purchase, e.g.: "The goat project is sponsored by Authentic Morocco Tours and Treks (contact details) and led by Association Hannan (contact details)."

Their response blew me away:

"More focus on the impact on children: We understand that, at least in the beginning before the goat project can take off and produce cheese for sale, it will first and foremost serve a nutritional purpose for children and women in the recipient families. Hence, we would like you to specify more how you will make sure (as much as possible) that children and women are the ones that drink and benefit from the milk. I know it is probably very difficult to monitor that kids nutritional indicators such as growth measurements and other health and child development indicators improve (unless you are a health/nutrition specialist) but this is the final outcome that we are after and hence the project should build in indicators along the results chain as much as possible towards this outcome. For example you should monitor if the goats produce milk, who in the households drinks the milk, and ask mothers if they think the milk makes a difference in the welfare of the kids (and women for instance if they are pregnant or anaemic). Please describe how you will monitor and report on these aspects."

How could we possibly monitor that? If I were staying in Morocco, I would certainly do it myself by establishing milking times and observing their consumption. The fact was that children and adults loved milk and even at the family or friends' gatherings it was served at the table. The only problem was that they couldn't afford to drink it regularly. My view on this was not to monitor the daily intake of milk, as I was certain they would, but to teach them how to drink it without sugar.

And as they suggested to "source the more expensive" goats, we were quoting the prices of the more expensive goats, but indicating that there were the estimated prices and not necessary the actual cost. Anyhow, the prices weren't trumped up but given by a goat breeder.

Their email irritated me but I knew it was down to my exhaustion as looking at it now I would have loved to continue with a little study making appropriate charts or health checks and perhaps it all might have led to other exciting findings.

Hannah assured them that the whole process of monitoring would take place and that we would prefer to have fewer but better quality goats. The project was resent and we waited for their response.

******

The feeling of loneliness, exhaustion and helplessness came with the recent events and hit me hard again. At home I missed Hakima who was sacrificing days and nights taking care of her mum, Rkia; then I felt disappointed with Papa's unresolved stomach problem and his stories. Next sad news arrived with Alla who had a camion accident; but luck was on his side though and he did not suffer any serious injuries apart from bruises and small cuts. A lack of friends and Mohamed's volatile character was also responsible for my over-sensitive reaction to Rkia's condition. She was at the hospital for a few days and I bravely went to see her. Her physical and mental discomfort and anguish was unbearable for me to look at. She was still conscious but might have not recognised faces that were with her all the time, the hands that were lifting her up making her feel more comfortable, the hands that were changing her hygienic pads every day and night, the bodies that were sitting behind her on the bed supporting her back and making her sit up, the eyes that were looking at her and drown in tears as they saw more of the end then the continuity.

There was no special bond between me and grandma Rkia owing to the fact that she was constantly on the move; but when she was with us, she would sit and ask questions in Amazigh and she would always laugh at my answers to them. She was a person of a compromising and peaceful nature, the least complying and demanding of all the elderly people that I had met there. She might have carried on with a long night chat keeping me awake or had never flushed that nasty squat toilet, but she was quickly forgiven, usually the very moment when her chat would stop and the toilet would be cleaned.

Here, in front of me, on that bed, there was not much of grandma left. Who was that woman who took control over her body and her mind? I didn't know her. It wasn't Rkia. And yet, I sobbed over the unrecognisable bones, skin, and mind. "Look at her," said Itto, Bassha's wife to Hakima pointing at me. Yes, I cried. I couldn't help looking at another human being tortured by pain that no one could stop or cure. Would it help if I was born here? Would I get accustomed to suffering like Mohamed did?

"Mohamed, Mohamed…" the fragile and scared voice was calling. And she trembled. "Mohamed, Mohamed…" she was calling that name repetitively as she was looking for Papa's company or some reassurance. "He is here… *la bas, la bas,*" the voices around her were calming her down. Her feet and legs were swollen and she passed blood with urine. Some said she had cancer. "Rkia is dying because we don't have money to afford a doctor's visit," said Papa. To the best of my belief it was too late for the visit but he had a point. Had she been referred to the doctor few months before, she might have had a chance of longer life with less pain.

In total distress I left the hospital one hour later. I could stand no more. I needed a hug. A real proper hug. And Mohamed was waiting for me and here I had a chance to get it... oh no, I couldn't, we were in the centre surrounded by other people and the hug would be most inappropriate.

"Why actually do you want to stay with me?" I asked. "Because of your "sagesse," he said adding, "I want to learn from you." I thought that was noble but at least expected. "I believed people stay together because they love each other. You can find many intelligent individuals in your life and learn from them, easier to find and it doesn't hurt," I said and felt tired. "Of course there are other reasons," he added. "That is very good, Mohamed.""

What happened to our connection that was flawless before we had decided to try to make sense of what we felt? Is it the expectations that were stopping us from growing? I expected him to love and respect me as making a life-time commitment based on my mind wasn't convincing enough; it could change with another person equally wise or wiser. What then?

"There is no force in the world but love, and when you carry it within you, if you simply have it, even if you remain baffled as to how to use it, it will work its radiant effects and help you out of and beyond yourself: one must never lose this belief, one must simply (and if it were nothing else) endure it!"

******

Papa Mohamed put his white djellaba on and started praying. He even went to the mosque. Hakima who was at home today was laughing at him saying that he only prayed for money.

To sit in the park or any public place by myself was always a task. Today, I was joined by a friend of Mohamed, a mute, young girl and her girlfriends. They were all to become hairdressers. The mute girl, sadly her name escaped my mind, was in love with Ali but Ali wasn't in love with her. Apparently he made some effort by studying sign language but a few times he stood her up. She was very open about her femininity and her bare cleavage had attracted a few "dragueurs" on the street and she had to be rescued. Even for me the way she dressed was a little bit too provocative for this town, and taking into account her disability, she was making herself twice as vulnerable as she was. On the other hand, it might have been the only way to attract men, the problem was she was attracting the wrong type who would take advantage of her and then abandon her. But she was always beaming with joy and I admired her high-spirited nature.

When the girls had left, the young Simo with his friend spotted me sitting there and joined me. The sun was strong. "Would you like to come with us to the "Complex Centre"?" asked Simo. "I'm happy sitting here reading and doing Sudoku." Simo went off and came back five minutes later. "Shouldn't you go?" I asked. "I changed my mind. Do you want me to leave you alone?" "You can keep me company, if you want." He did find Khénifra dull but tried to do everything to keep his mind occupied. "I'm a stage comedian and I perform in Amazigh," he said. "We have something in common; when I was at university I was also a stage comedian. Can I see you performing before I go away?" He wrote down a name of a club in the zone where he lived, took my telephone number and promised to confirm and give me more details on the forthcoming spectacle.

I kept reading the newspaper and listening to the music, when out of blue a man appeared in front of me. "Tu es belle." "Thank you very much, but I don't want to talk to you." "Why not?" he looked at me as there was something wrong with me. "I don't have the "envie."" "Why not? What is your name?" he continued. "Please, leave me alone," I said and had "envie" to kick his balls hard. Finally he understood, backed off and sat down on the opposite bench observing.

The next one was a "watchman." "What time is it?" Without a word, waving my arms, I showed him no watch on my wrist. Luckily for me he was not very proactive. He left. After him, a beggar who stunk of alcohol demanded money. "I don't have it, *smhli*." He touched my arm, said "no problem" and was about to leave when his hand reached out for my pen wanting to write something down. "I'm not interested, sorry."

A few minutes later another fellow was standing in front of me trying to sell some sun cream protection and the next one came out of his car that he had parked right in front of me. I continued listening to the music, doing Sudoku and paying no attention to that man whatsoever. He stood next to me, leaned against the metal bar, took his shoes off and said something that I ignored. He carried on talking though. I took my headphones out. "Are you talking to me?" "Yes, are you French?" "No." His French was impeccable. He was living and working in France as a merchant but disliked Europe. He repeated the same phrase that my "one afternoon friend" had said once: "People in Europe are racists and everything is too expensive." He offered his help with information about Berbères and was willing to show me around. He was kind but I refused.

In the meantime I kept receiving messages and phone calls from Mustapha who badly wanted to see me before I go away. "Je veux vérité," he said. "What vérité?" I asked. "Je suis malade," he said. "Then you need to go and see a doctor," I advised him. "Mais, toi, tu es médicament pour moi," he continued with his love tale and I was at the end of my tether.

I was sitting in my room, when the same night I heard a music coming from outside that indicated a marriage ceremony and later on some dreadful lament that indicated death. The crowd that gathered at the square in La Scierie was participating in a spectacle provided by a few well-dressed women that were holding massive bright-coloured plates. On the first plate there was a pair of red high heels, on the second - a dress and the third one looked full of sweets and it was carried by a young energetic woman who was performing a very strange dance with it: shaking the whole plate and making circles when moving forward towards the house.

Around midnight I heard a noise that made me think: someone must be dead. I had never heard anything like it before: the lament, the scream of children and adults, even the tears were heard. It stopped around 1.00am but restarted in the very early hours of the next morning. I came downstairs. "What is going on? Is someone dead?" "Yes, I will be going there soon. Do you want to come with me?" asked Hakima. I wasn't sure. I went up to the rooftop to see what was happening and saw men dressed up in their djellabas standing at the corner of our street; and that unceasing lament. I didn't go. I had had enough of seeing people in pain.

Instead, I packed everything that I was not going to take with me and went over to Mohamed's. He invited me in. When I was waiting for him at the rooftop, I felt a sudden and strong pang of sadness when all those moments of the past time had flashed in front of me: the tagine we made together, countless teas, dances, intimate moments, walks, reading and discussions. "How changeable everything is," I thought out loud. And then when he walked in, I became silent, I could no longer speak. The words were strongly entangled with the emotional pang that I felt and I could no longer make sense of what the heart beat and how fast. "You wanted all those videos that we made in Timdghass and the photos. Let's go downstairs to copy them on to your computer." While it was being copied, he turned the music on making me breakdown under the lightness of *"Inas, Inas"* musical notes that took me straight back to the past time. I was a wreck. "I have to go home," I said. "Stay. I want you to stay. Don't go. Don't leave me, please. I can't stand thinking that you may be gone forever," said Mohamed. I sobbed with pain, exhaustion, I sobbed with everything I saw and experienced and I couldn't hold it back. It was too fresh.

That afternoon we spent together; having coffee, watching films and answering questions. "Madeleine, I have not seen you for a long time, what happened?" asked his dad. "Mohamed and I have not been harmonious," I explained. "No, no, you two must stay together." "It's not easy sometimes." His dad might have understood but the fact was that there was always either black or white and no grey colour for him.

"Shall we catch a taxi to go to Aglmam tomorrow?" I asked. "It's not easy to find a transport for Aglmam but we could try." He was right. To find the taxi was impossible. One man wanted 120DH from us but we weren't willing to pay that much. "Let's just get into that bus," I pointed to the one that was about to go somewhere. The bus took us to Arougou for 7DH where we drank tea in my favourite outdoor café, had two delicious greasy animal organs' sandwiches fried on the outdoor barbecue and long walks across the wild fields of Arougou. What a beautiful and peaceful day we had.

The only thing that was on my mind that day was the nasty cough that came back and a strange rash on my chest and the face. "O goodness me, what is this?" I was worried. "Shall we go to the hospital?" asked Mohamed. "I have seen too much, I don't think I'll trust any doctor here. I'll wait. I'm sure I'll get better at home, in Europe."

******

This country is vast and wild but there is hardly any place where one can find solitude. The scattered houses have eyes, in fact, a few pairs. A picnic in the middle of nowhere would always be in the middle of somewhere, there would always be someone who would pass by or graze sheep or who had a house nearby. One could never be left alone; the eyes of society were always open. With spring that came grass would grow, the higher it would grow the better for the solitude-seekers. Mohamed and I would pass by a well-flattened nest scented with pleasure and a group of boys drinking and smoking in a second well-padded nest. That high grass was the best hiding place during the warm, fresh and seductive springtime evenings. The high grass would make them believe that the eyes of society saw nothing but in fact they saw everything. "There is so much hypocrisy in that society," I thought. Everybody knew about the alcohol and hashish consumption, about men's promiscuity and all those hiding places where they themselves hid but at the same time they criticised others who would do the same. "You can do it here, but there … or it's dark now, it's a good time."

"Your mum must know that you drink and smoke, but she would not allow you to have a drink at home?" I asked while hiding a glass of wine behind a sofa. "No, she wouldn't. It's against Islam." "What about if we take a look at the map and will pick up a place that we have never been to? We will not have to hide for a day or two" I asked. We took the map out and I looked at the north of Morocco. "Would you like to go to the sea?" "It would be a long journey and there are only a few days left," said Mohamed. "What about this place? I have read in the guidebook that it's beautiful. It's called the blue city." "That is Chefchaouen, I have never been there. It's a very touristy place though but if you want, we could take a bus to Chefchaouen." "Great. We could find out the bus timetable tomorrow and book a riad, would you be happy?" The idea was great. We both loved travelling and we both felt happier outside Khénifra.

We visited a few cities that evening… being the armchair travellers and discussed some oddities of some other places, for example *Berkane*, the north of Morocco, had more showers than *hammams*. "Why is that? Are people there more westernised, meaning they don't have time to spend in the *hammam*?" "I don't know, but people from that area seem different. They look different." "How?" "The consequences of French occupation: more mixed up marriages than anywhere else." "Do they also migrate to France?" "This part tends to migrate to Holland, whereas people from here go to France." "Interesting." "From Ujdar or Nador they migrate to Spain or Holland and from area of Benin Mellal to Italy," he said.

Melilia, the Spanish place in Morocco, is closest to Nador. Only residents of Nador can enter Melilia without a visa, all other of Moroccans require one. "People from Nador have developed their own language that no one else can understand. So if you go there and you don't speak

Nadorian, the chances that you would be served tea are very slim," said Mohamed. "Almost like Welsh," I added. "But Nadorians are not good people, they are conceited racists," he said.

"Both Melilia and *Ceuta*, a city close to Tanger, are Spanish cities in Morocco. The government of Morocco has requested from Spain the sovereignty of Ceuta and Melilia but the Spanish position is that both Ceuta and Melilla are integral parts of the Spanish state, and have been since the 15th century, centuries before Morocco's independence from France in 1956. Morocco denies these claims and maintains that the Spanish presence on or near its coast is a remnant of the colonial past which should be ended. The United Nations list of Non-Self-Governing Territories does not include these Spanish territories.

Melilia, like Ceuta, was a free port before Spain joined the European Union. The population is made up of Christians, Muslims (chiefly Riffians), and a small number of Jews. Both Spanish and Riffian are widely spoken, with Spanish as the only official language. What's interesting is that both cities have declared the Muslim holiday of *Eid al-Adha* or Feast of the Sacrifice, as an official public holiday from 2010 onwards. It is the first time a non-Christian religious festival has been officially celebrated in Spain since the Reconquista.

When in 2007, for the first time in eighty years, a Spanish Monarch, King Juan Carlos I and Queen Sofia visited the city, a massive flow of demonstrations, not only from the public, but also from the Moroccan government, had been sparked. Nowhere else but in Melilia one can still see a statue of General Francisco Franco."

******

The next morning we went to find out the bus timetable, booked a riad, packed the essentials and took a night bus to Tanger where we would change for Chefchaouen. His mum packed for us some dinner leftovers, a few eggs, bread, cakes, and tea.

But before I had left the house, I was shaken by a couple of visitors: Jamal's parents, parents of the man who abused Malika and who some time ago fled the police and his whereabouts had been unknown since. That morning Papa Mohamed hinted that they may be coming. *"La! La! La! La!* Why? The case is in police hands and I have nothing to say to them. Besides, why would they come here? *La!"* I strongly disagreed hoping that Papa would understand the sensitivity of this case. He didn't.

At first when I was called to come downstairs for tea, I had no idea who they were. Hakima called me over to the kitchen. "Jamal, Mohamed *mochkila*," she commented. "No?!" I couldn't believe it. The awkwardness of this situation made me quickly drink tea and leave the room. "Where are you going?" asked Papa. "I have to pack," I answered and walked off. Within a short while Papa came to my room. "They are Jamal's parents, they want to talk to you," he said. "I told you, I have nothing to say to them." Unfortunately I had to enter that room to get my shoes, and when I did, Papa and Alla insisted that I sit with them and talk. How? None of the people who were in the house spoke either English or French. How on earth could I explain that I had nothing to do with his disappearance? Irritated, I spoke. "I don't understand why you are here! What do you want me to do? This was not me who abused Malika, it was your son. It's not my fault that he ran away; if he had not been guilty, he wouldn't have fled."

It was upsetting that my family, at least Papa and Alla, put blame on me for the current situation and in all of that they only saw a guy and not the girl, the actual victim. The question was why did they get involved in all of that? I quickly left the house and met up with Mohamed. "I'm so angry with Papa. He has no idea what he is doing! I'm so glad that we are going away," I said trying to compose myself.

It took us ten hours to get to Chefchaouen but however tired this journey was I treasured one aspect of it: the closeness. We were able to sit arm to arm, hold hands, kiss… something that was normal for me but abnormal for Mohamed. We changed in Tanger in the morning and went through Tetouan that looked absolutely breath-taking from the bus window to Chefchaouen, the bleu city. When we finally found our riad and tried to check in, we were asked for the marriage certificate. "We are almost married," I said. This nice gentleman looked at me and smiled. "By law I need to see your marriage certificate to accommodate you in the same room," he said adding, "but… I can register you under two single rooms and give you the best double room in our riad." The room was comfortable but nothing extraordinary. In fact, the price was too high for the standard of that room: we were trembling from cold at night and in the morning there was not enough hot water to take a shower. Perhaps the bed with spotty tiger bedding that was embedded into an ornamented colourful wooden palace was indicating the sumptuous better-off side of that riad.

The residents of Chefchaouen are beautiful people and the particular style of wearing an elongated straw hat with garish woollen elements attached to it and good quality woollen pieces of fabrics that go over their arms and the bottom part make them stand out. A picturesque town set against the dramatic backdrop of the Rif Mountains filled with white-washed homes with distinctive, powder-blue accents.

"Chef Chaouen" derives from the Berber word for horns, Ichawen and refers to the shape of the mountain tops above the town that look like the two horns (chaoua) of a goat. The history says that it was painted blue by the Jewish refugees who lived there during the 1930's. The beauty of Chefchaouen's mountainous surroundings is enhanced by the contrast of the brightly painted medina. It is this beauty and the relaxed atmosphere of the town that makes Chefchaouen very attractive to visitors. The main square in the medina is lined with cafes and filled to the brim with locals and tourists mingling easily. Another reason why backpackers love Chefchaouen is the easy availability of drugs, a prolific source of kif. Hashish is subsequently sold all over town, but is mostly the domain of native Chaouenis. Chefchaouen is a popular shopping destination as well,

as it offers many native handicrafts that are not available elsewhere in Morocco, such as wool garments and woven blankets. The goat cheese native to the area is also popular with tourists. A nearby attraction is the Kef Toghobeit Cave which is one of the deepest caves in Africa."

It was certainly easy to come across a man who offered us hashish. And when the same man was asked about a bottle of wine, he wanted to walk us to a place that was selling whisky for 450DH. And he would persist and come back, in case we changed our minds.

The downside of that place was a low quality of food and high prices. With more tourists coming, the more fast-food places were becoming a standard. That particular one in the centre that offered us some seafood was dreadful and the owner was arrogant and rude. Not even had we finished with our meal when he had come up and started cleaning up… in front of us. The hygienic standards of that place were of a great concern to me when seeing and not even using the lavatory room. With regret we had to pass our complaint to a boy who trapped us in that restaurant with a promise of a good quality time.

"I have to buy that hat and something for my family," I said to Mohamed. And I got my hat along with a beautiful fabric that could be used as a tablecloth or a piece of outfit when wrapped around the hips or arms.

In the evening we had equally dreadful pizza and instead of a glass of wine, which I thought it would be easy to get in such a touristic town, we had two, instead of one, badly brewed pots of teas, a simple mistake made by the waiter.

The following morning it was time to go back home, to Khénifra, to spend one more day with my family, pack and leave the town at the night time as Raba airport was calling.

Our home was sad and even my colourful hat and equally colourful piece of fabric that I bought as a present did not manage to bright it up.

The following morning, Khadeja and Hajar, a girl who has been sponsored by Hmad and Hannah, came to ask for money. "You have been sponsored for many years and you know that the Association doesn't give the money but clothes." "No, no, we want money, why can't we have money?" demanded Khadeja. "Because this is the policy of Hannan School and it is how it works; you both know that very well," I said annoyed with their nagging. Apparently, they had paid Mohamed, the vice-president, a visit at home accusing him of corruption and demanding money that Hajar's sponsor had sent her. "This is out of order. You need to do something about it or she will lose the sponsor," Mohamed put his foot down.

The last day of my stay in Khénifra was pretty busy. I intended to go to El Borj to see the children and say goodbye to the teachers. However, for about one hour I had tried to catch a taxi but for some reason not a single one wanted to drive there as there were not enough passengers. It was around 10.30am when Samira, the teacher, bubbling with irritation came out of a yellow taxi just in front of a grand taxi stand. "I don't know what is going on? They don't want to drive to El Borj?" We were both sitting in an empty taxi and waited for four more passengers when another one that was going to Mrirt stopped. Having had a spare seat, the driver was willing to drop one of us off at El Borj. "You have to go," I said to her. "The children are waiting for you." "I'll stay, I don't have to go. *Bslama*."

I sat down at the café "Martil" and sent my last email to Hannah.

"Hannah, this is my last day! I feel extremely emotional. Mohamed and I have worked through our crisis and it's even more difficult to leave this country now. I want to go home but at the same time I don't. Difficult to explain. Thank you very much for everything, your support, your heart, your advice…"

Hannah could not believe it was the end of our co-operation. She kept thanking me for all the help and work I had done and was very happy to hear that Mohamed and I had worked though our problems and she understood the difficulty of leaving. "Somehow despite the difficulties these people and their country get under your skin," said Hannah quite rightly.

After a quick coffee, I went for a quick tea at Mohamed's and then ran back home as I still had packing and shopping to do. When after the *hammam* I came home, Meryam was waiting for me with a friend. "She is going to do proper henna for you," said Meryam. "I won't be able to walk or do anything for about three hours," I was thinking but didn't want to upset her. It was a very well-meant gesture. So I sat down in our cold living room, meaning I had to face up to an even longer process of drying henna, when that young girl was creating amazing patterns all over my feet and hands. It took about four hours for me to stand on my legs with not yet properly dried henna.

In the meantime, the two Fadmas came to bid me farewell bringing present and tears. That late afternoon, I finally managed to go to the medina and buy some presents for my family, mainly *babushki*, attractive and light to carry. "I was thinking," said Mohamed, "I'd like to have a ring; it would feel for me like we were married already, what do you think?" "Let's go and buy them," I responded cheerfully. The difficulty was to find a ring that would fit my finger, every single one was far too big; but the merchant was leading us from shop to shop, showing and trying different ones on until we found the one: a nice, simple, silver ring that fitted gracefully my finger. Ecstatic with our purchase we went off to Mohamed's for *chfnj* that his mum was baking for us. "Did your mum asked about Chefchaouen?" "Not much but she was curious where we were staying." "She must know about our intimate relationship but I see she doesn't approve of it. She seems a little bit tense lately." "She is probably tired," responded Mohamed. "Perhaps, but there is something that bothers her, I can sense it."

When we came in she was baking the *chfnj*. "Madeleine, I'm baking them for you, come on in," she said. We both sat with her in the kitchen. Mohamed took out the rings and showed them to her. There was no particular reaction but a question: who bought them and for how much. When I was saying goodbye to her, she said: "I hope you will come back, *Inchallah*."

I ran back home to pack my suitcases. "How is it possible that I have as much as I came with?" Packing is extra stressful when the mind is occupied with the onerous and strict rules of Ryanair. I was positive it was far too heavy and that they would charge me extra money. "And how do I carry my Chefchaouen hat and the backpack?" My quandary about packing was interrupted by Hakima who came to my room with a gift for my mum and to say goodbye to me. "I have to go to my mum's," she said and hugged me. "You are such a wonderful woman and thank you for being such a wonderful mum, I will miss you *bzzaf!*" I said it and wished she understood.

Then Meryam came in with a box of freshly baked cake and boucheyar. "I'm certain that I won't be hungry, what a wonderful gift, thank you. Now I have to go over to Mina's and say goodbye to her." She wasn't at home at that hour but soon I was informed through a message that she was back. It was before 10.00pm. I rang the door and saw mama Mina. "What is wrong with her face?" I thought. The way she spoke and greeted me was very different from what I was used to. Invited in, I walked up the stairs and when I looked at Mina I finally realised that she had no teeth. "What an awkward moment for both of us," I thought. I tried to behave as normal but all those hugs I was giving her and countless "thank you" I was expressing might have betrayed my shock at her toothless state. Frankly, I did not recognise mama Mina without her teeth. Nevertheless, with her teeth or without them I still loved her equally.

It was a very sad lifeless evening without Hakima, Papa who was on a job and crazy Mustapha who was no longer nagging us with his presence, so after a quick wash I was ready to get some sleep as the wakeup call was to be in three hours.

I woke up at 2.30am. Without waking anybody, I make myself a cup of coffee, did my final packing and was ready to leave. Mohamed was at my doorstep at 4.00am. "Look at you! You are so elegant!" He was wearing a proper jacket with a proper shirt and my black braces. I said goodbye to Meryam and left.

And here was another surprise. Mohamed came with his dad in his treasured car. "That is kind of your dad," I said while looking at the heavy suitcases.

His dad and his car equalled unity. The car did not exist without his father, the only person who could drive it, and his dad was dependent on the car, more emotionally then physically, or if we talked about his dad fiddling with the car almost every day then the physical dependence would equal emotional. His dad loved this old car so much that he was extra slow and extra careful giving way to cars on the roundabout even when it was him who had precedence over them.

When we arrived at the bus station after 4.00am and said goodbye to his dad, we took seats in the bus. When the bus was supposed to leave the station at 5.00am, there was still no sign of a bus driver, only the ticket inspectors were popping in controlling the number of passengers. When finally, after thirty minutes of delay the bus driver sat behind the steering wheel and left the station, one of the ticket inspectors got on a bike and cycled in front of it controlling its speed while looking for more passengers. The way they had been doing it always implied some sort of drama combined with action when the passengers picked up from the street had to jump inside the moving vehicle and were rushed by another ticket inspector.

The heavy rain helped us to sleep throughout the whole journey delivering us safely to the bus station of Raba five hours later. Our friend Mehdi was supposed to wait for us but there was no sign of him. We dragged ourselves to the bus station café and sat there waiting for Mehdi who arrived two hours later. We ordered caffee and had our little goodbye drink: a whisky with Coca-Cola that Mohamed was mixing under the table. He took the ring out and put it on my orange finger and I did the same, sliding it on his. I suppose we could call it an engagement. We were engaged to be married but how and where we still had no idea.

The tiny bottle of whisky was quickly emptied, so when Mehdi arrived we were a little bit tipsy, looking like a strange hybrid together: I dressed like a Western girl but wearing a Chefchaouen hat and having henna all over my hands, Mohamed – elegant but drunk. He was taking care of my backpack and I looked after the box with boucheyar, my hand luggage and a small backpack.

Mehdi had a craving for alcohol. "Shall we get to the supermarket?" "We can, we still have time." We took the metro and visited the first supermarket. I was very much convinced, looking at that bottle of whisky, that it was for later, but as soon as we left the supermarket the bottle was opened and mixed up with some leftovers of Coca-Cola. When we got to the Raba Ville Station, I had to look for a bus that could get me to the airport. At the information desk I was told that there was a bus, but no timetable was available. The bus cost only 20DH and it sounded like a perfect option in comparison to what we were getting from the aggressive taxi men who were quoting 150DH, then went down to 100DH and yet again to 70DH.

As it was far too early for us to go to the airport, we turned all those offers down hoping that we would find the right bus service. And when we were walking down the street, Mehdi had spotted the right bus and ran off after it coming back with the timetable. "No bus service between 4.00 and 7.00pm. How very weird and annoying!" I said adding, "we have no choice but to take a taxi; but before we do that, can we have a decent meal, please."

We walked and walked getting more and more tired and Mohamed more and more drunk. When we came across the first open restaurant, we decided to sit there. The front yard, through which we could get inside the restaurant, had a few tables. "Shall we sit outside?" We all agreed. A couple of waiters looked at us suspiciously. "You have got alcohol in that bottle," said one of them to Mehdi. Oh, no! What a mistake parading with it and tempting bad luck. "No, I don't," replied Mehdi whose face had gone red. If that man had opened it and sniffed it, we would have been in a big trouble. Fortunately, he allowed us to take a table but his eyes were on us all the time. We ordered some tagine when Mohamed wanted to use the toilet. "Can you give me one dirham?" he asked. "You don't need money, it's a restaurant's toilet," said Mehdi and I agreed with him. He walked off and said nothing. Then I followed him and used the same lavatory room and there was nobody there to ask or take money. When it was time to go, Mohamed grabbed my big backpack and shot off by himself. "What is wrong with him?" I asked Mehdi. Neither of us knew. "Mohamed slow down; what's wrong?" He neither slowed down nor did he look back, leaving me and Mehdi to find transport to the airport.

"Please, don't give him more alcohol," I begged Mehdi and he agreed with me. A great number of taxis were ready to take us to the airport but the price for such a short seven kilometres distance was still far too high. Mehdi was negotiating and getting into some rows with some taxi drivers, whereas Mohamed was standing looking angry. When a taxi agreed to take us for 100DH, Mohamed went straight for the front seat. "Come here with me." There was no reaction. His unexplained behaviour started annoying me but the first thing I had to do when we arrived at the airport was to weigh my backpack and the hand luggage. Nine kilograms over the limit had to be rearranged: a few books and some clothes were put inside my hand luggage which I hoped would not get weighed.

Exhausted and stressed I sat down. "What's wrong, Mohamed?" "Why didn't you both give me that one dirham?" "You really didn't need it," I said. He went off the handle. "I needed it and you didn't give me!" "If I had known, I would have given you. Here is more than one dirham," I gave him some money. The security guards who were walking around the airport were observing the whole scene. "You have to calm down because if not you will get arrested." He went even angrier and after a few fuming statements, he walked away without a word of goodbye.

Mehdi ran after him and managed to stop him far away while I went to check-in. Everything went well; I only had to empty my hand luggage of the nine extra kilograms. Yet again, I took a few books and some clothes out, managed to get the weight down to ten kilograms and walked off with my emptied hand luggage that I quickly refilled with all the excess clothes and books. That was massively draining. There was still some time left to the departure, so I sat down and waited for Mehdi to come. To my surprise Mohamed came back with him. "What about, I'm sorry for my irrational behaviour?" I asked. The sorry did not come, but what happened was a long and clear cry. He threw himself at me and sobbed like a baby while some security guards and travellers were observing us. But he needed to let out those emotions accumulated over months and to let out the fear that I may not come back. As complex and impossible as he was, I truly loved him. "I have to go. Let me go," I said. "Don't leave me," he was in a real state. "I have to leave you now but I will come back." I was slowly walking away and then disappearing mingling with other people who were getting in the queues behind me and when I turned my head around I could no longer see him. Being emotionally torn, crying my eyes out, I was gradually getting closer to the control point. It was a female officer. She looked at my passport and asked: "What did you do here?" "Voluntary work." She looked at my entry visa. "How long have you been here for?" "For five months." "You have been living here illegally for two months," she said. "Have I? Why?" "You visa is only valid for three months," she explained. "I had no idea. I'm sorry. I thought I could stay here as long as I wanted," I tried to justify my ignorance. "I can't let you out," she said. "I don't understand. I have another flight to catch from London, please I want to go home," I was begging her.

She left me waiting and came back with another male officer. He repeated the same questions and I repeated my story. "I have lived in Khénifra, I was registered there, I worked for a charity, I had truly no idea that I couldn't stay longer than three months," I was trembling with tiredness and powerlessness. "I'll call my family; will you talk to them, please?" He said he will so I called Meryam. Abdellah picked up the phone. "Get Meryam quickly, please." The officer talked to Meryam and I was hoping that this would resolve the problem. It didn't. Instead he said I had to go back to Khénifra. "Please let me go home, I can't miss my flight, I want to go home," tears were running down my face. "I'm sorry, that is the law, I can't let you go," he was emotionless. For a split second I had this crazy idea of bribing him, but the next minute it felt wrong to me. I looked at those sliding doors in front of me in the abyss of one or two meters, the doors that I had easily passed so many times before and that were not within my reach now.

I felt punished for all that time I had spent here voluntarily, for hours and weeks that I devoted to doing something good, to trying to improve, fix, to give myself to this country and its people. "What do I have to do? Who is going to pay for my lost flight?" I asked him feeling a complete resignation. "You have to go back to Khénifra, go to the police station and write PV and with that document you will be able to fly back home."

"Why is this happening to me? What went wrong?" I picked up the phone and called Mohamed. "I can't fly back home. Where are you?" "Still at the airport," he said. "Please, wait for me." "I'm here."

******

Everybody was crying today and especially the sky. It was not normal spring rain. I could imagine the sky sucking in all the reservoirs of water left on earth and pouring it over us in one big downpour. "I would rather be on that plane than get soaked wet," I was thinking out loud.

From a phase of complete resignation and exhaustion I moved to a phase of anger and frustration. "What happened?" shouted Mohamed who saw me dragging my hand luggage down the corridor and a police officer that was showing me out. "I can't go home," I said. Mohamed who was drunk and stunk of alcohol was trying to talk right at the face of that police officer while I was trying to push him away from him. "Keep your alcoholic distance."

"I need my backpack; also, can Ryanair rebook my flight?" I asked one of the crew members who was as emotionless and lacking compassion as the immigration officer who had turned me back. "1600DH for changing the flight," he said abruptly. "This is more than my ticket to London! And what about my London-Warsaw flight?" He didn't even answer but walked off to pass the information about my backpack to another crew member. I sincerely hate Ryanair. I hated them secretly before but now my hate had grown and no £10 voucher could change my feelings for this greedy, obnoxious, scrupulous, "blue people" who looked as ugly in those uniforms as they looked without them. Irreversible. "F… F… F…!" I don't know how many f… words I spat out that evening but it might have exceeded the whole number of f… words so far articulated. My head was exploding with pain and my nostrils were extra sensitive. "Oh Mohamed! The odour of that whisky may kill me! Don't come closer to those officers, they may arrest you."

It was about 8.00pm and I had no place to stay. I took my laptop out, sat down on one of those cosy seats in the corridor of the airport and started looking for a riad. Mohamed took a piece of pitta bread out and filled it with an egg. We were and behaved like little piggies: the crumbs were all over us and our seat; and then my jacket, the Chefchaouen hat, jumpers, magazines scattered all over the floor and my documents and passport were somewhere on top of it all; but we were and behaved like little piggies in love who weren't bothered by anybody who saw us kissing that evening and if we were arrested then it would resolve the problem of staying somewhere overnight. It would be ideal but this time, no matter how intimate we were, no one was even tempted to get us arrested.

Instead, I had to go and fetch my backpack. The female officer asked about my passport. "I don't have it with me, I don't know where it is," I responded with arrogance. "I'm sorry, it's not your fault, I'm just being tired," I apologised a minute later and she let me take my backpack without looking at my passport. Then I went back to our piggies' nests and restarted my search for a riad. "Why everything is so expensive? I'm not going to pay £300 for one night, I rather sleep here." It felt like it was the last straw.

In the meantime Mehdi made a few phone calls. "You will stay overnight with some girls in the dormitory," he said. "I don't want to stay with some girls, can't Mohamed stay with me?" The idea of making an effort to be kind to some strangers did not appeal to me. "No, he has to stay with me," said Mehdi adding, "men are not allowed there." Resigned and defeated I was slowly putting everything into my backpack and walking away from the airport to the bus that was about to leave in thirty minutes. We sat inside and waited, and while Mehdi tried to talk to some Americans who weren't keen on talking to him, Mohamed and I were sitting in silence. "I can't believe that I'm on this bus. I was supposed to be in London tonight and take another flight home in the morning," my thoughts were devouring me.

We got off in the centre of Raba and changed for a tram that took us to the students' house. The heavy rain did not cease. "I'm going to get off here to get some cigarettes and you both get off at this stop," he told us the name and left us. Freezing cold, exhausted, homeless, we were both standing in the rain waiting for Mehdi to come back. I couldn't believe this addiction. Three girls came up to us. "Is that you who need a room for tonight?" one of them asked me. "Yes, sorry to have bothered you," I said. Hasnae, a young girl who read Italian at university was pleased that we could communicate in French and Italian.

As those girls seemed terribly kind and I must have appeared terribly grumpy, I felt as if I owed them an explanation; so when Mehdi reappeared fifteen minutes later he explained in Arabic my frustration and somewhat offish attitude. "I'm very tired, so you must forgive me," I added.

"Don't look at the guard and behave like you were living here," said Hasnae when we were about to pass the gate to get inside a large student's complex; and without arousing any suspicions, we managed to get past it. "Shall we go and cook tagine?" asked Hasnae. "I'm not hungry at all, I just want to sleep," I said. "The girls wanted to make you tagine." "In that case, of course I'll join you. Do you mind if I have a quick wash first?" Hasnae took me to her room where we both were to sleep. "I have a flatmate but she is rarely here," she said. That girl was incredibly kind and thoughtful offering me everything that I would possibly need to wash myself or to use a lavatory room. "Would you like a pyjama to go out?" she asked. "You are very kind but I think my winter jacket keeps me warm." I got a kettle with hot water, washed my face and went out over to another unit of that large student's housing.

The two other girls had started preparing some vegetables to make tagine when we both joined them. They all were in their early twenties but had already experienced some romantic dramas. One of them who was a second year student of psychology had been with her boyfriend since she was seventeen years old. They were engaged to be married when her boyfriend had left to live and work in Italy but was regularly paying her visits. Once, when he was abroad, she called him. A girl picked up the phone. "Who are you?" she asked. "I'm his wife and who are you?" Apparently, her future husband had been married for over a year and throughout all this period pretended to be devoted to her and had clear intentions to marry this poor girl.

The second's girl's story was of an equal calibre. Her boyfriend, who was also a long-term partner, was proclaiming the same strong desire to build life with her. They had been together for a couple of years when she discovered, by chance, when talking to his neighbour, that her boyfriend, not a long time ago, got married to the same neighbour that she was talking to. Then was another one after him that was equally unfaithful picking up girls but declaring his ever-lasting love for her. "Moroccan men are merde," said Hasnae the only lucky one amongst them. She was in a happy relationship with ten years older man. "Moroccan men are merde and they go for merde girls," she said it twice. "They don't like ambitious women."

While waiting for the tagine, for over one and a half hours, the second girl was in a quandary about another guy who was sending her text messages and at the same time she was texting another one from her second mobile. She was reading aloud every message that she received and was answering with consent of her girlfriends. When one of the phones rang, she passed it over to her girlfriend. Apparently she was too upset to have a conversation with him but happy to hear his excuses through her friend. This girl was constantly texting them and it wasn't only me who got exhausted from watching her doing it. When the tagine was served and she continued with the monotonous action of taping, her friend put her foot down. "Stop it! He is not worth it," shouting at her she confiscated her phone.

That night Hasnae and her friend did everything to cheer me up, making me feel like at home with my real friends. The performance they both gave was worth watching. The predominant element of each female Berber dancer was the hips that were extraordinarily coordinated with the rest of the body, and this was what Hasnae and her friends were showing me; but at a certain point, having their long hair loose, they were on the floor curled up moving vividly their heads that were fully in charge of the movement of their hair. Their energy was simply spectacular and I utterly enjoyed watching them performing.

In the morning I bid Hasnae farewell, thanked her for her help and left to meet up with Mohamed who waited for me outside the student's house. He was sober but the strong stench of whisky did not leave him for a moment. We got to the station and took the 9.00am bus to Khénifra. "How are you feeling today?" I asked. "Fine," he responded. "Do you remember how you behaved last night at the airport?" He claimed he did but as far as he recalled there was nothing wrong with him or his behaviour. "You should at least say sorry for causing unnecessary stress," I added. He wasn't apologetic, so our journey seemed longer than usual as there was not much of an easy dialogue.

At 4.00pm we arrived in Khénifra, got off the bus that stopped close to the police station, and the bus drove off. "I forgot my hat!" I shouted knowing that I had no time to run after the bus. "Bugger!" A minute after, when we were still standing at the bus stop, a city bus pulled in front of us and Mohamed spotted his friend. With all the instructions given, his friend promised to go to the bus station and search for the hat.

The next step was to go to the police station. When the problem was explained to the police officer who stood at the door, we were instructed to see someone else who was supposed to help us. I walked to a room where there was one officer sitting. I made another explanation and with that explanation a demand for a written document that could get me out of this country. By the time I had elaborated on my problem, there were a couple of other officers who were actively listening. "We can't give you any document, that is not our job," said the first one I talked to. "I will not leave this place until you give me that document!" I shouted and continued. "I was told at the airport that it's you who was supposed to help me, just ring up Raba airport." They told us to sit in the corridor and wait. "I will not leave this building Mohamed until I will get this document." He understood and was fully supportive. "I will not mention any of my writing business here, just the voluntary work, if they asked." "That will be better," said Mohamed. They called me. "Were you registered with us? Where did you live?" asked me the officer. "I'll call my family and you can talk to them." He had a little chat with Meryam and then carried on asking questions. "Did you ever come to the police station to get registered?" "No. I did not know that I had to," I responded with all my honesty. "If I had known I would have done it," I added. "Do you know that you can stay in Morocco only three months?" "No. I don't. If I had known I wouldn't have stayed five months."

Some minutes later they came back with other questions. "So, you are a journalist," he said. "I'm not a journalist, but I write." "We have just contacted Mustapha and he told us you were a journalist," he continued. "I'm an independent writer," I confirmed my previous utterance. The officer walked off again and some time after Mohamed was called to come to the office. I followed him not understanding why they would interrogate him. "We don't need you now, just leave the room," said one of the three gathered there.

"What did they want from you?" I asked when he came back. "They wanted to know everything, every detail of my life: where I live, if I go to school or study, work, what is my relationship with you, they were asking about everything." "What did you say?" That you are my fiancée." "How did they react?" "They were just making notes."

At this point I was highly stressed. I did not want Mohamed to get into any trouble because of me. "I'm sorry for all of that and thank you very much for helping me. I know it's not easy. If you need to go home, I will understand," I said. "No, I'm staying with you."

One of the officers came to tell me that he needed to know what airport I was going to fly from. "I don't know. I haven't booked my flight yet." "Then we will contact Raba airport and you will have to fly from there," he said. "No! Because if I won't be able to find a flight from Raba, then obviously I won't fly from Raba," I protested. He walked off and a few minutes later came back. "Go and book you flight, you need to leave Morocco as soon as possible." "I understand, I have to find an affordable flight," I said. We reached a compromise. I was to book my flight tonight and come back tomorrow morning for the further investigation. "One of our officers will escort you to the airport," he said. "Why?" "We need to make sure that you will leave the country," he explained. "Merde! I feel like a criminal. Excuse my language officer."

After two hours spent at the police station, we were finally able to walk back home. "Mohamed, can you believe that? They will escort us to the airport. Isn't that ironic?" I asked him. "You are a very important person," said Mohamed laughing. "I came here to help and will leave this country feeling like a criminal," I added.

When we reached La Scierie, I saw Papa Mohamed from the distance. "Ba, Lo!" his well-known exclamation greeted me back at home. "Don't worry," he said, *"mochkil,"* and he recalled a couple of stories when he was stopped by police. "Perhaps it's not the same but yes, police can be intimidating." I left my suitcases at home, took my laptop with me and we both went to the café "Martil." "What are you doing here? Shouldn't you be in Europe?" Mustapha was a little bit shocked seeing my face. *"Mochkila* Mustapha," I said. He laughed and served me coffee.

As I had a great deal of help in searching for a flight while I was on a bus to Khénifra, from my two dear friends Toms, I had an idea of what sort of flight connections I was about to get.

Those flights had a couple of things in common: duration, as there was no direct connection, and price. The options were: either to travel to Paris or London, spend a night at the airport and take a morning flight to Warsaw, or fly to Oslo and spend twenty-four hours at Oslo airport. Purely, out of hatred to Ryanair, I choose the long stopover in Oslo. Not only were Norwegian airlines more flexible by offering two suitcases of twenty kilograms each instead of one of fifteen, but also were the cheapest of all of them. It hurt my budget at first but I was lucky to get the £260 reimbursed later by the Association Hannan.

The next morning I had to print off the confirmation of my flight, which did not arrive until after 10.00am, and give it to the police. When I finally got the document printed, I was asked to come to the office. The previous day's abrupt officer was rather kind to me today. His assistant, a young man, much more intelligent and sensitive, was sitting next to him. This time Mohamed's presence was not needed. They had to write a statement called in French PV which stands for procès verbal, stating firstly my ignorance for the law, she had no idea what she was doing, and then carrying on gathering information about my childhood, teenage years and the adulthood, meaning what schools, universities, diplomas, jobs, what countries, years, ending up here, in Morocco. "Why do you need all those information about my past? I could have told you anything." The nice officer smiled. "This is only to get you home safely," explained politely the first officer. "Mustapha said you were maybe a couple of times in El Borj." "Did he? That's funny because he doesn't visit El Borj often. However, if there was nothing for me to do at school, there was no point in going there," I said. "Tell me exactly what did you do?" And I did; step by step commencing with updating any paper work through trying to teach French, then explaining Malika's case and co-operation with Human Rights Organization, second-hand clothes collection, petitions, Timdghass, the goat and wood-burning stove project. "We are very grateful for your work here and we want you to go back home safely," said the officer and continued. "If you would like to come back and stay longer than three months, you must come to the police station and without a problem we would be able to extend your visa. You can also apply for three year residency here." *"Inchallah,"* I said. "Do you still need to escort me to Marrakesh airport?" "I think we can trust you," he responded. "Can you give me a contact number, in case I have any problems at the airport," I asked. "You will not have problems. The Marrakesh airport has been informed that you are coming and they will let you go." "I do hope so and thank you for your help," I said shaking hand with them. "Sorry for all your trouble and come back any time," they added politely.

We left the police station a little bit subdued. "Do you still want to go with me to Marrakesh?" I asked Mohamed. "Of course I want; but now we can have tea at my place and relax watching a film." We both deserved a break.

At his place there was only Hayat, his younger sister, who wasn't even surprised by seeing me back and later on his dad appeared in the kitchen. He asked Mohamed about the police investigation and worried about his son, predicting further difficulties for him. Oddly, his sympathy for me or my situation wasn't even proclaiming itself in an invitation to join him for tea that he had usually had with us; this time, however, he grabbed the pot and went off to "the Madeleine's room" as he called the unfinished one at the rooftop. "Is your dad ok?" I asked. "He worries about the whole police interrogation," he responded. "I bet he blames me for all of it." I said and convinced myself to my own suspicions when seeing him walking away without a word of goodbye. Just like that. And that hurt a little.

As soon as we sat down in the Madeleine's room and turned the film on, I heard my telephone ringing. "I bet it's Mustapha," I said but looked at the screen. "Abdellah, *la bas?*" I picked up the phone surprised. "Where are you?" he asked. "At Mohamed's having tea. I'll be at home soon. I still have to repack," I answered. "Rkia has died." "What?!" "Shall we wait for you at home or will go straight there?" "I'll go straight there," I was shocked when put the phone down. "Mohamed, will you come with me, please? Rkia is dead."

In that moment I was wondering what else could happen. How was it possible to endure these masses of pain laid out in front of me forcing me to stomp on them. "You fool! You will never be free from suffering." "This rings a bell," I said to myself. It felt as here there was no time to recover: one painful event comes and another follows. Perhaps this is how they get that thick skin that I lack?

I yet again had flashbacks from our trip to the mountains, and yet again saw grandma Rkia trampling that uneasy pathway. But what courage and extraordinary stamina she had! It would be most desirable to have a little bit of that valour too... if I ever reached her age.

"Mohamed, I shall put my black pyjama on, I can't go like this." We walked quickly to La Scierie. "Have you ever been to the funeral before?" I asked him. "I don't like funerals." "No one does but sometimes you don't have a choice." "The ceremony here is very strange, and what people do is either moaning or pitting the family of the deceased, asking what will happen to them, how will they live," he explained. "Wasn't that exactly what you said about Sanae's family when her dad died tragically?" I asked. "I did but her family is very poor." "But everyone is poor here, everyone struggles, perhaps their concerns are not fabricated?" "Maybe you are right," he admitted. "Would you like to come with me to see Rkia?" "I'll wait for you in a café and when you'll be ready to leave the place give me a ring." "What do I say to Hakima?" I asked. "Say: *Baraka Frassak.*"

At the front of the house, a large number of people were gathered. I recognised many faces and they recognised mine. Mama Mina was sitting close to the door. She hugged me crying and let me inside the house where I could find Hakima. The lament that I heard led me to her. She was at the far end of that corridor taking condolences from everybody who was coming in. Her tears and grief were contagious and real compared to the woman who had been taken out. That woman took her headscarf off and was pulling her hair while making a long-lasting lament and then she threw herself on the pavement hitting it hard with her clenched hands continuing with her lengthy powerful dirge. The moan continued but a couple of women managed to sit her on a chair when a few seconds later she slid down the chair fainting. The two women who assisted her moan put her back on it and she seemed to have been fine. The strangest of all for me was that there was not a single tear on her face. "Who was she?" I wondered.

I hugged Hakima and wanted to pass my Moroccan condolences but I forgot the word that followed *Baraka*. *"Smhli, smhli bzzaf,"* I said instead. "Come inside and sit," said Fadma. "I will soon be going, I can't stay long," I answered. "Where is Rkia?" I asked her. "She is in that room, do you want to see her?" "I'd like to." She led me to that room in which Rkia had spent hours with family and friends that had been looking after her. And there she was. Her body covered with a white bedsheet looked as if it had shrunk already. I was hesitant but I wanted to say goodbye to her. Fadma uncovered her head that was turned to her right, the headscarf was taken off and a few henna-dyed orange strands of hair were visible. The prominent cheekbones indicated her struggle with food. She looked in peace though. I touched her head and said *bslama*.

How hugely annoying that she had to go away and leave behind people who loved her, those whom she gave life. Was she aware of how hugely disappointing death felt in that moment?

"It has seemed to me for a long time that the influence of a loved one's death on those he has left behind ought to be none other than that of a higher responsibility. Does the one who is passing away not leave a hundredfold of everything he had begun to be continued by those who survive him – if they had shared any kind of inner bond at all? Over the past few years I have been forced to gain intimate knowledge of so many close experiences of death. But with each individual who was taken from me, the tasks around me have only increased. The heaviness of this unexplained and possibly mightiest occurrence, which has assumed the reputation of being arbitrary and cruel only due to a misunderstanding, presses us more deeply into life and demands the most extreme duties of our gradually increasing strengths."

I left the house, said goodbye to a few people and went back to Mohamed. "There was one woman whose grief did not feel real to me." "There will always be a woman who would scream like that, she is a professional moaner, she knows what she is doing and everybody else knows it's a performance" he said. "I wonder why? What do they do with the body?" I asked. "It must be buried within twenty-four hours."

"Moroccan funerals are done in conformity with Islamic customs. The body is prepared at home by the family and if needed someone from the community who has regrettably had that experience. The deceased is always placed facing Mecca towards the south when buried.

In all Islamic faiths, it is said Allah can bring them back to life if they are in the direction of Mecca for Judgement Day, so bodies are buried on the right side with the head facing south toward Mecca. In this position they are ready for resurrection by Allah on Judgement Day. It will then be decided if the soul will enter heaven or hell. Men are designated to chant Muslim professions of faith as they carry the body to the burial site.

Once the funeral has taken place, a couple of days later the family will gather for a formal get-together over food and some of the Koran is read out aloud. In Moroccan culture this meal is of utmost importance because it will give good vibes of charity for the spirit to take to the next world.

Traditionally women wear white while grieving and in addition to this it is the law that they abstain from sex for the forty days after their spouse has died. In ties with other Islamic groups in Africa and the Middle East the mourning period is forty days."

******

The grandchildren of Rkia, Achraf and Moad, seemed not to have been affected by her death. Achraf was outside playing with other children from the same neighbourhood and Moad was watching TV. I repacked, abandoned some more clothes and at around 11.00pm said goodbye. The last bus to Marrakesh was to leave at 2.00am but the time seemed to weigh down on us. I heard the clock ticking all those seconds that were adding up to minutes and then hours – too dear to be wasted. "Let me go!" I was rehearsing in my head what once again I was to say and I felt strangled by words. I should have felt relieved leaving behind all that struggle but somehow it now made perfect sense: I felt enriched, more courageous, stronger, different to who I was before. I did not want to be me standing in that airport corridor crying and saying: "Let me go!" I was happy to give that moment away to someone else who was ready.

We sat at the place near the bus station and ordered some tagine and chips. They served us a very "touristy meal." The tagine had clearly been standing on the burning charcoal for quite some time and the cold floppy greasy chips were almost inedible. "What a fantastic meal!" we both were saying it laughing. "And those heavenly crispy and hot chips are medicine to my poor soul," I said eating one by one.

There was a young, handsome man sitting next to us and I could feel his eyes on me, and then he disappeared. One hour later we had two young men standing in front of our table. "Hello, were you our teacher?" asked one of them. "Excuse me? Your teacher?" I looked at them perplexed. "The English teacher," he added. "I don't really remember that," I smiled. They apologised and left while that handsome man came out of the corner of the street, joined them, looked back at us and walked off with them. "Isn't that rather strange that they don't recognise their own teacher?" I commented. "They were clearly trying their luck."

It was 1.15am when we decided to walk to the station. Slowly taking our time, we got there within five minutes. A bus in front of the station with quite a number of passengers drew our attention. "What's that bus? Shall we go and find out?" I asked out of curiosity. "It's our bus," said Mohamed. "How come? It's forty minutes ahead of schedule. Imagine, if we came here on time ..." I said and couldn't believe our luck. The man took my suitcases and managed to put them inside the boot that looked pretty full already. We found two seats in front of a rather particular individual: a young man who not only stunk of alcohol, but was also listening aloud to one of the songs most loved by Moroccans, a soppy love song sung by Enrique Inglesias: "I can be your hero babe." "Mohamed, could you please, tell him to turn it down?" It was not a good time to listen to Inglesias moan. He did ask him but that drunken man said he needed that music like water. I sensed the broken heart problem. "How long?" I asked. "He is going to Agadir," said Mohamed. "Oh, no! Impossible!" I lamented. Mohamed took out his headphones and lent them to him. "Keep them until Marrakesh." He accepted and continued to torture himself leaving us, the passengers, feeling relieved.

Fifteen minutes later a ticket inspector came up to us and said something to Mohamed. "What does he want?" "He wants 10DH for the luggage that is in the boot." "This is clearly a joke," I said to that man. "So many times I have travelled and no one has ever asked for extra money," I was outraged by his cheeky attitude and added. "It's included in the ticket price." "What an opportunist!" I commented when he walked off.

I embraced my man, closed my eyes, instantly felt asleep and woke up when it was time to get off. "So early, so quick," the sudden wakeup call made me feel grumpy. It was around 6.30am when we arrived in Marrakesh. We found a café inside the bus station and slept for another twenty minutes at the table. "Shall we walk toward the Jemaa el-Fnaa and have breakfast there?" I asked when one hour went past. "We can leave all those suitcases here and explore the centre a little," said Mohamed. And we did.

The Jemaa el-Fnaa was quiet, no music, no performances, no stalls with food, only those countless stands with fresh orange juice were opened.

We sat down for coffee and *boucheyar* and were observing how quickly the square was filling itself with people. First the musicians were heard or one particular man with his flute and his one minute-lasting painfully repeated note. Then all those snake charmers and monkey trainers were seen and one had to be very careful not to come too close to them as their monkeys jump on you, sit on you head and demand money; how cleverly trained! Then when we were walking around the square, some story-teller warned us about the evil that we all carry inside us. That man wanted to chase the evil away and was rather cross with us when we had refused to have a spell put on us and carry on living with the evil he clearly saw in us.

All those stands with leather bags tempted us inside. "Come on in, come on in, look at this, just have a look," the merchant was pushing us. "I need a rucksack, maybe I can get it here," said Mohamed. We walked back to that man. "How much do you want for this rucksack?" he asked. "You can have this one for 70DH," the merchant quickly placed another one in front of us. "This one is nice, but I prefer that one, how much is it?" He did not want to say the price of that particular one. We walked off. He shouted: "350DH!" "That's too expensive." "200DH!" He went that low with the price. "Let's go back and negotiate," I said. "What about 100DH for that bag," we asked him. "You have here one for 80DH," he said adding, "a very good one." "This one does not seem like leather," we were a little bit suspicious. "It's a very good leather and for little," he was pushing us. "But I want to see that one," Mohamed pointed to a specific one hanging on the wall. "Why don't you want to show me that one?" he asked. This merchant was aggressive and wanted to sell us something that wasn't a leather bag. "No, we don't want that one," we walked off making him feel a little irate.

"I saw a programme on TV about merchants like him. It was a very canny way to do business. Firstly, they give people what they want, the expensive, beautiful bags that were supposed to cost for example 400DH, then after the negotiation the price went down to 300DH. What happens next is the merchant takes the bag with him in order to get a brand-new from the back of the shop and there he swaps with a brand-new looking like a leather bag but in fact it's a fake leather. And this guy knew we weren't stupid," recalled Mohamed.

In fact one has to be very careful not only with merchants like him, but anybody on that square. They simply want to trap you in any form of entertainment and if they manage, they leave you with no choice but to pay for it; but in spite of all those shrewd techniques of ambushing the innocent souls, the vibrancy and magnetism of that square, especially at night-time where everything comes to life, tempts and seduces letting the imagination get carried away.

"The Jemaa el-Fnaa is one of the best-known squares in Africa and is the centre of city activity and trade. It has been described as a "world-famous square", "a metaphorical urban icon, a bridge between the past and the present, the place where Moroccan tradition encounters modernity." It has been part of the UNESCO World Heritage site since 1985. The name roughly means "the assembly of trespassers" or malefactors. Jemaa el-Fnaa was renovated along with much of the Marrakech city, whose walls were extended by Abu Yaqub Yusuf and particularly by Yaqub al-Mansur in 1147-1158. The surrounding mosque, palace, hospital, parade ground and gardens around the edges of the marketplace were also overhauled, and the Kasbah was fortified. Subsequently with the fluctuating fortunes of the city, Jemaa el-Fnaa saw periods of decline and renewal.

Historically this square was used for public decapitations by rulers who sought to maintain their power by frightening the public. The square attracted dwellers from the surrounding desert and mountains to trade here, and stalls were raised in the square from early in its history. The square attracted tradesmen, snake charmers, ("wild, dark, frenzied men with long dishevelled hair falling over their naked shoulders") dancing boys of the Chleuh Atlas tribe, and musicians playing pipes, tambourines and African drums.

Snake charmers, acrobats, magicians, mystics, musicians, monkey trainers, herb sellers, story-tellers, dentists, pickpockets, and entertainers in medieval garb still populate the square."

All those souks around the main square would offer everything from brightly coloured sandals and slippers and leather pouffes to jewellery and kaftans. Then one would see stalls which would specialise in lemons, chillies, capers, pickles, green, red, and black olives, and mint, a common ingredient of Moroccan cuisine and tea. Similarly, dried fruit and nuts, including dates, figs, walnuts, cashews and apricots would attract the eye. All those individuals would sit there trying to sell hand-woven baskets, natural perfumes, knitted hats, scarves, t-shirts, ginseng, the green lipstick that changes into red or pink in contact with skin. The endless souks with carpets and rugs would stand out and blind one with its colours; and belts, and more belts.

"The Land of God" also gives one the opportunity to experience henna. And when we were chilling out sitting on the bench outside Jemaa el-Fnaa, a woman waiting for her henna to dry was sitting on the next bench and was clearly talking to herself. When we saw her scrapping if off, we interrupted her. "You should leave it for at least two hours otherwise it won't have any effect," we advised her. She stopped taking the henna off, stood up, came up to us and said in her broken French: "Give me 2000 francs for a taxi." "Sorry, we don't have it." She was certainly not a beggar, but looked a tiny bit mad; so when we refused giving her money, she walked off mumbling. "Well, she was still living in the era of frank's, good luck to her," I said and took my dictaphone out. We had some fun when interviewing each other, recalling the past time and stories from Marrakesh. A couple of memorable photographs and off we went, back to the station to find a bus to the airport. The taxi men offered 100DH for a ride. We refused. The cost of a bus ticket was only 20DH. We waited patiently as there was no rush. "Do you want to go to the airport?" we were approached by another man. "We are fine with a bus," we answered. "I take you for 45DH," he said. "Really? Then we will come with you," we agreed while being taken to his old Volkswagen minibus. When there was time to pay, I took 100DH out and got 50DH back. "Sorry, I don't have 5DH," clever I thought.

When I checked my baggage in, we still had some time for coffee. All the words that I wanted to articulate would not pass my throat area, they would all stop there; and when slowly one by one they squeezed themselves through, it was that one who sobbed. It wasn't me. I was strong but the words were weak. We went out and turned some music on and those notes happened to be as weak as the words. We were sitting under a poster that was giving people information about taxi fares, melting under the strong sun beams and feeling the weak musical notes and words. "I have to go now," I took a piece of toilet paper and blew my nose. "Be strong," said Mohamed. "I'm strong, it's not me who cries but words." "Be good to yourself," I said and disappeared into that overcrowded corridor quickly losing sight of him.

When I came to the passport control, the female immigration officer looked at my visa. "You've extended your stay here by two months. I can't let you out," she said and gave me heart palpitations. "I know but it was sorted, the police told me I won't have any more problems." She left the stand. The passengers behind me were getting agitated. I stopped looking back. She finally returned. "Sorry, we have to keep you here," she said and gave me almost heart attack. "I don't understand." "It was a joke," she added. "If you want to stay in Morocco, you must marry a Moroccan man," she smiled. I showed her my ring.

"Where are you Mohamed?" I called him back immediately. "I'm still on the bus going back to the airport," he said. "I was pensive and did not notice that the bus had arrived in the centre," he explained. "They let me out but we will see each other soon." *Inchallah.*

******

Notes:

1 (p. 252) "Letters on life," Rainer Maria Rilke, The Modern Library New York, 2006, p. 187.

2 (p. 256) Berkane is a city in the northeastern Morocco in the area of Trifa and is considered the capital of the citrus fruit industry of Morocco, and high-quality fresh fruit and vegetables are plentiful year round. It is known for its farms of clementines, also a large statue of an orange is at the center of town. It is very close to Saïdia, a popular beach resort town on the Mediterranean, as well as Tafoughalt, a small village in the nearby mountains known for its healthy air and herb markets. Berkane is also famous for being the birthplace of the Olympic athlete Hicham El Guerrouj who holds the world record for the fastest mile but unfortunately, he has never been a major social player in the development of his native town.

3 (p. 256) Melilia and Ceuta: wikipedia.org.

4 (p. 258) Chefchaouen: amusing planet.com.

5 (p. 269) Mochkil/ machi, in Darija, no problem.

6 (p. 272) "Letters on life," op.cit., p.107.

7 (p. 272) From the article: "Funeral Traditions in Morocco,"2014.

8 (p. 275) Jemaa el-Fnaa: wikipedia.org.

End of Part Eight

Glossary:

Äami – lit. my paternal uncle; when it stands in front of a name, it expresses a great deal of respect for an elderly person.

Aji! - Come!

Amen - water

Arbiya - Arabic

Baba - grandfather

Blatti! - Wait!

Boucheyar/ Mssemen - Moroccan pancakes

Brwita/carozza – trolley

Bsha/bessaha - for good health

Bslama - goodbye

Bzzaf - very

Chfnj/sfnj – donate ring

Chokrane - thank you

Chouf! - Look!

Chwya/chwiya - a little

Djaja – bag

Elben – sour milk

Epo – mother

Flouss - money

Forno - wood-burning stove

Fota – towel

Habibi/Habeebi - my beloved, darling, also a friend

Hrira - the traditional Moroccan soup

Hubz - bread

Hut – fish

Iben - white cheese

Idren – acorns

Inchallah - if God wills/permits

Koul! - Eat!

La - no

Layssahel - lit. God will ease you

Malhababic - welcome

Mika – bag

Mochkil/ machi - no problem

Nafha - black tabacco

Salam ali-koum, La bas? Bikhir? Henya? - Hello. How is going? How are you? Is it going well?

Smhli - I'm sorry

Torta - cake

Wakha, yes, ok

Wyih! - a joyful way of saying yes

Zwina, zwin - beautiful

A barbecue inside the house with Papa Mohamed and Mustafa

In the forest of Ajdir with, from left, Hakima, one of Papa Mohamed's sisters and Fadma.

ART . TRAVEL . CAREERS .

SOCIAL STUDIES

Published by Cv Publications

www.tracksdirectory.ision.co.uk